———— SPANISH EXPEDITIONS INTO TEXAS, 1689–1768 ————

SPANISH EXPEDITIONS INTO TEXAS, 1689–1768

WILLIAM C. FOSTER

UNIVERSITY OF TEXAS PRESS

AUSTIN

TO MY CHILDREN
William Crozier, Ebba Birgitta, Eric Lindh, and Claire Kearney

Publication of this work has been made possible in part by a grant from the Program for Cultural Cooperation between Spain's Ministry of Culture and United States Universities.

First edition, 1995

Requests for permission to reproduce material from this work should be sent to Permissions, University of Texas Press, Box 7819, Austin, TX 78713-7819.

∞ The paper used in this publication meets the minimum requirements of American National Standard for Information Sciences—Permanence of Paper for Printed Library Materials, ANSI Z39.48-1984.

LIBRARY OF CONGRESS
CATALOGING-IN-PUBLICATION DATA

Foster, William C., 1928–
Spanish expeditions into Texas, 1689–1768 / by William C. Foster. — 1st ed.
    p.   cm.
Includes bibliographical references and index.
ISBN 0-292-72488-8. — ISBN 0-292-72489-6 (pbk.)
1. Texas—Discovery and exploration—Spanish.   2. Spaniards—Texas—History.
3. Texas—History—To 1846.   I. Title.
F389.F69   1995
976.4'02—dc20   94-37235

CONTENTS

PREFACE

In the late 1980s, the DeWitt County Historical Commission undertook to have a county history written and published. The book, co-edited by Rosemary B. Sheppard and Patsy Goebel, included a prehistory introduction, an article on Spanish expeditions into South Texas in the late seventeenth and eighteenth centuries, and several summaries and sketches on the more recent Anglo period. This book grew out of the article on the Spanish colonial period that I prepared for the county history, which was published in 1991.

My study of the Spanish epoch in Texas and the Spanish expeditions into the province from northeastern Mexico might have ended with the publication of the county history if I had not been so intensely frustrated during my research by the widely conflicting projections of the Spanish expedition routes across Texas. During the past ninety years, the state's most distinguished historians have uniformly extolled the significance of these early Spanish expeditions, but disagreed widely on the routes followed on every expedition from that of Governor Alonso de León in 1689 to that of Fray Gaspar José de Solís in 1768. These starkly divergent route projections were made despite the availability of one or more detailed diaries written by experienced military leaders, engineers, and padres, giving the direction and distance traveled each day and the names of campsites used and rivers crossed.

This uncertainty in the expedition routes has confused archeologists and anthropologists interested in the exact location of a repeatedly used Indian campsite, traditional river crossing, or Indian rock carving reported by the diarists. I found no rational justification for scholars such as Herbert E. Bolton, Carlos E. Castañeda, Robert S. Weddle, and the experts who prepared the 1991 studies for the Texas Highway Department differing by as much as 50 miles on where Alonso de León crossed the Nueces, the San Antonio, and the Guadalupe on his trek to Matagorda Bay in 1689 and 1690 or by 50 to 60 miles on whether Captain Ramón (1716), Brigadier Rivera (1727), and the Marqués de Rubí (1767) crossed the Brazos in Milam, Burleson, or Washington County.

All historical accounts of Spanish expeditions into Texas during the colonial period and all expedition diary annotations are plagued with wide variations in route projections. No one has previously tracked the daily line of march with cross-document analysis and located the nightly campsites on each of the eleven major expeditions in chronological order for the 500- to 800-mile trek across northern Mexico and Texas, using all available manuscripts, typescripts, and published expedition diary accounts with on-site route verification. This book does that.

To complete this study required enormous help, which was given by many. Jack Jackson's sympathetic encouragement and active participation were the most critical. Jack's skillfully prepared sketches, carefully designed to reflect accurately and in detail the dress, costumes, weapons, and manner of living of the period, substantially strengthen the book. John V. Cotter's maps may give a clearer picture of the expedition routes and Indian trade routes than the text. Finally, the fascination of the subject, the location, and the time provided the real motivation to resolve the route dilemma.

Other Texas historians and anthropologists gave substantial assistance along the way, including Professor Thomas N. Campbell, Professor David J. Weber, Robert H. Thonhoff, and, in ways perhaps unknown to him, Robert S. Weddle. Dorcas Baumgartner, archivist for Gonzales County, was available to struggle with me mile by mile over the most troublesome route projections. Spanish translation support was received from a number of sources, including principally Adela Pacheco Cobb of Washington, D.C. My special friend David Adams helped me see the similarity between Indian signs and American Sign Language, and Blair James showed me the way with canoes. When the way was temporarily blocked or densely clouded, Frankie Westbrook was close at hand with advice that only an experienced and caring editor could give.

One of the most exciting discoveries for me in the study was the richness and depth of the Spanish materials in the Library of Congress, including the Hispanic and Manuscript Divisions, in Washington, D.C., where much of the research was conducted. The excitement in finding unexpected historic records, however, was matched by the thrills I found on the numerous trips with friends and family by pickup, canoe, and helicopter to verify my route projections. To my initial surprise, the river bends, creek junctions, densely wooded areas, and prairies have remained sufficiently stable over the past 300 years to permit route verification. We found that the ancient Indian trade routes out of Mexico and across the state make as much sense geographically today as they did centuries ago when thousands of Indians from below the Rio Grande annually walked across vast parts of Texas to trade, hunt, and raid. They moved from modern Chihuahua and Coahuila in northeastern Mexico across Texas from one water hole to the next creek or river, along high, open ground, often protected by dense woods from the mounted Apache or other enemies to the north, and crossed rivers at fords with rocky shallow bottoms marked by a sharp turn or fork or high bluff.

In carefully reading the early diary accounts and related materials, I found other information about the area now called Texas. Indian tribes were identified by name and described in each diary; the wild animals and vegetation were frequently reported in detail. The diaries also include comments on weather and notes on the spread of epidemics. These parts of the diary accounts have not been ignored in the text. I believe that experts have far too quickly dismissed such diary information. Certainly the diaries must be read critically; all writers, including diarists, can be biased and imprecise. Nevertheless, I firmly believe that the expedition diaries should be accorded the highest respect, and my deepest appreciation and gratitude is reserved for the Spanish diarists who made this book possible.

SPANISH EXPEDITIONS INTO TEXAS, 1689–1768

FIGURE I
Precontact Jumano travel along a familiar trade route to visit their allies in Central and East Texas.

ONE

INTRODUCTION

The discovery and early exploration of North America in the late fifteenth and early sixteenth centuries ignited a European power struggle that engaged principally England, Spain, and France. One of the areas of intense regional conflict between Spain and France during the later part of the seventeenth century was the northern Gulf of Mexico. The Gulf was considered a Spanish sea in the 1680s, and the lands known today as Mexico, New Mexico, and Texas were subject to a firm Spanish claim. Nominal Spanish occupation extended north from Mexico City to military and mission outposts in present-day northern Nuevo León (at Cerralvo ca. 1583), Coahuila (near Monclova), West Texas (at El Paso and Presidio), and New Mexico (at Santa Fe in the 1580s). Since the Spaniards Francisco Vázquez de Coronado and Hernando de Soto (with Luis de Moscoso) had explored but found treasures in neither northwestern or northeastern Texas in the middle sixteenth century, that vast area was claimed by Spain but basically remained without an established Spanish presence.[1] An attempt in 1632 to start a mission for the Jumano Indians on the Concho River near present-day San Angelo lasted only six months. Other efforts to establish missions in Texas around El Paso and near the junction of the Rio Grande and the Mexican Conchos River in the 1680s were more successful.[2]

The Mississippi River drainage area east of present-day Texas was subject to a French claim established in 1682 by René Robert Cavelier, Sieur de La Salle. Returning to the New World again in 1684, La Salle sailed—intentionally or by navigational error[3]—not to the Mississippi Delta but to the Texas coast. La Salle landed his colony, which numbered about three hundred, including nine women, some with young children, at Matagorda Bay, thus staking out a new French-Spanish battlefield. This book deals with the major Spanish overland expeditions undertaken in response to this threat, which lasted from La Salle's arrival in Spanish Texas to the end of the French presence. These expedition routes (and the Indian trade routes they followed) became the first Spanish road system across Texas and have been woven into the present state highway network.

Reports of the French settlement, at first unconfirmed, sent shock waves from Mexico City to the Spanish outposts in northern New Spain. The Spanish viceroy in Mexico City issued orders to send expeditions by both land and sea in search of La Salle's colony,

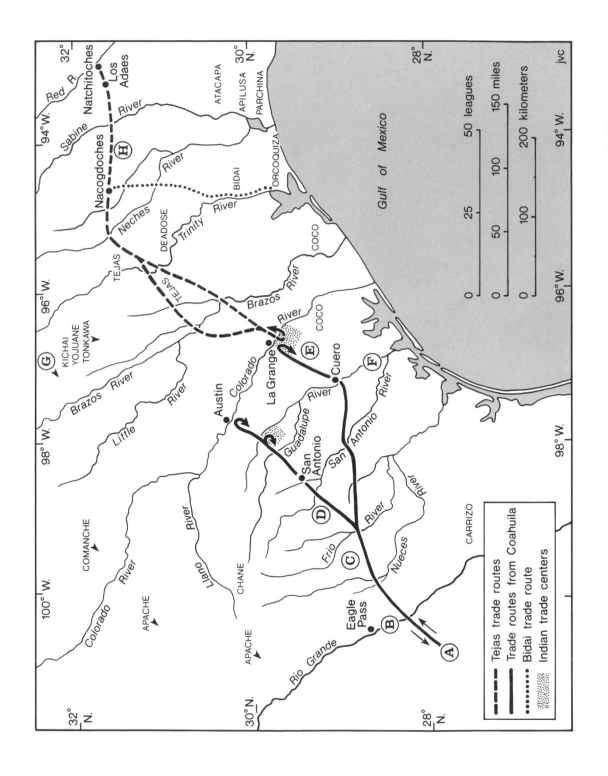

MAP I

Indian Tribes and Trade Routes in Texas according to Expedition Diaries, 1689–1768

The geographic area in which Indian tribes were found on the Spanish expeditions into Texas is indicated either by a circled capital letter (representing several tribes) or by the name of a single tribe. An arrow indicates the projected direction that the tribes were moving during the period they were encountered. Circled capital letters and tribal names shown without arrows suggest that the tribes were likely found near their native residential area.

A. Roving tribes from Coahuila and Chihuahua. Tribes principally from Coahuila and Chihuahua (Vizcaya) that traveled north of the Rio Grande to trade, hunt, or serve as guides along trade routes that led to the Colorado River: Borrado, Cacaxtle, Catquesa, Caynaaya, Chalome, Cibola, Jumano, Mescal, Mesquite, Pacpul, Quem, Saquita, Sijame, Simaoma, Siupan, Timamar, Tlaxcalan, Toboso.

B. Rio Grande tribes. Local tribes found principally along either side of the lower Rio Grande: Agualobe, Alachome, Cacase, Chaguan, Ervipiame, Hape, Momon, Ocana, Odoesmade, Paac, Pacuache, Piedras Blancas, Salinero, Xiabu, Yorica.

C. Frio River tribes. Local tribes found principally near the Nueces and the Frio rivers: Aguapalam, Apaysi, Papanac, Parchaque, Pastaloca, Pataguo, Patchal, Patsau, Payaguan, Pitabay, Sacuache, Samampac, Sampanal, Tepacuache, Vanca, Xarame.

D. Medina River tribes. Local tribes found principally near and immediately southwest of the Medina and the upper San Antonio rivers: Pamaya, Pampopa, Pastia, Payaya.

E. Trans–Colorado River tribes. Local tribes found principally between the lower Guadalupe and the Colorado rivers: Aname, Aranama, Caisquetebana, Cantona, Cava, Emet, Mayeye, Muruam, Naaman, Sana, Tacame, Tamique, Tohaha, Toho.

F. Karankawan tribes. Local coastal Karankawan tribes: Coapite, Copane, Cujane, Karankawa.

G. Norteños. Principally Wichita tribes moving southwest: Taguaya, Tawakoni, Yscani.

H. Hasinai (Tejas) and related East Texas tribes. Local western and southern Caddoan tribes found principally between the Neches and the Red rivers: Adaes, Ais, Nabidacho, Nacogdoche, Nacono, Nasoni, Natchitoche, Neche.

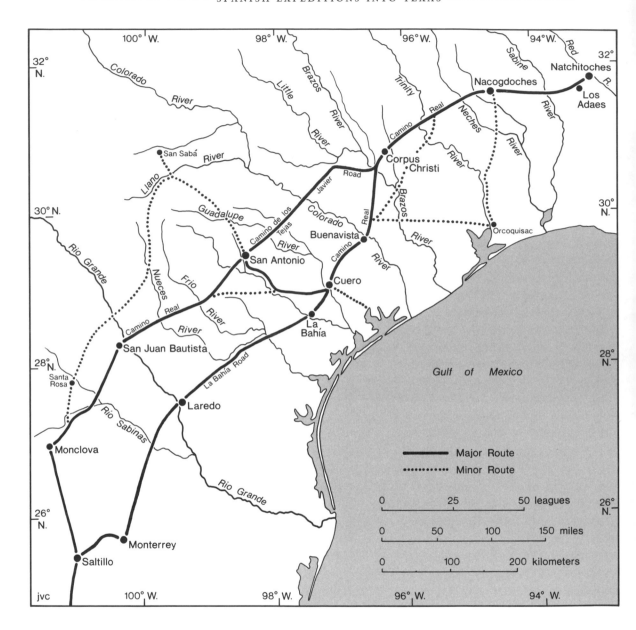

MAP 2

Spanish Road Network in Northeastern New Spain according to Expedition Diaries, 1689–1768

which was thought to be somewhere along the Texas coast. One marine expedition from Veracruz in early 1687 was successful in locating and identifying a French vessel in Matagorda Bay (named *San Bernardo* on the expedition), but the expedition leaders—Martín de Rivas and Pedro de Iriarte—decided that the ship, acknowledged to be one of La Salle's, posed no actual threat because the colonists were presumed to have perished. The colonists were actually gathered near a fort located a few miles upstream on a creek that entered the bay.[4]

Despite the report from the 1687 marine expedition, overland expeditions continued. One such expedition from Presidio de Conchos in northern New Spain south of the Big Bend was led by Captain Juan Fernández de Retana in early 1689. After passing the mission at La Junta (near present-day Presidio, Texas, on the Rio Grande), Retana continued northeast about 100 miles to the Pecos River, where his party met a large number of Cibolo and Jumano Indians returning from their annual hunting trip and "visit to the Tejas trade fair" in Central or East Texas.[5] The well-recognized Jumano leader, Juan Sabeata, told Retana of reports that the French settlement on the coast had been destroyed. As evidence, Sabeata showed the Spaniards some papers written in French and wrapped in lace. The captain decided to return home for further orders.

While Captain Retana awaited instructions, another expedition was underway near the lower Rio Grande. The Spanish outpost closest to the area where the La Salle settlement was reportedly located was Monclova, about 120 miles south of the Rio Grande in the modern state of Coahuila. The captain of the military post or presidio recently established at Monclova was Alonso de León, an officer who earlier had led unsuccessful expeditions from Nuevo León to and beyond the Rio Grande in search of La Salle's colony. On his trip in June 1686, De León had followed the lower Rio Grande to a point near the present-day city of Brownsville; in 1687, he had crossed the Rio Grande and ventured up the Gulf Coast as far as a large river or bay area that he was unprepared to cross or to circle.[6]

But events along the lower Rio Grande in 1688 and early 1689 greatly improved the prospects of locating the French settlement. The most significant occurrence was the capture of Jean Géry, a Frenchman apparently from La Salle's colony, who was found living among the Indians at De León's doorstep, about 50 miles northeast of the Rio Grande, probably in the Zavala-Uvalde-Kinney County area.[7] Géry said he would guide De León and his *entrada* to the French settlement, accurately estimating that the trip could be made in about twelve days.

The Spaniards who interrogated Géry referred to him as a "demented Frenchman," and this characterization has been accepted by at least some Spanish colonial historians.[8] But the old Frenchman proved to be a helpful guide and a loyal and trusted friend to De León. He is one of the most intriguing figures associated with the early expeditions.

As promised, Géry, with the assistance of a local Pacpul and a Quem Indian guide, led De León to the French settlement. De León's expedition in the spring of 1689 was the first of a series of dramatic journeys during the next eighty years from northeastern Mexico into country new to the Spaniards, but well known and traveled by Indian tribes from Chihuahua and Coahuila. The Spaniards later called the country the "Province of the Tejas." Between 1689 and 1768, the Crown financed or otherwise promoted eleven elaborately planned overland expeditions into Central and East Texas. With each expedition the Spaniards' knowledge of the region north of the Rio Grande and its native people expanded. The following chapters retrace these eleven expedition routes day by day from their origin in what is today northeastern Mexico into Spanish Texas.

Historians of the early Spanish period in Texas have written extensively on the significance of these late-seventeenth- and eighteenth-century expeditions, but have offered widely different projections of the routes traveled by De León and by the leaders of subsequent expeditions. Historians such as Herbert E. Bolton, Carlos E. Castañeda, J. W. Williams, and Robert S. Weddle as well as the recent state-sponsored expedition route study by the Texas Department of Highways have differed by as much as 60 miles in their projections of where De León forded each of the first five major rivers he crossed in Texas: the Nueces, the Frio, the San Antonio, the Guadalupe, and the Colorado. Spanish colonial historians have repeatedly acknowledged that Indian tribes from West Texas and northeastern Mexico annually attended Tejas Indian trade fairs in Central and East Texas, but the Indian trade routes across Texas have never been located and the precise sites where the survivors of La Salle's colony were recovered by the Spaniards have never been accurately identified. In the early eighteenth century, five expeditions crossed the Brazos at the same river junction, where there were large Indian encampments collectively referred to by the Spaniards as the Ranchería Grande, but studies disagree on whether the Brazos de Dios crossing and the nearby Ranchería Grande were located at the Little River junction in Milam County, at the junction of the Little Brazos in Brazos County, or about 40 miles downstream near the Navasota junction in Grimes County.

Some of these differences may have resulted from attempts to project the route by the use of one diary alone, from a misunderstanding of the names of rivers used in the diaries, or from a general lack of confidence in the distances and directions reported by the diarists; but, as David J. Weber and Donald E. Chipman have noted, distorted projections may well have been perpetrated by local communities attempting to capitalize on history by promoting expedition routes close to home.[9] These points of contention are specifically mentioned at relevant places in the text.

Probably the most basic reason for the confusion in the expedition routes, however, has been the absence of any multiexpedition study that utilizes cross-document analysis for the daily movement of all eleven expeditions, considered in chronological order, including a comparison of the names for rivers, creeks, and campsites. Because these names were generally (although not always) used on subsequent expeditions, such an analysis of the routes is critical to understanding the development of the earliest road system across Texas. The basic route map becomes more precise with the information added by each new expedition. Failure to study carefully the chronological changes in the names used by expedition diarists for the same rivers and campsites can lead route projections far astray.[10]

Another factor that has perhaps discouraged any detailed chronological comparison of the early routes has been the warning by prominent Texas historians that the directions and distances given in diary accounts could not be relied upon to reconstruct the routes of early expeditions. In 1911, Eleanor Claire Buckley stated that no common route pattern could be found in the diary reports for the early expeditions.[11] Writing in the 1930s, Carlos E. Castañeda echoed this sentiment by stating that no dependence could be placed "on the direction of travel as recorded in the [De León's] comprehensive diary."[12] More recent warnings have come from several contemporary Spanish colonial historians, such as Professor Donald E. Chipman, who has characterized the charting of De León's path across Texas as "at best pure guesswork."[13]

One of the best-known studies of expedition routes in Texas is the extensive account written by J. W. Williams and edited and compiled by his friend Kenneth F. Neighbors.[14] In contrast to the present study, which is limited to expedition routes from northeastern New Spain into Texas during an eighty-year period, Williams made independent studies of a wide selection of journeys through Texas beginning with Cabeza de Vaca in the 1530s and closing with mail routes and wagon train trails of the late nineteenth century. Both favorable and critical comments on the accuracy of route projections offered by Williams are included in the text. Other published accounts of expedition trails include historians' projected locations of isolated campsites or river crossings on selected dates along the route, the 1991 state-funded study of expedition routes generally known as the Old San Antonio Road, and the annotations and maps provided in translations of several diaries.[15]

THE METHODS USED TO DOCUMENT ROUTES

The central purpose of this study is to track as precisely as possible the route followed on each of the eleven expeditions. In projecting the daily line of march, two comparisons have been used: a cross-document analysis of the information given in the diaries kept for each of the expeditions and a comparison of that information with contemporary topographic maps, reinforced by on-site verification from the ground and from the air of particular features mentioned in the diaries.

I have plotted the daily directions and distances recorded in the seventeen diaries (kept on the eleven expeditions) throughout the 600- to 800-mile trek from Monclova and Saltillo to Matagorda Bay, East Texas, and in some instances on to Los Adaes in present-day western Louisiana. This multiexpedition approach allows a comparison of the routes and the named campsites used on successive journeys. Contemporary U.S. Geological Survey topographical maps, in which heavily forested areas are colored, have been used to check the accuracy of distances between rivers and between identified camp locations and to verify diary reports of heavily wooded areas. Aerial photographs and on-site inspections have provided verification of sites, particularly in remote areas.

This study assumes that expedition diaries are the primary and most reliable source for determining the route that the expeditions followed. There are sound justifications for this assumption. These diaries were official Spanish documents, mandated by the Crown to be kept on each expedition. Diaries were usually signed under oath by the diarist and attested by at least two responsible members of the party. On six of the eleven expeditions, more than one expedition diary or account was kept, giving an additional means of verifying the line of march.

Expedition leaders customarily received detailed orders that specified the manner in which the diary accounts were to be kept. Two notations of the number of leagues (one in the written diary entry and the second on the margin of the page) and at least one indication of the direction traveled each day were required. In addition, the orders required other information to be included in the diary, such as the names of streams and campsites. The diarist was also supposed to list the fauna, flora, and Indian tribes encountered. This systematic method of maintaining a diary record is also found in the journal of the Frenchman Henri Joutel, who faithfully recorded the daily direction and distance traveled on La Salle's last journey in Texas.[16]

But any dependence on Spanish diary accounts requires not only a review of the English translation of the diaries, but a careful study of manuscript and typescript versions, where available. As noted in the text, several diary translations dropped one or more daily entries, so that manuscript and typescript copies had to be consulted to determine the direction and number of leagues traveled on those days.

Most of the expedition diaries were translated into English decades ago; De León's 1689 diary was translated in 1905. Until recently, the diaries of only Salinas Varona (1693), Pedro de Rivera (1727), and the Marqués de Rubí (1767) remained untranslated. However, the *Southwestern Historical Quarterly* published Salinas Varona's expedition diary in the fall of 1993.[17] The editors of the translation of Salinas's diary, Jack Jackson and I, have prepared an annotated English translation of the Rivera and Rubí diaries, included in *Imaginary Kingdom: Texas as Seen by the Rivera and Rubí Military Expeditions, 1727 and 1767*, forthcoming from Texas State Historical Association.

The diarist used a compass to determine the direction traveled, and the expedition leader (with the diarist and perhaps others) estimated the number of leagues traveled daily. The basic method of establishing distance was probably to multiply their travel time by an experienced estimate of the speed of march that day. The weather, terrain, and size and composition of the expedition party all affected the speed of travel and thus the distance covered on any particular day. This proved to be a reliable way to estimate distance when used by experienced travelers.[18]

The Spanish diarists and expedition leaders were frequently skilled frontiersmen, familiar with the use of the compass (and the astrolabe) and with estimating distances traveled. Nevertheless, the accuracy of the daily entry of the number of leagues traveled seems to vary according to the experiences of the diarist, the condition of the terrain, the severity of the weather, and whether the route was along a new pathway or one that had been used repeatedly.

The compass direction, recorded at least once a day, was sometimes general ("eastward") but usually specific—"to the north-northeast" (with a projected accuracy of 22.5°). A reader is still required to exercise judgment in projecting the location of each campsite day by day.

Although the diarist did not explain the method used to arrive at the number of leagues his party traveled each day, it can be demonstrated that most daily distances given are reasonably reliable. First, it appears that all diarists employed the Spanish league customarily used in New Spain at the time (approximately 2.6 miles) as the standard measurement of distance.[19] A comparison of the total number of leagues recorded by diarists between two locations with the distance measured along the same line of travel using large-scale contemporary United States and Mexican government maps supports this conclusion.[20] For example, in the movement between Monclova and the Francia crossing area on the Rio Grande in 1689, De León recorded traveling 49 leagues. The next year, the governor estimated 47 leagues; in 1693, Salinas reported 51 leagues; and in 1727, Rivera gave 52 leagues as the distance through the comparatively open country between the same two points. The measured distance on contemporary topographical maps along the same route is about 125 miles or 48 leagues.

For the journey between the Francia crossing area and the ford on the Nueces, several miles north of present-day Crystal City, De León recorded 18 leagues in 1689 and 19 the following year, Salinas reported 19 leagues in 1693, and Aguayo gave 21 leagues in 1721. The measured distance is about 52 miles or 20 leagues. From San Antonio northwest to the Colorado River crossing below Austin, Espinosa recorded 32 leagues in 1709; Aguayo reported 36 in 1721. The measured distance is about 88 miles or 34 leagues. Farther east, in the movement through a forested area between the Brazos and the Trinity, Espinosa recorded 33 leagues in 1716, Alarcón noted 34, and Rivera 35. The straight-line distance is about 83 miles or 32 leagues. This rather consistent pattern of estimating distances, with an accuracy range within 10 to 15 percent of actual distance, indicates that the distances recorded by the diarist should be given substantial weight in the absence of conflicting evidence such as a diarist's pattern of understating or overstating distances (as in the case of Terán and Solís).

The diary accounts must be read and studied sequentially to find the names first used for the rivers and creeks and to understand the modern streams to which these names apply. The various accounts must then be adjusted for deviations and errors in the names of rivers actually crossed and the directions and distances recorded. Carlos Castañeda characterized his confusion in trying to understand the various names used for rivers in Texas as a "nightmare" and added that Pichardo and Fray Morfí were likewise baffled.[21]

It is virtually impossible to trace accurately the route of a single expedition since no single diary provides sufficient information, and every diary has some "mistake," such as omitting the distance or direction traveled that day or assigning the wrong name to a river or campsite given another name on a previous expedition. But by comparing the seventeen diaries kept on the eleven expeditions, an accurate route can be worked out for each of them. The pattern of the routes emerges clearly as the named rivers and campsites are repeated on successive journeys.

Each expedition built on the experience of preceding ones, often using the same named campsites (*parajes*) or referring to them by name in passing. Road signs were carved in trees and on stone and were constructed in the form of wooden crosses and piles of rock or cairns. This study concludes that the riverbeds of the larger rivers have not been changed substantially by natural causes in the last 300 years—nor have the inland prairie areas or the tree lines bordering the coastal prairies. Therefore, verification of route projections has also been enhanced by the use of contemporary topographic maps, aerial photographs, and on-site inspection. Most features reported by the diarists—such as a river junction, significant turns in a river's direction, a dense woods, or a treeless prairie—can be found and verified on contemporary maps or by observation today.

Frequently, several senior members or Indian guides included in a new expedition party had accompanied earlier expeditions along the same route. The continuity of personnel on successive expeditions is impressive. In 1689, De León was accompanied by Fray Massanet, Alférez Martínez, and two identified Indian guides. The same four (including the same Pacpul and Quem guides) were with De León again in 1690, as was Salinas. Massanet, Martínez, Salinas, and the same two Indian guides were on the 1691–1692 journey with Terán, for all or part of the way. When Salinas returned to East Texas in 1693 with a relief convoy, therefore, he covered a route that he had twice traveled earlier.

The same continuity of personnel is found in the expeditions in the early eighteenth century. Espinosa, who was one of the leaders and the diarist for the 1709 expedition to the Colorado, accompanied Ramón and kept his own diary account again in 1716. Both Espinosa and Ramón (with their own experienced Tejas guides) joined the Alarcón expedition in San Antonio in 1718 on the march to East Texas, and Espinosa was with the Aguayo expedition in 1721 from the Rio Grande to the Sabine. It is reasonable to suggest that the route reports by these experienced travelers, who repeatedly used the same river crossings and campsites, were quite accurate.

The interpretation of the daily entries in the diary accounts is simplified by two factors. All expeditions between 1689 and 1727 crossed the Rio Grande at the same crossing area, about 35 miles below Eagle Pass, and all expeditions that went beyond the Brazos had as one of their points of destination a small valley (San Pedro) in northeastern Houston County, a few miles west of the Neches River. This firm fix on the points of departure and destination gives the diary reader significant benchmarks to use in projecting the route patterns.

Tracing the line of march across northern Coahuila and Texas was also simplified by the geography of the region traversed. The terrain covered along the routes was rather flat, with no mountains to climb. The vegetation was relatively sparse in the southwest, but rainfall was higher and frequent flooding occurred in the thickly wooded areas of the eastern sector. David J. Weber has called attention to recent studies by climatologists indicating that the Spanish expeditionary period into Texas occurred during a "Little Ice Age," a 300-year-period (ca. 1550 to 1850) when Europe and North America experienced colder and wetter conditions than we have today.[22] Susan L. Swain has described the adverse effects of the Little Ice Age on agricultural production in colonial Mexico.[23] Some unusually frigid and wet weather reports from South Texas and Coahuila in the expedition diaries tend to confirm the harder evidence of the Little Ice Age found by geographers and climatologists in the expansion and contraction of glaciers during the period.

As the expeditions moved northeast from the Rio Grande, the belted nature of the soil, particularly across the central part of Texas, created grassy prairies or corridors that influenced the selection of routes in some of the more heavily wooded regions, such as the Monte Grande northeast of the San Antonio area. The most significant physical features, however, were the large rivers that flowed to the southeast, following the tilt of the land toward the Gulf of Mexico. Had the Texas coast offered several deep natural harbors and access by river to inland destination points (as the French found in Louisiana), some of the Spanish overland expeditions might never have been undertaken or repeated, and the routes of communication during the colonial period would have been dramatically different.

Standard orders not only directed the expedition leader to maintain a diary, but also required expedition parties to use experienced Indian guides at all times. These guides were not asked to blaze new trails, but to lead the expedition party along known Indian trails to the destination. The mandate to use Indian guides was realistic and wise, being based on 200 years of Spanish expansion experience in the New World. But this reliance on Indian guides necessarily meant that no early Spanish expedition routes would be blazed through previously untrod wilderness. Instead, the first Spanish trails followed the best available Indian trade routes. Although this conclusion is not novel,[24] many Texas historians have discussed route projections without acknowledging the expedition leader's dependence on Indian guides or noting the specific linkage between expedition routes and early Indian trade routes.

Spanish authorities required each expedition not only to use Indian guides at all times but to record the Indian tribes encountered on the trip and to describe the wildlife and vegetation seen along the route each day. This study, which is directed primarily at locating expedition routes, uses the method of cross-document analysis and verification by employing contemporary sources and comparative materials to examine the extensive reports in the diaries on the location and movement of Indian tribes and the presence and range of wildlife and vegetation.

The route maps in each chapter depict the results of the route study. In the following chapters, each expedition party is tracked daily along its route across Texas, as the expedition diarist identifies the Indian tribes encountered and describes the terrain, wildlife, and vegetation, giving occasional reports on the weather and epidemics.

INDIAN TRIBES AND THE ENVIRONMENT

The ancestors of the tribes covered in this study arrived in the Southwest via Alaska from Asia ca. 10,000 B.C.[25] They had spread through the Americas and outnumbered the Europeans by the early 1500s, when the Spaniards arrived in central Mexico. The Spaniards thus had been in the New World for almost 200 years (and in northeastern Mexico for over a century) when the first expedition crossed the Rio Grande to meet the French threat. Consequently, they knew the Indians of New Spain very well. Two of the foremost Spanish historians who wrote about Indians on the northeastern frontier in the 1600s were Juan Bautista Chapa and Alonso de León (the elder). These two historians joined Fernando Sánchez de Zamora in writing a classic history of Nuevo

León which included extensive comments on the Indians. Chapa and De León described in detail their manner of living and named over two hundred and fifty tribes that resided at that time in the area between the Rio Grande and Monterrey.[26] In their respective essays in the *Historia,* both Chapa and De León identified graphically the most critical physical weakness or vulnerability of the Indians—their lack of any natural defenses to resist the deadly and highly contagious European diseases, such as smallpox.

De León tells the story of a young Spaniard in 1646 recuperating from a bout with smallpox (*viruelas*) who ignited a one-year epidemic near Monterrey that killed over 500 Indians and Spaniards. The local Indians reportedly fled in fear of the deadly smallpox, thereby spreading the disease to more distant tribes and depopulating Indian villages (*despobló rancherías enteras*).[27]

Chapa's account of the local Indians' vulnerability to European-induced diseases predicted that all Indians in New Spain would die from the diseases and all tribes would soon be annihilated (*va aniquilando*). In his discourse on natives in northeastern New Spain, Chapa listed by name 47 tribes that once lived near Monterrey, 44 other tribes that lived near Cadereyta (a city east of Monterrey about 70 miles below the Rio Grande), and 70 other tribes that lived closer to the Rio Grande, near the city of Cerralvo. These 161 tribes had all resisted Spanish occupation and had been defeated or otherwise had become extinct. Chapa then listed by name another 95 tribes that would also soon vanish. The chronicler's reason for the depopulation of the native tribes is perhaps best rendered in his own words:

> In the future these tribes [the second list of 95 tribes] will also disappear and it will be necessary to collect others because any Indian who falls sick will die, even if you care for him. . . . It will come to pass in this realm as it was told by Don Francisco López de Gomara . . . that, of a million and a half natives that were on the Island of Hispañola, in less than fifty years they were all gone. . . . These local tribes are [now] being annihilated and in time all the Indians of New Spain and Peru will disappear, as they have done in other places.[28]

As the Spanish colonial historian David J. Weber notes, some experts today estimate that in 1500 the population of the Americas was within a range of 70 million to over 100 million, more than the population of Europe, estimated at about 70 million. These demographers project that during the sixteenth century the Indian population in central Mexico was reduced substantially (perhaps as much as 90 percent), primarily by European diseases.[29]

Contemporary demographers have estimated that by the time the first Spanish expeditions were launched into Texas to meet the French threat (1680s), the Indian population in some areas involved in this study, such as Nuevo León and Coahuila (including parts of South Texas) and the western Caddo (the Tejas) in East Texas, had already been reduced in population to only a small fraction (one-eighth to one-tenth) of their size in 1520–1540, the time of first European contact.[30] David E. Stannard refers to the population collapse of the American Indian as the worst demographic disaster in the history of the world.[31] The Spanish expeditions into Texas covered by this study were initiated during the later stages of the Indian depopulation in North America.

The health of the native population and the impact of European diseases and epidemics on the Indians, as well as on the French and Spaniards, were noted by the expedition diarists. Epidemics affected each trip differently.

As indicated by Chapa and De León, the Indian tribes (termed "nations" by the Spaniards and the French) in northeastern New Spain were numerous and diverse, yet they were interrelated through trade and periodic aggressive engagements. Although the names of approximately 140 Indian tribes are given in the eleven diaries, the total number of tribes in the region covered by the expeditions, and in some instances even their tribal name and language, may never be known. As additional evidence is collected and studied, it appears that the lifestyle of the individual tribes that lived or passed through the 600-mile-wide area varied as greatly as the climate and vegetation.

Some Indian tribes from Coahuila and from below the Big Bend area of the Rio Grande were highly mobile hunters and traders who traveled 500 to 800 miles annually across much of northeastern New Spain and present-day Texas following distinct trade routes. They traded, hunted, and communicated with other Indians from northern Mexico and West Texas to Central and East Texas. Long before the arrival of the Spaniards, Indian trade fairs were held at locations near the southwestern edge of the traditional Tejas hunting grounds in the lower Colorado River area. Agriculture was well developed by the Caddo Indian communities in East Texas, such as the Tejas, and crops were also grown by the Jumano and other Indians along the Rio Grande and the Conchos River in northern Chihuahua. Beans, corn, and squash were staples in both locations before the first visit of a Spaniard.[32]

In Coahuila, and also between the Rio Grande and the San Antonio River, the expeditions encountered numerous small nomadic tribes that had been depopulated and survived principally by hunting and gathering food by 1700. Although some preliminary studies have been made of these Coahuiltecan people,[33] less has been published about the Indians who lived between the middle San Antonio River area and the Trinity. This deficiency may be met in part by the ongoing publication of the *Handbook of North American Indians,* which is scheduled to include as a subject area the Indian tribes in Central, North, and East Texas. As Thomas N. Campbell has stressed, the tribal situation at the time of Spanish exploration in Texas was also complicated by Indian migrations into and out of the Central Texas area as Spanish and Apache pressure was exerted, principally from the southwest and north.[34]

The instructions given to the expedition leaders and diarists required them to record more information than the basic route and Indian tribes encountered. The formal instructions to Governor Terán in 1691 and to the two military inspectors, Brigadier Pedro de Rivera (1727) and the Marqués de Rubí (1767), demanded information on the types of fauna and flora found in the provinces of northern New Spain. The information in the appendixes on flora and fauna and on Indian tribes encountered is derived primarily from diary entries.

The results of this study will be useful to those interested in a systematic and reliable approach to the reconstruction of expedition travel routes. Since these expedition diaries give detailed firsthand accounts of the Indian tribes, vegetation, wildlife, and the weather along the route traveled, the study and analysis will also interest archeologists, ethnohistorians, anthropologists, biogeographers, climatologists, historical demographers, and other scholars. The historian David J. Weber has recently stressed the importance of extracting and analyzing baseline information on vegetation and wildlife found in Spanish colonial documents, such as expedition diaries, against which changes can be measured.[35]

The precise location of an identified crossing or encampment is frequently critical to scholars who use information recorded at successive points along the route. For example, there can be no successful archeological investigation of an Indian campground or a river crossing used by local Indian guides on the early expeditions until there is some certainty as to where the diarist was on the date of the encampment or when the crossing occurred. The confusion caused by contemporary anthropologists' reliance on inaccurate route projections by historians is seen in William W. Newcomb, Jr.'s 1993 comments on the location of the Mayeye Indians in Central Texas. Newcomb, citing Herbert E. Bolton, says the Mayeye were seen in 1727 (by Pedro Rivera) near the city of Temple in Bell County, whereas Rivera actually reported meeting the tribe 60 miles to the south-southeast in Burleson County.[36] It is therefore encouraging that historians, anthropologists, and archeologists have begun to focus their respective disciplines on common questions.[37]

Alonso de León's 1689 expedition, guided by Géry and two Indians from Coahuila, was the first Spanish *entrada* to venture from northeastern New Spain beyond the San Antonio River, but it went no farther than the west bank of the Colorado across the river from the present city of La Grange in Fayette County. Still, this expedition again brought the Spaniards into contact with the friendly Tejas Indians of East Texas, who thereafter served as the essential local connection in the Spaniards' coming confrontation with the Apache on the frontier and with the French in Louisiana.[38]

It was the threat of the French, more than any consideration of the Indians themselves, that controlled the pattern and flow of Spanish *entradas* during the following eighty years. The period of Spanish expeditions from northern New Spain that began in the 1680s ended soon after the French threat disappeared in the 1760s as a result of the transfer of French Louisiana west of the Mississippi to the Spaniards after the British defeat of the French in Canada and the close of the Seven Years' War in Europe. Spanish expeditions that crossed Texas after 1768 (and several before that date) tended to originate and be conducted within the area, rather than being sent into or across Texas from New Spain.

During the period after the 1760s, Indian power rather than the French imperial threat dominated colonial policy in northeastern New Spain. This new Indian power was generated not from within the depopulated ranks of local Texas tribes, but principally from the more nomadic, well-armed horsemen who rode in force off the Plains from the north, driving the Spanish to positions along a defensive corridor that generally followed the Rio Grande and driving the Central and West Texas Apache deep into northeastern New Spain.

As the chapters covering each expedition unfold, our familiarity with and respect for each diarist grows; in effect, the diarist serves as a present-day guide. Generally, the diary accounts were composed daily, while the impressions of that day were still fresh. The diarist not only directs our steps, but reveals the very earliest glimpses of the Province of Texas. Governor Alonso de León, our first diarist and guide, inspires such confidence. He was not only one of the most daring expedition leaders, but also one of the most accurate recorders of distance and direction and of scenes long since past.

FIGURE 2
Alonso de León leads his men toward the French fort on modern Matagorda Bay in 1689.

TWO

IN SEARCH OF LA SALLE

Governor Alonso de Léon's 1689 Expedition

On March 23, 1689, the governor of the Province of Coahuila, Alonso de León, left Monclova (in northeastern New Spain) to lead the first Spanish *entrada* to search beyond the Nueces River for La Salle's French colony, thought to be located somewhere on the present-day Texas coast.[1] Although there had been four unsuccessful Spanish overland expeditions and five unsuccessful marine excursions to locate the French colony, expectations were high.

De León—who had recently been promoted to the governorship of Coahuila—had captured Jean Géry, a 50-year-old Frenchman living among the Indians a short distance north of the Rio Grande, probably in the Kinney-Uvalde County area.[2] Under questioning by the Spanish, Géry testified that he had arrived with René Robert Cavelier, Sieur de La Salle, at the Texas coast five years earlier and had been sent to "pacify" the Indians near the Rio Grande. Géry, who would serve as both a guide and an interpreter, knew the route from the Rio Grande to the French colony on the bay. The Frenchman understood the language of the Indian tribes living near the Rio Grande (probably a Coahuilteco dialect) and could also speak a second Indian language (probably Sanan) with several Indian tribes living between what are presently the Guadalupe and Colorado rivers.

This chapter is based on three accounts of the expedition. The first is De León's personal diary translated into English by Elizabeth H. West, Texas State Historical Association Quarterly 8 *(January 1905), 199–224, republished in Herbert E. Bolton, ed.,* Spanish Exploration in the Southwest, 1542–1706, *388–404. The second is Juan Bautista Chapa's diary account,* Historia del Nuevo Reino De León de 1650 a 1690, *142–157. The third is Fray D. Massanet's 1690 letter to Don Carlos de Sigüenza, translated into English by Lilia M. Casís,* Texas State Historical Association Quarterly 2, *no. 4 (April 1899), 253–312. The manuscript copy of De León's diary,* Texas Documentary History, *vol. 1, Mexico (Viceroyalty), [AGN] Provincias Internas, in the Manuscript Division of the Library of Congress was also consulted.*

The high expectations were reflected in the size and composition of this *entrada*[3]—eighty-five armed soldiers, a French-speaking interpreter (Alférez Francisco Martínez), two padres, twelve mule drivers, thirteen servants, and an unspecified number of Indians, in addition to over seven hundred horses, two hundred head of cattle, and pack mules carrying eighty loads of flour, five hundred pounds of chocolate, and three loads of tobacco. The principal representative of the church was Fray Damián Massanet, who kept no diary but recorded his narrative of the expedition in a detailed letter to Don Carlos de Sigüenza y Góngora in 1690 and gave a further account of the existing Indian trade routes and his recommendations for developing the region in another letter to the viceroy.[4] Also on the journey was Juan Bautista Chapa (sometimes known as "Autor Anónimo"), an old acquaintance of the governor and the governor's father, Alonso de León (the elder). Chapa wrote his own account of the trip and apparently took the astrolabe readings along the way.[5] Chapa had accompanied De León on his expedition to the Gulf Coast in 1686, recording locations along that earlier route by the use of the astrolabe.[6]

De León's expedition marched about 21 leagues (55 miles) downstream along the bank of Coahuila Creek, which runs north from Monclova to the junction with the Salado de Nadadores River, then along the right bank of the Nadadores between two high bluffs called Baluartes, past a lone tall cottonwood (at a site later called Alamo), to the junction with the Sabinas River (*Monclova*, G14-4, and *Nueva Rosita*, G14-1). The route from Monclova north was east of the line of march Fernando del Bosque followed to the Rio Grande in 1675; it was closer to the one De León had taken the year before to recover Jean Géry. From the river crossing near the junction (March 27), the guides directed De León north for another 18 leagues across open plains to the Rio Grande. De León had received formal training and a certificate as a navigator, enabling him to maintain an exceptionally accurate account of the line of march.[7]

As the party approached the river, also called the Río Bravo, about 35 miles below modern Eagle Pass, the governor secured a guide and interpreter, a Quem Indian who had recently spent a week at La Salle's colony while searching the coastal area for his kidnapped wife. Earlier, a leader of the Pacpul Indians (Géry called him "Brother") had been retained as a guide by Massanet.

To the surprise of De León and his troops, about 10 miles below the Rio Grande crossing some 500 Indians gathered to meet the expedition and to celebrate the arrival of their dear friend, the old Frenchman Géry. The Indian encampment included several tribes with whom Géry was living when De León captured him, including the Jumano and Mescal, who were also encountered over 200 miles north of the Rio Grande on later expeditions. The other two nations identified were the Hape and Xiabu (or Ijiaba). The Hape were a friendly tribe that Fernando del Bosque had met in 1675 north of the Rio Grande and that helped later expedition parties ford the Rio Grande, but the Xiabu were not identified in subsequent expedition diaries or reports. It is significant that De León referred to the Indian tribes as "nations," acknowledging their sovereignty.[8] The French did the same.[9]

The Indian encampment provided Géry with a prominent place of honor covered with buffalo hides for the evening, in keeping with the accommodations he had enjoyed

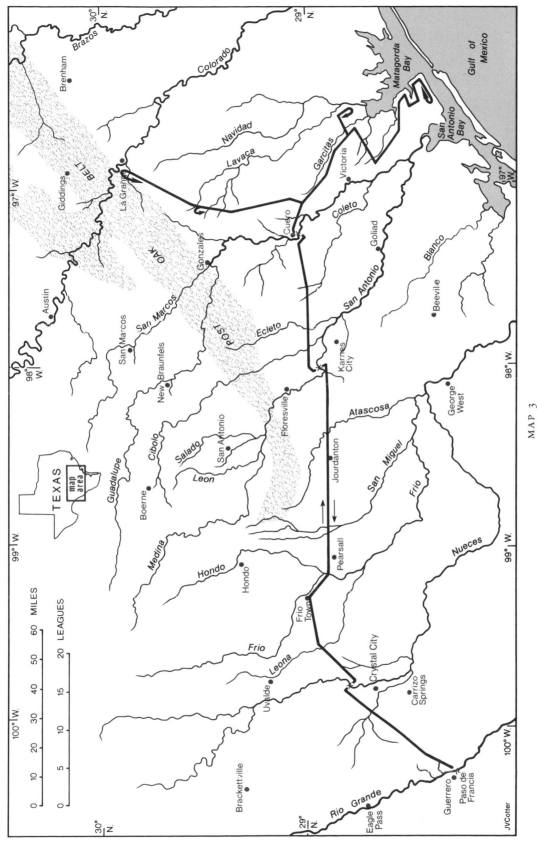

MAP 3

Governor Alonso de León's 1689 Expedition

TEXAS
map area

MILES
LEAGUES

Brazos
Brenham
Colorado
Giddings
BELT
La Grange
Navidad
Lavaca
Garcitas
Victoria
Cuero
Coleto
OAK
Gonzales
Goliad
San Antonio
Blanco
Austin
San Marcos
San Marcos
POST
Ecleto
Beevile
San Marcos
New Braunfels
Karnes City
Floresville
Atascosa
George West
Cibolo
Salado
San Antonio
Jourdanton
San Miguel
Boerne
Leon
Frio
Guadalupe
Medina
Pearsall
Nueces
Hondo
Hondo
Frio Town
Frio
Crystal City
Leona
Uvalde
Carrizo Springs
Brackettville
Guerrero
Paso de Francia
Eagle Pass
Rio Grande

Gulf of Mexico
Matagorda Bay
San Antonio Bay

97° W.
98° W.
99° W.
100° W.
30° N.
29° N.

JVCotter

the year before when De León captured him. Chapa added that Indian maidens gathered around Géry as a part of the warm reception and that some tribal members were away from the encampment hunting bison.[10]

In response to the favorable welcome by Géry's friends, De León distributed clothing, blankets, beads, and knives, and furnished five head of cattle to barbecue for a celebration feast. The governor reported that thirty-two hollow eyes in sixteen dried human skulls securely hung on individual pegs on a ten-foot pole glared down on the festivities, a perhaps unintended but nevertheless stark warning to the Spaniards.

They probably crossed the Rio Grande at a point identified as the Francia crossing, about 5 miles east-southeast of modern Guerrero, Coahuila, and about 30 miles south of Eagle Pass (see Map 3 and *Piedras Negras*, H14-10). The *entrada* represented one of the most impressive displays of Spanish military power ever marshaled in the area north of the Rio Grande.[11] The troops and supporting entourage were undoubtedly an impressive sight, spreading in a column for over a mile with Governor De León, in armor or mail, leading the procession. An armed battle with the French forces waiting at the settlement (named Fort Saint-Louis) near Matagorda Bay was expected within the next two weeks.

It took the governor three days, April 2 through 4, moving to the northeast through mesquite brush and cacti, to reach the present-day Nueces River, which the governor named Río de las Nueces because numerous pecan trees lined the riverbank. De León named the campsite used the first night El Paraje de los Cuervos for the flock of crows (estimated at 3,000) that appeared that evening.[12] On the second evening, the governor's campsite was located at a creek called Arroyo de Ramos. At this encampment located on a tributary of modern Comanche Creek, near the intersection of Maverick, Zavala, and Dimmit counties, De León and his companion Chapa (whom he calls "el Autor") took a reading with an astrolabe acknowledged to be defective that indicated the party was at 26°31' latitude, a latitude that actually falls 20–30 miles south of Monclova. The rough journey ahead did not improve the impaired condition of Chapa's astrolabe: readings taken later along the route continued to be far afield. Because of the consistent northeast direction taken during all three days and the number of leagues reportedly traveled (a total of 18 or about 47 miles), the crossing of the Nueces is projected to be about 8 miles north of present-day Crystal City, the county seat of Zavala County (see Map 3).[13]

The party traveled only about 18 miles on the following day and made many turns and detours, including an early turn back a short distance downstream. They used axes to cut a path through the thickets of mesquite and prickly pear. Camp that evening was on the present-day Leona River, which was given the name Río Sarco by De León. This river is a western tributary of the larger Frio River system and is the only major river 18 miles northeast of the Nueces from the location where this party crossed the previous day.[14]

On April 6, De León traveled only 13 miles, again to the northeast. This route took the party through open pasture with occasional mottes of oaks to the bank of the present-day Frio River at a point near Frio Town in the northwest corner of Frio County, as illustrated on Map 3 (see also *Crystal City*, NH14-11, and *San Antonio*, NH14-8).

De León named the present Frio River Río Hondo.[15] That afternoon, the party found some large white rocks with carved crosses and other skillfully made figures that the governor said had been cut into the stones many years earlier (*al bajar al río hallamos unas piedras grandes blancas y en algunas de ellas vimos algunas cruces grabadas y otras figuras hechas a mano con mucha perfección y al parecer son de mucho tiempo*). Such petroglyphs were frequently used to mark Indian trade routes.[16] De León's notation suggests that his Indian guides were probably leading the expedition party along an old trade route that connected the Indian communities from below the Rio Grande with those in Central Texas and perhaps beyond.

On the following day (April 7), the party did not cross the Frio but instead turned downstream 10 miles, following the right bank east and southeast to camp a few miles below the junction of the Frio with present-day Hondo Creek.[17] This location on the Frio was the fording area used by every subsequent expedition that traveled from the Francia crossing area on the Rio Grande used by De León toward East Texas or Matagorda Bay on the Gulf Coast, with the sole exception of Terán in 1691. Terán crossed the Frio near De León's April 6 campsite in northwestern Frio County and then cut across what are presently Seco and Hondo creeks in south-central Medina County as he moved toward the present-day San Antonio area.

At the close of De León's entry for April 7, the governor commented that his party had not encountered any Indians since meeting the five tribes near the Rio Grande, but had found Indian trails that had been made much earlier (*fuimos atravesando algunas veredas de indios, eran de mucho tiempo y no pareció ninguno*). Again, De León confirmed by this comment on his line of march that his party was not blazing a new road but rather following known paths that Indians had used for many years.

On Friday, April 8, De León reported that he and his troops crossed the Frio River and marched through mesquite brush another 20 miles generally toward the east and northeast. The governor commented that around midday the party crossed two deep ravines, which suggests that the party passed the two parallel branches of the present San Miguel Creek that run north to south about two miles apart at this point a few miles above their junction. When De León passed the same stream the next year on his second expedition, he named the creek (the present San Miguel) for his traveling compadre Chapa. The camp that evening was probably near the Frio-Atascosa County line on a small tributary of San Miguel Creek.

Holy Saturday turned out to be a festive day. De León traveled only 13 miles, generally to the northeast, before fixing camp and cracking a keg of wine for the troops. Around the campground tall pecan trees and numerous oaks supported thick grapevines. In honor of the occasion, the stream (the present Atascosa River) was named Arroyo del Vino. The campsite was a few miles south of the modern city of Pleasanton. Perhaps the wine flowed too freely: the horses stampeded at nine in the evening, even though fifteen soldiers had been assigned to guard the remuda. By the time a count was made in the sober light of Easter Sunday morning, 102 horses were missing. Easter was spent rounding up the strays, and the search continued until vespers.

On Monday, the governor moved out for a long day's march 31 miles east through woods of oak and pecan trees and then northeast to the present San Antonio River, which De León named Río de Medina. The governor described the river as very large, although there was not much water at the time, and as having a good ford, which implies shallow water and a firm bottom. The site was probably the solid rock shelf that extends from bank to bank at the Conquista crossing above present-day Falls City, in Karnes County (see *Crystal City,* NH14-11).

A number of prominent Texas historians, including Carlos E. Castañeda and Robert S. Weddle, have also suggested that De León crossed the San Antonio River in the same general area in Karnes County; Weddle identifies the crossing site as 8 to 10 miles downstream, closer to Panna Maria or Runge. The 1991 Texas State Highway Department history of the Old San Antonio Road is the only study that mistakenly projects that De León crossed the river near the present-day city of San Antonio, approximately 35 miles upstream.[18]

On April 12, the party crossed the San Antonio River very easily, although there was a 50- to 60-foot descent to the river. (The present banks are as high as 60 feet at locations near Falls City.) The party then marched east over low, open hills and crossed several deep ravines or creeks through formations of red and yellow clay (perhaps the Marcelinas Creek area) and a dry stream most likely associated with present Cibolo Creek. After marching about 13 miles, the party found a good campground and stream (modern Cibolo Creek), which was named Arroyo del León because a dead mountain lion or cougar was found nearby.

The next morning Governor De León and his troops moved east-northeast. After marching only a mile, the party passed a small hill with a motte of oaks to the right. Among the trees, the scouts or guides found small handmade piles of stones or cairns (*estaban en ella unos montecillos de piedras puestas a mano*). During this period, a small pile or pedestal of rocks along a pathway was used by both Indians and Spanish explorers to mark trails or as a memorial. For example, in September 1718, Governor Alarcón placed a cairn on a small hill near the Guadalupe River below present Gonzales in order to mark his trail. Because these small stone markers found in the woods were not prominent, the Indian guides and possibly the old Frenchman Géry may have searched for the rock marker to confirm that the party was still following the old Indian route. During the Spanish interrogation of Géry in Mexico City the year before, the Frenchman insisted that he knew the route from the Rio Grande to the French settlement because the trail was marked.[19]

After traveling through about 5 miles of woods and then through a more open stretch, the party reached a campsite on a small creek. De León spent that evening on a branch of one of the larger tributaries of Coleto Creek northeast of Yorktown and about 15 miles from the Cibolo Creek camp (see Map 3). In this area of western DeWitt County, a major tributary of Coleto Creek is identified on current government maps (see *Seguin,* NH14-9) as Salt Creek.

The governor followed the same east-northeast direction and traveled the same distance the next day. The company went through country that De León described as the most pleasant the party had crossed. They passed a large herd of bison, the first they had seen on the trip. (Bison were reported on later expeditions in the seventeenth century ranging well below the Rio Grande. See the entry "Bison" in Appendix I.) The party killed six bison for food.

The Quem guide told Massanet a great river would be found that day. As predicted, at two o'clock in the afternoon, De León reached the river, which was then known as La Rivière de la Madeleine by the French and Río de Magdalena by the Spaniards. The governor renamed the river Nuestra Señora de Guadalupe in honor of the protectress whose picture had been painted on the royal standard or flag carried on the *entrada*.

Map 3 shows the governor's position on the Guadalupe at a point a few miles below the mouth of present Sandies Creek, near the place later identified by the Marqués de Rubí as Vado del Gobernador when he crossed the Guadalupe at the same ford in 1767. The crossing is also identified by the same name and location on a ca. 1807 map by Manuel Agustín Mascaró.[20]

Herbert E. Bolton, Carlos E. Castañeda, Robert S. Weddle, and Donald E. Chipman have projected that De León's crossing of the Guadalupe River was near or a few miles below present Victoria.[21] The projection that the ford was below Victoria, about 40 miles downstream from Vado del Gobernador, conflicts sharply with repeated diary accounts of the distance (about 17 leagues) and direction (east-northeast) recorded by De León on the three-day trip from the San Antonio River to the Guadalupe. It also cannot be reconciled with the specific distance and direction recorded between the Guadalupe crossing east to the bay and from the same Guadalupe crossing north to the Colorado River crossing. This triangular measurement of distance and direction from the Guadalupe crossing east to the bay and north to the Colorado gives substantial support for the present projection.

On April 15, the party traveled a total of only about 5 miles—2 to 3 miles downriver to reach the river crossing and another 2 to 3 miles beyond the river, to a campground on the left bank of a small creek.

Early on Saturday morning (April 16), a Mass of Thanksgiving was sung in honor of the Blessed Virgin of Guadalupe. De León then divided and reorganized his forces for the advance upon the French fort. The Quem guide had assured the party that the distance to Fort Saint-Louis along a pathway was only about 15 leagues (39 miles). This proved to be a close estimate.

The reorganized troops—an advance party of sixty soldiers led by the governor, followed by the main party or rear-guard—had traveled in an easterly direction only about 8 to 10 miles when a soldier with the rear-guard sighted a lone Indian in the woods. This was the first Indian the party had encountered north of the Rio Grande.

The Indian appeared unafraid of the Spanish soldiers, and Géry stepped forward to serve as interpreter. The Indian guides from south of the Rio Grande, who probably spoke Coahuilteco, were not familiar with the local Sanan language.[22] According to Massanet, this Indian was the first to inform De León that the French colony at the bay had been ravaged "two moons" earlier. The local Indian reported that most inhabitants had been killed by coastal Indians and that several children had been taken captive. After questioning the Indian through the old Frenchman, De León left his main camp in place and was led to a nearby village inhabited by Emet and Cava Indians, tribes that lived principally between the Guadalupe and Colorado rivers at that time. According to Massanet, this village was only 5 miles off the path that De León's party was following to the French settlement.

At the camp, the Indians' first reaction to the sudden appearance of De León's troops was fright, in contrast to the delight expressed by the Jumano, Mescal, and other Indians who had greeted Géry a few miles below the Rio Grande. The Emet and Cava Indians immediately fled to hide in the nearby woods. Only their camp dogs, laden with bison hides, failed to escape. At that time, local tribes in the Guadalupe Valley seldom had horses, but some did train young wolves and coyotes as pack animals.[23] When the village leaders were assured that no harm was intended, the Indians extended to the Spaniards a greeting that has become associated with the name of the state: "Techas! Techas!" they shouted—meaning, according to Massanet, "Friends! Friends!" "Tejas" or "Techas" was used by several tribes to identify themselves as enemies of the Apache.[24]

The villagers told De León that four Frenchmen had visited their camp (near present Irish Creek) a few days earlier with some Tejas Indians and that the French party had left traveling north to the Tejas nation. After the village leaders agreed to furnish two guides to help De León find the Frenchmen, the governor distributed tobacco and trinkets to the local residents.

There was evidence at this encampment that the Indians had not only heard about the destruction of the nearby French colony but had been there to loot. According to Massanet, a large young villager wearing a friar's robe appeared before De León and the mortified padre. Presumably, the robe had been taken from one of the priests killed during the massacre at the colony.

In the early afternoon, De León decided to leave his main base-camp in place at its location about 13 miles east of the Guadalupe crossing. With a force of sixty men, Jean Géry, Chapa, and the two local Indian guides, De León proceeded north, following the trail of the four Frenchmen and their Tejas companions. The guides led the governor about 20 miles that afternoon to a location near the DeWitt-Lavaca County line. Here, at sunset, De León's party reached a second village, populated by more than 250 Toho and Tohaha Indians.

At this village, De León heard in more detail how the French colony first had been ravaged by smallpox and finally had been decimated by the coastal Indians several months earlier. According to Chapa's account, the Indians said that most of the French community earlier had died from an attack of smallpox (*un achaque de viruelas*).[25] This report of a smallpox epidemic was later confirmed by two Frenchmen captured by De León. Medical experts have reviewed these and other French accounts of La Salle's voyage and concluded that the settlement was reduced by other diseases as well, including typhoid fever and one "syphilitic in nature."[26]

De León also found at the encampment additional evidence of looting of the colony by these local Indians. One Indian was dressed in French clothing and other villagers had French books, including a Bible. De León and his troops spent the night with the Indians near the village. The second village campsite for the evening of April 16 was on a headwater creek of the Lavaca River near modern Yoakum, in the vicinity of a Spanish *paraje* later called Padre Campa's Pond.

The following morning (April 17), the governor and his contingent, still using their local guides, continued north to a third Indian camp along the Indian trade route that Nicolás de Lafora later called the Camino Real. This village of Emet Indians was on what is presently the Lavaca River, between Shiner and Moulton near the Lavaca-Fayette County line and close to the Spanish *paraje* later called Lavaca (see *Seguin*, NH14-9).

These three encampments visited by De León are marked distinctly on the map of De León's 1689 expedition prepared by Carlos de Sigüenza.[27] Herbert E. Bolton correctly suggested that the creeks crossed by De León north of the Guadalupe in 1689 (and again in 1690) were the upper waters of the Lavaca River.[28] Just as the Indians sought village sites near fresh flowing streams or ponds to bathe, as was their custom in the early morning, the Spaniards required camp locations where their horses and pack animals could be watered nightly The Spaniards later called the overnight camp locations or *parajes* along this stretch of the Camino Real Piélago del Rosal, La Mota del Padre Campa, Los Ramitos, Lavaca, Navidad, and Breviario.

To De León's surprise, the Emet Indians in this third encampment recognized and greeted (apparently in Sanan) the Frenchman Géry as an old friend as the Indians below the Rio Grande had greeted him. Géry was able to converse easily with them and to learn in detail about the four Frenchmen. Toward evening, an Indian visitor from a village up the trail leading northward came specifically to talk with his friend Géry. De León, who was obviously puzzled by the sudden appearance of the Indian visitor and by the warm reception given Géry, surmised that the neighbor must somehow have heard that Géry was at that village and came to pay his respects.

At the Emet Indian village on the headwaters of the Lavaca River, over 200 miles northeast of the encampment that greeted the old Frenchman with such affection and respect three weeks earlier near the Rio Grande, both De León and Chapa were amazed to witness and were moved to record the same expression of the Indians' admiration. The charismatic quality of Géry was summarized in Chapa's observation that no less than thirty tribes—separately identified by name by the chronicler—gave their allegiance (*su devoción*) to Géry along the 175-mile stretch of the Indian trade route that ran from the Rio Grande to the Colorado.[29]

It should be noted that earlier, after being captured and then taken to Mexico City, Géry had testified that La Salle had sent him out from the French colony to pacify the Indians near the French colony and later to pacify the Indians to the west near the Rio Grande.[30] These two favorable receptions suggest that Géry's testimony was accurate and that he was at least a popular and trusted figure across a wide area of South Texas at the time.

At this point, De León decided to return to his base-camp in DeWitt County and not to continue pursuing the Frenchmen. A local villager, who had just returned from escorting the four Frenchmen and the Tejas Indians, reported that the river to the north (the Colorado River) was flooded and that De León's large party could not cross it. The Indian did agree to take a message, translated into French by Alférez Martínez, requesting the four Frenchmen to return to meet the Spaniards. The Indian messenger assured the Spaniards that he knew the Indian trade route to the Tejas and that he could find the Frenchmen. He promised to return with a written reply from the Frenchmen in a few days and to join the governor at the ravaged French fort on the bay. De León agreed to give a horse to the Indian if he returned as promised.

The messenger was obviously familiar with the old trade route that followed the relatively flat and open ridge of the Oakville Escarpment to the north-northeast from the Guadalupe crossing in DeWitt County to the Colorado ford near present La Grange in Fayette County and on to the junction of the Navasota and Brazos rivers, along which the Frenchmen and their Tejas party would camp. The Indian pathway extended past the Brazos crossing into Grimes County northeast to the Tejas Indian villages beyond the Trinity River in Houston County. The guide also knew the location of the former French colony near Matagorda Bay, which was about 80 miles south of his village, because he collected a horse from De León eight days later (April 17–25), at the ruins of the fort after he had returned from the Tejas and delivered to the governor a written reply from one of the Frenchmen, Jean L'Archevêque.

On the way back to the Guadalupe base-camp near Irish Creek (April 18), the governor received a report, brought by an Indian, that there had been a stampede at the base-camp. More than one hundred horses and a soldier named Juan de Charles were missing. The following two days, April 19 and 20, were spent near the Irish Creek camp recovering the lost soldier and most of the horses with the help of Indians from several local villages. The Indians who helped were given tobacco, which was their favorite reward. It is curious that the Spaniards, who were introduced to tobacco by the Indians on their arrival to the New World in the 1490s, were distributors of that commodity to Indians in Texas 200 years later. Blankets and beads were also parceled out to those who aided in the search.

While waiting for the recovery of Juan, Chapa made another observation of the sun at the Irish Creek camp and the party found itself at 28°41' north according to De León. Chapa corrected De León's diary account and personally reported 28°4'. According to the contemporary government map, it appears that the camp was located at about 29°3' latitude and about 97°10' longitude (but no reading of longitude was attempted and reported in expedition diaries until 1727, when Brigadier Pedro de Rivera and his engineer gave their professional observations).

Juan de Charles actually was not found by the Spaniards but was returned to his camp by an Indian bison hunting party who had found him near camp. Juan was kept overnight, but during the evening he injured himself by igniting his own gunpowder. The next morning, after treating Juan's injuries, the Indians led him back to a ridge near De León's base-camp and quickly disappeared. De León was pleased but surprised that Juan survived the night with "the savages," who, according to the soldier, treated him with great kindness. These "savages" apparently did not trust the Spaniards either.

On April 21, the governor left the Irish Creek base-camp with his full force including his Indian guides and proceeded toward the former French colony on Garcitas Creek. At least one local Cava was still serving as a guide. Early that morning, the party saw and crossed present Chicolete Prairie, the open, flat coastal plain that Massanet described as being treeless for long stretches. Chicolete Prairie today begins a few miles southeast of the Irish Creek area and extends to the coast (see *Seguin*, NH14-9, and *Beeville*, NH14-12). The party reached upper Garcitas Creek after marching about 20 miles. They saw herds of buffalo, and the padre reported that they met a small band of about twenty unidentified Indians. De León camped that night near a pond or small tributary of Garcitas Creek.

Early the following morning, the governor found the former French settlement 8 miles down Garcitas Creek "toward the east." The scene at the ruins of the settlement was one of horror. After La Salle had left on his last journey toward the Mississippi from this colony, only about twenty-five inhabitants remained, less than 10 percent of the initial settlement population. Two of them were priests, according to a young boy, Jean-Baptiste Talon, who survived the slaughter and was later rescued.[31]

Three deteriorated bodies, one of a partly clad woman, were found and buried. The "coastal Indians" (Karankawa) had killed all the adults and a small baby. They captured and took with them four young boys and one or two young girls. De León speculated that the bodies of many residents had been devoured by some of the alligators seen in the vicinity.

Clothing and personal effects were scattered about, and the six small houses, roofed with buffalo hides, had been sacked and looted. On the frame of the door of the fort was inscribed "1684." The one remaining iron cannon was buried. The two-story fort remained standing, and De León intentionally did not burn it. The only life in the devastated settlement was found in the fenced garden, where some corn, asparagus, and endive were still growing.

During the following two days, De León explored the western shoreline of Matagorda Bay, the head of which was about 4 miles downstream from the old fort. Géry served as the guide on De León's tour of the bay area. His services as a knowledgeable guide there dispel for me any question of whether he had arrived with La Salle or was of sound mind. The old Frenchman led De León and thirty troopers from the campsite on Garcitas Creek to the southwest 12 miles away from the mouth of the creek and the bay and then well around the headwaters of two other creeks (present Placedo Creek and Chocolate Bayou), circling almost 20 miles before turning east again about 8 miles back to a campsite close to present Magnolia Beach.

The next morning, the party followed the bay shore around many small lagoons and Powderhorn Inlet for another 20 miles. The horses could not be ridden through the deep sand at times, as the party pressed on to present Pass Cavallo at the mouth of Matagorda Bay. Dewberries and grapes were abundant along the way, according to Fray Massanet. The troops explored the mouth of the bay area, venturing southwest down the coast a distance of perhaps 6 to 8 miles, and then began the return trek along the same route.

On the night of April 24, De León and his scouting party camped along a brackish creek (present-day Placedo Creek) near an abandoned Indian camp, where they found several Indian canoes, which led to the later name Arroyo de las Canoas (Canoe Creek).

By noon the next day, the party was back in camp on the Garcitas, having covered a reported total of 52 leagues (135 miles). The projected route along the bay shore is shown on Map 3. There De León found waiting the Emet messenger, who had returned from East Texas with a reply from one of the Frenchmen living with the Tejas east of the Trinity. The reply, written in French, explained that two of the four Frenchmen had accepted De León's invitation and were coming to join the governor.

The Emet was awarded his promised horse. At that time, the local Emet, Cava, Toho, Tohaha, and coastal Karankawa Indians did not usually possess horses, as did the Tejas Indians to the east, the Apache further to the northwest, and the Jumano and some other Indian tribes from West Texas.[32] A horse was no doubt a great prize for the local Indians, and mounts were eagerly sought in exchange for some valuable service or the return of a hostage.

It is well documented that the local Indians including the Emet and Toho kept themselves in excellent physical condition—swimming, bathing, and running each day. There are reports of these Indians outrunning horses and deer on a long and exhausting chase.[33] But this Emet messenger was perhaps exceptional. At about noon on April 17, he had left camp near present-day Shiner, about 30 miles southwest of La Grange on the Colorado. He raced on foot to the Colorado, swam it, and then trotted up the trail some 60 miles to the Brazos River crossing, then some 60 miles further to the Trinity, and finally some 40 miles beyond the Trinity to the Tejas camp. He received the written answer there and returned along the same pathway to Shiner and from there down the Indian pathway some 80 miles to the bay. This round-trip trek of some 440 miles, which included swimming three large rivers, was made in eight full days—from noon on April 17 to midday on the 25th. The Indian messenger had covered on foot the distance of two marathons a day for eight consecutive days.[34]

The next day, April 26, the main camp moved back upstream 8 miles to the former campsite on Garcitas Creek to secure better water and to explore the area north and eastward toward the present Lavaca River. Géry was again the guide, this time leading De León and twenty men 8 miles northeast to the present Lavaca River, which De León named the San Marcos. This designation of the San Marcos River in 1689 also led De León to identify the modern Colorado River as the San Marcos in 1690. When De León arrived at the present Colorado the following year on his trip to East Texas, he thought the river was an upper stretch of the one he had named San Marcos the year before near the bay.

After reaching the Lavaca, the party proceeded with some difficulty downstream to a little hill about a mile and a half from the mouth of the river. They estimated that the distance between the mouth of the Lavaca and the mouth of the smaller Garcitas Creek was about 4 miles and that it was the same distance between the mouth of Garcitas Creek and the former colony upstream. Near the mouth of the river, Chapa again took a reading with his defective astrolabe with mixed results. De León reported that the latitude reading taken by Chapa was 26°3'; Chapa himself reported 29°3', a figure much closer to the correct reading of the bay area, which extends from about 28°25' to 28°40' based on the contemporary USGS map (see *Beeville*, NH14-12). It is interesting to note that the French monk Christian Le Clercq had reported a reading of 27°45' for the bay, illustrating the difficulties cartographers had in preparing accurate maps at that time.[35] De León returned to the Garcitas camp for the evening, having covered a total of 15 leagues (39 miles).

The next day, the party returned toward the former campsite near Irish Creek. Although the diary record is not clear, apparently the party split near the old campsite (according to Massanet), with the principal group continuing about 12 miles upstream to the Guadalupe crossing and the original base-camp near present Cuero to wait for De León. The governor took a command of thirty soldiers north from the Irish Creek campsite along the same Indian trail that he had used the week before toward the Colorado River in search of the Frenchmen.

With the assistance of local guides, De León traveled northward more than 25 leagues (65 miles) up the path across De Witt, Lavaca, and part of Fayette County to a Tohaha village near the Colorado River across from modern La Grange, where the Frenchmen and some Tejas were found camped. The governor returned to the Guadalupe camp with only two of the four Frenchmen; the other two had decided that it was safer to remain with the Indians than to risk an uncertain surrender to Spanish troops.

The French captives who returned were naked, covered heavily with tattoos, and carried only an antelope skin. The two men, Jean L'Archevêque and Jacques Grollet, along with a chieftain of the Tejas Indians and eight of his men, returned to the base-camp near the Guadalupe crossing with Governor De León to meet for two days and to give testimony using Alférez Francisco Martínez as the interpreter.

Jean L'Archevêque was interrogated first. He stated that he had arrived with La Salle at the bay five years earlier, where they had placed a large cross with the coat-of-arms of the king of France so all would know of their presence. He and several others, including his partner, had become ill on their journey with La Salle toward the Mississippi. The sick men were required to remain with the Tejas Indians in East Texas while La Salle and his party moved on to the northeast in search of the Mississippi. After La Salle's death, Jean had returned to the bay with his Tejas hosts only to visit but found the village devastated.

Jacques Grollet testified next.[36] He said that he was among some 250 men who initially arrived at the French colony. But of those who survived he knew of only a man and a boy (probably referring to Pierre Meunier and Pierre Talon) still left with the Tejas. He added that the Karankawa told him that they held two young girls and three boys. According to rumor, one of the girls had been killed. Both depositions were formally attested by two witnesses who signed the document that evening.

De León noted in his diary account that the Frenchmen told about an epidemic of smallpox at the community on the bay during the months before the surprise attack by the coastal Indians. Chapa also wrote in his separate account that, after the depositions were over and on the following day when the horse herd was being reorganized, the Frenchmen recounted how the smallpox epidemic had killed over one hundred residents of the French community.[37]

These two reports, combined with the statement about the smallpox epidemic made earlier by the Indians, confirm that the deadly virus was present in the bay area and may have spread from the French community to the Indian population with whom they were in direct contact.[38]

The statements made at the Guadalupe base-camp were supplemented in Mexico City later that year. At that time, the two Frenchmen explained in greater detail how and why they had continued to live for almost two and one-half years in a Tejas Indian village about 220 miles from the French settlement. They had not returned home to the French colony because they did not know the way and because hostile Indians would have been encountered en route.

The two witnesses added that their friends and hosts, the Tejas, had finally agreed to take them to a village of Indians (probably in Coahuila) where missionaries resided. This testimony is not surprising. The Tejas Indians were familiar with the old Indian trade route leading from Central Texas southwest to the Rio Grande and into Mexico and West Texas. Tejas Indians had been found near the Rio Grande by the Spanish in the 1670s and there recruited (or forced) into service in the missions in northeastern Nuevo León and Coahuila.[39] There is also evidence that Tejas leaders had personally visited the Jumano in West Texas.[40]

During the early part of this journey toward the Rio Grande, along the route near the Guadalupe crossing, the Tejas Indian party with the four Frenchmen recognized the road to the colony along a trail they were following near the Guadalupe crossing. Their Tejas hosts agreed to allow the Frenchmen to visit the colony. But when the party arrived at the fort, they found the remains of the massacre. The party then decided to change plans and return to the Tejas country rather than continue west.

The Tejas Indians and the four Frenchmen were apparently returning home to East Texas along the Indian trade route when De León arrived on the scene and sent written word for them to come back to the bay and join the Spaniards. It is significant that the trail between the Guadalupe and the Colorado rivers was the route followed earlier by the Tejas Indians on their planned visit to West Texas and was also used on their return to East Texas. This is a pathway along an open, high ridge area, from which Peach Creek (Gonzales County) drains to the north and the Lavaca-Navidad watershed (Lavaca County) drains to the south. The Tejas apparently also followed an established path along the east side of the Guadalupe from the crossing near Cuero across Chicolete Prairie to the bay, visiting the friendly villages along the way. The Indians later returned west from the bay along the same path to the Guadalupe crossing area and then north-northeast to the Colorado, the Brazos, and the Trinity. The marathon runner, as noted, apparently followed much of the same road.

After the completion of the two interrogations on the Guadalupe, De León and Massanet spoke at length with the Tejas chieftain. The Indian leader—with whom the four Frenchmen had been staying—displayed an elementary understanding of religion, and perhaps even of the Catholic faith. The Tejas chieftain requested that De León and the priest return the next year and establish a mission among his people. He also promised to send, at a later time, an appropriate Tejas delegation south to meet with Spanish officials. This promise was kept.

According to Chapa, the day after the meeting was over, the Tejas Indian leader stood on the banks of the Guadalupe to signal farewell to De León when the expedition party began to retrace its route to Monclova. De León's diary, however, does not include a daily itinerary for the return march. The governor carried with pride his two captive Frenchmen, a report that the French colony was no longer a threat to Spain, and word that the Tejas wanted the Spaniards to return the following year and establish a mission among them.

TABLE I

Governor Alonso de León's 1689 Expedition

Date	Distance Leagues (Miles)	Direction	Campsite (COUNTY)
4/1	—	—	Río Bravo (Rio Grande) [1]
4/2	5 (13)	N, NE	El Paraje de los Cuervos (Cuervo Creek, MAVERICK) [1]
4/3	5 (13)	NE	Arroyo de Ramos (Comanche Creek, DIMMIT) [1]
4/4	8 (20.8)	NE	Río de las Nueces (Nueces River, ZAVALA) [1]
4/5	7 (18.2)	—	Río Sarco (Leona River, ZAVALA) [1]
4/6	5 (13)	NE, E	Río Hondo (Frio River, FRIO) [1]
4/7	4 (10.4)	E, SE	Río Hondo (Frio River, FRIO) [1]
4/8	8 (20.8)	E	(San Miguel Creek, FRIO) [2]
4/9	5 (13)	NE	Arroyo del Vino (Atascosa River, ATASCOSA) [2]
4/10	—	—	(Remained in camp)
4/11	12 (31.2)	E, NE	Río de Medina (San Antonio River, KARNES) [1]
4/12	5 (13)	E	Arroyo del León (Cibolo Creek, KARNES) [1]
4/13	6 (15.6)	ENE	(Salt Creek, DEWITT) [1]
4/14	6 (15.6)	ENE	Río de Nuestra Señora de Guadalupe (Guadalupe River, DEWITT) [1]
4/15	2 (5.2)		(Guadalupe River, DEWITT) [1]
4/16	5 (13)	E	(Main camp remained at Irish Creek camp, DEWITT) [2]
	8 (20.8)	N	(Governor's party moved north, LAVACA) [2]
4/17	5 (13)	N	(Governor's party moved north, Lavaca River, LAVACA) [2]
4/18	13 (33.8)	—	(Governor's party returned to base-camp, DEWITT) [2]
4/19	—	—	(Search for missing soldier)
4/20	—	—	(Continued search)
4/21	8 (20.8)	E, NE	(Garcitas Creek, VICTORIA) [1]
4/22	3 (7.8)	E	(Fort Saint-Louis on Garcitas Creek, VICTORIA) [1]
4/23	18 (46.8)	SW, E	Bahía (Magnolia Beach, CALHOUN) [2]
4/24	30 (78)	—	(Placedo Creek, VICTORIA) [2]
4/25	4 (10.4)	—	(Fort Saint-Louis, VICTORIA) [1]
4/26	3 (7.8)	—	(Garcitas Creek, VICTORIA) [1]

[De León retrieved the Frenchmen near the Colorado River and returned to the main camp on the Guadalupe River in DeWitt County to interrogate the Frenchmen until May 4, when he commenced his trip back to the Rio Grande. De León's diary notes only that the party returned along the same route followed earlier: northeast from the Rio Grande to the Guadalupe.]

*Numbers in brackets indicate measure of confidence in camp location, from 1 to 3.

FIGURE 3
The Talon children are reunited by De León's 1690 expedition at a site near Cuero.

THREE

A MISSION FOR THE TEJAS

Governor Alonso de Léon's 1690 Expedition

Governor Alonso de León, under orders from the viceroy, Conde de Galve, broke camp on March 27, 1690, at the Villa Santiago de la Monclova to lead the second expedition to present-day Matagorda Bay and then northeast. The area to be visited northeast of the Medina (or the San Antonio River) would later be called the Province of the Tejas.[1] Within a week of this date one year earlier, the governor had left Monclova on the first major *entrada*. De León's charge this time was to torch the remains of La Salle's former Fort Saint-Louis on Matagorda Bay (Espíritu Santo Bay), which he had located and named the previous year. He was also to search for remaining members of La Salle's colony, particularly any surviving children reportedly held by the Karankawa who had ravaged the settlement. Then, if the Tejas chieftain (whom the governor had met the year before) requested their presence, the *entrada* was to escort Fray Damián Massanet and his three fellow priests to the Tejas nation, near the Neches River in present Houston County, to establish a mission there.

De León's 1690 expedition would follow the route he had taken the year before from Monclova to the Rio Grande and on to the same crossing of the San Antonio River and the same base-camp near the Guadalupe River. While the main supply unit remained at base-camp near the Vado del Gobernador crossing, a small contingent again would visit the site of La Salle's settlement and return to base-camp. The entire party would then march north to the Colorado crossing near La Grange where the governor had met the Tejas chieftain and the Frenchmen the year before. The Indian route east of the Colorado River toward the Neches River, however, would be new to him.

This chapter is based primarily on Alonso de León's diary account of the expedition translated into English by Herbert E. Bolton, ed., Spanish Exploration, *405–423. A typescript copy of the manuscript of the diary,* Texas Documentary History, *vol. 1, Mexico (Viceroyalty), [AGN] Provincias Internas, in the Manuscript Division of the Library of Congress, was consulted as necessary. Juan Bautista Chapa's comments on the trip (Chapa,* Historia, *163–167) and Fray Massanet's letter describing the trip (*Texas State Historical Association Quarterly *2, no. 4 [April 1899], 253–312) were also consulted.*

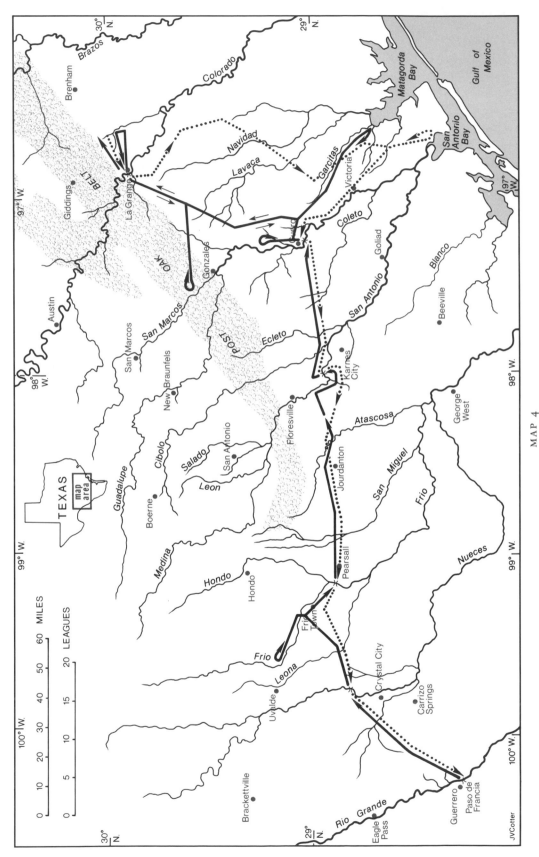

MAP 4

Governor Alonso de León's 1690 Expedition, Part 1

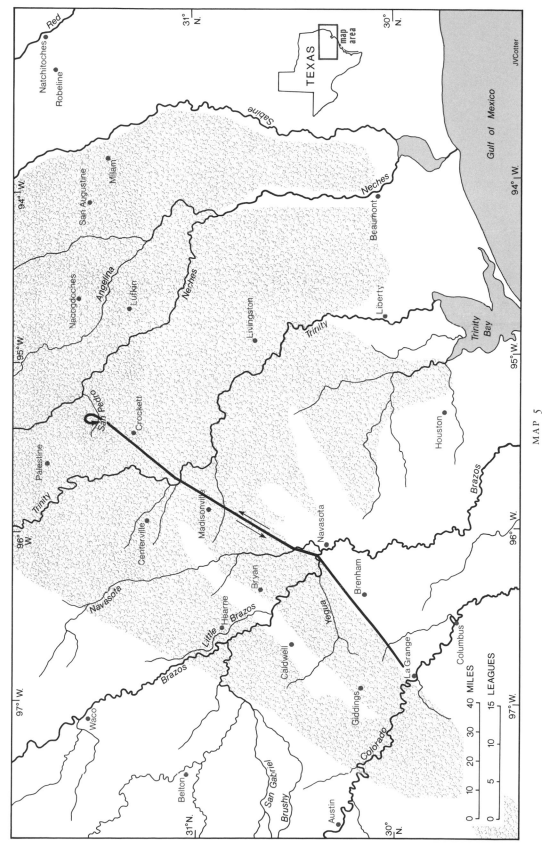

MAP 5

Governor Alonso de León's 1690 Expedition, Part 2

Eight days (and about 120 miles) after De León's party left Monclova headed north, they camped on the banks of the Rio Grande. The party again followed the Coahuila River (the present-day Monclova River) and the Nadadores for the first 70 miles, through the pass called Baluartes, past El Alamo, and through *chaparros* and lechuguillas to the same ford of the Sabinas River. The caravan then moved over level country and through more chaparral another 50 miles to the Rio Grande. The day before reaching the Rio Grande, April 3, the governor paid his respects to the Indian village that had greeted the Frenchman Jean Géry and De León's company so warmly the previous spring. The governor referred to the tribes (presumably the Hape, Jumano, Mescal, and Xiabu) in his diary as "the Indians of the Frenchman," although the Frenchman himself was not on this trip. The party, led by the same Indian guides used the year before, was directed to the same ford on the Rio Grande, but this year they also found bison. The previous year, no bison were encountered until the day the party reached the Guadalupe River.

The ford used the previous year is about 5 miles east and downstream from present-day Guerrero, Coahuila. The crossing was probably at or near the ford later called Paso de Francia, one of the principal fords that served the future site of the mission and presidio San Juan Bautista.

The party crossed the river without incident on April 6. The line of march toward the north-northeast through mesquite brush generally followed the route taken the previous spring. The second evening was spent at Arroyo Ramos, where the governor had stopped the year before. On the next evening, however, the party camped at a new location that the governor, perhaps in a spirited mood, named Caramanchel, which is Spanish for an outdoor public bar.[2] Regardless of its derivation, the same name for the creek was used by later diarists; about forty years later, Brigadier Pedro de Rivera called the same creek (present-day Comanche Creek) or one of its tributaries Caramanchelito.

After traveling about 50 miles northeast from the Rio Grande, the party found the ford of the Nueces River on Sunday, April 9. The direction taken and distance traveled confirm that De León crossed the Nueces approximately 8 miles upriver from the present town of Crystal City. This general route of march was followed, with few variations, by each of the later expeditions that crossed the Rio Grande at or near Paso Francia.

The following day, the governor marched another 18 miles northeast through more mesquite brush and again reached the Río Sarco (present-day Leona River). The mileage traveled from the Nueces to the Leona was identical to that of the previous year. On the following day, about 15 miles beyond the Leona, De León reached the modern Frio River, which he again called the Río Hondo. The campsite is near the point where the Frio intersects the four corners of present-day Zavala, Frio, Uvalde, and Medina counties.

Because De León recorded traveling 15 miles between the Leona and the Frio River, in contrast with the 12 miles recorded in 1689, the campsite was most likely approximately 3 to 5 miles farther upstream to the northwest (see Map 4). The main party camped at that location on the Frio for three days. The governor, Captain Salinas, and twenty soldiers scouted west about 16 miles to investigate a reported Indian encampment where an unidentified Frenchman (most likely Jean Géry) had once stayed or lived.

The location of this Indian camp is near the left bank of the Frio River in southern Uvalde County. It was in the same general area in 1688 that the governor had captured Géry, whose services had proved very valuable on the governor's first expedition. After that trip, Géry had dropped out of Spanish control near the Rio Grande,[3] which was also near his former Indian friends and family. The governor may have been searching for his missing friend.

The friendly Indians in the village along the Frio had news of two Frenchmen living beyond the Guadalupe River, and one Indian had a French musket, which suggests that the village might have had direct contact with the Indians living near the French settlement on the bay. At least the Indians passed on accurate information about the movements of the two young Frenchmen, Pierre Talon and Pierre Meunier, whom De León would find beyond the Guadalupe the following month. Diary accounts of the expedition leaders frequently reported receiving accurate and helpful information from Indians along the route. After distributing gifts to the Indians, De León returned to his main camp, accompanied by a few of his Indian friends.

On April 15, the party broke camp and continued to trace the path taken the year before. The *entrada* turned to the east, going about 15 miles downstream along the right bank of the Frio toward its junction with Hondo Creek, just as De León the year before had turned east and southeast 10 miles downstream to the same river crossing. The ford is below but near the junction of the Frio River and Hondo Creek.

After Mass on Sunday, De León crossed the Frio and traveled about 20 miles northeast. This coincides closely with De León's comparable movement of 8 long leagues toward the east and the crossing of the Chapa (San Miguel Creek) the previous year. The campsite is projected to have been at a tributary of San Miguel Creek east of Pearsall near the Atascosa County line.

The *entrada* again moved northeast and east the next day and, after marching 13 miles, arrived at a creek that De León called Arroyo de los Robalos or Bass Creek. Herbert Bolton correctly notes that this stream was apparently the one called Arroyo del Vino where De León had camped on April 9, 1689.[4] De León gave no reason for changing the name from Arroyo del Vino or Wine Creek to Robalos, but perhaps the former name was associated with the Saturday night wine party and the embarrassing loss of horses the year before. The line of march and distance traveled on April 17, 1690, and April 9, 1689, coincide very closely: east or northeast for 13 miles. The campsite was on the Atascosa River in north-central Atascosa County.

The similarity between De León's 1689 and 1690 *entradas* becomes even more apparent at this point. At the same camp location the year before, De León temporarily lost 102 horses in a stampede. On the evening of April 17, 1690, 126 horses stampeded. Near the same campsite on De León's return trip, the governor encountered a Toho Indian encampment, the possible source of the excitement leading to the two stampedes in the same area. As a result of the last stampede and recovery effort, the company could move only about 10 miles on April 18. Since the guide also lost his way, the party simply continued a short distance north.

After setting out toward the north on the morning of April 19 and traveling a total of about 18 miles, the party "arrived at the Medina [San Antonio] River above the ford" and camped the following day. The next day, the party moved downstream along the river "toward the *east* and, at a distance of 2 leagues, [we] reached the ford of the river" (emphasis added). At the projected crossing of the river, near Falls City, the San Antonio River takes a very unusual and abrupt change in direction toward the east, in contrast to its general south-southeast flow.

This combined three-day movement of about 34 miles toward the northeast between April 18 and 20 tracks the same general route that De León recorded for one day, April 11, the year before, when he reported traveling 31 miles to the east from Arroyo del Vino to the Medina (San Antonio) River crossing. The 1690 crossing was most likely near the Conquista crossing below the bend of the San Antonio River close to the Wilson-Karnes County line.

After crossing the San Antonio River, the governor continued to follow his 1689 route 13 miles east on April 21 to Arroyo del León (Cibolo Creek). The next day he camped about 15 miles farther along present Salt Creek, a brackish tributary of Coleto Creek northwest of present-day Yorktown in western DeWitt County. The governor commented on the salty taste of the stream near the campground; on his return, he avoided the camping location but named the stream. A small stream off the Guadalupe was the campsite for the following evening. The next day, the party crossed the Guadalupe River, probably at Vado del Gobernador, and camped near the governor's 1689 Guadalupe River base-camp.[5]

On April 25, De León, Fray Massanet, Captain Gregorio de Salinas Varona, and twenty soldiers left the supply party at base-camp and proceeded east toward La Salle's old Fort Saint-Louis. Massanet had been the dominant clerical figure in the 1689 *entrada*, while Captain Salinas was not on the earlier expedition. The reconnaissance party reached the former French settlement and bay after marching about 14 leagues on April 25 and another 7 leagues the next day. The year before, the governor had given the direction as first east, then east-northeast, and finally east from the Guadalupe camp to the bay, rather than simply east, but De León recorded traveling about the same distance—19 leagues, rather than 16 leagues in 1689.

After torching the remains of the fort, the party moved downstream a few miles (about 2 leagues) and revisited the bay. There the young Spanish troopers from Monterrey swam in the salty water of Lavaca Bay and bottled some water to take home to their families, who had probably never seen the Gulf of Mexico or tasted sea water. The party camped near Garcitas Creek on the night of April 26. According to Chapa's account, while at the bay, Salinas and Martínez attempted to correct the 1689 observation, which was known to be unreliable because it was made with a warped astrolabe. However, cloudy weather prevented the reading from being taken.[6]

The next day, the governor's troops made several short side excursions and detours, searching for a local Indian guide as they returned up Garcitas Creek for a total distance of about 52 miles. The small party crossed the open Chicolete Prairie and passed Irish Creek, returning to the Guadalupe base-camp. The need for a local Indian guide was acute. The Quem and Pacpul Indian guides who had proved so valuable the year before again accompanied them, but they were unfamiliar with the territory and the languages of the tribes north of the Guadalupe. Jean Géry—who not only was familiar with the local territory and language but had been well received the year before by the Emet and other local Indians—would have been most welcome. De León later expressed in a letter to the viceroy his personal sadness over the loss of his faithful friend Géry, who had been invaluable in first locating the French colony.[7] Robert Weddle speculates that Géry may have returned to his Indian family and friends in southwestern Texas, where the Spanish had first captured him.[8] As mentioned, De León's brief side trip on April 12–14 near the Frio may have been to search for the Frenchman.

De León spent a fruitless day on April 28, sending smoke signals to advertise for an Indian guide while he wandered about 15 miles upstream and then back downstream, along the left bank of the Guadalupe, moving generally from present Cuero to McCoy Creek and back. The captain, who was very familiar with Indian customs in New Spain but not with the native lifestyle in the Texas coastal area, apparently acquired the local means of communicating with smoke signals quickly. The next day, the governor led his camp east, still without the aid of a local Indian guide, and then north a total of about 15 miles to a location near the Irish Creek campsite he had used the previous year. De León was apparently attempting to retrace his route in 1689, when he had left the Irish Creek area with local guides to travel north along the old Indian trade route to the Colorado River. This time he gave the Irish Creek location a name: San Pedro Mártir. Here the governor left the supply party to await the arrival of some twenty stragglers who were to join the expedition from Coahuila. The fact that this separate tardy company could be expected to find the Irish Creek camp from the Rio Grande suggests that De León's route was becoming well known. The trail should have been reasonably clear to the late arrivals since they were following an 800-horse remuda.

On April 30, De León (probably with Captain Martínez and Captain Salinas) and a squad of sixteen soldiers with Fray Massanet left the supply camp at San Pedro Mártir and moved north. The troops served as an advance party, hacking a passage across dense Little Brushy Creek and Big Brushy Creek near modern Yoakum, continuing north along the Indian trail taken the previous year through the area near Shiner and Moulton in Lavaca County. The advance party found no guide but apparently located the pathway, as suggested by De León's report of passing numerous small streams (the upper Lavaca and Navidad), where he found several deserted Indian villages that he had visited in 1689.[9]

After an indirect route covering 91 miles (35 leagues) in three days, with numerous detours because the party had no experienced Indian guide, De León reached the Río San Marcos (Colorado River) near La Grange on May 2. This reference to the present Colorado as the San Marcos was the first naming of the river, which the governor apparently thought was an upper extension of the river (the present Lavaca) that he had named the San Marcos near Matagorda Bay the year before. At this point, De León was close to the site of the Toho Indian encampment where he had found the two Frenchmen the year before.[10]

After crossing the Colorado, De León proceeded 13 miles. He camped and waited five days for word from the Tejas leader who had invited him to visit. In contrast to the trip the year before, on this expedition De León saw no Indians between the Guadalupe River and the Colorado. During the same month the year before, the governor had visited or contacted at least four occupied villages or encampments in the same area. Near the camp on the east side of the Colorado, the party met several Tejas Indians who were hunting bison. At that time, the area east of the Colorado crossing in Fayette County was a Tejas hunting ground. De León asked them to return to the Tejas nation and to request that the chieftain visit his camp. One Tejas messenger was given a horse to make the trip. He used the horse not to ride, however, but as a pack animal to carry home the bison meat taken in hunts between the Colorado and the Brazos.[11]

On May 9, without having received word from the Tejas leader, but having seen smoke signals in the south from his advancing supply party that he had left at San Pedro Mártir, the governor retraced his route, moving southwest to recross the Colorado to meet them. On the west bank, De León greeted Captain Francisco de Benavides and his supply company near a hill he called Jesús María y Joseph Buenavista. The hill is identified as the very prominent rise and bluff referred to as Buenavista on several later expeditions and now called Monument Hill near the Colorado opposite La Grange (see *Seguin*, NH14-9). This hill is also near the location of the Indian camp where the governor had first met the Tejas chieftain and the two Frenchmen the year before.

The supply company had remained at San Pedro Mártir in central DeWitt County, awaiting the arrival of the stragglers. The augmented troops from the camp at San Pedro Mártir had marched north across Lavaca County and part of Fayette County about 60 miles in three days to rejoin Governor De León near the Colorado River. After marching about 15 miles, their first overnight stop (May 7) had been at a location named San Miguel Arcángel, which was probably on the upper Lavaca River near Shiner. The campsite on the next evening was named San Gregorio Nazianzeno, located on the upper Navidad near Flatonia about 25 miles north of San Gregorio. On the next day, May 9, the supply party met De León in the afternoon near the hilltop location called Buenavista.

Near Buenavista was a large Indian camp. Massanet reported that it included the Toho, Emet, Tohaha, and other unidentified Indians. The governor's party had found these same tribes the year before in encampments along the upper Lavaca and Navidad, on the trail between the Guadalupe and the Colorado rivers.

At this camp, the governor found a local Indian linguist who spoke several languages including "lengua Mexicana." Because this was the native language understood by De León's Quem guide and interpreter, his services again became useful. The report that a local Emet, Toho, or Tohaha native could speak the second language (perhaps Coahuilteco) suggests more than just casual or infrequent contact between the tribes near the Rio Grande and those who lived principally between the San Antonio and Colorado rivers.

The local Indians informed De León that two young men from La Salle's colony were nearby. This information confirmed the earlier report De León had received from the unidentified Indians on the Frio River that two Frenchmen were living beyond the Guadalupe. One French boy (Pierre Talon), the local Indians reported, was with some friendly Indians, probably Toho, at a camp two days' journey to the west, and a second young man (Pierre Meunier) was at an Indian camp, probably Tejas, a short distance beyond the Colorado to the east.

Several years earlier, La Salle had taken Meunier and Talon to the Tejas Indians to live with them and learn their language. Being an experienced explorer, La Salle appreciated the importance of having and even training his own guides, interpreters, and sometimes spies. The French explorer placed the two boys among the Tejas Indians to the northeast of the bay colony for the same reason he had earlier sent Géry (according to Géry's own testimony) to the southwest to live with and to pacify the Indians nearby.[12]

That same afternoon, De León and Captain Salinas with a small contingent of eight soldiers and the Indian interpreter-guide proceeded southwest, retracing their earlier route down the old Indian trade route about 30 miles, at which point they camped for the evening. The next morning, the party continued a short distance south and then turned sharply west, moving across modern Peach Creek to an area near present Canoe Creek on the left bank of the San Marcos River near the Gonzales-Caldwell County line. In 1693, Salinas followed the same line of march (June 26, 27) on his return trip from East Texas.

The governor peacefully recovered the French boy, 14-year-old Pierre Talon, and returned to a campsite along the trade route near the one used the evening before.[13] Although Pierre later testified to French authorities that he had attempted to escape from the Spaniards at the time of his capture, De León's diary records that the recovery was made voluntarily, with the cooperation of the boy's Indian friends and without any exchange or customary ransom.

Several years later, Pierre Talon also testified that he had joined the Toho Indians, close neighbors and friends of the Tejas, after La Salle was killed.[14] Pierre lived with the Toho and even fought in their skirmishes with other Indians.

By May 12, the governor and his small group had retraced their route north and again crossed the Colorado River, moving northeast several miles to a new campsite named San Joseph y San Ildefonso. The governor's supply party was waiting for him there.

The following day, three Tejas Indians brought 20-year-old Pierre Meunier to the governor's camp without a struggle. Like Pierre Talon, he had been living among these local Indians. Earlier Meunier had been frightened by the prospect of being captured by the Spanish troops, and the friendly Tejas Indians had helped protect and hide him. But now the Indians cooperated with the Spaniards and returned Meunier, just as they had returned the two Frenchmen the year before.

The day after Meunier was rescued, the governor—now reunited with his full party—continued, with his Tejas friends and the young Frenchmen as guides and interpreters, toward the Brazos River and Tejas country. Massanet reported that a Tejas Indian arrived in camp who was very familiar with the area and showed the party the path to the country of the Tejas until they met the chieftain. It is significant that De León would not venture far east of the Colorado until he had one or more guides and escorts who knew the old Indian trade route that he wanted to follow to East Texas from the Colorado. Neither the king nor the viceroy asked their expedition leaders to blaze new trails; they were too prudent to ignore the existing Indian trade routes known by their Indian guides. Moreover, this journey did not involve the customary forced entry into new territory, as did the usual *entrada;* this trip was by invitation and thus required an escort.

On May 13, De León left San Joseph y San Ildefonso and proceeded east-northeast. During the next two days, they followed the relatively clear area below the southern border of the Monte Grande, passed a creek that De León named San Francisco de Asís, and moved on to the Brazos, which the governor himself referred to as the Colorado but renamed Espíritu Santo. The two names for the present-day Brazos continued to be used on later expeditions, and it was not until the early 1700s that a third name, Brazos de Dios, was added. The distance along the roadway between the Colorado and Brazos River was recorded very accurately by De León as 21 leagues (about 55 miles). De León's ability to measure precisely the distance he traveled each day was not matched by many later expedition leaders or diarists (see *Austin*, NH14-6). De León crossed the Brazos on May 15, a few miles above the junction of the Navasota River, which he referred to as Arroyo San Juan.[15]

After crossing the Brazos and the Navasota, the party turned north-northeast, still following the Indian pathway that continued through present Grimes County, along the southeastern boundary of the thick wood, and into Madison County for a total of 51 miles (in four days) to reach the Trinity River (which De León named Río Trinidad) near the Madison-Leon County line. De León named the campsites for each evening: Beato Salvador de Horta (May 16), Arroyo San Diego de Alcalá (May 17), Valle de Santa Elvira (May 18), and a valley, Monclova (May 19). By May 22, the party had marched through groves of live oak and pine 47 miles beyond the Trinity and passed several Tejas villages to reach the location of a settlement (pueblo) De León named San Francisco de los Tejas (in present San Pedro Creek valley in northeastern Houston County; see *Palestine*, NH15-1).

After giving the Tejas chieftain a staff with a cross and the title of governor, De León helped construct a church and a mission residence for the padres. According to Chapa, the two captains, Martínez and Salinas, took a reading and found that the "provincia de las Tejas" was 34°7' north.[16] The San Pedro Creek area in present Houston County where De León constructed the first mission in East Texas is closer to 31°30' latitude. The reading of 34° north latitude would place the location north of the Red River. Because of these problems in taking readings, attempts to use the readings to locate an expedition route or even an encampment are fruitless and frustrating. By June 1, the governor was ready to return. Massanet reported that the party retraced "the same road" used on the trip east.

Over the next sixteen days, the party, accompanied by a small delegation of Tejas Indians who could also serve as guides, proceeded along the Indian trade route back toward the Colorado crossing. The four-man Tejas delegation included the Tejas governor's brother, cousin, and a nephew, according to De León. They retraced the same road with precision, each night using the identical campsites they had used or passed on the trip east. On June 14, the party crossed both the Navasota (Arroyo de San Juan) and the Brazos (Río Espíritu Santo) and the next day reached the camp where the governor had waited fruitlessly a week for the Tejas chieftain to arrive in early May.

The following day, De León passed Real de San Joseph y San Ildefonso (where he had camped on May 11) and stopped for the evening at a creek a few miles northeast of the Colorado. Jesús María y Joseph de Buenavista (present Monument Hill), off the west bank of the Colorado, was reached on June 17. This easily identifiable hill high on the Colorado across from La Grange was cited as Buenavista on several subsequent expeditions, including the side trip on Terán's 1691 expedition made by Captain Martínez from the Colorado to the bay the next summer. It has, of course, been a significant landmark throughout the centuries.

This Indian trade route between Buenavista on the Colorado River and the Tejas Indian country beyond the Trinity served to complete the last leg of the first Spanish road that ran from Monclova to East Texas, the only road from northeastern New Spain (principally Monclova) that was used repeatedly by expeditions in the late seventeenth century.

On June 18, the governor visited Indians from a nearby large settlement (or gathering) of several Indian tribes, including the Cantona, Tohaha, Sana, Cava, Emet, and Toho. A month earlier, Indians in the same area and from some of the same tribes had reported the location of Pierre Talon and Pierre Meunier. They now reported that three French children were being held by the coastal Indians and offered to send a guide part of the way. A similar statement about coastal Indians holding French children hostages had been made the year before by the Emet and the Cava and by the captive Frenchman, Jacques Grollet. Pierre Talon identified the children as his three siblings, being held by the Karankawa, and asked De León to rescue them.

The governor decided to divide his command again and to send his supply company south along the old Indian route back to the Guadalupe base-camp near Cuero. Several officers could lead the supply company because they were familiar with this Indian path between the Colorado to the Guadalupe, having traveled the trade route, or major parts of it, several times with De León over the previous fifteen months.

The governor and Captain Salinas, accompanied by a local Indian guide from the Buenavista area and a detachment of sixteen soldiers, left the Buenavista camp on the same day (June 18), proceeding first southeast near the western (right) bank of the Colorado River. After traveling about 25 miles, the party passed a Toho Indian camp west of present Columbus in western Colorado County. That afternoon, they saw large herds of bison on the broad plains between the Colorado and Navidad rivers and made camp on upper Sandy Creek in present Colorado County.

On June 19, the party picked up several new Indian guides as it moved west across the lower Navidad-Lavaca watershed, distributing tribute to three more friendly Indian encampments. The first was inhabited by "Có oé," probably Coco. Although the Coco were primarily coastal Indians, they also lived in the open areas of the upper reaches of Sandy Creek (in Jackson, Wharton, and Colorado counties) and the area east of the Colorado. The residents of the second Indian camp visited that morning identified themselves as Toho, members of the same tribe found at the large gathering near La Grange. The third was another large camp of Indians called "Na aman," located on the Navidad. According to one transcript of De León's diary, there were about 3,000 Indians in this camp near the Lavaca-Jackson County line.[17] This tribe may be the same or associated with the Aranama Indians who were later found in the area or with the Aname Indians later found in the area who asked Governor Alarcón in 1718 for a mission near the bay.

Early the next day, June 20, De León picked up four new guides from a friendly Indian tribe called the Caisquetebana, who had a camp near present Arenosa Creek. The governor's small party then moved south across a creek that De León identified as "the arroyo of the French" (Garcitas Creek) and past "the old settlement" (the ruins of Fort Saint-Louis). Continuing a short distance south, De León crossed a stream (the present Placedo Creek) that he called Arroyo de Canoas or Canoe Creek, mentioned by him in 1689. He camped that evening further south on a second creek (present Chocolate Bayou) at a location possibly 5 miles upstream from Lavaca Bay.

Early the next morning, De León advanced about 15 miles south toward the Karankawa camp, determined to recover, by force if necessary, the three French children whose young lives had been spared when the local Indians had killed the other residents of La Salle's community and who had been held captive for over a year. Marie Madeleine was only sixteen, and the boys were eight and five years of age.

When the captain reached the encampment, the Indians, who were obviously agitated, began to demand a heavy ransom for the children's release. With few troops but impressive and noisy firepower, De León was in no mood to pay dearly for the release of children. A fight ensued, the only serious skirmish with Indians reported on any expedition. Four Indians were killed by blasts from the muskets or pistols of the troops. Two arrows struck De León in the side but were deflected by his protective mail. Several of De León's horses were also killed by the Indians. Pierre Talon later testified that the fight erupted in part because the Karankawa insisted that De León pay a ransom of two horses for Pierre's sister, rather than just one horse as for each of the younger brothers.[18]

Herbert E. Bolton incorrectly states that the Indian camp where the children were rescued was "far south of the Garcitas River, on the coast of Matagorda Bay."[19] Robert Weddle says that the three children were recovered on the west side of Matagorda Bay.[20] De León reported that the recapture took place about 6 leagues (15.6 miles) south of the second creek (Chocolate Bayou) campsite, "on the *headland* of a *small bay*" (emphasis added).[21] Map 4 shows that the Karankawa camp where the children were recovered was 15 miles south of Chocolate Bayou at the head of San Antonio Bay.

After the skirmish, De León withdrew with the three children to the Chocolate Bayou campsite used the prior evening. Because he was uncertain whether the Karankawa would give chase the next morning, June 22 was probably an anxious day for De León's small rescue party, particularly for the three young children. Camp broke at early daylight. The party (now perhaps twenty-two in number) rode hard to the north for about 14 leagues or 36 miles throughout the longest day of summer, probably without a local Indian guide. The troops and children raced up the Guadalupe past modern Victoria, through the treeless, open Chicolete Prairie, and into the edge of the protective woods along the river. At nightfall, "about ten o'clock," they camped. Because neither La Salle's French colony nor the Karankawa had horses, the youngsters had probably never ridden horseback, much less for fifteen hours in one day. The camp that evening was near the mouth of present-day Price's Creek on the DeWitt-Victoria County line. The following day, after finding the trail of some of his scouts from base-camp and completing a short ride of about 13 miles up the Guadalupe, the governor joined his main supply company near present Cuero.

On this leg of the journey from the bay up the Guadalupe, De León needed no guide. He had ridden the 50 miles between Fort Saint-Louis and his Guadalupe camp on four different occasions over the previous fifteen months. On this final trip between the two locations, he stated accurately that the party traveled up the river in a northerly direction. The directions reportedly taken on June 22 and 23 help clarify the direction from the Guadalupe crossing to the French settlement: in a more southeasterly direction, rather than toward the northeast as recorded on Sigüenza's 1689 route map.

At the Guadalupe camp, the Talon children faced each other for the first time since their older brother, Pierre, was taken from the colony by La Salle several years earlier to live with the Tejas Indians. The similarity in their darkly tattooed faces renewed their family bond, although the two younger boys could speak to their older brother only in the language of the Karankawa through their sister, who translated their speech into French. The younger boys had forgotten much of their native language after eighteen months with the Indians. Although the Karankawa left the children indelibly marked with tattoos on their faces and bodies and with the memory of the massacre of their mother and over twenty other members of La Salle's colony, the children also took from their captors the memory of being tenderly loved. One of the two remaining French captives, who was rescued the following year,[22] reported that the Indians were moved to tears when the children departed.

The next day, De León broke camp on the Guadalupe for the last time. Although the governor's diary from the year before includes no entries for the daily movements on the return march to Monclova from the Guadalupe, his 1690 diary contains entries noting the number of leagues traveled each day. The diary does not specify the direction taken, but, in addition to distance, gives the names of campsites and the rivers and creeks crossed between the Guadalupe and the Rio Grande.

The route west from the Guadalupe River to the San Antonio River crossing followed the path that the party had taken eastward only two months earlier. The first evening, they camped on present-day Yorktown Creek, a tributary of Coleto Creek. The next day, De León intentionally rode past the campsite he had used earlier on modern Salt Creek, but in passing named it Real de Agua Salada. Moving southwest the next day, the party camped again on Arroyo del León (Cibolo Creek). De León recorded that the distance from the Cibolo to the San Antonio River was about 13 miles, the same distance recorded on the earlier trip. They reached the San Antonio River on June 26 at the ford (near Conquista crossing) used earlier that year and the year before, upstream from Falls City in Kansas County.

The party forded the San Antonio River and traveled about 20 miles to the west the next day. On the following day, the party journeyed 13 miles and arrived at an encampment of Toho Indians above the ford of the Robalos (the present Atascosa River) at a point about 32 miles from the San Antonio crossing near present Falls City. This is the only report made on any expedition that locates the Toho Indians south of the San Antonio River. The company went past Real del Aire on June 29, to camp 13 miles south and west of the Atascosa River. At this point, twenty-five exhausted men and over two hundred tired horses were left to return at a slower pace; but the French children continued with De León.

The following day, after crossing the Hondo (present-day Frio River), De León reached a campsite that he referred to as Las Cruces (The Crosses), located about 8 miles "above the ford" of the Frio River. They had marched a total of more than 20 miles that day. The name probably refers to the crosses and other inscriptions that the governor had seen on a white rock formation near that location during his march east in the spring of 1689. The return to the marked location on the Frio suggests that the governor was continuing to follow the old Indian trade route.

On the following day, July 1, the party veered southwest 13 miles to the Río Sarco (Leona River), approximately the same distance traveled between the two streams on the earlier trips that year and the year before. Near the Leona River crossing Captain Salinas may have carved or otherwise left a cross that he later mentions finding on his resupply mission in 1693.

The party crossed the Nueces River the following day and continued southwest for a total of about 20 miles to an unnamed watering pond. According to De León, the company traveled 26 miles on July 3, crossing Arroyo de Ramos and arriving at another watering pond. After journeying more than 20 miles the following day, the expedition reached the banks of the swollen Rio Grande. De León waited a week at this spot for the river to recede. Although the river was still high, the governor, followed by Massanet and Pierre Meunier, swam his horse across. The company reached Monclova on July 15.

Once the expedition had returned, Padre Massanet wrote a detailed letter to the viceroy recommending that a number of missionaries be sent to the Tejas Indians, but that only one Spanish settlement should be established—on the Guadalupe, serving as a halfway station between Coahuila and the Tejas missions.[23] The Tejas Indians in East Texas near the Neches River were the focus of this new mission because they were considered to be very receptive and relatively advanced. They raised and stored both corn and beans. Massanet noted that they cultivated squash and watermelons, weeded their fields with wooden hoes, sat on wooden benches, and slept on raised canopy beds.

After encouraging the viceroy to support Christianizing these Indians, Massanet added that East Texas was very accessible by an existing Indian road protected from Apache attack. He described the existing Indian trade route connecting northeastern New Spain with the Indians living between the Rio Grande and the Guadalupe and further north to the Tejas. The padre began, "Above all, I would like to mention to His Excellency . . . the existing road" to the Tejas. After listing the rivers crossed and the associated Indian tribes from the Río del Norte (Rio Grande), to the Nueces, the Hondo (Frio), and the Medina (San Antonio River), Massanet accurately estimated that the Guadalupe was "about 20 leagues" beyond the Medina crossing. Again accurately, he added: "To go to the Tejas from the Guadalupe River, one goes north and after 30 leagues, one finds the San Marcos River [the Colorado]." Because of his trip from the Guadalupe to the Colorado in 1690, the priest knew both the correct distance and direction and that along the way "there are many creeks with good water," a reference to the numerous Lavaca and Navidad headwater tributaries along the route. "From the San Marcos River [the Colorado] the road goes north to the Tejas."

Actually, De León's direction for the three-day march in 1690 between the Colorado and the Brazos was more to the north-northeast. In describing the Indian trade routes beyond the Colorado, Massanet wrote that there were two roads. "The Apache come to the road, and they are enemies of both the Tejas and the Spaniards. There is another road to go to the Tejas, and it is farther east." This lower, more easterly route was the one Massanet took with De León in 1690; he would take the more northern route with Terán in 1691. The path "farther east," or the lower road, "is safer, though it takes longer, because the Apache do not get there because of all the thick woods [the Monte Grande] and the distance." He concluded his discourse on the Indian trade routes in Texas by adding that there were two rivers between the Colorado and the Tejas, the Espíritu Santo (Brazos) and the Trinidad (Trinity). Massanet confirmed in his letter that he and De León were following a clear Indian route to the Tejas country.

Although De León did not revisit the Guadalupe and his Tejas friends in East Texas, some members of his party would return to follow parts of the old Indian trade route. Captain Martínez returned the next year, leading Governor Domingo Terán de los Ríos from the crossing of the Colorado near La Grange along the Indian path south to a Guadalupe base-camp area (September 2–8, 1691), before meeting Captain Salinas (who had come by sea with additional troops) at the bay. Later that year and in early 1692, Terán followed De León's route on his second trip to East Texas and on his return to the bay. (Pierre Meunier served with Terán as an interpreter on the same 1691–1692 *entrada*.) In March or April of 1692, Martínez possibly took Terán's troops from Matagorda Bay along parts of De León's road back to Monclova at the close of Governor Terán's *entrada,* but no diary account of that trek has been uncovered to date.

Salinas, as governor in 1693, followed De León's trail from Monclova to the San Antonio River, the Guadalupe, the Colorado, and then to East Texas during his resupply mission. In 1714–1715, Pierre and Robert Talon and their Tejas friends probably passed over parts of the route while serving as interpreters and guides for Louis Juchereau de Saint-Denis on his first visit to San Juan Bautista. In returning to Mobile, the Talons most likely again visited Matagorda Bay to determine its distance from the Spanish "mines" at Boca de Leones, which they reported to Governor Cadillac.[24]

It seems clear that De León's route—which followed the tracks of the Quem and Pacpul guides and the Frenchman Géry along the old Indian trade route between the Rio Grande and the Guadalupe River and proceeded along the pathway from the Guadalupe to La Grange and on to the Brazos and Mission San Francisco de Tejas beyond the Trinity—was the principal route across Texas used by the Spaniards in the late seventeenth century. It was bypassed only once, when Governor Terán's expedition moved east from the Frio to the present-day site of San Antonio and then to the Colorado and on to East Texas along an alternate route in early 1691; on his second trip to East Texas, Terán used De León's route.

There was no Camino Real through San Antonio and the Bastrop area in the seventeenth century; the earliest Spanish trail to East Texas followed the Indian trade route from the Rio Grande in southern Maverick County toward the Gulf Coast and Matagorda Bay, turning north at Vado del Gobernador on the Guadalupe and continuing across the Colorado near La Grange and across the Brazos and the Navasota near their junction and across the Trinity near the Madison-Leon County line.

TABLE 2

Governor Alonso de León's 1690 Expedition

Date	Distance Leagues (Miles)	Direction	Campsite (COUNTY)
4/6	8 (20.8)	N, NE	(Unnamed creek, MAVERICK) [1]
4/7	3 (7.8)	NE	Arroyo de Ramos (Comanche Creek, DIMMIT) [1]
4/8	3 (7.8)	N, NE	Arroyo Caramanchel (Comanche Creek, ZAVALA) [1]
4/9	5 (13)	N, NE	Río de Nueces (Nueces River, ZAVALA) [1]
4/10	7 (18.2)	E, N	Río Sarco (Leona River, ZAVALA) [1]
4/11	6 (15.6)	N	Río Hondo (Frio River, FRIO) [1]
4/12	—	—	(Remained near camp searching for two lost soldiers)
4/13	—	—	(Base-camp remained, De León camped 5 leagues upstream)
4/14	—	—	(De León returned to base-camp)
4/15	6 (15.6)	E Downstream	(Frio River crossing, FRIO) [1]
4/16	8 (20.8)	E, NE	(San Miguel Creek, ATASCOSA) [2]
4/17	5 (13)	NE, E	Arroyo de los Robalos (Atascosa River, ATASCOSA) [2]
4/18	4 (10.4)	Lost	El Real del Rosario (Atascosa River, ATASCOSA) [2]
4/19	7 (18.2)	N Downriver	Río Medina (San Antonio River, KARNES) [1]
4/20	2 (5.2)	E	Río Medina (San Antonio River, KARNES) [1]
4/21	5 (13)	E	Arroyo del León (Cibolo Creek, KARNES) [1]
4/22	6 (15.6)	E, NE	(Salt Creek, DEWITT) [1]
4/23	5 (13)	E, NE	Río Guadalupe (Guadalupe River, DEWITT) [1]
4/24	2 (5.2)	Downstream	Río Guadalupe (Guadalupe River, DEWITT) [1]
4/25	14 (36.4)	E	(Garcitas Creek, VICTORIA) [2]
4/26	14 (36.4)	Downstream, upstream	(Unidentified creek, Garcitas Creek, VICTORIA) [2]
4/27	20 (52)	Upstream, detours	Río Guadalupe (Guadalupe River, DEWITT) [1]
4/28	12 (31.2)	Upstream, downstream	Río Guadalupe (Guadalupe River, DEWITT) [1]
4/29	6 (15.6)	E, NE	San Pedro Mártir (Irish Creek, DEWITT) [2]
4/30	9 (23.4)	—	(Mustang Creek, LAVACA) [2]
5/1	12 (31.2)	—	(Lavaca River, LAVACA) [2]
5/2	14 (36.4)	—	Río San Marcos (Colorado River, FAYETTE) [1]
5/3	7 (18.2)	—	(Cummins Creek, FAYETTE) [1]

[From May 4 to 8, De León waited in camp for the Tejas chieftain.]

Date	Distance Leagues (Miles)	Direction	Campsite (COUNTY)
5/9	19 (49.4)	W, S	(Unidentified camp, FAYETTE) [2]
5/10	27 (70.2)	W and return	(Unidentified camp, FAYETTE) [2]
5/11	16 (41.6)	NE	(Cummins Creek, FAYETTE) [1]
5/12	6 (15.6)	NE	San Joseph y San Ildefonso (FAYETTE) [1]
5/13	6 (15.6)	E, NE	San Francisco de Asís (WASHINGTON) [1]
5/14	6 (15.6)	NE	Río Colorado (Brazos River, BRAZOS) [1]
5/15	5 (13)	NE	Arroyo San Juan (Navasota River, GRIMES) [1]
5/16	4 (10.4)	NE	Beato Salvador de Horta (GRIMES) [1]
5/17	6 (15.6)	NNE	Arroyo San Diego de Alcalá (Bedias Creek, MADISON) [1]

Date	Distance Leagues (Miles)	Direction	Campsite (COUNTY)
5/17	6 (15.6)	NNE	Arroyo San Diego de Alcalá (Bedias Creek, MADISON) [1]
5/18	8 (20.8)	ENE	Valle de Santa Elvira (MADISON) [1]
5/19	1.5 (3.9)	NNE	Río Trinidad (Trinity River, LEON) [1]
5/20	7 (18.2)	ENE	Arroyo San Bernardino (HOUSTON) [2]
5/21	6 (15.6)	ENE	San Carlos (HOUSTON) [2]
5/22	5 (13)	ENE	San Francisco de los Tejas (San Pedro Creek, HOUSTON) [1]

[De León and Massanet met with the governor of the Tejas Indians and established Mission San Francisco de los Tejas in the valley of San Pedro Creek during the period May 23 to June 1, when the return trip commenced.]

6/1	5 (13)	"same road"	San Carlos (HOUSTON) [2]
6/2	6.5 (16.9)	—	Real de San Bernardino (HOUSTON) [2]
6/3	6.5 (16.9)	—	Río Santísima Trinidad (Trinity River, HOUSTON) [1]

[From June 4 to 10, De León waited to cross the flooded Trinity River.]

6/11	3 (7.8)	—	Santa Elvira (MADISON) [2]
6/12	9 (23.4)	—	(Unnamed creek, MADISON) [2]
6/13	8 (20.8)	—	Arroyo de San Juan (Navasota River, GRIMES) [1]
6/14	8 (20.8)	—	(Unnamed creek, WASHINGTON) [2]
6/15	7 (18.2)	—	(Unnamed camp, FAYETTE) [2]
6/16	6 (15.6)	—	(Unnamed creek, FAYETTE) [1]
6/17	5 (13)	—	Jesús María y Joseph de Buenavista (Monument Hill, FAYETTE) [1]

[From Buenavista, the main force returned south-southwest to the Guadalupe campground at the crossing near Cuero. The governor and a small unit proceeded to Matagorda Bay to recover the French children then traveled upstream along the left bank of the Guadalupe to rejoin the main force.]

6/18	17 (44.2)	NE, E	(Probably upper Sandy Creek, COLORADO) [2]
6/19	15 (39)	S, W	(Probably Arenosa Creek, VICTORIA) [2]
6/20	14 (36.4)	E, S	(Probably Chocolate Bayou, VICTORIA) [2]
6/21	12 (31.2)	S, N	(Returned to campsite of June 20) [2]
6/22	14 (36.4)	N upriver	Río Guadalupe (Price's Creek, VICTORIA) [1]
6/23	5 (13)	N upriver	Río Guadalupe (Guadalupe camp, near Cuero, DEWITT) [1]
6/24	7 (18.2)	—	(Yorktown Creek, DEWITT) [1]
6/25	7 (18.2)	—	Arroyo del León (Cibolo Creek, KARNES) [1]
6/26	5 (13)	—	Río Medina (San Antonio River, KARNES) [1]
6/27	8 (20.8)	—	(Probably San Miguel Creek, FRIO) [2]
6/28	5 (13)	—	Río Robalos (Atascosa River, ATASCOSA) [2]
6/29	5 (13)	—	(Probably San Miguel Creek, FRIO) [2]
6/30	8 (20.8)	—	Las Cruces (Frio River, FRIO) [1]
7/1	5 (13)	—	Río Sarco (Leona River, ZAVALA) [1]
7/2	8 (20.8)	—	(Nueces River, ZAVALA) [1]
7/3	10 (26)	—	(Unidentified watering ponds, MAVERICK) [2]
7/4	8 (20.8)	—	Río Grande (Rio Grande near Francia crossing, MAVERICK) [1]

[De León waited on the north bank of the Rio Grande from July 5 to 12 for the water to recede. The governor's party crossed the river on July 12 and arrived in Monclova three days later. De León's diary includes no entries for the trip from the Rio Grande to Monclova.]

FIGURE 4
Fray Massanet conducts services near the future site of San Antonio on June 14, 1691.

FOUR

SAN ANTONIO DE PADUA

Governor Domingo Terán de los Ríos's Expedition,
1691–1692

Domingo Terán de los Ríos commenced the third Spanish expedition from the Presidio of Coahuila on May 16, 1691. The destination of this *entrada* was the newly established Province of Tejas. A disappointed Alonso de León, who had led the first two expeditions beyond the Guadalupe, was passed over and died two months before the expedition began.[1]

Terán's expedition differed from the previous two in several respects. Most significantly, the leadership of this one was openly split between the military mission under Governor Terán, who also held the first office as governor of the Province of Tejas, and the spiritual mission under the experienced Fray Damián Massanet. Therefore, the description of the daily itinerary and activities of Terán's party is based on diaries and related documents prepared by both the governor and by the padre.[2] Governor De León had been the undisputed leader of the previous two expeditions.

To clarify the division of responsibility, Spanish authorities issued detailed instructions for the expedition, including a requirement that a detailed diary be kept. The diary recording was to be made daily with the cooperation of all senior officials "who seem to be most intelligent" and to be approved by the governor. The character of the country, the kinds of animals and plants, the climate, the principal rivers (including the distances

This chapter is based on three diary accounts of the trip. The primary account is Terán's personal diary, translated into English by Mattie Austin Hatcher, Preliminary Studies of the Texas Catholic Historical Society *2, no. 1 (January 1932), 10–48. The manuscript copy of his diary,* Texas Documentary History, *vol. 1, Mexico (Viceroyalty), [AGN] Provincias Internas, in the Manuscript Division of the Library of Congress was also consulted. The second diary account, covering only the first trip to East Texas, was written by Fray Massanet. This diary was also translated into English by Mattie Austin Hatcher in* Preliminary Studies *2, no. 1 (January 1932), 48–67. The third diary covered only the sidetrip Captain Martínez led from Terán's camp on the Colorado to Matagorda Bay. Martínez's diary has not been translated into English; a manuscript copy of his diary is in* Texas Documentary History, *vol. 1, Mexico (Viceroyalty), [AGN] Provincias Internas, in the Manuscript Division of the Library of Congress.*

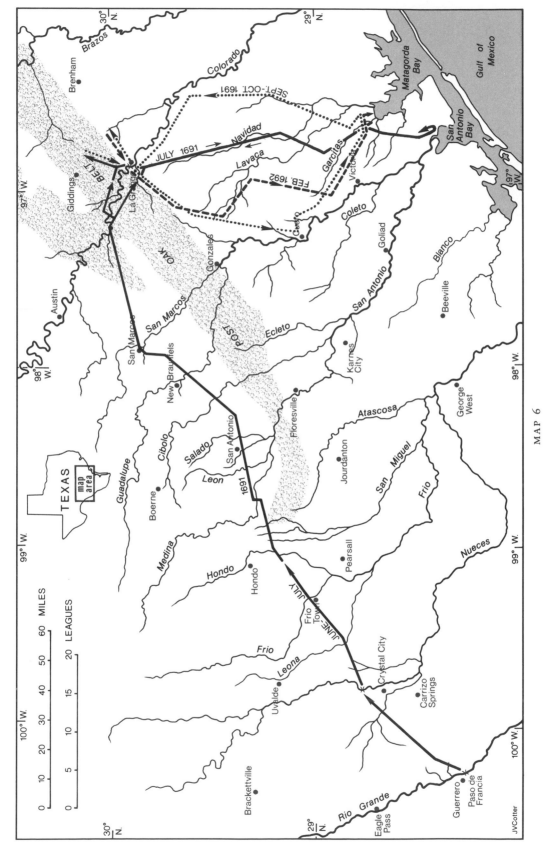

MAP 6

Governor Domingo Terán de los Ríos's 1691–1692 Expedition, Part 1

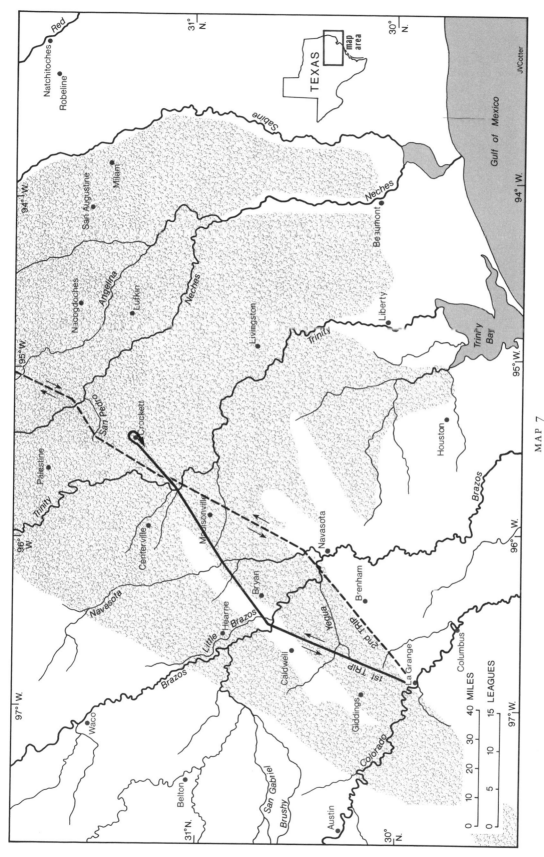

MAP 7

Governor Domingo Terán de los Ríos's 1691–1692 Expedition, Part 2

between them), and the Indian tribes were to be noted. These instructions to record the native population and the natural environment encountered on the trip set clear high standards which most later Spanish expedition diarists followed. The diary accounts therefore give some of the clearest vignettes of native Texas 300 years ago.

The military effort on this *entrada* included the addition of a new marine element composed of fifty men under the command of Captain Gregorio de Salinas Varona. Salinas was directed to meet Captain Francisco Martínez, from Terán's overland expedition, at Matagorda Bay. Although the trip was a new experience for Terán, Captain Salinas, Captain Martínez, and Father Massanet had been on De León's 1690 *entrada*. Martínez and Massanet also had been on the first expedition in 1689.

By May 24, the procession had worked its way northeast from Monclova to the campsite called Pescado, tracking the route established by De León in 1689 and followed again in 1690. Terán's party had followed the south bank of the Nadadores River beyond the mountain cliffs called Baluartes and passed the large cottonwood tree (*álamo grande*). They crossed the Sabinas River, lined with *tarayes,* above the junction with the Nadadores and marched 7 leagues farther north to Pescado. Here Padre Massanet had been waiting for several days. Although no Indians were reported along the route across northern Coahuila, Fernando del Bosque encountered local tribes each day on his 1675 march north from the Nadadores to the Rio Grande.[3]

The padre with his delegation and experienced Pacpul and Quem guides had left the Caldera mission in eastern Coahuila on May 16. In three days, the church group had traveled 16 leagues north, through mesquite brush, across the Sabinas River, which Massanet said was lined with cottonwood and ash trees. The route north of the Sabinas carried the party past salt flats and clumps of prickly pear and catclaw to the designated rendezvous at the Fish Ponds (Charcos del Pescado). For the next 500 miles, from Pescado to the Trinity, Terán and Massanet rode together, but not in comfort or without friction.

On May 27, Governor Terán and Massanet found the creek near the Indian village that happily received the Frenchman Jean Géry in 1689. The governor reported that the Indians in the area included the Mescal, Odoesmade, and Momon. The Mescal tribe had been identified at the same location earlier by De León. Massanet said that some Mescal, Yorica, Jumano, Parchaca, Alachome, and Pamai Indians accompanied the caravan that day. This pattern of Terán and Massanet recording different Indian tribes at the same location on the same day was repeated several times along the expedition trail. On each occasion, the padre's accounting was the more detailed. The creek, called Juan's Creek by later diarists, was only about 15 miles from the Rio Grande, which the party reached the next day.

Both Terán and Massanet report that large herds of bison were found near the south bank of the Rio Grande and that the troops killed several for food. Massanet described the flora: there were tall reeds along the river, particularly at the crossing, as there are today. Terán added that he saw more *tarayes* and catclaw.

The ford was about 15 miles from the point where Terán first set the royal standard on the banks of the river. Map 6 places the approximate location of the crossing near Paso de Francia, used by De León.[4] The river was up and rising, making the crossing difficult. Immediately after the party crossed the Rio Grande, a violent late spring storm struck the camp, scattering everything from animals to tents. Because it took several days for the large party to cross the river and regroup, the march did not continue until June 3.

El Charco del Cuervo (Pond of the Crow) was the campsite for the first evening northeast of the river crossing. The company reached the campsite after marching about 10 miles from the Rio Grande crossing. Map 6 places the location on present Cuervo Creek, which De León also visited and named. The padre described the camp as being in a woods of mesquite and tall hackberry trees with bison feeding along the creekbed. Cuervo Creek today trickles through more barren terrain with sparse vegetation. Terán and Massanet's descriptions of plant and animal life along the Rio Grande in Maverick County 300 years ago contrast with the flora and fauna known in the area today—now the area is too dry to support the heavily wooded areas and vegetation required by large bison herds.

On June 4, the *entrada* continued north-northeast another 13 miles to a location shaded with tall oaks on a stream that Terán called Ramos. Governor De León had referred to the same creek as the Arroyo de Ramos on April 3, 1689. The following day, after another 10-mile journey to the north-northeast through mesquite bush, Terán camped at the creek called Caramanchel (present Comanche Creek), which had been named by De León the year before. Massanet said that the Quem, Pachul, Ocana, Chaguan, Pastaluc, and Paac Indian nations came out to see them. Terán omits any reference to Indians visiting the camp that day.

They reached the Nueces on June 6, after a 10-mile march north-northeast. Because Massanet recorded that the movement that day was 15 miles to the northeast, the exact location is uncertain, but the crossing was probably several miles north of Crystal City. Massanet reported that large herds of bison were seen near the Nueces; mesquite, oak, and pecan trees lined the banks of the stream. Terán also noted the large pecan trees, along with the mesquite and catclaw.

The general direction traveled and the total distance of about 44 miles recorded by Terán between the Rio Grande and the Nueces are consistent with De León's route, although the number of leagues noted is somewhat smaller. De León had traveled 47 miles (18 leagues) to the northeast between the Rio Grande and the Nueces in 1689, and 49 miles (19 leagues) to the north-northeast on the same trek in 1690. Terán continued to understate the distance traveled each day.

From the Nueces, north and east, Terán generally continued to follow the trail of De León, moving more than 15 miles through a very heavy woods of mesquite and catclaw on the next day, first toward the east for 5 miles through large pecan trees and later back toward the northeast. Terán did not mention in his diary that the party camped that evening on a stream, which was normally required for the stock. The journey was delayed a day because of the loss of cattle and the straying of the *ganado menor* (sheep and goats). Massanet's entry for the same day reported that the party marched 15 miles through heavy woods toward the north-northeast, then east-southeast, and finally east; that evening, according to the padre, they camped on the Río Frío after fording the stream.

De León had named the stream the Río Sarco on April 5, 1689, and referred to it by that name again on April 10, 1690. It should be clear that the stream where Terán's party camped on June 7 and 8 was only 15 miles from the Nueces crossing above Crystal City and therefore could not have been the present Frio River, which is over 30 miles northeast of the Nueces crossing. This early confusion caused by calling the present-day Leona River the Río Frío has plagued a number of studies of expedition routes. Map 6 places the June 7 and 8 campsite on the present Leona River in central-northeast Zavala County, the same stream referred to as the Río Frío by Massanet and the Sarco by De León on both his expeditions.

On June 9, the party traveled north some 15 miles to the river called El Hondo on De León's two previous expeditions. Massanet also recorded camping on the Río Hondo that evening. They were camping near and perhaps slightly upstream from Las Cruces, the campsite on the present Frio that had been named and used twice by De León, near the place where De León had found the mysterious figures and crosses carved on rock. At the Frio encampment, Massanet lists thirteen Indian nations that visited and received tobacco, rosaries, knives, and beads.[5] Terán makes no report of any Indian visitors.

From this location, the Terán route diverges from that taken by De León in 1689–1690. Terán noted on June 11, after crossing the Frio, that his men moved north to a stream (perhaps modern Seco Creek) "which had not been named in previous expeditions, as we were traveling in a different direction." Massanet echoes this report, stating that on Monday "we started for the Tejas, our route pursuing a direction different than the one followed by the two previous expeditions [De León in 1689 and 1690]." On those two earlier expeditions, De León had marched 10 to 15 miles downstream on the Frio, toward the southeast, to camp for the evening below the junction of Hondo Creek and the Frio River. De León, however, had been moving east toward Matagorda Bay. In contrast, this expedition was destined to establish missions in East Texas, so Terán's company crossed the Frio and continued north. Terán also commented, "It was considered a shorter and easier route to the Tejas. Besides, there was a different guide."

Leaving the Frio River crossing, Terán marched a total of 11 leagues northeast across present Medina County to reach the Medina River; this took only two days (see *San Antonio*, NH14-8). The *entrada* covered 16 miles on June 11 and 13 miles on the next day. On the second day, the governor reported correctly that they had discovered a new road (or found another Indian trade route). The royal standard was planted that afternoon on a stream "which, at various points, on previous trips, had been called the Medina." Massanet's account did not note reaching the Medina on June 12; he said only that the Indians call the stream "Panapay." The padre added that along the route north of the Frio the party had seen mesquite, cedar, oak, cottonwood, and mulberry trees and also more bison and deer.

It should be clear from Map 6 and the maps accompanying subsequent chapters that the route taken by Terán from the Nueces to the Medina was never followed again on any expedition covered in this study. Governor Salinas, in 1693, followed De León's route to East Texas and crossed the present San Antonio River near Falls City in Karnes County, the Guadalupe near Cuero, and the Colorado near La Grange. On Salinas's return, he visited the San Antonio area and found Terán's trail, but he did not follow it west of the Hondo. Salinas instead moved south from the Medina along a route that ran between the present-day Hondo and the San Miguel and then crossed the Frio at the ford De León had used before below its junction with Hondo Creek.

Terán's party continued the next day (June 13), moving along a pathline from the Medina east toward the present-day city of San Antonio. After marching 13 miles, they camped at a location that Terán and Massanet both named San Antonio de Padua because, as the padre mentioned, it was this saint's day. Under the orders issued dividing responsibilities on the expedition between Terán and Massanet, Terán alone was granted the authority to give official names to camps and rivers previously unnamed. Thus, officially, Terán was the one who gave the location the name San Antonio de Padua.

Near San Antonio de Padua was a river (later named Río de San Antonio de Padua by Padre Espinosa) that, according to Massanet, was bordered with cottonwoods, oaks, cedars, mulberries, and vines. Terán reported cypress trees and some siene bean bushes along the stream. Prairie chickens and buffalo were so numerous that the horses became frightened and stampeded. The following day (June 14), the troops rested to observe Corpus Christi Day. Both leaders reported finding a large village of friendly Indians of the Payaya nation. Two years later, in the summer of 1693, Governor Salinas encountered the same tribe of Indians when he was moving through the San Antonio area on his return trip from East Texas. The identification of Indian tribes along the way is significant in tracking expedition routes, as Thomas N. Campbell and Donald Chipman have emphasized, because the presence of identified tribes in a location helps scholars assess the validity of the route projection.[6]

At this point, the party was only about 30 miles from the Guadalupe and 55 miles from the San Marcos River, near the present city of San Marcos. But it should be recalled that the Guadalupe had been crossed earlier by Spaniards only at the ford called Gobernador (in DeWitt County) and the present-day San Marcos River was, at that time, known only as a branch of the Guadalupe. Terán's group accomplished this trek between San Antonio de Padua and the present San Marcos River (called the Guadalupe by both Terán and Massanet) without significant incident in five days of slow travel. From June 15 to 19, they inched east and northeast, toward the San Marcos crossing.

The route, as reported by Terán, proceeded from San Antonio in an easterly direction that took the expedition below present New Braunfels. Although several creeks were mentioned, neither the governor nor the padre even noted in their diaries that they crossed the Guadalupe River where it runs between present Seguin and New Braunfels. This is not surprising, because earlier Terán had omitted any references to crossing the Leona River and Massanet had failed to mention the Medina. The two diarists reported seeing bison each day and crossing several large unidentified creeks and streams, some with alligators, but not until the fifth day of travel, after marching 21 leagues (about 55 miles) from San Antonio de Padua, did Terán note that they reached a branch of the Guadalupe (the present San Marcos).

On June 19, when Terán and Massanet were approaching the San Marcos, they encountered a very large gathering of 2,000 to 3,000 Indians.[7] Terán identified the Indian nations as the Jumano, Cibolo, Cantona, and Casquesa (see Appendix IV entry for "Catquesa"). They were well-recognized tribes. Massanet added that the Chalome and Chaynaya tribes, visitors from below the Rio Grande, were there too. Sixteen years later, the Chalome and two other tribes guided Espinosa from the San Antonio area past San Marcos to the Colorado crossing in Travis County.

The Indians were mostly distant visitors from south of the Rio Grande and West Texas on their annual trading and hunting excursion to Central Texas. They were not only mounted (at a period when few local Indians had horses), but were riding in saddles with stirrups, which Massanet noted as unusual. Five years earlier and about 100 miles to the southeast, La Salle had encountered a similar or perhaps the same large party of Indians mounted with saddles and stirrups, wearing boots and spurs. They also told La Salle of their contacts with the Spaniards to the west in northern New Spain.[8]

Massanet commented in his diary account that the same tribes customarily remained near the headwaters of the San Marcos to hunt each year until winter, when they would return west. The padre also observed that the Indian tribes that lived west and south of the Guadalupe River spoke the same language but that the tribes that lived between the Guadalupe and the Colorado spoke different languages. He added, however, that the Central Texas tribes communicated and maintained a friendly relationship with each other.

The only previous Indian gathering that numbered 1,000 or more had been reported by De León the year before, on June 19, at a village of Indians (perhaps Aranama or Aname) on the lower Lavaca River. But this gathering of several large tribes that Terán met was not a local village community; rather, this assembly included several visiting tribes that annually moved from West Texas and the Rio Grande area to hunt buffalo near the Guadalupe and Colorado rivers and to trade with their friends in the area and with the Tejas Indians in East Texas. The Indians from the west annually made the trek to exchange items—including Spanish horses and goods from Chihuahua and New Mexico—with the Tejas and with local tribes. The historian Elizabeth John refers to these exchanges as occurring at trade fairs.[9] In the spring of 1686, La Salle's party also had seen evidence of substantial trade between the Tejas and the tribes from the New Mexico area. Father Anastase Douay reported that Spanish money, silver spoons, lace, clothes, and horses all were found in the villages of the Tejas (or Asinai).[10]

Some of the Indian leaders Terán met had close connections with Spanish authorities in northeastern New Spain and several Indian leaders, referred to by Massanet as captains, spoke fluent Spanish. The tribal captains apparently held some form of written understanding from Spanish authorities in Vizcaya (the present state of Chihuahua) and New Mexico acknowledging that the Indians possessed a right to occupy or use certain lands. The Spanish term used by Terán for the written grants held by the Indians was *patentes formales;* but the governor did not elaborate further, other than to say that the Indian captains wanted the same form of formal instrument from him. He delayed action, effectively denying the request.

Terán did not trust these chieftains, but he spoke with them at length. He considered them intelligent and brave, but haughty. Nevertheless, he prepared an impressive barbecue for them. The Indians responded by conducting a well-organized parade.

The parade was one of the most dramatic and dazzling displays of Indian pomp and ceremony witnessed on any *entrada*. According to Massanet, near present San Marcos, at a place the Indians called Canaquedista (meaning headwaters), several thousand Indians marched and rode in columns, two by two. Reportedly, each of four principal Indian leaders led his tribe past the priest to kiss his habit or his hand and receive presents.

First in the parade according to Massanet was Captain Don Juan Sabeata, the old captain of the Jumano from West Texas. Sabeata was a widely known Indian leader who remained on the Texas scene for another fifteen years. In April 1689, he had notified the Spaniards of the demise of La Salle's settlement a short time before Governor De León discovered the remains.[11]

The second column was led by a captain of the Cantona Indians, who carried an old but well-preserved wooden or cane cross. The Cantona captain was later met by Fray Espinosa (1709) not far away, on the Colorado, displaying the same or a similar old, well-preserved cane cross. The third group was guided by the chief of the Cibolo tribe from the West Texas–Rio Grande area, accompanied by some Chalome and Chaynaya Indians carrying a banner with an image of Our Lady of Guadalupe. The banner apparently had been given to the tribe by Massanet or De León the previous year. The last column, headed by an Indian carrying a similar image or banner of Our Lady of Guadalupe, was led by Captain Nicolás of the Catqueza, another Indian nation that probably resided to the southwest.

Captain Nicolás was one of the Indians who seemed to interest Massanet most. The padre noted that Nicolás could speak a number of "Mexican dialects" (probably meaning Aztec) and the Spanish language as well, "understanding everything that was said to him." The captain had been reared in the Spanish town of Parras (located about 120 miles south-southwest of Monclova) and had spent time in New Mexico. Nicolás was highly regarded among his people, Massanet said, because Indians admire a man who is expert in cruelties and in war. Massanet seemed to think the Catqueza nation was a local tribe rather than one from West Texas, but the detailed background of their captain and his association with the Jumano and the other West Texas tribes suggest otherwise. Terán's comment that the Catqueza held some form of written permit to use land from the governors of Vizcaya and New Mexico supports the thesis that they were from an area south of the Rio Grande or West Texas.[12]

This display of the image of Our Lady of Guadalupe by the Indians probably pleased Massanet and certainly did not surprise him. On the 1690 trip, the padre reported that six such banners were presented to deserving Indian leaders. Massanet also gave presents to the participants on this occasion—men were given knives and tobacco; women received earrings, beads, and red ribbons.

The celebration was marred, however, by two letters that the Indian leaders delivered to Fray Massanet. The letters were from the padres who served at the East Texas mission among the Tejas Indians, with whom the West Texas Indians had been visiting and trading. The East Texas padres, following the example of the Tejas earlier, used the Jumano chieftain as postman to take messages west for delivery to Spaniards in the missions in either West Texas or New Mexico. The sad message revealed that a serious epidemic had struck the mission area and many Indians had died. One priest also had died from a fever that lasted eight days. In reaction to the epidemic and loss of life, the Tejas had turned against the church. The message prompted Massanet to suggest that the governor proceed in a more urgent manner.

On June 20, Terán's party arrived at a stream that is presently known as the Blanco River; both the governor and Massanet referred to it as another branch of the Guadalupe. The governor was again impressed by the large number of trees that grew along the riverbanks in the region; he found pecans, cypresses, willows, siene bean bushes, and many other, unnamed trees. That evening, after a strange disturbance (perhaps caused by the Indians), the governor's horse herd stampeded. This caused a serious delay. After searching for four days, Terán could recover only thirty-five of the one hundred missing mounts.

By June 26, after marching east for another two days, the party reached the present Colorado at a crossing below Onion Creek, a few miles downstream from the Travis-Bastrop County line (see *Austin*, NH 14-6). Terán observed that the river had been called the San Marcos and Colorado on earlier expeditions. Actually, De León had consistently referred to the present Colorado River as the San Marcos and to the present Brazos as either the Espíritu Santo or Colorado. Further confusion in the names of Texas rivers was assured by Terán's mistaken comment.

Near the Colorado, Massanet observed a thick forest (later called the Monte Grande) crowded with oaks, cedars, brazilwoods, cottonwoods, pines, and grapevines, and the padre carved a cross and the date on a large hackberry tree. The party immediately worked its way downstream, crossing and recrossing the river skirting the edge of the forest several times,[13] and moving southeast to a campground near a large, long lagoon with a plentiful supply of both fish and alligators. There are today a number of extended lagoons along the Colorado in the vicinity of Smithville (see *Seguin*, NH 14-9). On Map 6 the campsite near the third river crossing is located about 26 miles (10 leagues) upstream from present La Grange. Although it is not specifically mentioned in the diary account, Terán and Massanet apparently moved the main supply party about 7 leagues farther downstream during the next two weeks while Captain Martínez traveled to Matagorda Bay to meet the supply ship from Veracruz and the marine reinforcements under the command of Captain Salinas Varona.[14]

Governor Terán and Fray Massanet gave no account of Captain Martínez's excursion to the bay, but the captain kept a diary himself.[15] On July 3, according to his diary, Martínez left Terán's base-camp on the Colorado with his French guide Pierre Meunier to rendezvous with Salinas at Matagorda Bay and return with the marine resupply party. The captain was well acquainted with the area along the Colorado River near La Grange and the bay because he had been with De León the year before on the trip to the bay to recover the three Talon children.

Captain Martínez reported that he took twenty soldiers, fifty-six mules, and almost three hundred horses to use as mounts and pack animals for the fifty troops and supplies that were to arrive with Captain Salinas. The first day, Martínez moved downstream along the right bank of the Colorado past live oak groves and other oaks for about 26 miles (10 leagues), to the campsite named Jesús María y Joseph Buenavista by De León the previous year. The captain confirmed in his journal that he was familiar with the site.

He had passed the location with De León, once (May 11, 1690) when crossing the Colorado traveling to East Texas and again (June 17) on the return march. The site of Buenavista is an easily distinguished hill—presently called Monument Hill—directly across the river from the city of La Grange. It provides a beautiful view of the surrounding countryside, as the captain stated in his account.

On July 4, Martínez proceeded down the Colorado toward present-day Columbus and then turned west over open grasslands to camp on an upper tributary of the Navidad River, which he named Arroyo San Laureano. On that day, the captain was able to secure by force the assistance of an unidentified local Indian guide, who was brought into camp by two troopers. At 5:30 the following morning, the party moved south down the Navidad for about 28 miles to an overnight camp on a large creek off the lower Navidad that he named Arroyo San Eugenio.

Martínez marched west for about 8 miles on July 6 to the lower Lavaca River. Elms and cottonwoods were seen along the trail. The captain reported that the French had named the river the Creek of the *Caña* or Canes. His source for this information was Pierre Meunier, who accompanied him as a guide. The Talon brothers, Pierre and Jean-Baptiste, later confirmed that the joined Lavaca and Navidad rivers were called the River of Canes.[16] The party moved about 4 miles past the Lavaca to spend the night on a second creek, probably the Arenosa, which Martínez named Santa Lucía Mártir.

The captain went south across Victoria County about 12 miles the following day to the Creek of the Frenchmen (Garcitas Creek). The captain's diary account supports the conclusion that the French settlement was on a creek about 16 miles west of the Lavaca River or the River of Canes; therefore, the fort could not have been located on the Lavaca River in Jackson County as some historians have argued.

About 5 miles down the creek riding east toward Matagorda Bay through flat land the captain encountered an Indian who said that he was from a village located on another bay "where the French girl [Marie Madeleine Talon] had been recovered" the year before (nearby San Antonio Bay). Soon thereafter, the captain selected a spot near the former French colony on Garcitas Creek as the initial base-camp and named it Don Gaspar.

That afternoon, Martínez traveled about 4 miles south down the creek to present Lavaca Bay, which he called De Todos Santos. This was a name briefly used for modern Lavaca Bay, as Espíritu Santo was used for modern Matagorda Bay. When Juan Enríquez Barroto visited the bay by sea in 1687, however, he named it San Bernardo Bay—a usage which eventually replaced De León's Espíritu Santo. Today, Espíritu Santo Bay is the small waterway connecting Matagorda Bay and San Antonio Bay, so the name has not been lost, just reassigned, like the early names of many Texas rivers (see *Beeville*, NH14-12).

Martínez saw no vessel at the bay and returned to his base-camp near the former French fort. He found that his Indian guide had departed, leaving word that he was going to locate one of the French boys.

Captain Martínez moved his Garcitas campsite on Sunday, July 8, about 4 miles west up a nearby creek (probably Placedo Creek) to a lagoon of good water. Six members of the camp were detailed to build fires and to send smoke signals advising Captain Salinas's vessel of Martínez's camp location. The Spaniards had adopted the Indian practice of using smoke signals as a means of communication. De León and his troops had used smoke signals, and later, in 1709, Fray Espinosa employed them while searching for the Tejas Indians near the Colorado.

The next day, Martínez, eight soldiers, an interpreter, and Pierre Meunier left camp to survey the area farther west. About 10 miles from camp, they spotted several Indians who were spying on their small reconnaissance party. After traveling another 4 miles east-southeast, the party found an Indian village near the head of San Antonio Bay. The captain observed that this was the area where Governor De León had recovered the Talon children. Martínez's diary account supports the conclusion reached earlier that the Talon children had been rescued by De León at an Indian village on the headwaters of San Antonio Bay and not on the western shoreline of Matagorda Bay. The captain's diary entry also confirms that he had been with De León during the skirmish and recovery of the three Talon children the year before. Although De León's diary account of the recapture does not mention whether Captain Martínez was with him, the governor had taken Martínez along on other side trips when a hostile encounter with Indians was expected or a French translator might be needed.

At the Indian camp, the conscripted Indian interpreter and Meunier moved quickly ahead of the party and called to the Indians, declaring that no harm was intended. Slowly, the Karankawa returned to meet with the captain. Upon questioning, they reported that no ship had been seen for five "moons." Martínez then insisted that the Karankawa bring him the other two French boys and one French girl they were holding. The captain offered horses in exchange and threatened hostility if the children were not returned. The Indians replied that they were not holding French children at their own village, but said they would pass the word to nearby camps.

The captain then left a written note addressed to Captain Salinas that was to be taken by the Indians to the mouth of Matagorda Bay. Upon returning to base camp about the time of 3:00 P.M. prayer, Martínez received word that one French boy would be returned the following day at the Lavaca Bay shore near his camp. As a sign of the good intentions of the Karankawa, the Indian messenger left two arrows and a piece of buffalo rawhide.

The captain and sixteen of his twenty soldiers moved the next morning about 2 to 3 miles to the bay shore to meet with the Indians. At the bay, some of the Indians whom Martínez had seen the day before delivered a young French boy, Eustache Bréman. In exchange, the captain gave the Indians a horse and a few presents, but held three of them overnight. The following day, only two of them were set free and were told that the third Indian would be released when the remaining French boy and girl hostages were brought to camp. After answering that the girl had been taken by other Indians within the "corra" (which probably meant the circular inland bay area), the two released Indians left camp. The captain continued to send up smoke signals and had an Indian climb a tall oak to see if the ship carrying Salinas and his men could be seen. The Indian reported only that some Indian smoke signals, which he could not read, were being sent from a village on the opposite side of the bay.

The returned captive, Eustache Bréman, was one of the five or perhaps six children who survived the Karankawa massacre at the French colony in late December 1688. Eustache had been a captive for two and one-half years: the first eighteen months with the three Talon children who were rescued the year before, and the full two and one-half years with the Talons' oldest brother, Jean-Baptiste. The five young captives had developed a strong friendship and gave each other support, as reflected in the story told under questioning in 1698, after the Talons returned to France. Jean-Baptiste recalled that the Karankawa men, on one occasion, wanted to abuse his sister, Marie Madeleine, whom he described as quite pretty and well built. But, when the Indians came in force, Eustache resisted their efforts by convincing them that the young girl's God would make them all die if they did violence to her. The ploy succeeded, according to her brother.[17]

Around noon on July 12, the two Indians who had been released to seek the other French girl and older French boy returned with only the boy, Jean-Baptiste Talon. In exchange for his release, the Indians were given two horses and some tobacco. The Karankawa reported that there were no more French children being held there. For Martínez, this report closed the case, and the existence or fate of the second girl captive remains uncertain. The final comments made about her by the Indians perhaps suggest that she was being held elsewhere, which, in effect, supports the earlier statements that the second girl had not been killed.

The recovery of the oldest Talon brother, Jean-Baptiste, does not end the saga of the five captive Talon children. Robert S. Weddle has made exhaustive studies and presented fascinating accounts of the Talon family.[18] One or more members remained on or near the Texas scene during the following twenty-five years. In 1698, when Jean-Baptiste was questioned in some detail by French officials about his early life at La Salle's colony, he described his experiences with the Karankawa Indians. Jean-Baptiste was one of only a few who had firsthand knowledge of the lifestyle of the Karankawa at this time. He gave a detailed account of a Karankawa raid on their traditional enemy the Tejas, executed while he and the other French children were being held captive.

Jean-Baptiste said that the "Clamcoeh" band of Karankawa, which was the tribe with whom the children were living, initiated a surprise raid from their village near the old French settlement. According to their custom, he said, the Indians first took the entire village—including women, children, and the elderly—to find a safe, yet convenient, refuge for those who were not to be engaged in the actual raid. The Karankawa paddled in canoes past the River of Canes (Lavaca River), east toward present Carancahua Creek and the Colorado River, the lower stretch of which leads north toward the Tejas villages between the Trinity and Neches rivers. The coastal area near the mouth of the Colorado provided a secure location for the camp along the general route taken for the East Texas raid. The five French children and the Karankawa women, children, and aged waited at this location for six weeks for the return of the raiders.

When the men (and perhaps some women) returned, it was evident that victory was theirs. The result was demonstrated by the display of fifty to sixty scalps and thirty to forty captured Asinai or Tejas slaves. The holding of hostages and slaves was not an uncommon practice for the Karankawa and for other Indian tribes in the area. Jean-Baptiste added that some of the captured slaves were eaten at a feast that extended for over three days, during which the French youth fasted because human flesh was the sole fare. This form of ritual cannibalism was rather widely practiced among Indians in the Gulf coastal area. Jean-Baptiste modified the stigma by explaining that the Karankawa were cannibals only toward their Indian enemies and would never eat a Frenchman.[19] Fray Solís later suggested that the Karankawa had no such reservation about roasting Spaniards, especially Spanish priests. During an earlier period, Alonso de León (the elder) wrote in convincing detail of widespread cannibalism in northeastern New Spain, giving specific references to Nuevo León natives who ate both friend and foe.[20]

On July 12, advised again by his Indian tree climber that no sign of any vessel could be seen, Martínez ordered a return march to the Colorado along the same path used on the way down to the bay. By July 19, Martínez's party had found Terán's new base-camp, closer to La Grange. There a vote was taken among the senior members of the expedition to proceed immediately to the land of the Tejas and relieve the stricken mission, although Terán wanted to send Martínez immediately back to the coast to await Salinas and his troops.

On July 22, as directed by the majority, Terán left the Colorado camp in Fayette County with his full *entrada* (not including Salinas and his troops) and moved north-northeast, following "a narrow trail with woods on either side." Robert Weddle correctly comments that the governor "seems to have been a little off the course of the later Camino Real, which Terán is credited with marking."[21] The Camino Real referred to by Weddle much later crossed Bastrop County near the modern city of Bastrop about 30 miles north of Terán's camp and line of march.

Both Massanet's and Terán's accounts of the party's movement from the Colorado indicate that this route was north toward the Brazos and the Little Brazos junction rather than more eastward toward the Navasota junction used earlier by De León and Salinas. Massanet wrote that the Tejas leader Bernardino who accompanied the party and several other Tejas and Cantona Indians were along to serve as escorts.

After four days' travel 47 miles north-northeast, through dense oak woods, later called the Monte Grande, the party reached the Brazos River, which Massanet correctly identified as the Espíritu Santo and which, Terán said, "the natives call the Colorado."[22] This further confounded the problem of the nomenclature of Texas rivers, with the present Colorado being called the San Marcos and the present San Antonio being called the Medina, not to mention the Hondo-Frio mix-up.

Although the river was down, both Terán and Massanet noted that a smaller second stream (perhaps the Little Brazos) was crossed a short distance after fording the larger Brazos River. The guides from the Tejas country who had met the expedition on the third day's movement east of the Colorado continued to lead the *entrada* through the open corridor in the Monte Grande, past the customary crossing of the Brazos in Burleson County, and along the pathway that then led northeast to the Trinity.

During the trip to the Trinity, Terán and Massanet continued to record their separate daily accounts of the journey. The governor suggested that he was following a road in a corridor through a dense wood and over a rough country. In Fray Massanet's account, which is much more detailed, explicit, and accurate, the padre gave the Asinai name used for each river and large creek crossed from the Colorado to the Trinity, confirming that the Tejas Indians who accompanied the ecclesiastical group were familiar with and could identify the route and the streams by name. When Massanet crossed the Navasota River on July 28, he recorded that the natives called the river the Babototo. He added that the party was crossing the river well above the ford he had used to cross the same river the year before with De León when they were following the lower Indian trade route and crossed downstream, a few miles above the mouth of the Navasota.

Terán's party was probably moving along the Tejas trail through the natural clearing or corridor in the middle of the Monte Grande that Espinosa also would follow on later expeditions with his Tejas guides. The same open corridor is seen on contemporary topographic maps prepared by the USGS and the Texas General Land Office. Immediately after crossing the Navasota, both Terán and Massanet mention passing two large lakes or lagoons. A lake (named Santa Ana by Espinosa in 1716) located a few leagues east of the Navasota River was a campsite used on later expeditions by Alarcón and Rivera. Although the route is not without question, the references to the Babototo River and the nearby large lakes tend to confirm that Terán was following the more northern route from the Colorado to the Trinity on his first trip to East Texas.

The confidence that can be placed in Massanet's daily account (in contrast with Terán's diary) is clearly illustrated in the approximately 40-mile movement of the expedition between the Navasota River and the Trinity. Terán unrealistically reports that the trip was made in one day, August 1, having marched 5 leagues (13 miles). Massanet says that the trip took three days (July 29–31) and they traveled 16 leagues (42 miles), which closely matches the straight-line measurement of the distance between the Navasota and the Trinity across southern Leon County. The acrimonious relationship between the governor and the head priest continued to separate the two leaders and may help explain the differences in their daily diary accounts of the distances traveled.

By August 1, the party had reached the Trinity, where the padres with the Tejas contingent abruptly left the governor with his main body of troops and advanced along a route that was familiar to the Tejas escorts or to Massanet from his visit the year before. Terán traveled another 26 miles east of the Trinity before he met, on August 4, some of the few troops left by De León. He stopped there before reaching the mission area, well short of the Neches. The thick woods of oak, *nogales* (see Appendix II entry for "Pecan"), and pine surrounded his camp for a distance of about 65 miles and continued, the governor said, to the northeast for "60 leagues" (about 156 miles) to the Cadodache nation. The governor did not realize then that he would be directed by the viceroy to return and visit the area later that year.

After meeting the Tejas governor, Terán rested his troops in camp for about three weeks before commencing his return. No details are given in the diary of the day-to-day activity during his stay. Massanet, however, noted with great sorrow the large number of Indians who had died during the epidemic.

This was not the first serious epidemic the Tejas had suffered from highly contagious and deadly European-introduced diseases such as smallpox, measles, and typhoid. Experts estimate that by the time Massanet and De León first arrived among the western Caddo (or Tejas) in 1690, the population of the larger Caddo nation, which occupied parts of Oklahoma, Missouri, Arkansas, and Louisiana as well as northeastern Texas, had been reduced by a series of epidemics to only a small percentage (perhaps 10–20 percent) of its population before the first European contact with the Caddo by the De Soto–Moscoso expedition in 1542.

Timothy Perttula reports estimates of a decrease from a Caddo population of 200,000–250,000 in 1520 to a population of only 8,500 in 1690. He adds that the projection in depopulation of the Caddo is in line with projections for the depopulation of Indians in the southeastern states who were similarly exposed to epidemic diseases.[23] The projection is also close to that made in 1980 for the depopulation of Indian tribes in Coahuila, Nuevo León, and Vizcaya by Peter Gerhard.[24] This striking demographic loss in the native population in northeastern Mexico and East Texas was probably not confined to only the local Indians, because there is strong evidence to support the thesis that these contagious diseases were transmitted between the Tejas and the numerous visiting Frenchmen from La Salle's colony and from tribes who journeyed along established trade routes from Mexico to exchange goods, horses, and slaves. The Indian and European traders from the Gulf Coast, northeastern New Spain, and West Texas may have exchanged unseen European-introduced viruses as well as goods.[25] The numerous reports of epidemics in the early and middle 1600s in Texas, Nuevo León, and Coahuila suggest the need for further demographic studies of this region.[26]

On August 24, the governor began his return march to what he called "the Old Fort" on Matagorda Bay. Massanet remained in the mission field. Apparently Terán's camp beyond the Trinity had remained near the same location, because the governor marched only 26 miles (10 leagues) again on his return trip from the campground to the Trinity crossing. Terán's diary entries on the distance and direction traveled each day to the Colorado, as noted in Table 3, do not permit any precise estimate of the location of Trinity crossing, but it would appear to be several miles above De León's earlier crossing.

From the Trinity the governor reported traveling southwest. Before he arrived at the Navasota, Terán camped again at the two lakes he had named San Isidro Labrador on July 31. He again refers to the Brazos as the Colorado, as did De León. The summer heat and the drought was taking its toll—the 1,000-head remuda of horses (all, he said, under five years of age) was exhausted; the governor now was riding a mule. Since leaving Coahuila, the party had received only two rain showers, and the country was without water or grass. The governor noted each day that the terrain he was passing was similar to that seen on his trip east. The party found the Colorado crossing on August 31 at La Grange and remained in camp until September 2.

It was Governor Terán's plan on his return trek from the Colorado first to take the main body of his troops, horses, and supplies to the Guadalupe campground and Vado del Gobernador crossing used by De León (DeWitt County). Although the governor had not been there himself, Captain Martínez was very familiar with this trail down the Indian trade route from La Grange to the old Guadalupe crossing; he had followed the path, or major parts of it, on at least five occasions with De León's party within the previous two years. Martínez had camped near the Vado del Gobernador crossing with De León in both 1689 and 1690. The governor planned to leave the main body of troops and supplies there with Captain Martínez and then to take a few men to the bay to see if Captain Salinas had finally arrived. If Salinas was not waiting at the bay, the governor planned to retrace his steps to the Guadalupe crossing and proceed overland back to Monclova.

On September 2, Terán left the Colorado and traveled southwest 13 miles. He reported that the camp location and stream there had been called Las Tres Cruces (Three Crosses) on previous journeys, which is consistent with the later identification of Tres Cruces in the vicinity of Buckner's Creek by Governor Salinas (in 1693) and others. Although the origin of the name Tres Cruces is uncertain, it may derive from the three paths that crossed near this location—two headed north and northeast to East Texas and one south to the Guadalupe River ford and west to Coahuila.

The following day, "marching for the Guadalupe," the party continued southwest about 10 miles, through a large herd of more than 4,000 buffalo. They camped on a tributary of the Navidad that Terán named San Sebastián. The following day (September 4), the party veered more to the south about 13 miles because of the difficult terrain near the headwaters of the Lavaca River. The governor complained that he was traveling the "road followed in the previous expedition [De Leon's 1689 and 1690 expeditions], which could only have been opened by a man in his sleep." He acknowledged, however, that De León's route led toward the Guadalupe. The camp that night was probably on Brushy Creek near the Lavaca-DeWitt County line. Perhaps it should be noted again that Terán's daily distance projections in number of leagues traveled were not as accurate as the distance estimates made by De Leon, Massanet, or Salinas in 1693. The governor frequently understated the distance traveled and actually covered a greater distance than his diary entries reflected.

On September 5, the party continued south-southwest more than 15 miles and arrived at the Guadalupe River. Because the number of leagues entered by Terán in his diary entry suggests a shorter distance than the one he actually traveled, the precise location of Terán's Guadalupe camp is difficult to project with certainty, but it was in the vicinity of De León's earlier camps near Vado del Gobernador. There the governor left Captain Martínez, as planned, with the main body of his troops, provisions, and supplies to await orders for the return to Monclova.

Terán and a small unit proceeded on September 7 toward the old fort on the bay, moving from the Guadalupe camp a total distance of 26 miles: 5 miles northeast, 8 miles east, 8 more southwest over level open country (Chicolete Prairie), and finally 5 miles southeast. On the open prairie, they again saw herds of more than 1,000 buffalo.

The next morning, the party continued to the southwest, still moving across open prairie. Along the way, they contacted some troops from Captain Salinas's command, who had been sent up the Garcitas either to man a sentry post or to scout for the governor's party. On the banks of the Río de los Franceses (Garcitas Creek), they found Captain Salinas, who reported that he had been waiting since July 2. The captain had orders from the viceroy directing the governor to return to the Tejas country and to explore farther east. Terán immediately sent two aides back to the Guadalupe base-camp to bring Captain Martínez and the remaining troops, supplies, and horses to the bay. With the marine reinforcements, a new expedition was to be organized.

Governor Terán's diary record omits any references to the activities that occurred between September 8 and 27. By the latter date, the expedition party was reorganized and ready to head back to East Texas from the camp at Santa Margarita de Buenavista, a location unidentified by Terán but apparently near the old fort area.

On September 27, Terán's troops (augmented by Captain Salinas's men) left the encampment near the former French fort. The mounted troops first veered north a short distance to get fresh water for the horses, probably at present Arenosa Creek, and then moved a total of 13 miles northeast to camp on the Lavaca River. The campsite for the evening was named San Opio. The next morning, the troops rode northeast more than 20 miles to camp near the Navidad River, which the governor named San Exuperio. No description of the terrain is given because, the governor explained, he had given a description earlier in the diary. Actually, the party was moving in a new direction, north from the bay area, across the lower Lavaca and Navidad in Jackson, Wharton, and Colorado counties.

Early the next afternoon, they stopped at a location named San Miguel, about 21 miles north-northwest of the previous camp. The same direction was followed on September 30, 18 miles to a campsite near a pond, San Gerónimo de la Mota. On October 1, after traveling 13 miles, Terán completed his unintended circle of the Colorado–Guadalupe–Matagorda Bay area, returning to a campsite near the Colorado crossing called Rosario. He would return to this encampment the following February on his final trek home. Captain Salinas also camped at the *paraje* Rosario near the left bank at the Colorado River crossing on his return from East Texas in 1693.

Near the Colorado River crossing, the governor obtained the services of the old Indian leader called captain of the Cantuna and three of his men to serve as guides to the Tejas. This captain was probably the Cantona Indian leader whom Terán had met near San Marcos at the Indian parade earlier in the year, who later (1709) would guide Espinosa to a large gathering of Indians a few leagues east of the Colorado near the Travis-Bastrop County line. Terán now also had the services of Captain Salinas, who had traveled the same route from the Colorado crossing near La Grange to the Neches with De León in 1690. Their route from the Colorado this time followed the one De León and Salinas had taken earlier, rather than the more northerly route that Terán had taken on his first trip to East Texas. Massanet had earlier reported to the viceroy that there were two routes from the Colorado crossing to the Tejas.

The first campsite (1.5 leagues northeast of the river) was named Padre San Francisco. Terán said the campsite was where he had previously met with "the Reverend Fathers," meaning Massanet and his padres, who had voted on July 21 to proceed to the East Texas missions rather than to send Martínez back to the bay as Terán strongly preferred. This reference helps locate the campsite used at the time Terán proceeded east of the Colorado on his first trip in July. At some point while Martínez was traveling to Matagorda Bay, Terán's party apparently had moved downstream to camp a few leagues north of the Colorado crossing near La Grange.

Terán's party traveled 17 leagues northeast in the next three days (October 5–7) to the Brazos crossing near the Navasota junction.[27] The projection that Terán was following a different route to East Texas on his second trip is supported by the fact that he was marching in a different direction, northeast rather than north-northeast (the direction that led to the Little Brazos River junction), and the named campsites were new. The continuing dry weather had reduced the Brazos, making the crossing boggy rather than wet, and had made the Navasota appear to the governor to be only a small branch of the larger Brazos River.

After crossing both the Brazos and the Navasota on October 7 and moving north and northeast, Terán's party continued toward the Tejas missions. Suddenly, the drought was broken by heavy rains. The trip northeast was interrupted for a total of twelve days along the pathway between the Brazos and the Trinity to permit Terán's troops to construct a bridge near a *paraje* called Melancio. The camp was approximately 30 miles north-northeast of the Navasota crossing (above its junction with the Brazos) and approximately another 30 miles west of the Trinity, which they forded on October 25. Bedias Creek—which runs from west to east and is located about half the distance between the two river crossings—had apparently flooded, causing the delay. The name of the camp becomes significant because Governor Salinas mentioned the *paraje* Melancio on his trip to resupply the East Texas mission and on his return from the mission in 1693. He undoubtedly remembered the week's delay in 1691 and the construction work.

After crossing Bedias Creek, Terán moved north-northeast, probably crossing the Trinity near the ford he had used on his first trip. The governor either deliberately or by mistake marched to the Mission María on the Neches, about 5 miles northeast of Mission San Francisco, where Fray Massanet was serving. His openly hostile relationship with Massanet seems to offer the best explanation for bypassing Mission San Francisco and bivouacking his troops at nearby María.

The governor remained in the mission area until early November, probing the river and preparing to visit the Cadodacho nation farther northeast. No expedition from New Spain had attempted a systematic exploration of this region, much less in the winter, which arrived in force just as Terán's party prepared to begin the journey.

The trip to visit the Caddo who lived near the Red River in southwestern Arkansas took another month. The projection of Terán's route is based on his diary account of the directions and distances traveled, but it should be repeated that the governor's diary accounts of the number of leagues traveled were not consistently reliable; he frequently misstated or understated the distances he actually traveled (see *Palestine*, NH15-1; *Tyler*, NI15-10; *Shreveport, La.*, NI15-11; and *El Dorado, Ark.*, NI15-8).

Four priests, including Fray Massanet, joined Terán on November 6 as he commenced the journey. The party moved slowly northeast, 10 to 12 miles a day, and reached the Sabine River on November 13. Turning north, they were slowed, and at times delayed for a day or two, by the ice, snow, and exhausted pack animals. The company constructed a bridge to cross icy Cypress Bayou northeast of present Marshall and a second bridge over the Sulphur River where Terán and thirty troopers left the main camp to move north-northeast.

Terán's account of the distance and directions traveled beyond Cypress Bayou between November 18 and 29 is not sufficiently clear to permit a confident projection of where the party crossed the Sulphur River and located the village of the "Cadodacho Nation" on the Red River, but the village appears to have been in Miller County, Arkansas. There Terán found the young chief or "Caddi" of the Cadodacho Indians and remained near the river until early December.

On December 5, Terán began his return trek southwest to the East Texas mission area near the Neches. It was an extremely hard journey: the weather had turned bitter cold and the men, as well as the horses and pack animals, were exhausted. Desertions also became a problem. Terán spent a day searching for his young "Negro" bugler, who had escaped.[28] Terán's comment is not the only reference to African Americans or mulattoes in Spanish expedition diaries and related colonial documents. Captain Domingo Ramón (1716) lists a "Negro" by the name of Juan de la Concepción in his expedition party; a mulatto served as a herd driver for Saint Denis's party in 1717; and Alarcón (1718) mentioned that his black cook almost drowned in the Trinity River. These references to African Americans are not surprising, because there are reports that mulattoes accounted for a substantial segment (up to 20 to 30 percent) of the municipal population of Monterrey, Sabinas, and Linares in the 1730s.[29] Peter Gerhard refers to reports of a large population of African Americans or mulattoes in Coahuila in the late 1700s.[30]

By early January, the governor was at Mission San Francisco, the weather bitterly cold, and the troops even more exhausted and discouraged. Still, Terán was ready to continue his journey "in the direction of the bay in search of El Real de Santa Margarita de Buenavista" (his former campsite near Matagorda Bay). Six missionaries who had been with Fray Massanet decided to leave the mission field with the expedition. With travel conditions aggravated by the ice and snow, the governor seems at first not to have been following any clear road. His diary entry on February 1 illustrates the difficulty of the march and the confusion. Everyone began searching for the shortest and quickest route; after consulting the reports from each of the prior expedition leaders, Terán accepted a Tlaxcalan Indian as his guide.

It is significant that in deep East Texas the governor selected a native of Coahuila as his guide. The choice of a Tlaxcalan Indian to serve as the principal guide for a trip from East Texas to Matagorda Bay suggests that some Indians other than the Jumano and Cibolo from northern New Spain were familiar with the trade route from Coahuila to East Texas and the bay. It should be remembered, however, that the Tlaxcalan Indians had been on friendly terms with the Spaniards in Mexico and northeast New Spain for decades and frequently had fought with and supplied guides to the Spanish military.[31]

By February 11, Terán had reached the Brazos near the Navasota junction. Along the route (on February 5), Terán again passed the campsite San Melancio, confirming that he was following the same road he had used on his second trip to East Texas in the fall of 1691. At the Brazos, Captain Francisco de Benavides gave Terán a full personnel, supply, and commissary report. Benavides was an experienced supply officer who had also served under De León.

Terán marched 19 leagues southwest from the Brazos to the customary Colorado crossing, which he forded on February 26, after constructing a float. Terán again established his camp at Rosario, where he received the horses that he had entrusted earlier to the Cantona Indians.

On February 28, the party marched about 16 miles southwest, to the *paraje* called Las Cruces. This probably was the location earlier called Tres Cruces, the first camp used by Terán east of the Colorado in October 1691. As was his custom, Terán renamed the spot, calling it La Cruz de San Román. The direction and distance given suggest that it was near Buckner's Creek.

The following day, the governor continued to move southwest for another 15 miles, reaching a place on the upper Lavaca River in Lavaca County that he named San Miguel. Terán wrote that the camp received news from the bay that one soldier and five seamen had drowned, which indicates that he had intermittent contact with the Spanish forces waiting at the bay for his return. On March 1, Terán recorded only that they continued their journey and avoided the heavy woods along "the direct route." The party presumably moved in a more southerly direction, crossing the Lavaca River tributaries a few miles farther downstream from the old Indian trade route between La Grange and the Guadalupe. The camp for the evening was named El Angel de la Guardia.

The party followed a route south-southwest for about 15 miles on March 2. At this campsite, named Las Bocas de San Pablo, a search party was sent out to find three missing men; only two were recovered. The next day, local Indians reported sighting the third man, who apparently was injured, but the governor left the soldier among the Indians (quite possibly he preferred to remain there). On March 4, the party continued "along the route and road to the south" for only a few miles because there was a shortage of fresh horses. San Casimiro was the name given the camp located in southern Victoria County.

On March 5, the governor and his exhausted men and horses moved toward the same Real de Santa Margarita de Buenavista campsite they had used to regroup the expedition forces the previous fall. Below the present Victoria-DeWitt County line, 8 miles south-southwest of San Casimiro (a few miles from the location where Terán met Salinas's troops the year before), Terán's troops met soldiers from the ship waiting at the bay.

Terán remained at the bay until March 24, when he and Captain Salinas sailed into the Gulf, having turned the command of the camp over to Captain Francisco Martínez, who later led the remaining troops and padres overland southwest to Monclova. Unfortunately, no diary account of Martínez's return march has been discovered. It is presumed that he went by way of the Guadalupe crossing. This, at least, was the plan before Terán received the viceroy's instruction to visit the Caddo Indians east of the mission field. It was also the only route that Martínez knew, having followed it twice with De León.

Governor Terán and his troops, with most of the priests who had gone to East Texas with Massanet, left the new Province of Texas in a troubled, sick, and uncertain state. So fragile was the condition of the mission and the Spanish presence there that another expedition was required soon after Terán returned. Captain Salinas was appointed governor of Coahuila and shortly thereafter undertook the assignment to resupply Massanet at the distant East Texas mission designed to win souls and maintain Spanish claims to the province, should France attempt another venture like La Salle's.

TABLE 3

Governor Domingo Terán de los Ríos's 1691–1692 Expedition

Date	Distance Leagues (Miles)	Direction	Campsite (COUNTY)
6/3	4 (10.4)	NNE	El Charco del Cuervo (Cuervo Creek, MAVERICK) [1]
6/4	5 (13)	NNE	Arroyo Ramos (Comanche Creek, MAVERICK) [1]
6/5	4 (10.4)	NNE	Arroyo Caramanchel (Comanche Creek, ZAVALA) [1]
6/6	4 (10.4)	NNE	Río Nueces (Nueces River, ZAVALA) [1]
6/7	6 (15.6)	N, E	Río Frío (Leona River, ZAVALA) [1]
6/8	—	—	(Remained in camp to recover missing stock)
6/9	6 (15.6)	N	Río Hondo (Frio River, FRIO) [1]
6/10	—	—	(Remained in camp to recover missing horses)
6/11	6 (15.6)	N, NE	Arroyo San Simón (probably Hondo Creek, MEDINA) [2]
6/12	5 (13)	E	Arroyo Medina (Medina River, MEDINA) [2]
6/13	5 (13)	E	San Antonio de Padua (near modern San Antonio, BEXAR) [1]
6/14	—	—	(Remained in camp to celebrate Corpus Christi Day)
6/15	5 (13)	E	San Ignacio de Loyola (probably Cibolo Creek, BEXAR) [2]
6/16	4 (10.4)	E	Santo Domingo (unidentified stream, GUADALUPE) [2]
6/17	4 (10.4)	ENE	San Pedro de Alcántara (unidentified creek, GUADALUPE) [2]
6/18	4 (10.4)	E	Santa Rosa Peruana (unidentified creek, GUADALUPE) [2]
6/19	4 (10.4)	E	Río Guadalupe (San Marcos River, HAYS) [1]
6/20	4 (10.4)	ENE	Río Guadalupe (Blanco River, HAYS) [1]
6/21–24		—	(Remained near camp searching for missing horses)
6/25	5 (13)	E	Arroyo Santo Tomás (unidentified creek, BASTROP) [2]
6/26	4 (10.4)	ENE	Río San Marcos (Colorado River, BASTROP) [2]
6/27	—	—	(Rest stop)
6/28	—	—	(Rest stop)
6/29	3 (7.8)	Downstream	Río San Marcos (Colorado River, BASTROP) [2]
6/30	—	—	(Remained in camp to rest small stock)
7/1	6 (15.6)	Downstream	Río San Marcos (Colorado River, BASTROP) [2]
7/2	—	—	(Remained in camp)
7/3*	10 (26)	SSE	Jesús María y José de Buena Vista (Monument Hill, FAYETTE) [1]
7/4*	6 (15.6)	E, SW	Arroyo San Laureano (Navidad River, FAYETTE) [2]
7/5*	11 (28.6)	S	San Eugenio (Navidad River, COLORADO) [2]
7/6*	4.5 (11.7)	W	Santa Lucía Mártir (unidentified creek, JACKSON) [2]
7/7*	9 (23.4)	S, E, SW	Don Gaspar (Garcitas Creek, VICTORIA) [2]
7/8*	1.5 (3.9)	W	(Placedo Creek, VICTORIA) [2]
7/9*	11 (28.6)	W, ESE	(Placedo Creek camp, VICTORIA) [2]
7/10*	—	—	(Remained near camp)
7/11*	—	—	(Waited to recover French children)
7/12*	6 (15.6)	Return	(Lavaca River, JACKSON) [2]

Date	Distance Leagues (Miles)	Direction	Campsite (COUNTY)
7/13*	6 (15.6)	Return	(Navidad River, JACKSON) [2]
7/14*	6 (15.6)	Return	(Navidad River, LAVACA) [2]

[Terán moved his camp about 7 leagues downstream while awaiting Captain Martínez's return from the bay. Terán left the Colorado River on July 22, 1691, to continue northeast to East Texas. Massanet reported that his party left the Colorado on July 21 and traveled north 7 leagues.]

Date	Distance Leagues (Miles)	Direction	Campsite (COUNTY)
7/22	5 (13)	NNE	San Emeterio y San Caledón (FAYETTE) [?]
7/23**	3 (7.8)	NNE	Arroyo San Carlos (LEE) [2]
7/24	6 (15.6)	NNE	Arroyo Santiago (BURLESON) [2]
7/25	4 (10.4)	NNE	Río Colorado (Brazos River, BURLESON) [2]
7/26	—	—	(Constructed bridge)
7/27	1 (2.6)	—	Arroyo San Bernardino (probably Little Brazos River, BRAZOS)
7/28	6 (15.6)	NNE	Arroyo San Cypriano (probably Cedar Creek, BRAZOS)
7/29	—	—	(Rested small stock)
7/30	—	—	(Rested small stock)
7/31	6 (15.6)	NNE	San Isidro Labrador (lakes near western LEON) [2]
8/1	5 (13)	NNE	Río Trinidad (near Trinity River, LEON) [2]
8/2	—	—	(Troops rested and padres moved east of Trinity) [2]
8/3	5 (13)	NNE	Arroyo San Salvador (HOUSTON) [2]
8/4	5 (13)	—	(Camped about 0.5 league from first Tejas village, HOUSTON) [1]
8/5	—	—	(Waited in camp)
8/6	—	—	(Marched undisclosed distance to meet Tejas delegation)

[Governor Terán remained near camp, delivering supplies and meeting Indian leaders, until the commencement of his return trip on August 24.]

Date	Distance Leagues (Miles)	Direction	Campsite (COUNTY)
8/24	5 (13)	SSW	Arroyo San Salvador (HOUSTON) [2]
8/25	5 (13)	SW	Río Trinidad (Trinity River, HOUSTON) [2]
8/26	5 (13)	—	San Ysidro Labrador (lakes, LEON) [2]
8/27	4 (10.4)	S	San Ysidro Labrador [sic] (BRAZOS) [2]
8/28	6 (15.6)	SSW	Arroyo Santiago (BRAZOS) [2]
8/29	5 (13)	SW	Río Colorado (Brazos River, BURLESON) [2]
8/30	5 (13)	SSW	(Unnamed creek, BURLESON) [2]
8/31	8 (20.8)	SSW	Río San Marcos (Colorado River, FAYETTE) [1]
9/1	—	—	San Marcos (remained on east bank of Colorado River) [1]
9/2	5 (13)	SSW	Las Tres Cruces (Buckner's Creek, FAYETTE) [1]
9/3	4 (10.4)	SSW	Arroyo San Sebastián (Navidad River, FAYETTE) [1]
9/4	5 (13)	SSW	(Lavaca River, LAVACA) [2]
9/5	6 (15.6)	SSW	Río Guadalupe (Guadalupe River, DEWITT) [2]
9/6	—	—	(Main camp at Guadalupe camp)

Date	Distance Leagues (Miles)	Direction	Campsite (COUNTY)
9/7	10 (26)	SW	Unidentified Creek (Little Brushy Creek, DEWITT) [2]
9/8	—	SW	Río de los Franceses (Garcitas Creek, VICTORIA) [1]

[From September 9 to 26, Governor Terán remained at Real de Santa Margarita de Buenavista in Victoria County to prepare for new journey to East Texas.]

9/27	5 (13)	NNE	San Opio (Lavaca River, JACKSON) [2]
9/28	8 (20.8)	NE	San Exuperio (Navidad River, COLORADO) [2]
9/29	8 (20.8)	NNW	San Miguel (Navidad River, COLORADO) [2]
9/30	7 (18.2)	NNW	San Gerónimo de la Mota (Navidad River, FAYETTE) [2]
10/1	5 (13)	NE	Río Rosario (Colorado River, FAYETTE) [1]

[Governor Terán remained on the west bank of the Colorado River, waiting for the river to recede, on October 2 and 3 and crossed the river on October 4.]

10/4	1.5 (3.9)	NE	Padre San Francisco (FAYETTE) [1]
10/5	7 (18.2)	NE	Santa Caterina (FAYETTE) [1]
10/6	6 (15.6)	N	San Bruno (WASHINGTON) [1]
10/7	4 (10.4)	NE	San Martín (Navasota River, BRAZOS) [1]
10/8	7 (18.2)	NNE	San Pedro de Seville (GRIMES) [1]

[Between October 9 and 12, Terán was delayed by rain.]

10/13	3 (7.8)	ENE	San Fausto (GRIMES) [1]

[Between October 14 and 21, Terán's troops constructed a bridge over Bedias Creek.]

10/22	1 (2.6)	—	Melancio (GRIMES) [1]
10/23	4.5 (11.7)	NE	San Servando y San Germano (MADISON) [1]
10/24	7 (18.2)	NNE	Arroyo Frutos (LEON) [1]
10/25	6 (15.6)	NE	Arroyo San Frontón (HOUSTON) [2]
10/26	10 (26)	NNE	Mision Santísimo Nombre de María (Neches River, HOUSTON) [1]

[From October 26 to November 6, Terán remained near Mission María. From November 6 to 28, his party marched principally northeast and met the Cadodacho. Terán remained with the Cadodacho until December 5, when he commenced his return trip. The governor's diary entries give no daily distance and direction traveled on his return. He arrived at Mission Santísimo Nombre de María on December 30. On January 4, 1692, Terán's party returned to Mission San Francisco, "one and one-half leagues southwest." On January 9, Terán commenced his return trip to the bay, giving no daily entries for the distance or direction traveled until he passed the Trinity. They apparently followed the same route east used in the fall of 1691. On February 24, the party reached the Colorado. They crossed the river and made camp at El Rosario on February 26. Two days later, they began the journey to the bay.]

Date	Distance Leagues (Miles)	Direction	Campsite (COUNTY)
2/28	6 (15.6)	WSW	Las Cruces (Buckner's Creek, FAYETTE) [1]
2/29	6 (15.6)	SSW	San Miguel (Near Moulton, LAVACA) [1]
3/1	—	S	El Angel de la Guardia (Big Brushy Creek, DEWITT) [3]
3/2	6 (15.6)	SSW	Las Bocas de San Pablo (Little Brushy Creek, DEWITT) [3]
3/3	—	—	(Near camp to search for missing men)
3/4	1.5 (3.9)	S	San Casimiro (VICTORIA) [3]
3/5	3 (7.8)	SSW	Real de Santa Margarita de Buenavista (Lavaca Bay, VICTORIA) [1]

[After Governor Terán had traveled about 7.8 miles, he met a scouting unit that had been sent from the bay to escort him to his awaiting ship. On March 24, 1692, the governor left the bay. Captain Francisco Martínez was left in charge of the command to return overland to New Spain.]

---

* Captain Martínez's diary does not account for the balance of his return trip to the Colorado main camp.

** The entry for July 23 was omitted in Hatcher's translation. The translation omits any notes on the distance traveled on October 7, but the manuscript copy provides the information.

FIGURE 5
Salinas prepares his men for a possible attack by the local Muruam Indians on Peach Creek in present Gonzales County.

FIVE

TO RESUPPLY THE MISSION

Governor Gregorio de Salinas Varona's 1693 Expedition

Gregorio de Salinas Varona, the governor of Coahuila, left the city of Monclova in northeastern New Spain on May 3, 1693, to resupply Fray Damián Massanet and the missionaries remaining in East Texas.[1] As a captain, Salinas had visited the mission area near the Neches River twice, once with De León in 1690 and again in late 1691 with Governor Terán's expedition. He had spent most of the three previous years in Texas. To add to this impressive military service in the recently designated Province of Tejas, Salinas headed the marine expedition that surveyed Espíritu Santo Bay (present Matagorda Bay) in the fall of 1690, between his overland trips with De León and Terán.

Salinas was therefore one of the most experienced leaders of any overland expedition into Texas from New Spain. Only De León was a veteran of more campaigns on the northeastern frontier. None of the major military and political figures who led later expeditions into Texas in the early eighteenth century—Captain Aguirre (1709), Captain Ramón (1716), Governor Alarcón (1718), Governor Aguayo (1721), and Brigadier Rivera (1727)—was as experienced as Salinas.

The route Governor Salinas chose on his ten-week journey to East Texas and back to Monclova was primarily the same one he had followed northeast in 1690 as a captain under De León.[2] Salinas's 1693 expedition party was composed of only twenty escort soldiers, one lieutenant, two alféreces, a sergeant, several (probably four) Indian guides, and a chaplain. The party was supported with 180 horses and 137 mules, mostly loaded with mission supplies, and an undisclosed number of mule drivers and herders. The daily

This chapter is based on the manuscript copy of the diary of Governor Salinas held in the Archivo General de Indias, Sevilla (AGI), Audiencia de Guadalajara (Guad.) 151 (old 67-4-11). A typescript of the manuscript copy is held in the Manuscript Division of the Library of Congress, Sevilla, [AGI] Guad., 67-4-11. The diary has been translated into English and annotated by William C. Foster and Jack Jackson, eds., and Ned F. Brierley, trans., "The 1693 Expedition of Governor Salinas Varona to Sustain the Missionaries among the Tejas Indians," Southwestern Historical Quarterly 97 (October 1993), *264–311.*

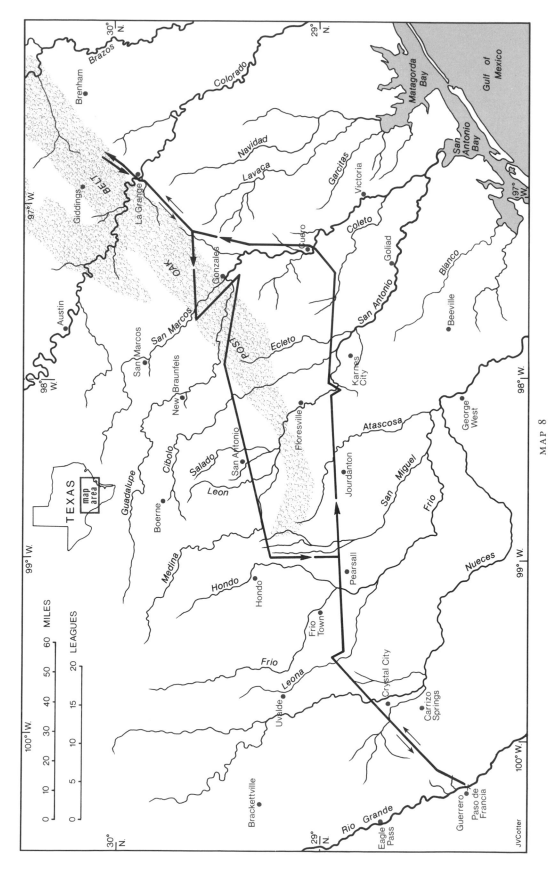

MAP 8

Governor Gregorio de Salinas Varona's 1693 Expedition, Part 1

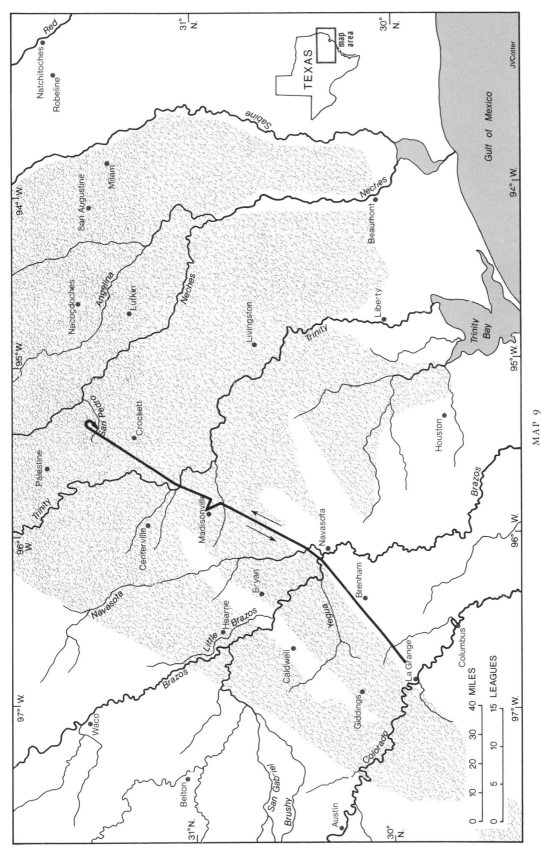

MAP 9

Governor Gregorio de Salinas Varona's 1693 Expedition, Part 2

normal routine during the expedition was to arise early, observe Mass, and depart from the camp by 6 to 7 A.M. The party would stop at about 3 in the afternoon to prepare a campsite for the evening.

Salinas's strict military character and discipline can be seen in his daily notations of the time he departed in the morning and the time of arrival at his next campsite. The governor was also one of the most accurate diarists in faithfully recording the direction taken and distance marched each day. His retracing of De León's route, campsite to campsite, allows a very close reexamination of De León's first path from Coahuila to East Texas and consequently a confirmation of the early Indian trade route connecting present-day northeastern Mexico and East Texas. Salinas was also a diligent reporter of the flora along the route, identifying the trees and bushes seen each day.

Salinas left Monclova following the creek (the modern Monclova) that runs north through the city. His party tracked the route taken by both De León and Terán north about 60 miles, through mesquite brush, past the junction with the Salado de Nadadores, the mountain ridges and pass called Baluartes, and the large cottonwood grove called Alamo Gordo to the junction with the Sabinas River (which runs generally from west to east in this region, parallel to the Rio Grande). Between the Sabinas and the Rio Grande, the party lost sight of the mountains to the south and crossed open mesquite brush country with occasional salt flats and islands of prickly pear and lantana for another 50 miles, past Real Pescado toward the Rio Grande crossing a few miles below present-day Guerrero. The encampment at Pescado was used earlier by Governor Terán and Fray Massanet in 1691 and was used later by Captain Ramón in 1716.

On May 9, the day before reaching the Rio Grande, the company crossed a creek identified as Juan the Frenchman—named for Jean Géry, who had met some of his Indian friends on the creek on De León's first *entrada*. The creek was called Juan's Creek on later expeditions and is identified as La Salada Creek on contemporary Mexican government topographical maps (see *Piedras Negras,* H14-10). Near the Rio Grande the Spaniards encountered the Cacaxtle, Ocana, and Piedras Blancas Indians and gave them the usual tribute of tobacco, small bells, and blankets. Salinas found several Cacaxtle Indians a few weeks later about 250 miles northeast, near La Grange along the old Indian trade route. William B. Griffen considers them residents of western Coahuila and eastern Chihuahua, although Spanish troops engaged them in northern Webb and Duval counties in the 1660s.[3] In 1675, Bosque met Ocana Indians near the same Rio Grande crossing or a few leagues upstream.[4]

On the afternoon of May 9, Salinas sent an advance guard of five soldiers to check the condition of the Rio Grande crossing. Later that evening, the scouts reported that although the river was high, the ford was in good condition and could be used.

The following day, the party traveled only about 8 miles to the river and then upstream to the crossing. They saw more Indians, from a rather large encampment of Agualohe. By crossing the river carefully with one load at a time, Salinas was able to transfer everything to the left bank without mishap. On the left bank, he met another large gathering of Agualohe who said that they frequently used the same crossing. Map 8 places this crossing near Paso de Francia, 5 miles below present Guerrero, which is the same fording area used by Governor de León (with Salinas) in 1690.

From the Rio Grande, moving northeast through more mesquite brush, Salinas continued to track De León's route. This was the only route to East Texas that Salinas knew: he had not been on this overland leg of Terán's *entrada* in 1691, the only seventeenth-century expedition that passed through the present San Antonio area.

Salinas took three days to reach the Nueces River at the customary crossing about 50 miles to the north-northeast of Paso de Francia. The distance and direction that Salinas traveled between the two river crossings follow closely those recorded by De León in 1689 and 1690 and by Terán in 1691. Between the two rivers, Salinas identified familiar creeks, including Caramanchel (present Comanche Creek), 12 miles to the southwest of the Nueces crossing. Map 8 shows the crossing at a point approximately 8 miles above present Crystal City.

During the three-day march, Salinas reported seeing bison grazing among the large mesquite trees and meeting some Pacuache Indians. This tribe was encountered repeatedly near the Rio Grande and as far north as the Frio River on later expeditions, including those led by Fray Espinosa, Captain Ramón, and Governor Alarcón. De León and Terán had reported bison ranging below the Rio Grande. No expedition diarist after Terán mentioned encountering bison below the Rio Grande, and Fray Isidro de Espinosa later suggested that the herds below the river had been depleted through wasteful slaughter by his countrymen.

The Pacuache warned Salinas of an ambush plan: the Jumano and Toboso Indians planned to attack his supply caravan and steal all its cargo and animals. The warning included the exact location of the ambush: the crossing of the Colorado River. This suggests that both the Spaniards and Indians knew rather precisely the trade route the expedition would take, including the location that Salinas would use to cross the Colorado River.

The Indian camp at which Salinas received the warning was over 250 miles from the Colorado River ford, but the threat was real. Salinas indeed intended to cross the Colorado at the location that De León had used, near present La Grange. The warning may also have sounded plausible to Salinas because the Jumano and Toboso from Chihuahua and West Texas were known to travel widely together to hunt and trade. The Spaniards knew that these tribes from the Big Bend area hunted each summer along the Colorado River and traded with the Indians along their trade route which extended into East Texas.

On the following day (May 12), Salinas reported meeting Indians from two other tribes, the Tepacuache and Sacuache, settled in a thicket of mesquite and lechuguilla near Comanche Creek, where the governor camped. Salinas gave them tobacco. The following evening, after traveling only 5 leagues, camp was made at a clearing "where previous expeditions had stopped on the bank of the [Nueces] river."

On May 14, Salinas continued northeast through pecan trees and scrubby chaparral to the present Leona River, about 16 miles beyond the Nueces crossing. The governor referred to the river as the Río Frío, the name used by Massanet, rather than the Sarco, the name used by De León. After crossing the Leona, Salinas followed the river downstream along the left bank, which was lined with live oaks (*encinos*) and other oaks (*robles*) (see Appendix II entries on "Live Oak" and "Oak"), where he saw another gathering of friendly Pacuache. He also found the cross he had placed near the riverbank on De León's expedition three years earlier. Salinas had crossed the present Leona twice on De León's 1690 expedition, first going northeast, and again later that year marching southwest on the return trip to the Rio Grande and Monclova. It appears more likely that the cross was left or marked on his return trip (see Map 4).

At six the following morning (May 15), the governor continued from the Leona campsite (marked by the cross) northeast more than 20 miles to the ford of the present-day Frio River, which he called the Hondo. This route from the marked Leona campsite straight to the crossing of the Frio River cut a bypass across west-central Frio County that was followed by Espinosa and all later expeditions from San Juan Bautista. The pathway was described as very rugged over numerous ravines and through more thorny chaparral (*chaparros de espinos*) and scrub oaks but also taller trees, such as live oaks. Salinas named his camp location on the Frio San Isidro and passed the same named campsite on his return. Map 8 places the campsite for the evening of May 15 at the Frio River crossing in a relatively flat and open area a few miles below its junction with Hondo Creek. This was the crossing area used by De León in 1689 and 1690; Terán (1691) had crossed the Frio about 15 miles upstream and then headed toward San Antonio rather than Matagorda Bay.

The next day, Salinas crossed the Frio River and proceeded first northeast and then southeast to the creek called Chapa, which De León had named on April 16, 1690. This creek, about 12 miles east of the river junction crossing, is the present-day San Miguel, which divides into two creeks, Black Creek and Elm Creek, both running from north to south. After crossing the creek, lined with oaks, the party continued east for a short distance and made camp on a small stream more than 5 leagues from the Frio near the present Frio-Atascosa County line.

The expedition moved 21 miles east-southeast through Atascosa County the next day (May 17), passing the water hole that De León called Aire and going beyond the Atascosa River, earlier called Robalo by De León. The campsite was along a tributary of the Atascosa River, between the present cities of Poteet and Pleasanton. They marched only 6.5 miles east on May 18, because a soldier became very ill.

The party moved 26 miles on the following day and reached a camp near the San Antonio River, traveling first east, then northeast, and finally southeast. The pathway, which at times seemed unclear, led the party through a sandy plain studded with live oaks and pecan trees, following a course that led through several ravines and thick mesquite. On that day, when approaching the Medina (San Antonio River) in Wilson County, the governor reported that the party—including his Indian guides—had traveled too far north and had "missed the river crossing more than three leagues." Thus, they first moved south downstream 5 miles to a sharp bend in the river and then northeast about 2 or 3 miles, apparently near Conquista crossing just above Falls City, where they "found the crossing" that the governor had used before.

This is the only stretch of the San Antonio river that bends decidedly to the northeast from the river's general southeasterly flow. In 1690, Governor De León had complained of the same directional problem of striking the Medina (the San Antonio River) at a point too far upstream. De León also moved southeast downstream about 5 miles and then east along the riverbank to find the ford. Salinas commented that the bank at the crossing was very steep. De León had made the same observation and had estimated the descent to be about 50 feet, which is a noticeable variation at a sea level elevation of about 250 feet. Map 8 marks the crossing above present Falls City near the Wilson-Karnes County line, near the location of the ford used by De León in his 1689 and 1690 expeditions.

On May 20, Salinas began to track the same stream and river crossings that De León used between the San Antonio and Guadalupe rivers. The governor's party moved about 15 miles that day, primarily east, as had De León. Salinas said that the camp that evening was on De León Creek, which was the same stream (the present Cibolo) named Arroyo *del* León by Governor De León because of a dead cougar found nearby in 1689. Salinas altered the name so it appears to be named for Governor De León rather than for the mountain lion. Espinosa, in 1709, possibly adopted this name when he identified the first creek or spring east of the Medina in present Bexar County as Arroyo de León; Alonso De León was never close to San Antonio.

The next afternoon, the governor found the Salado, the creek De León had named Real de Agua Salada when traveling between the Guadalupe and the San Antonio rivers on his return to Coahuila from East Texas with Salinas on June 25, 1690. Salinas used this salty stream, presently identified as Salt Creek in western DeWitt County, as his second *paraje* on the movement from the San Antonio River toward the Guadalupe (see *Seguin*, NH14-9). The party marched southeast about 20 miles that day (May 21) through more oak and mesquite.

Unlike De León's *entradas* in the years 1689 and 1690, which sighted no Indians between the San Antonio and Guadalupe rivers, Salinas's party encountered some hostile Indians near Salt Creek on the upper Coleto, a short distance from the present cities of Nordheim and Yorktown. As they had been warned, an angry band of painted Jumano carrying oval leather shields and bows and arrows confronted the convoy, but there was no engagement. That night Salinas found eight Indians hiding near the Salt Creek encampment and held them for the evening; they were released the next morning. Under interrogation the captured Indians denied that they were Jumano, leaving open the question of whether they were Toboso.

The appearance of the Jumano (and perhaps Toboso) Indians was not a surprise. The governor had been warned that they planned to ambush him and was traveling along the trade route that the Jumano and other Indians had followed for decades, maybe longer, to the customary trade grounds west of the Colorado in present Fayette County. This immediate area near the DeWitt-Karnes County line is where the stone marker was found on De León's 1689 journey along the northeast leg of the trade route. On June 23, Governor Salinas would again meet the Jumano with some of their East Texas friends, the Tejas, at a *paraje* called Rosario west of the Colorado crossing.

On May 22, the resupply company reached the Guadalupe, after moving another 21 miles east, and the governor "found the river crossing at three o'clock in the afternoon." This was probably the same ford used by Governor de León (Vado del Gobernador), a few miles below the mouth of modern Sandies Creek. Both De León (in 1689 and 1690) and Salinas traveled east 20 to 22 leagues from the crossing of the San Antonio River to Vado del Gobernador, later used and referred to by name by both Rubí and Lafora.

When Salinas reached the Guadalupe on May 22, it was very high. To cross the river with the heavy supplies, his men constructed a barge or float. But the first barge was overloaded, and the crossing proved to be a disaster. Most of the cargo was lost, including half the corn, three plates of lead, two suits of armor, three swords, and an arquebus, the musket of that time. Subsequent attempts fared better: the soldiers loaded the barges more lightly and escorted them across the river by swimming or floating at each of the four corners of the barge. This was the same cargo river crossing technique used by the "Nadadores" Indians when Aguayo first crossed the Rio Grande with his sizable convoy in early 1721. The troops unloaded the float on an island in the middle of the river. From the island to the opposite bank, the water was sufficiently shallow to allow mules to carry the cargo. Even at this point, one mule loaded with corn was taken by the current and lost, and a load of sugar was soaked. Although there were no human fatalities during the crossing, several soldiers almost drowned in the swift current.

The next day, May 24, was a Sunday. The party rested on the riverbank, diving and searching for lost equipment and drying their clothing and gear. The governor was near (or a few leagues below) Vado del Gobernador, a Guadalupe River ford shown on Mascaró's ca. 1807 map.

Early Monday morning, after Mass, the troops left the Guadalupe. First they moved upstream a short distance northwest along the bank, then turned northeast, and finally proceeded due north. Captain Salinas was apparently seeking and subsequently found the old Indian trade route that led from the Guadalupe crossing near Cuero to the Colorado ford near La Grange. After leaving the Guadalupe and traveling more than 20 miles, the party camped the first night somewhere on the upper tributaries of the Lavaca River, perhaps on Big Brushy Creek near present Yoakum. At this campsite, they cut two crosses on large white trees, probably sycamore or hackberry.

Traveling another 21 miles north the next day, May 26, the governor camped on the upper Navidad, where he found an encampment of local Sana Indians. Salinas met them again on his return trip. He gave the Sana tobacco and small bells. The Indians in turn advised him that at Tres Cruces, a well-known *paraje* and creek lying immediately ahead on the Indian trade route a few leagues south of the Colorado crossing, there was a gathering of Simaoma, Mescal, and Tohaha Indians. From this report, it appears that the Simaoma and Mescal, both from south of the Rio Grande, were visiting and perhaps trading with the local Tohaha. The presence of these two visiting tribes from Coahuila suggests that a number of tribes other than the Jumano and Toboso were familiar with the old trade route out of Mexico that led to the trade center and crossing of the Colorado west of present La Grange.

Salinas was familiar with the location of the meeting place that the Indians called Tres Cruces. He had been with Terán on September 2, 1691, when their expedition party camped on a stream that Terán identified as one "which in the preceding journeys had been called Las Tres Cruces." Later, Salinas correctly identified the location of Tres Cruces in a letter to the viceroy.[5] The stream and campsite was about 12 miles southwest of the Colorado River crossing, probably near Buckner's Creek. When Terán was returning to the bay on February 28, 1692 (again with Captain Salinas in his company), he left the *paraje* Rosario, which was near the west bank of the Colorado across from present La Grange. Traveling about 12 miles southwest, Terán and Salinas reached the place called Las Cruces.

The troops under Governor Salinas left at five o'clock the following morning, May 27, and continued crossing small creeks and tributaries of the upper Navidad to a hill covered with live oaks and other oaks from which the Colorado River could be seen. After traveling a total of 21 miles, Salinas camped by the river at a location he named Mártires de Pamplona. He would again pass this *paraje* about a month later (June 24), on his return trip. Near the river the governor described reaching a hill "that can be seen from a distance" (present-day Monument Hill). From the hill he crossed a deep little creek, Buckner's Creek, and proceeded a short distance to his camping location at a clearing near the water. The riverside camp was visited by several Cacaxtle Indians, the same tribe that he had seen earlier near Rio Grande. These Coahuiltecans too apparently used the same Indian trade route to the local trade fair area.

Thus, in an area stretching about 20 miles west of the Colorado crossing, Salinas reported encountering no less than five Indian tribes—two local (Sana and Tohaha) and three from the area below the Rio Grande (Simaoma, Mescal, and Cacaxtle). Salinas's report that tribes from below the Rio Grande gathered west of the Colorado crossing is supported by Father Anastase Douay's 1686 account that La Salle's party encountered near the same area mounted Indians (with boots and spurs) from below the Rio Grande.[6] William R. Swagerty has studied the significance of identifying regional trade centers or "rendezvous" and his map depicts protohistoric Indian trade networks from northern Mexico into Arizona, New Mexico, and West Texas, but not across Central Texas to the Tejas and other Caddoan tribes as suggested by this study.[7]

The following day, Salinas wrote that he "found the crossing of the San Marcos [Colorado] River"; a few days later, he called the Brazos the Espíritu Santo, as had De León, Massanet, and Terán.[8]

Salinas completed the crossing of the Colorado without the difficulty he had encountered at the Guadalupe. His party then traveled several miles beyond the crossing to a *paraje* called San Francisco de Buenavista, probably the same location as that named Padre San Francisco by Governor Terán on October 4, 1691, about 4 miles northeast of the Colorado River crossing.

Beyond the Colorado, Salinas continued to follow De León's 1690 route, moving swiftly northeast through oak forests toward the Brazos: 18 miles on May 29, 18 miles again the next day, and 13 miles on May 31. The direction and the distance of 21 leagues between the Colorado and the Brazos are the same as those recorded for the same movement by De León (May 11–14, 1690). The crossing of the Espíritu Santo (present Brazos River) was made a few miles above the junction of the Navasota, which he called the Colorado. This is near the location De León had used to ford the same streams. Thereafter, the governor continued to follow the old Indian trail north to the Tejas.

On June 3, moving beyond the Brazos crossing north-northeast, the party crossed a creek Salinas called Terán, to camp at "Melacio." When Salinas was on Terán's second trip to East Texas from the bay (in the fall of 1691), they had followed De León's road east. After crossing the Brazos, Terán had stopped near the same location for a week to build a bridge and ford the same creek (present-day Bedias Creek). Salinas used the same name, Melacio (Melancio), to identify the *paraje* and named the stream for the former governor.

During the following two days, the party became lost in the maze of small creeks feeding the present Bedias Creek. Instead of continuing northeast, the party veered northwest into the Monte Grande which Salinas called the Forest without End (Monte sin Fin). But Salinas recognized his mistake on June 5, retraced his steps, and noted that "the Indian guide found the road, which we followed along an old trail." On the next day, the governor reported that he was "always following the trail of the Indians, which continues all the way to the Tejas nation."

Salinas made a quick turnaround at Mission San Francisco, which the party reached on June 8 after marching about 12 leagues (31 miles) east of the Trinity River crossing. The road wandered through thick stands of pine, oak, and walnut trees. Six days after arriving at the mission, the governor headed home, back along the same road.

Governor Salinas had followed the same Indian route to the Tejas that he had followed first with De León in 1690. This northern leg of the route was probably also followed by the long-distance Emet runner who had delivered De León's message to the four Frenchmen in East Texas in 1689. This Indian trade route was the first Spanish road across Texas, chartered by De León (1690), later followed in part by Terán (fall of 1691), and now followed along its full course by Salinas.

In his diary, Salinas mentions nothing about the recurrence of the epidemic as a factor in the deterioration of the mission; but during the summer and fall of 1692 (after Terán and Salinas had left), the epidemic apparently broke out again, claiming another missionary and many more Indians. The tribe became convinced that the holy water used in baptism caused the deaths and on several occasions threatened to kill the padres.[9] In a 1693 letter to Viceroy Galve, Salinas wrote that the padres wanted to leave because of the threats of the Indians and that two friars returned with him to Monclova.[10]

The governor's diary entries for his return trip southwest cite the names of each of the overnight campsites used on his march to the northeast. The *paraje* Frailes (east of the Trinity) used on June 7 was mentioned again on June 14, and Melacio on Bedias Creek was again the campsite on June 18. San Juan de Ortega east of the Brazos, named on June 2, was cited on the return trip on June 20. On the same day, the party crossed the Brazos, which was high, but Salinas reported that he avoided "the problems he had on our two previous journeys" (with De León in late 1690 and with Terán in late 1691). This reference helps establish that Terán followed De León's route on his second trip to East Texas.

Salinas continued the same pattern of repeating the named campsites used between the Brazos and the Colorado as he continued his march southwest. San Fernando, named on May 30, was cited on June 21; San Félix, named on May 29, was cited again on June 22; and finally, at the crossing of the Colorado, the governor reported passing San Francisco again on the east side of the river and camping a few leagues beyond the west bank again at Rosario, on June 23.

On the west side of the crossing of the Colorado, about 8 miles west of the river across from present La Grange, the governor found a large gathering of local Cantona Indians who were hosting a meeting with some Jumano visitors from the Rio Grande and West

Texas and some of their East Texas (Asinai) friends. The area west of the Colorado crossing was a popular Indian convention center for the exchange of information (and perhaps stories) and a trade fairground for the exchange of goods, animals, and captives. La Salle's men and Spaniards who visited the Tejas several years earlier had seen a wide assortment of Spanish items. The Tejas had Spanish horses from Chihuahua and New Mexico, and most tribes held and traded other Indian and sometimes Spanish captives. In 1691, the Jumano traded five captive Muruam youths for horses with Terán at the fairgrounds near modern San Marcos, as noted by Massanet. The Cantona apparently played host at the La Grange fairground area south of the dense woods as well as the one near San Marcos immediately north of the Monte Grande.

The diaries of Governors De León, Terán, and Salinas confirm that the old Indian trade routes connected the East Texas Tejas and associated Caddo Indians not only with their Central Texas tribal friends (the Tohaha, Sana, Cantona, Toho, Emet, and others) but also with the friendly tribes from Coahuila, Chihuahua, and West Texas, including the Mescal, Cibola, Mesquite, Simaomo, Cacaxtle, Toboso, Jumano, and Cacquite (or Saquita).

On June 24, Salinas moved several miles past the site of Santos Mártires de Pamplona (which he had named on May 27) and camped on Buckner's Creek. Near the creek, the governor found another Indian tribe from below the Rio Grande, the Simaomo (whom the Sana had reported seeing earlier), meeting with some Tejas (Asinai) Indians.

From this familiar spot, the governor decided to cut a new route, rather than follow De León's road south. Did he seek a shortcut or did he simply want to see the area near present San Antonio that Fray Massanet and Governor Terán had visited? His plan, apparently, was first to retrace the route that he had followed with De León in the spring (May 9 and 10) of 1690 from this same Colorado River crossing, when they had traveled two days west to recover Pierre Talon near the San Marcos River above present Gonzales. Following this projected route, he would cross the Guadalupe close to Gonzales, 30 or more miles upstream from Vado del Gobernador. The San Antonio River would be reached at a point near the present city of San Antonio, where Terán had crossed when he journeyed east in 1691.

In executing this movement, which represents the only departure from De León's pioneering route, Salinas traveled all day, keeping a line of heavily wooded hills (the Monte Grande) on his right. No direction was recorded, but the march covered more than 15 miles and passed two associated Indian camps, one of the local Sana and the second of some Saqui or Saquita. The second encampment provided Salinas with a very knowledgeable guide who was fluent in Spanish. Unlike the Sana, the Saquita were not a local tribe, but rather were visitors from below the Rio Grande. The guide probably had learned the Spanish language through some contact with a mission in his residential area. The fact that the borrowed guide knew the route to San Antonio and south so well suggests that the Saquita were visiting, hunting, or trading in the area along the Indian trade route.

The next morning, June 26, Salinas with his new guide continued south-southwest for a short distance, with the same line of wooded hills on his right side. The line of low hills and woods that he followed is identified as the south shoulder of the hilly and heavily wooded area south of present Peach Creek that forms a southwestern extension to the post oak belt. The party then turned west and "away from the road" (the old Indian trade route to the Tejas) and marched through some round hills to what is presently upper Peach Creek in Gonzales County. The round hills and woods are identified on contemporary topographic government maps (see *Seguin,* NH14-9). The recently acquired Indian guide accurately advised that camp should be made on Peach Creek because there was no other campground with adequate water between the creek and the San Marcos River.

The party traveled more than 15 miles that day (June 26) and found a large Muruam village near Peach Creek.[11] The Muruam tribe had been in the area for decades, perhaps centuries. That afternoon, over one hundred warriors, armed with bows and arrows, approached Salinas's encampment. The Spaniards also detected some hiding Indian reinforcements. The troops remained on alert all afternoon and into the evening, most mounted and wearing their protective metal-mesh gear. Salinas's approach, as usual, was to treat the Indians with cautious respect. Nevertheless, the Indians managed to rattle the governor and steal four of his horses. He acknowledged in his diary that day that he and his men might not be able to disengage themselves from the situation.

The troops broke camp earlier than usual the following morning, at 5 A.M., and continued west then southwest until they reached the San Marcos River. They were probably near present Canoe Creek and close to where De León and Salinas had recovered Pierre Talon in 1690. Following Terán's identification of the San Marcos in 1691, Salinas referred to the river as a branch of the Guadalupe River.[12] The fact that they were able to cross on the trunk of a fallen tree also suggests that the river was the smaller San Marcos rather than the larger Guadalupe, which had been high a few weeks earlier. The party traveled a total of 21 miles that day and made camp near the west (or right) bank of the San Marcos River on a rocky hill in a motte of live oaks just below the Gonzales-Caldwell County line.

Governor Salinas turned and marched to the southeast on June 28. During the morning, they traveled with a line of hills on their right side—covered with live oaks mixed with other oaks—and the present San Marcos River on their left. By noon, the party had found a crossing of the Guadalupe, presumably upstream of the present city of Gonzales and near the ford shown as Vado de las Juntas de St. Marcos con Guadalupe on Mascaró's ca. 1807 map. The small party camped about a mile farther upstream on the southwest side, beyond the right bank of the Guadalupe, after having traveled more than 15 miles down the right bank of the San Marcos.

On the following day (June 29), the company moved west and then northwest more than 20 miles upstream along the southern (right) bank of the Guadalupe toward present Seguin. The Guadalupe was to their immediate right all day. They established camp at three that afternoon near a prominent round hill, which indicates they were in the vicinity of Capote Hills. Salinas noted that he did not proceed farther that day because the dense woods continued for some distance to the west. The same heavily forested area is found today between Capote Hills and San Antonio (see *Seguin,* NH14-9). Salinas could not have anticipated that the forested area continued west without the advice of some knowledgeable person such as the Indian guide.

Near the Capote Hills camp another vacant Indian village was found. This one was within 10 miles of an abandoned Indian camp that Governor Alarcón found in 1718, which may suggest that some Indians in the area (perhaps Toho or Emet) preferred to withdraw temporarily into the thick woods when intruders appeared, rather than to confront them as the local Muruam had.

The governor veered more toward the west the next day, crossing at noon a creek that he was able to identify correctly (perhaps with the guide's help) as a branch of the Medina (the San Antonio River). The stream was most likely present Cibolo Creek. After traveling a total of over 18 miles, the governor established a campsite that afternoon several leagues beyond the Cibolo.

By noon on the following day (July 1), Salinas reached a second stream which he also identified as a branch of the Medina or San Antonio River, probably the present Salado Creek. They continued to move west all day, traveling a total distance of over 20 miles. The party crossed a number of smaller streams and a large river (the San Antonio River) that Salinas called Río de Nuestra Señora de la Visitación. Mulberry trees, willows, live oaks, and other oaks were in the area near the river, the same trees that were mentioned along the San Antonio River by other diarists.

Finally, by mid-afternoon, Salinas found "the road that was taken by Don Domingo Terán" near a stream that was probably the modern Medina River. Salinas does not report how he knew that he crossed Terán's path, but his assessment was accurate. This point on Salinas's route matches the location of the Medina crossing that Governor Terán used in 1691, when he moved east from the Hondo to the Medina toward San Antonio (see Maps 6 and 8). This accuracy suggests that Salinas had a rather clear picture of the routes taken on prior expeditions, even those in which he was not a participant.

Salinas made camp near a village of Payaya Indians, the second village of the tribe visited that afternoon. The first was near the San Antonio River. In 1691, Fray Massanet and Terán had also seen the Payaya Indians living in the same area. The repeated references to the Payaya on the Medina help confirm the projected route and may suggest that this location was more settled than some of the temporary Indian encampments near the Rio Grande.[13]

The governor continued his rapid march across South Texas to the Rio Grande. On July 2, the party marched more than 20 miles southwest, crossing several streams lined with cottonwoods, and arrived at a creek that Salinas was able to identify correctly as the upper present-day Hondo Creek. On the following day, the party did not cross the Hondo, but instead veered south between the Hondo and San Miguel creeks, passed some hills that Salinas called Cacaxtles, and camped at the familiar creek crossing named Chapa. Salinas's comment on the name of the hills suggests that the Cacaxtle Indians, a tribe he had met earlier near both the Rio Grande and the Colorado, also occupied the hilly area near the San Miguel south of San Antonio at that time.

Salinas reported that here he picked up the "old road" of De León, which he had used moving east earlier. This two-day movement (July 2–3) south and southwest from the Medina near San Antonio established the route between the Frio crossing and the Medina that Espinosa would use going north on the next expedition, in 1709. All later expeditions from San Juan Bautista followed the route to San Antonio initiated by

Salinas, the northern leg of the route Herbert E. Bolton and others have called an early Camino Real (or Pita Road) to San Antonio from San Juan Bautista.

After moving west along the old road and finding the usual ford, Salinas crossed both the Hondo (the present Frio) and the Río Frío (the present Leona) on July 4. Early that day, he crossed the Frio at a location called San Isidro. This is also the crossing location (named on May 15) that the governor used on his eastward trek. Salinas then crossed the Nueces the next day near the place he had forded earlier that year. He covered the approximately 54 miles between the Nueces and the Rio Grande along the usual route, camping at the *parajes* Santa Deota and San Ubaldo to interrupt three long days of travel. The party reached the Rio Grande at noon on June 7, but high water delayed a crossing for five days. Salinas mentions that the Mescal, Hape, and Cacase collectively assisted his party to cross the raging river by skillful use of hides to support the rafts they constructed.

Governor Salinas's 120-mile return trip south from the Rio Grande to Monclova took him five long days and he apparently followed the route he had taken northward earlier that spring. He repeated the same campsites that he used before, including Pescado, where on his return he reported seeing some friendly Yorica Indians.

The completion of Salinas's resupply expedition signaled the end of the initial period of Spanish occupation of East Texas in the late seventeenth century. However, the Spanish late-seventeenth-century road system (which followed known Indian trails and trade routes) lasted well into the nineteenth century. Texas highways today follow some of the same early Indian pathways.

Although Salinas left Fray Massanet with several fellow priests and a few soldiers in East Texas, the threats by their Tejas hosts, who had turned hostile, soon forced the padre and troops to leave. Sad is the story of Massanet's tortuous retreat during the winter of 1693–1694. The distraught missionary was lost for weeks in the thick Monte Grande, apparently somewhere between the Trinity and the Colorado, but was eventually rescued by some friendly Cantona Indians. In describing Massanet's ordeal, William E. Dunn identifies by name the four troop escorts and concludes that the padre returned to Monclova in February 1694.[14]

There is also the fascinating story of one of Massanet's troop escorts, José Urrutia, a soldier who survived the winter ordeal with Massanet and stayed with the Cantona Indians for seven years as an Indian captain. Urrutia was one of the very few Spaniards who was able to live for an extended period with the Indians and then return to prominent military service with the Spanish government. It is remarkable that this man of the frontier proved himself capable of living among the Indians as one of their leaders for several years and yet was able to regain the military discipline necessary to hold the position of a presidio captain.

Although the close of Salinas's resupply expedition ended the first mission experiment in East Texas, his return did not signal a reduction in the Spanish mission and presidio expansion program along the central Rio Grande. Between 1699 and 1703, the Spaniards established a presidio (San Juan Bautista) and three missions (San Juan Bautista, San Francisco Solano, and San Bernardo) near the Rio Grande crossing area that had been used on the earlier expeditions.[15]

From the recently founded presidio, a brief military foray into Texas to the Nueces River was conducted in March 1707 by Captain Diego Ramón. One purpose of this limited exercise was to replenish the Indian population, decimated by the local smallpox epidemic at the Rio Grande missions.[16] Padre Isidro Félix de Espinosa, who served as chaplain on the twenty-six-day trip, later reported in great detail how devastating the epidemic was not only to Indians in the mission but also to those in the nearby countryside.[17] Although the military operation was brief, its mission was accomplished. At least ten male Indians were killed in two skirmishes, but three were taken alive along with at least thirty-two women, boys, girls, and babies.[18] This military field operation was one of the most fully documented, although limited, ventures that the Spanish made into Texas from San Juan Bautista between Salinas Varona's expedition in 1693 and Fray Espinosa's very significant reconnaissance trip to the Colorado River in 1709.

TABLE 4
Governor Gregorio Salinas Varona's 1693 Expedition

Date	Distance Leagues (Miles)	Direction	Campsite (COUNTY)
5/11	7 (18.2)	NE	San Ubaldo (Comanche Creek, MAVERICK) [1]
5/12	7 (18.2)	NE	Arroyo Caramanchel (Comanche Creek, ZAVALA) [1]
5/13	5 (13)	NE	Río de las Nueces (Nueces River, ZAVALA) [1]
5/14	6 (15.6)	NE	San Bonifacio (Leona River, ZAVALA) [1]
5/15	8 (20.8)	E, NE	Río Hondo (Frio River, FRIO) [1]
5/16	5 (13)	NE, SE	San Eubaldo (San Miguel Creek, FRIO) [1]
5/17	8 (20.8)	ESE	Santísima Trinidad y San Pascual (Atascosa River, ATASCOSA) [2]
5/18	2.5 (6.5)	E	San Félix (Atascosa River, ATASCOSA) [2]
5/19	10 (26)	NE, SE	Río Medina (San Antonio River, KARNES) [1]
5/20	6 (15.6)	ESE	Arroyo del León (Cibolo Creek, KARNES) [1]
5/21	8 (20.8)	SE	Corpus Christi y San Secundino (Coleto Creek, DEWITT) [1]
5/22	8 (20.8)	E	Río Guadalupe (Guadalupe River, DEWITT) [1]
5/23	—	—	(Crossed Guadalupe River)
5/24	—	—	(Remained near camp, searching for missing supplies)
5/25	8 (20.8)	NE	Santa María Magdalena (Big Brushy Creek, LAVACA) [1]
5/26	8 (20.8)	N	San Felipe Neri (Navidad, LAVACA) [1]
5/27	8 (20.8)	NE	Río de San Marcos (Colorado River, FAYETTE) [1]
5/28	4 (10.4)	—	San Francisco de Buenavista (Cummins Creek, FAYETTE) [1]
5/29	7 (18.2)	NE	San Félix (FAYETTE) [1]
5/30	7 (18.2)	NE	San Fernando (WASHINGTON) [2]
5/31	5 (13)	NE	San Diego de Venecia (WASHINGTON) [1]
6/1	—	—	(Delay to clear roadway)
6/2	5 (13)	NE	Río Colorado (Navasota River, GRIMES) [1]
6/3	8 (20.8)	NNE	San Melancio y San Spidio (Bedias Creek, GRIMES) [1]
6/4	6 (15.6)	NW	San Deciano (LEON) [2]
6/5	8 (20.8)	SE, NE	San Sancho (LEON) [2]
6/6	8 (20.8)	NE	San Norberto (MADISON) [1]
6/7	8 (20.8)	N	Arroyo Frailes (HOUSTON) [1]
6/8	5 (13)	NE	Misión San Francisco (San Francisco de los Tejas Mission, HOUSTON) [1]

[Between June 8 and 14, Salinas delivered supplies and prepared for the return trip.]

Date	Distance Leagues (Miles)	Direction	Campsite (COUNTY)
6/14	9 (23.4)	"same road"	San Basilio (HOUSTON) [1]
6/15	10 (26)	—	San Francisco (MADISON) [1]
6/16	—	—	(Delayed to search for animals)
6/17	—	—	(Rain delay)
6/18	7 (18.2)	—	San Melancio (Bedias Creek, MADISON) [1]

Date	Distance Leagues (Miles)	Direction	Campsite (COUNTY)
6/19	6 (15.6)	—	San Gervasio (GRIMES) [1]
6/20	8 (20.8)	—	San Florentino (WASHINGTON) [1]
6/21	7 (18.2)	—	Santa Demetria (WASHINGTON) [1]
6/22	8 (20.8)	—	San Paulino y Cervera (FAYETTE) [1]
6/23	5 (13)	—	Nuestra Señora del Rosario y San Juan Mártir (FAYETTE) [1]
6/24	3 (7.8)	—	San Juan Bautista (Buckner's Creek, FAYETTE) [1]
6/25	6 (15.6)	—	Santa Orosia (Navidad River, FAYETTE) [1]
6/26	6 (15.6)	SSW	Santa Perseveranda y San Pelayo Mártires (Peach Creek, GONZALES) [1]
6/27	8 (20.8)	W, SW	San Zoilo (San Marcos River, GONZALES) [1]
6/28	6 (15.6)	SE	San Sereno Mártir (Guadalupe River, GONZALES) [1]
6/29	8 (20.8)	SW, W	San Pedro y San Pablo (Capote Hills, GONZALES) [1]
6/30	7 (18.2)	SW, W	San Marciano (Cibolo Creek, GUADALUPE) [2]
7/1	8 (20.8)	W, SW	San Eugenio (Medina River, BEXAR) [2]
7/2	8 (20.8)	SW	Nuestra Señora de la Visitación (Hondo Creek, MEDINA) [2]
7/3	10 (26)	SW, S	San Marcos Mártir (San Miguel Creek, FRIO) [1]
7/4	9 (23.4)	—	San Bonifacio (Leona River, ZAVALA) [1]
7/5	9 (23.4)	—	Santa Deota (Comanche Creek, ZAVALA) [1]
7/6	10 (26)	—	San Ubaldo (Comanche Creek, DIMMIT) [1]
7/7	7 (18.2)	—	Río Grande (Rio Grande near Paso de Francia)

[Governor Salinas remained on the northeast bank of the Rio Grande waiting for the water to recede until July 13, when the crossing was made. He reached Monclova on July 17.]

FIGURE 6
Fray Espinosa is affectionately greeted by a large group of Indians under Captain Cantona near the Travis County crossing of the Colorado River in 1709.

SIX

NEW ROAD TO THE COLORADO

*The 1709 Expedition of Fray Isidro de Espinosa, Fray
Antonio de Olivares, and Captain Pedro de Aguirre*

On April 5, 1709, Fray Isidro de Espinosa, Fray Antonio de Olivares, and Captain Pedro
de Aguirre—accompanied by fourteen soldiers—left the Franciscan Mission San Juan
Bautista and the Presidio San Juan Bautista on the lower Rio Grande on a brief
reconnaissance expedition to the Colorado River.[1] This was the first Spanish expedition
sent beyond the Frio River since the Tejas had forced Fray Massanet to abandon the East
Texas mission in the winter of 1693. It was also the first major expedition into Central
Texas to be launched from the new Presidio San Juan Bautista and the associated
missions.[2] The purpose was not to rout the French or to establish or resupply any
mission. Rather, it was a limited reconnaissance, initiated by a report that the Tejas
Indians (who had driven the missionaries out of East Texas sixteen years earlier) were
now prepared to move from their traditional residential area near the Trinity and the
Neches to the present Colorado River, some 100 miles to the southwest, if the Spaniards
would establish a mission for them there.

The limited scope of the expedition is evident in the size of the party. The military
leader was a captain (not a governor) and only fourteen soldiers served under him. Two
prominent church officials, Fray Espinosa and Fray Olivares, composed the ecclesiastical delegation. Both padres later played major roles in Texas expeditions and mission
work. But the key figure was Espinosa, who later led or accompanied the expeditions
of Captain Ramón (1716), Governor Alarcón (1718), and Governor Aguayo (1721–
1722). Fray Espinosa, as diarist, carefully recorded the route and events each day.[3] The
padre was also one of the few diarists who could match the accuracy of De León and
Salinas in recording the distances traveled each day. His colorful descriptions of the
Indians and detailed notations on the wildlife and vegetation surpass those given on any
prior expedition. Later, the padre authored one of the most detailed and engaging

---

*This chapter is based on Fray Espinosa's diary, translated into English by Gabriel Tous,
Preliminary Studies of the Texas Catholic Historical Society 1, no. 3 (March 1930),
3–14. The typescript copy of the manuscript diary held in the Manuscript Division
of the Library of Congress (Sevilla, [AGI] México, 62-2-29) was also consulted.*

chronicles of mission life as it revolved around the local Indians in northeastern New Spain and the Province of Texas.[4] Espinosa was in charge of the mission of San Juan Bautista, and Captain Aguirre was the commander of Presidio Río Grande del Norte, located a few miles away.

The composition and purpose of the excursion were so modest, compared to earlier expeditions, that a relatively unproductive venture was anticipated. However, the thorny (*espinosa*) padre and his small entourage made an extremely significant contribution to the early Spanish road system in Texas. Espinosa's party charted a new route that future expeditions from San Juan Bautista to San Antonio would follow and then charted the route between San Antonio and the Colorado later followed by Ramón, Aguayo, and Rivera, called the Road to the Tejas. Contrary to what some authorities have stated, the route followed on the 1709 expedition was not the one already explored by Terán in 1691.[5]

The first day of travel was brief, commencing in the early afternoon. Espinosa crossed the Rio Grande near Paso de Francia, the fording area used by De León, Terán, and Salinas on their expeditions between 1689 and 1693. He moved beyond the river a distance of only about 10 miles, even though the river was low, which made the crossing easy. They stopped at Cuervo Encampment, a creekside *paraje* named by De León in 1689. The stream runs for about 30 miles, generally from north to south, and enters the Rio Grande a few miles upstream from the Francia crossing.

Cuervo Creek today flows intermittently but has pools or water holes much of the year. The creek is identified by name on contemporary government maps (see *Crystal City,* NH14-11) and is shown on the March 1878 map of Maverick County prepared for the Texas General Land Office. The Maverick County map places Cuervo Creek approximately 10 miles north-northeast of a Rio Grande crossing named Pacuache Pass on the map, which is consistent with the location of De León's ford called the Francia crossing a few miles downstream.

Espinosa's party moved east during the next two days, through mesquite brush and oak groves, past Comanche Creek (called Arroyo Caramanchel) to the Nueces River; both streams were described as lined with ash, elm, oak, mulberry, and pecan trees. The thorny shrub *cocolmecalt* and alfalfa grew in the open fields. The only tribe encountered during the day's march was a small Pacuasian hunting party. Espinosa reported that the Indians were hunting rats or mice (*ratones*), which were frequent menu items of the Indians of the lower Rio Grande area.[6] Other Indians in the area did not approach the expedition party but sent up thick smoke signals and disappeared deeper into the dense brush and woods. Although Comanche Creek was dry when the company passed, the fresh and clear Nueces provided plenty of fish for the evening meal. The campsite was several miles above the present town of Crystal City, close to De León's earlier crossing location.

The party continued for 18 miles on April 8 to the river De León had earlier named and Espinosa called the Sarco (the present Leona). The diarist also mentioned that the local Indians, in their native language (perhaps Coahuilteco), referred to the stream as the cold river or in Spanish Río Frío, as did Fray Massanet in 1690 and Salinas in 1693. Although the party marched through some very thick mesquite brush that day, they were

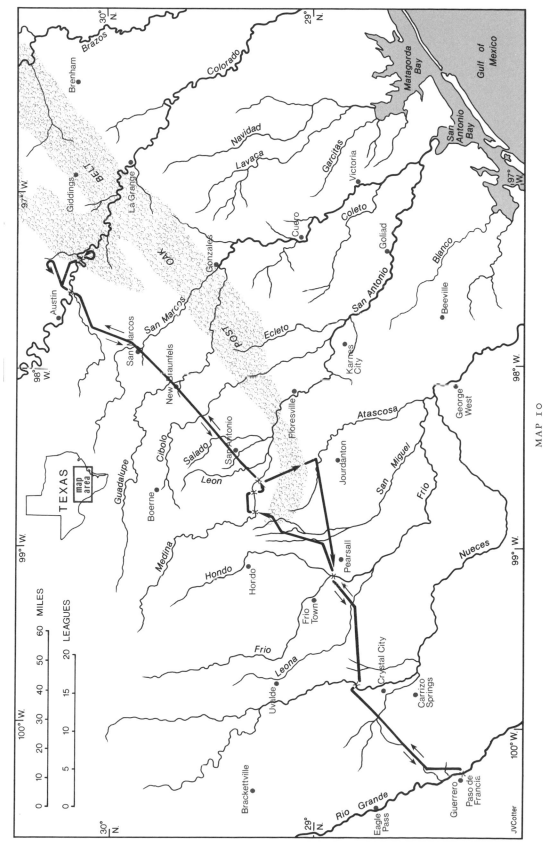

MAP 10

The 1709 Expedition of Fray Isidro de Espinosa, Fray Antonio de Olivares, and Captain Pedro de Aguirre

following a path that led across the Nueces and several minor tributaries of the river. Along the streams the diarist reported mulberries, elms, mesquites, and oaks.

At the Leona, a small party of Indians appeared that included two Xarame and about twenty more Pacuasian, members of the same Indian tribe encountered about 25 miles to the southwest two days earlier. The Xarame were also residents of the Rio Grande area and northern Coahuila. The fact that Espinosa separately identified only two Xarame may suggest that they were temporarily visiting their neighbors or peacefully passing through the area along the traditional Indian route across South Texas that the padre was following. The distance of 18 miles and the direction taken agree with those cited by Salinas between the Nueces and the Leona.

The expedition left the Leona on April 9, moving northeast toward the present Frio River. The Frio crossing was a short distance below its junction with Hondo Creek, the fording area used by both De León and Salinas. The party continued northeast beyond the Frio to the large creek that the padre correctly identified as the Chapa (San Miguel Creek) but did not cross. De León had named this creek in 1690, and Espinosa recognized it as the first creek northeast of his Frio River crossing. Espinosa recorded that the troops advanced north along the right or west bank of the San Miguel about 5 miles upstream through cypresses, elms, and live oaks. This route places the party that evening on the present San Miguel Creek a few miles below the Frio-Medina County line in north-central Frio County.

Espinosa had consciously decided not to travel to San Antonio de Padua via Terán's route, which crossed the Frio at a point about 30 miles due west, in the northwest corner of Frio County (see Map 10). The padre chose to cross the Frio where De León and Salinas did, below the Hondo Creek junction. Then he moved up the San Miguel and north toward San Antonio.[7] This became the new route that later expeditions would follow instead of Terán's trail. Even the menu that day was new: the evening meal changed from fish to fresh turkey. Some of the troops hunted during the day and provided seven birds for supper. Although earlier expedition diarists had identified bison herds below the Rio Grande and along the expedition route, this was the first to identify wild turkeys, which at the time were apparently plentiful throughout northern Nuevo León and Coahuila and much of South Texas (see Appendix II entry on "Wild Turkey").

Espinosa and his escort continued east, through valleys filled with mesquite clumps and oak groves, then north 21 miles on April 10 to the headwaters of present Atascosa River. They camped at the headwaters of a stream called Arroyo of the Robalos (Atascosa River). The Atascosa was renamed Robalos by De León in 1690, after he first had named it Arroyo del Vino in 1689. De León and Salinas, however, had crossed the Atascosa River much farther downstream to the southeast in east-central Atascosa County.

A march of about 13 miles the following morning (April 11) brought the party to the Medina River, where they found a small encampment of the Payaya Indians. Espinosa noted that the camp was located in a clearing along the river bordered by cottonwoods, elms, and pecan trees that provided food for all the Indians who lived along the banks of the river. The Payaya were found in the same area in 1691 by Governor Terán and by Governor Salinas on his return trek from East Texas in 1693. These friendly Indians later were charter members of the missions established near San Antonio.

The party crossed the Medina a few miles downstream from present Castroville and then moved east through a plain, but did not stray far from the river, which they recrossed and later that day crossed a third time. Along the way, they met another tribe, the Pampopa, who would later also congregate at the several missions near San Antonio. The Spaniards stopped at the Pampopa village to inquire about the availability of Indian guides and the location of watering places on the planned route toward the Colorado.

Espinosa wrote that a Pampopa Indian on horseback voluntarily joined them as a guide from the village and that twelve additional tribesmen accompanied them on foot. Espinosa's notation that only one local Indian had a horse tends to confirm the current view that many local Indians in South Texas at the beginning of the eighteenth century were not customarily mounted, as were the Apache and some of the other Indians residing in West Texas and New Mexico at that time.

Espinosa called the first stream crossed the next day east of the Medina Arroyo de León. Since Terán, Massanet, and Salinas did not refer to the creek by name, Espinosa was the first diarist to call the stream by name.[8] The diarist also recorded at the crossing of the León that the party was within a short distance of where "General Gregorio Salinas" had crossed the stream earlier. Espinosa's observation was quite accurate, which confirms that the padre had a very clear picture of the route Salinas had followed. Salinas, as seen in Map 8, crossed Leon Creek on his return trip from East Texas in 1693. The reference also suggests that Espinosa was particularly mindful of Salinas's route, which he had been carefully following since he left the Rio Grande.

The second stream Espinosa crossed was associated with the present San Pedro Springs; the padre named it Agua de San Pedro. He observed field work, resembling an irrigation ditch with taps or sluices for water control, near some terraced areas (April 13). The padre's description is very explicit: *dimos en una acequia de agua muy poblada de arboles que era suficiente para un pueblo, y toda llena de tomas de agua por estar alta la acequia y colgadas las tierras pusimosle por nombre el agua de S. Pedro.*

Although Espinosa was not a casual or inattentive observer, his comments on water control may still be questioned. Contrary to conclusions drawn in some recent studies, the comment could be interpreted to suggest that the Indians in the San Antonio area were agricultural during precolonial times or the early European contact period. However, a recent assessment of agricultural practices among Indian communities in North America at the time of first European contact excludes the San Antonio area.[9] The subject requires further study. Additional historic evidence suggesting that water control was practiced in the area between the middle San Antonio and Colorado rivers in the initial European contact period is found in the two diaries of Governor Alarcón's expedition in 1718.

In the immediate area, Espinosa also identified a large encampment of more than 500 Siupan, Chaularame, and Sijame, tribes from below the Rio Grande. These Indians were camped on a river that Espinosa correctly said the Spaniards had not named; he named it San Antonio de Padua. Tall pecan, cottonwood, elm, and mulberry trees followed the riverbank, just as Salinas reported in the area when he first called the river Visitación on July 1, 1693. Both Massanet and Terán had given the name San Antonio de Padua to the location (not the river) on June 13, 1691. The fact that Espinosa gave the river the same name that Terán had earlier given the location along the river suggests again that he knew exactly where he was.

After traveling that day about 21 miles from the Medina, the party camped that night (April 13) east of San Antonio River on a creek with briny or salty water (the stream was called Salado by Espinosa on the return trip). Four Indians from the large encampment of the three tribes acted as guides for Espinosa as he prepared to move northeast toward the Guadalupe and the Colorado. As Massanet (1691) reported meeting the Chalome near San Marcos with other highly mobile tribes from below the Rio Grande, these Indians could serve as knowledgeable guides.

The accuracy of Espinosa's diary entries on the distance and direction traveled is clearly illustrated on his movement from the Frio crossing to the Medina and on to the Salado. The straight-line measured distance between the streams on contemporary government maps is within 10 percent of the distance that Espinosa gives in Spanish leagues: 17 leagues (44 miles) from the Frio crossing to the Medina crossing and 8 leagues (21 miles) between the Medina and the Salado. The straight-line measured distance between the Frio crossing and the Medina is 40 miles and between the Medina and the Salado crossing is 20 miles.

After Sunday Mass on April 14, the small party marched northeast toward New Braunfels and the Comal River, referred to correctly by the diarist as a branch of the Guadalupe. Again, Espinosa was not following Terán, who had moved east from San Antonio, crossing the Guadalupe River at an unidentified location below New Braunfels. Terán never noted crossing the Guadalupe east of San Antonio on his movement in 1691, whereas Espinosa (with his local guides) stated that he set out in search of the two nearby branches of the Guadalupe the day after crossing the Salado. Later expeditions (see Maps 11, 15, and 17) all followed Espinosa's route from San Antonio to New Braunfels and on to the crossing of the San Marcos River near the present city of San Marcos and then to the Onion Creek crossing of the Colorado, rather than following Terán's way.

The Espinosa party continued to the present Guadalupe to camp on April 14, traveling a total of 23 miles from Salado Creek. During the day, there was another turkey hunt, with some success. However, one of the soldiers shot himself in the hand. The group caught a wide variety of fish which they prepared that evening. They also spotted alligators along the riverbank. Again Espinosa noted thick stands of cypress, elm, cottonwood, and willow along the river. He reported that the party waited for some Sana Indians to bring news of whether the Tejas were on the Colorado, but the local Sana scouts did not return that evening. The Sana were a very active and mobile tribe that De León and Salinas saw on several occasions in the area to the south between the Guadalupe and Colorado rivers; they later would serve as scouts for Aguayo.

The following day, Monday, the company continued northeast in search of the Colorado River, setting mesquite brush fires along the way as friendly signals to the Tejas. Suddenly, to Espinosa's surprise, they arrived at a river that they thought was the Colorado after marching only about another 15 miles beyond the Guadalupe.

At this point in Espinosa's diary, names and references to rivers become confusing. From the beginning of the expedition, the party was searching for the Colorado River, which at that time was called the San Marcos. De León had named the present Colorado River the San Marcos when he first crossed it in 1690. The present San Marcos River was unidentified by any name other than the Guadalupe (by Terán) or the "first branch of the Guadalupe" (by Salinas). Thus, when Espinosa's party thought they had reached the river "sooner than we had anticipated," their surprise is understandable. In fact, they had not reached the San Marcos or modern Colorado, but only the present San Marcos River, which until then had not been recognized as a named river but only as a branch of the Guadalupe. Nine years later, in May 1718, Governor Alarcón was surprised under similar circumstances when he made the same mistake, thinking he had reached the San Marcos or Colorado, only to discover later that he had reached the present San Marcos River.

On April 16, the company crossed the San Marcos River near its source, still moving east. By the end of the day, another 21 miles had been covered and camp was made on present-day Onion Creek, called Garrapatas (Ticks), by Espinosa and by later explorers as well. After another 13-mile march to the northeast the next day, the small party camped near the banks of the present-day Colorado River. Espinosa, who thought he had crossed the Colorado at San Marcos, now thought he had moved farther east to the Brazos River. He therefore called the river "the Río Colorado or the Espíritu Santo (which are the same)." In 1690, De León had said that the present Brazos was called the Colorado and renamed it the Espíritu Santo, and it retained both names throughout the early eighteenth century. About 20 miles downstream from Austin, Espinosa established a base-camp. Although confused in the identification of the rivers crossed, the padre (with the help of Indian guides) had selected the location of the principal fords of the Guadalupe, San Marcos, and Colorado that would be used on later expeditions. They followed Espinosa's route, not Terán's.

Thus, Espinosa followed De León's route to the crossing of the Frio then very deliberately veered north and followed Salinas's route to San Antonio, and from there charted (with Indian guides from San Antonio) a new trail northeast to present New Braunfels, San Marcos, and the Colorado River crossing a few miles below Austin. Captain Ramón in 1716 (with Fray Espinosa), then Governor Aguayo in 1721 (also with Espinosa), and finally Brigadier Rivera in 1727 would later follow the full course of Espinosa's 1709 route.

The Espinosa party divided the next day (April 18). Seven soldiers went with Captain Aguirre and the padres across the river, while the other seven soldiers remained near base-camp. Along the riverbank, across from the camp, the captain's party found an abandoned Indian camp. It was arranged in the shape of a half-moon, with more than 150 large, well-made circular huts. The fact that the huts in the encampment had been left apparently intact suggests that the Indians may have detected the arrival of the Spanish party and simply withdrawn into the protective woods. This response was similar to that witnessed by De León in 1689 at a Cava and Emet village near the Guadalupe in central DeWitt County and by Alarcón in 1718 when he encountered an Indian village of comparable size (more than 120 huts) on the present San Marcos in northern Gonzales County about 35 miles to the southwest of Espinosa's Colorado River camp. Regrettably, neither Espinosa nor Alarcón described the huts in any detail.

The captain and his small group moved east another 15 miles downstream, to recross the river a second time, and then moved northeast an additional 5 miles along the riverbank. The party traveled a total of 23 miles, mostly downstream, that day, but the camp was still 6 to 8 miles above present Bastrop. Along the Colorado the party saw the same trees they had seen on the San Marcos and Guadalupe rivers (cypress, cottonwood, and elm), but also wild grape vines that were much higher and larger than those of Castile.

That night (April 18), Espinosa complained that he suffered much from the cold. This complaint in mid-April is not surprising because Espinosa's expedition, like other Spanish expeditions, was undertaken during the Little Ice Age (ca. 1550–ca. 1850), when North America, as well as Europe, was experiencing colder and wetter weather than we know today. According to the United States Geological Survey, the Little Ice Age ended, and a warming trend began, in the central United States in the 1860s.[10] Thus, it is also not surprising that Alonso de León (the elder) and Espinosa both described the winter months in northern Nuevo León and Coahuila, an area about 40 miles south of the Rio Grande, as a bitter cold season that brought freezing conditions and snow for extended periods.[11]

On Friday, April 19, to the surprise of the troops, they saw many bison. No bison or even bison tracks had been seen between the Rio Grande and the Colorado. Aguirre's small party returned to the base-camp after dark that day to find an Indian who identified himself as Captain Cantona, a chieftain well known to Spaniards. This was probably the same captain of the Cantona who had been one of the parade leaders near San Marcos in early 1691 and who had served as Governor Terán's guide to East Texas on his second trip in September 1691. Although Espinosa does not explain this connection in his diary account, he does elaborate on the relationship between Captain Cantona and leaders of earlier expeditions in his later written works.[12] Captain Cantona was accompanied by forty members of the Yojuan, Simomo, and Tusonibi tribes.

It is unclear why Captain Cantona was the leader of these three tribes. Recognized leaders of one Indian tribe occasionally were selected as the chieftain of another tribe, however, as was the case of the Apache Mocho, who served as the chief of the Tonkawa in the early 1780s. The Cantona were a widely recognized tribe seen frequently near the Colorado River between Austin and La Grange, meeting and trading with both the East Texas Tejas and tribes from along or below the Rio Grande. But Espinosa did not report the presence of the Cantona Indians, only the presence of a Captain Cantona.

The Indians met by Espinosa have been identified as immigrants (not hunters, traders, or visitors) to the Bastrop area by the leading anthropologist Thomas N. Campbell. Campbell says that the Yojuane had moved into the area from north of the Red River and that the Simaoma and Tusonibi had immigrated from northeastern Mexico.[13]

The troops who remained at base-camp reported that the Indians first approached their camp from the river, in single file, carrying a well-made *otate* (cane) cross. The cross-bearer was followed by three other Indians, each with an image of Our Lady of Guadalupe, two painted and the third an old *grabado* (engraving). The spectacle was, in miniature, similar to the Indian parade numbering 2,000–3,000 participants that Terán and Massanet witnessed near San Marcos in 1691.

These Indians bowed, petted the Spaniards' faces, and embraced the soldiers and priests. They said that they first feared that the Espinosa encampment was an Apache camp, but that they knew it was a friendly party of Spaniards when they saw the red waistcoat of the alférez (a rare diary entry indirectly noting the uniforms worn by the Spanish officers in the field). Captain Aguirre gave Captain Cantona a silver-topped cane, a symbol of Spanish recognition of authority.

The Indian visitors were from an encampment only 10 miles away, but they asked to spend the night with the Spaniards and did. The padres knew that Captain Cantona and his followers frequently visited the Tejas in East Texas and would know where they were. In answer to Captain Aguirre's questions, the captain reported that the Tejas and their chieftain, called Bernardino, were three days' journey away. The Tejas nation, the captain said, had not moved west to the San Marcos River, as suspected and hoped by the padres. However, the fact that the Tejas chieftain was Bernardino, probably the one who led the movement to chase Padre Massanet from East Texas in 1693, discouraged the fathers. Espinosa added that he knew that the chief of the Tejas was antagonistic toward the faith and added that the chief had escaped from a Rio Grande mission. The comment makes the identification of Bernardino uncertain, because the earlier Tejas leader named Bernardino who returned with De León in 1690 to Coahuila was escorted back to East Texas by Terán in 1691.

The next morning, Espinosa and his party followed the Indians northeast back to their large encampment. Gabriel Tous, who translated Espinosa's diary, incorrectly locates Espinosa's base-camp between present Bastrop and Smithville. The camp location is a few miles north of Bastrop (see Map 10) and the Indian camp was on Wilbarger Creek.[14] Tous's translation includes a map of Espinosa's route which differs from Map 10 in several other significant respects.[15]

All the Indians came from their huts to greet the Spaniards with their hands raised or crossed. They wore little clothing; almost all were entirely nude. Shouting for joy, they caressed the faces and arms of the Spaniards, doing the same among themselves, and passed the hands of the Spaniards over the faces of their babies. The padres shed tears of joy to be among the 2,000 Indians. This large encampment was comparable in size to the gathering of Indians reported by Terán and Massanet near San Marcos in 1691. The Spaniards gave tobacco to the women and lumps of brown sugar to the boys and girls.

When the meeting was over, Captain Cantona returned to base-camp with Aguirre and the company. From there Espinosa's party proceeded back southwest toward the Rio Grande. On Sunday, April 21, "following the same route by which we had come," the party reached the present San Marcos River after marching about 23 miles. At this point in Espinosa's diary, the padre digressed to give one the most colorful descriptions of Central Texas offered by any diarist on an early-eighteenth-century expedition.

Espinosa's comments were addressed to "Your Excellency," the viceroy, Duke of Albuquerque. After noting the variety of flowers, hemp, and fruit trees including wild persimmons, wild grapes, and mulberries, he described the pecan trees. The pecans, he said, surpassed the nuts of Castile—the meat was tastier and the shells were softer and more easily cracked, although they were longer and thinner. To keep the nuts from year to year, the Indians buried them in the ground or threaded them on long strings, but often stored them in small leather sacks.

The padre continued his comments on the natural history of the area by offering observations on the wildlife. Deer were reported to be so numerous that they resembled flocks of goats and were everywhere. Bison and wild turkeys were equally abundant. In its hump that reached from the neck to the rump, the buffalo, said Espinosa, holds "six loins concealed," superior to the loin of Castilian beef in taste and lightness. In his later history of the missions in Nuevo León, Espinosa noted that the large bison herds that had earlier roamed south of the Rio Grande in Nuevo León had been slaughtered and eliminated by Spanish settlers, who sought only the tongue and tallow of the beasts.[16] Although Espinosa stressed that bison constitued a critical component of Indian life, he did not describe how they killed this large and swift animal. The only account of an Indian bison hunt by La Salle's journalists was offered by the leader's brother, who recorded witnessing in the Lavaca-Fayette County area 150 mounted Indians with lances tipped with sharpened bone chasing bison in a fashion that resembled multiple bullfights.[17] The ancient ancestors of the Indians ca. 10,000 B.C. may have killed mammoths with spears in Texas, but these early hunters were on foot.

Espinosa's central Texas wildlife list included bear, mountain lion or cougar, jaguar (*tigre*), and fox, all present in amazing numbers. A plentiful supply of fish—*bobo,* catfish (*bagre*), bass (*robalo*), *besugo,* eel (*anguila*), and *mojarra*—were found not only in the river but in the smaller creeks as well. The padre added that a large fish called *piltonte* (yellow catfish) was taken in the Rio Grande.[18]

Espinosa's extensive notes to the viceroy also included a brief commentary on the numerous local Indian tribes. The diarist pointed out that the natives were too numerous to count. His party had seen about fifty local tribes, but this number did not include "those tribes that visit from the interior," meaning, the padre said, the region to the west that borders on New Mexico. Espinosa's reference to Indian tribes from the areas of West Texas and New Mexico visiting the Colorado River area and his earlier comments about the Cantona captain and his followers frequently visiting their friends the Tejas in East Texas confirm that the padre correctly understood the highly mobile character of many of the Texas Indian tribes at that time.

With reference to communications between the tribes, Espinosa restated Massanet's observation in 1691 that natives local to the immediate area (Central Texas) spoke different languages. Nevertheless, most communicated easily and with skill and drama by the use of sign language. The natives, Espinosa added, also learned Spanish with ease. In fact, several prominent Indian leaders then spoke Spanish. The use of Indian sign language permitted the exchange of information and, Espinosa continued, facilitated the trading of fancifully painted deer or buffalo hides for Spanish goods or items from other tribes. The Indians' propensity for trade, as noted by Espinosa, complemented the French designs for expansion and control of the natives by trade. This interest in trade was resisted as inimical to early Spanish colonial policy, which sought Indian control through the establishment of presidios and missions.

After leaving the San Marcos and still following in reverse the earlier route, Espinosa marched 13 miles west the following day to the Guadalupe, a few miles below present

New Braunfels. The next day, Tuesday, was a long one, and the group covered 36 miles. They first passed a stream that Espinosa called and probably named Arroyo Salado. Then the party crossed the Río de San Antonio, the San Pedro, the Arroyo de León, and, finally, the Río de Medina. Thus, from expedition diary accounts alone, it appears that Espinosa named Leon Creek, San Pedro Creek, the San Antonio River, and Salado Creek in 1709.

Below the Medina River on the following day, the party became lost, their Indian guide having led them first toward the southeast rather than the south-southwest. An adjustment in direction late in the day brought the party to a tributary of the Robalos (Atascosa River) after the group had wandered some 42 miles, "16 leagues, according to our time." This is the clearest statement made by a diarist that travel time was a factor considered in estimating the distance traveled. The uncertainty of direction makes the precise location of the camp open to question.

On April 25, Espinosa corrected the mistake made in the direction taken the day before by marching directly west 23 miles to camp on the river Chapa (the San Miguel), at a location east of the ford of the Frio where he had crossed earlier and where Salinas had also passed after moving south-southwest from San Antonio in 1693. The following day, the party reached the Leona River after marching 20 miles. Two days later, they arrived at the Rio Grande, having forded the Nueces on April 27. The mission of San Juan Bautista welcomed them the next day.

The captain and the two padres were obliged to file a negative report—the Tejas Indians had not moved to the Colorado River as earlier suggested. Undaunted by this, and perhaps pleased by having charted a new route, the remarkable Fray Espinosa acclaimed that the party nevertheless returned "with health, success, and consolation, for all of which we thank God."

The report perhaps discouraged any further immediate plans to launch another large military expedition into Texas, but it did signal that a mission (with a supporting presidio and community) would be established someday near present San Antonio. There would be a delay of only seven years, not the sixteen-year lapse that occurred between Massanet's return in 1693 and the 1709 trip. The Spaniards finally had a more northern route to follow to the San Antonio area and on to the Colorado that had been used at least once in each direction. On the next expedition, the Spaniards would go to stay.

TABLE 5

The 1709 Expedition of Fray Isidro de Espinosa, Fray Antonio de Olivares, and Captain Pedro de Aguirre

Date	Distance Leagues (Miles)	Direction	Campsite (COUNTY)
4/5	4 (10.4)	—	Real del Cuervo (Cuervo Creek, MAVERICK) [1]
4/6	8 (20.8)	E	(Comanche Creek, DIMMIT) [1]
4/7	5 (13)	—	El Río de las Nueces (Nueces River, ZAVALA) [1]
4/8	7 (18.2)	E	Río Sarco or Río Frío (Leona River, ZAVALA) [1]
4/9	9 (23.4)	NE, N	Arroyo de Chapa (San Miguel Creek, FRIO) [1]
4/10	8 (20.8)	E	Arroyo de los Robalos (Atascosa River, northwest ATASCOSA) [1]
4/11	5 (13)	E	Río de Medina (Medina River, BEXAR) [1]
4/12	5 (13)	E	Río de Medina (Medina River, BEXAR) [1]
4/13	8 (20.8)	E	Arroyo "con agua salada" (Salado Creek, BEXAR) [1]
4/14	9 (23.4)	NE	Río Guadalupe (Guadalupe River, COMAL) [1]
4/15	6 (15.6)	NE	Río de San Marcos (San Marcos River, HAYS) [1]
4/16	8 (20.8)	E	Arroyo de las Garrapatas (Onion Creek, TRAVIS) [1]
4/17	5 (13)	NE	Río Colorado or Espíritu Santo (Colorado River, TRAVIS) [1]
4/18	9 (23.4)	SE	(Colorado River, BASTROP) [1]
4/19	9 (23.4)	—	(Colorado River, TRAVIS) [1]
4/20	8 (20.8)	NE	(Wilbarger Creek and returned to Colorado River campsite) [1]
4/21	9 (23.4)	—	Río de San Marcos (San Marcos River, HAYS) [1]
4/22	5 (13)	—	Río de Guadalupe (Guadalupe River, COMAL) [1]
4/23	14 (36.4)	—	Río de Medina (Medina River, BEXAR) [1]
4/24	16 (41.6)	SE	Arroyo de los Robalos (Atascosa River, eastern ATASCOSA) [1]
4/25	9 (23.4)	W	Arroyo de Chapa (San Miguel Creek, FRIO) [1]
4/26	8 (20.8)	—	Río Sarco or Río Frío (Leona River, ZAVALA) [1]
4/27	16 (41.6)	—	Arroyo Caramanchel (Comanche Creek, DIMMIT) [1]
4/28	—	—	Misión San Juan Bautista (near bank of Rio Grande) [1]

SEVEN

IN QUEST OF COMMERCE

Captain Domingo Ramón's 1716 Expedition with Espinosa and Saint-Denis

On February 17, 1716, Captain Don Domingo Ramón set out from the city of Saltillo, by way of San Juan Bautista, on an expedition to the Province of Texas to establish permanent missions and, more significantly, a presidio on the northeastern boundary of the territory claimed by Spain. Although the captain brought with him from Saltillo a sizable contingent representing the church, the principal ecclesiastical figures—Fray Isidro de Espinosa and Fray Antonio Margil—did not meet the party until it reached the Rio Grande. Captain Ramón and Fray Espinosa both kept diaries of the trip.[1] The account of the expedition by the experienced padre was the more accurate and detailed.

There had been no established Spanish presence in the eastern buffer zone of the Spanish claim for twenty-three years, since Fray Massanet was forced to abandon his mission by the Tejas chieftain Bernardino and his followers in 1693. The probability of success for the reestablishment of Spanish missions in East Texas was enhanced by including in this expedition party eight married soldiers with families among the twenty troopers. Soon after leaving Saltillo, Ramón's party celebrated the birth of a new member. Later, the number of married couples increased by one as the caravan rode across South Texas.

The priests escorted on the expedition represented two groups of Franciscans—Espinosa led the priests from the College of Querétaro, and Fray Antonio Margil was the senior member from the College of Zacatecas. Margil, however, was seriously ill when the expedition was launched and followed the party later. Ramón listed by name

---

This chapter is based on two accounts of the trip. The first is Fray Espinosa's diary, translated into English by Gabriel Tous, Preliminary Studies of the Texas Catholic Historical Society 1, no. 4 (April 1930), 4–24. A typescript copy of the manuscript diary held in the Barker Texas History Center (AGN, Provincias Internas, vol. 181) was also consulted. The second account is the diary of Captain Ramón, translated into English by Paul J. Foik, Preliminary Studies of the Texas Catholic Historical Society 2, no. 5 (April 1933), 3–23. A typescript copy of his manuscript diary held in the Barker Texas History Center (AGN, Provincias Internas, vol. 181) was also consulted.

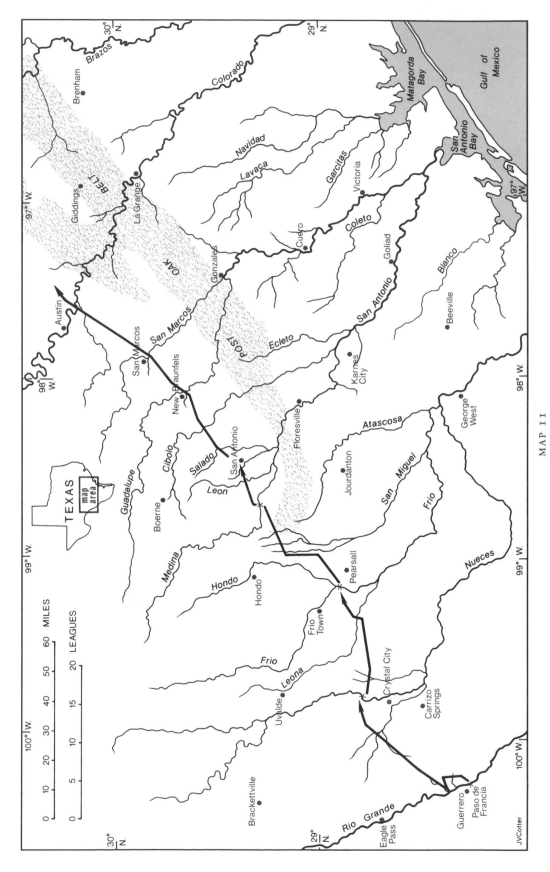

MAP II

Captain Domingo Ramón's 1716 Expedition with Espinosa and Saint-Denis, Part 1

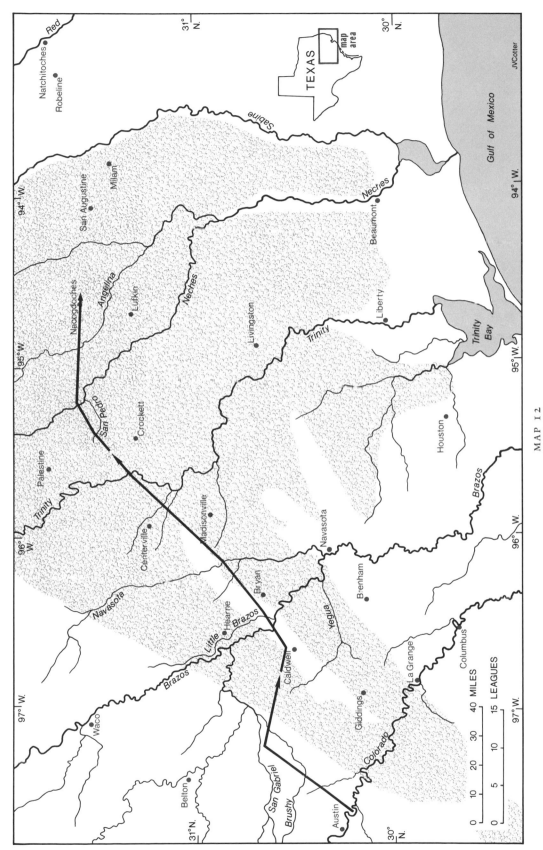

MAP 12

Captain Domingo Ramón's 1716 Expedition with Espinosa and Saint-Denis, Part 2

the sixty-five members of the expedition party, which included, in addition to the soldiers and priests, an African American named Juan de la Concepción, a six-year-old boy, a four-year-old girl, and two Indian guides.

Fray Espinosa, the diarist and a leader on the 1709 three-week expedition to the Colorado River from the Rio Grande via San Antonio, was qualified to serve not only as a diarist but more significantly as a guide.[2] The remarkable padre also demonstrated on the expedition that he had acquired or someone in his party had the ability to read the latitude through "observations with the sun." His reported readings with the astrolabe (the predecessor to the sextant) exceeded the accuracy of similar readings of latitude by Chapa on De León's 1689 expedition, by Captains Salinas and Martínez on De León's 1690 trip, and by the same two officers on Terán's expedition. The padre's position on this expedition is also reflected in his authority officially to name the campsites used and the streams crossed.

The expedition plan was to proceed to East Texas along the more northern route through present-day San Antonio. One of the three Frenchmen in the party, identified by Ramón as "Captain Don Luis de St. Denis, Chief Convoy," was expected to serve as an experienced guide along the route through the present San Antonio area and on to the Colorado River crossing and East Texas. The weakness of this part of the plan, however, was that Saint-Denis had never traveled to or from East Texas along the route now contemplated. Neither Ramón nor Espinosa was familiar with the territory beyond the Colorado River. The Frenchman had misled the Spaniards by suggesting that he knew the route through the San Antonio area but knew nothing of the Texas coastal area near Matagorda Bay, perhaps to quiet their concerns that the coastal area was vulnerable to French designs.[3]

To appreciate how useless Saint-Denis would be as a guide on this expedition, it is necessary to review briefly how he first arrived on scene at San Juan Bautista. In early 1714, the enterprising Frenchman had made his way from Mobile to East Texas to visit Indian friends among the Tejas and to stage his trading venture with the Spaniards. Accompanied by two of the Talon brothers—Pierre and either Robert or Jean—and Médard Jallot, Saint-Denis secured the services of the Tejas chief, Bernardino, and some of his men to guide the French party to the Rio Grande. The Talon brothers had traveled much of the same route together as guest travelers (or captives) and guides with De León in 1690 on his return from the Tejas in East Texas to the same Rio Grande crossing near San Juan Bautista. The Tejas chieftain called Bernardino is probably the same man who had traveled south along the Tejas trail to the Colorado crossing near modern La Grange and along the Indian trade route to the Rio Grande crossing with De León in 1690 and back northeast with Terán in 1691. A more competent group to guide the Frenchmen could not have been assembled.

The Tejas Indians were, of course, very familiar with the old Indian trade route from East Texas going south to the Colorado and on to the Rio Grande. They had followed it to hunt deer and bison between the Trinity and the Brazos and farther south and west to the Colorado for decades, possibly centuries. The Tejas had been found as far south as the lower Rio Grande, probably between modern Laredo and Eagle Pass, as early as the 1670s according to Padre Francisco Peñasco, who returned to the Mission

Santa Rosa in northern Coahuila with some of the Tejas in the summer of 1674. Tejas "converts" were at Mission Caldera in eastern Coahuila in 1683.[4]

This trade route is the one that was taken in 1689 by the Tejas and their four French companions across the Colorado at present La Grange where De León picked up their trail. Massanet said the Tejas chose this more eastern route because it put the protective and heavily timbered Monte Grande, the thick woods north of the road, between them and their mounted enemies, the Apache. The Tejas were never reported in the San Antonio area; they preferred the lower route along which De León had found a hunting party in 1690 and Salinas had seen several Tejas encampments in 1693.

Pierre Talon and his brother were very familiar with the lower coastal route, closer to Matagorda Bay, which had been their home for several years. The guides thus took Saint-Denis along the only route they knew to the Rio Grande: toward the bay and then west, many miles below the San Antonio area.

The conclusion that the earlier party led by Saint-Denis had skirted, if not visited, the bay area on the way southwest to San Juan Bautista is supported by Saint-Denis's own map of his trip and the report that they encountered and fought the coastal Indians, probably the Karankawa, after crossing the Colorado River. Accounts of the skirmish tell how the Tejas defeated the coastal tribe and pursued them to their village. There the coastal Indians agreed to allow Saint-Denis's party to advance without further interference.[5] With the aid of Pierre, who had lived with the Tejas, and his brother Jean or Robert, both of whom had lived as captives of the Karankawa, the Frenchmen were able to secure the cease-fire.[6]

Thus, it is unlikely that Saint-Denis had ever visited the San Antonio area, and his services as a guide to present-day San Antonio and the area to the northeast were of limited value.[7] But Saint-Denis offered other services. Captain Ramón and his son, who was also on the expedition, were interested in trading with the French, and their newly acquired relative by marriage, Saint-Denis, provided a valuable connection.[8] The reversal of the Tejas leader's distrust of the Spaniards might also have been traced to prospects for trade, with the Tejas serving as brokers between the French and Spaniards.

The trio of Diego Ramón, his son Domingo, and their new relative Saint-Denis assembled on the Rio Grande before the march began. On April 18, Domingo Ramón's party arrived from Saltillo and camped near Presidio del Río Grande, where Saint-Denis awaited. Captain Ramón's father, Major Sergeant Diego Ramón, met the expedition in his official capacity as captain of the presidio.

The two-month trip (February 17–April 18) made by Ramón and his party from Saltillo to San Juan Bautista had been frequently interrupted. Delays were occasioned by the birth of a child, the loss of horses and mules, the desertion of several soldiers, inclement weather, comforting a distressed young mestiza who had been abused by her master, and an unsuccessful search for a small boy who became lost along the way. When he approached the Sabinas River, the captain saw the first herd of wild horses reported on an expedition. As he approached the Rio Grande, Ramón picked up the route followed earlier by De León and Salinas, camping on April 13 at the *paraje* Pescado, the camp that Terán and Espinosa had used in 1691.

During the next two days (April 14 and 15), Ramón crossed first Juan's Creek and then nearby Amole Creek about 18 miles south of the Rio Grande. This reference to the two named creeks gives the first clear identification of the location of the creek frequently referred to in expedition diaries as Juan the Frenchman. Amole Creek, like Cuervo and Cueva creeks, has retained its name and is so designated on contemporary Mexican government maps (see *Piedras Negras*, H14-10). Nearby Juan Creek is now called Salada Creek.

Two days after arriving at the presidio near the Rio Grande, Domingo Ramón marched along the river to the pass called Francia. Map 11 places the crossing about 35 miles below the present city of Eagle Pass near the location of the crossing used by De León. The river was low and the crossing easy. Nevertheless, the party spent several additional days near the riverbank after the crossing, reporting thick growths of mesquite brush and prickly pear.

On Monday, April 27, the expedition left the Rio Grande and marched about 8 miles northwest and then 5 miles west, which brought the party back to the river at the Pacuache crossing that the diarist called Diego Ramón Pass. Espinosa explained that the party set out that day for the customary *paraje* Cuervo (which had been used or passed on previous expeditions), but lack of water along the way forced the return to the Rio Grande near a second crossing farther upstream. Heat and the drought continued to plague the party during most of the summer months. Ramón reported that a storm struck that evening. The tornado-force wind blew with fury against their three tents and picked up and threw a mounted sentinel and horse.

The next morning, the party proceeded 13 miles northeast from the river through green pastures to the creek Cueva del León (Lion's Cave). Cueva is a creek about 3 miles upstream from Cuervo Creek, at their junction with the Rio Grande. Both creeks, marked on a contemporary map (*Crystal City*, NH14-11), run from the north into the Rio Grande above the Francia crossing. The certain identification of the two named creeks on contemporary maps confirms the location of the original area where De León forded the river and shows that the early expeditions first moved to the north-northeast toward the Nueces along a line of march west of Carrizo Springs and Crystal City.

According to Espinosa, the party marched northeast another 13 miles on April 29, following a pathway through mesquite, prickly pear, and mottes of oak and live oak toward a watering place on Comanche Creek. The conflicting reports made by Ramón and Espinosa illustrate the problem of understanding what occurred on certain days throughout this expedition. Espinosa blamed five "Bozale" Indians for stealing some horses that day, but Captain Ramón reported that he recovered the stolen animals from some Pacuache Indians, whom he threatened to hang if the offense was repeated.

During the next two days, the party moved only 13 miles through flat land with prickly pear, wild *orégano* (lantana), and mesquite, stopping first at the Ponds of Carrizo and then at a spring, Ojo de Agua. (About a year later, on April 19, 1717, members of Ramón's command returned to the same campsite with Saint-Denis's partner, Sieur Derbanne, and a caravan with French goods on their way south to San Juan Bautista.) Both Ramón and Espinosa recorded that the party reached the Nueces River on May 2. The crossing of the Nueces was several miles above present Crystal City, near the crossing used by most earlier expedition leaders. Espinosa recorded moving 22 leagues from the Rio Grande to the

Nueces crossing, which closely matches the account given by both De León and Salinas. The padre had apparently retained the ability to estimate distance that he demonstrated in his 1709 diary account. A large unpopulated Indian camp was found in the pecan and oak grove near the river. The party remained in place on Sunday.

On May 4, the expedition proceeded about 5 miles to a watering pond east-northeast of the Nueces crossing. Espinosa referred to it as Tortuga (Turtle Pond). Captain Ramón called the same watering hole Ranas (Frog Pond). The camp was near the headwaters of the present Tortuga Creek, which originates in central Zavala County about 8 miles east of the Nueces River and then runs south generally parallel with the Nueces to join it in north-central Dimmit County. Earlier expeditions had skirted a few miles north of the ponds to strike the Leona farther upstream and thus earlier diarists never mentioned the Tortuga stream or campsite. But this *entrada* continued to follow the route that Espinosa had followed in 1709, not the slightly more northern route followed by De León and Terán. On later expeditions, Alarcón, Aguayo, and Rivera would all stop for a rest at Tortuga along Espinosa's way. The next spring, Ramón's troops also used the campsite, on their return with Saint-Denis's business partner, Derbanne.

As in the case of other creeks in the Rio Grande area (such as Amole, Cuervo, and Cueva), the name of Tortuga Creek has not changed over the past 250 to 300 years. The consistent use of the same names for creeks and streams can prove valuable in verifying expedition campsites and routes, whereas the switching of names (which also occurs) can be extremely confusing.

Another day of rest was called on May 5 to celebrate the marriage of Ana Guerra to a soldier, Lorenzo Mercado. On Ramón's trip from Saltillo to the Rio Grande, Ana, a young mestiza, and Lorenzo had requested the captain's blessing and protection to marry en route. To document that all necessary ecclesiastical requirements were properly observed, Espinosa noted in his diary that the announcement of the pending wedding had been duly made in the church before the expedition commenced.

The pause in the movement of the caravan may also have been needed for other reasons. The soldiers, including the captain, had been engaged with the Frenchmen in horse races and stunts along the way, resulting in several rather serious falls. In addition, the party needed time to round up a deserter, one José del Toro, an Indian soldier who was found hiding high in a tree a few miles away.

Espinosa recorded that during the next three days the party marched east-northeast, crossing the Leona and finally camping about 5 miles short of the Frio River on May 8 and 9. During this movement from the Leona to the Frio, the party saw heavy growths of brazilwood (*Brazil*) and grapevines and several large flocks of turkeys.[9] The group also passed three encampments of Pataguo Indians.[10] This tribe lived on both sides of the lower Rio Grande.

The day after Ramón's party visited the Pataguo Indians, an unexpected Indian traveler arrived at Ramón's camp from the northeast headed for a destination below the Rio Grande. He was a Mesquite who had been with some members of his tribe on the Brazos. The lone Indian was traveling southwest along the Indian trade route that Ramón's party was tracking toward the northeast. He reported that a large concentration of Indians was gathered near the Brazos. When Espinosa reached the Brazos River a few weeks later, he did find a very large Indian congregation, including some of the messenger's brethren, the Mesquite.

The following day, Espinosa crossed the Frio below its junction with Hondo Creek at a "very convenient ford" and marched northeast beyond the stream. Ramón's party was still closely following Espinosa's earlier route, crossing the Frio in the flat valley area near the customary ford used first by De León. Near the Frio ford Espinosa reported that "on observing the sun, the latitude was found to be 28°40'." (Espinosa had given no latitude readings on his 1709 journey.) According to present-day measurements on government maps, the crossing, a short distance below the Hondo Creek junction, is at about 28°50' latitude. One minute along the 28° latitude represents a little over 1 mile in distance, so the measurement by the astrolabe was reasonably accurate—within about 12 miles.

The padre reported that about 36 miles were covered during the following three days to reach the Medina River. The principal stop along the road was called the Ponds of Pita, where the party camped on May 12. The Spanish word *pita* means yucca and the encampment may have derived its name from that plant. Regardless of the derivation, the name later became associated with the Pita road to San Antonio that passed near the camp location.

Both Ramón and Espinosa, who had earlier repeatedly complained of the heat and drought, were relieved to rest near the freshwater stream and pond at Pita. The vegetation here was rich with large oak trees and grapevine; one vine measured about 3 feet in circumference, as witnessed by all the padres present.[11] The Pita campground was used on later expeditions by Alarcón, Aguayo, and Rivera. The Medina crossing is projected to be 10 leagues north-northeast of the Pita camp.[12] Pecans, willows, elms, and cottonwoods, some draped with grapevines, followed the course of the Medina River and both hemp and flax grew in nearby fields.

On May 14, the expedition again moved northeast. After traveling about 8 miles beyond the Medina River, Espinosa recorded crossing the Arroyo de León, the stream he first named in 1709. The San Antonio River, reached after traveling another 10 miles, was the camp for the evening. Espinosa explained that the location near the river was very suitable for settlement; the river offered an abundance of fresh water and fish. Along the river they found tall pecans, cottonwoods, palmettos, mulberries, willows, grapevines, and some yuccas, ferns (*culantrillos*), wild hemp, flax, and blackberries or dewberries (see Appendix II entries on "Blackberry Bush" and "Dewberry Bush"). As expected, Fray Espinosa referred to the river as the San Antonio, for he had named it when he passed that way in 1709. The padre commented on the clear water and the fish, which included catfish, *mojarras, piltontes,* and *catanes,* with a few alligators as well. The party remained there the next day.

Ramón continued 5 miles northeast the following day (May 16) to camp on Salado Creek, which Espinosa had also named in 1709. The padre found in the bed of the creek some grapevine stocks that appeared to him to have been planted by hand (*que parecía majuelo plantado a mano*). The observation about planted vines in the Salado near San Antonio is curious because a similar comment was made later by the diarist Peña with Aguayo on May 13, 1721.

On Sunday, the camp proceeded another 13 miles to an unnamed creek, probably the Cibolo. Saint-Denis, Médard Jallot, and a Indian guide left the expedition to proceed ahead to search for the Tejas Indians who were to meet the party and escort them to East Texas. Espinosa gave a latitude reading of 29°38' for his location on the Cibolo. This reading was also within a few degrees of the mark as measured on contemporary maps.[13]

Ramón's party reached the "first Guadalupe River" (the Comal River) the following day (May 18) after traveling 18 miles. Another short trek of less than 2 miles brought the party to the Guadalupe, at the same crossing location used by the padre in 1709. Alligators were as numerous here as they were on the San Antonio River.

On May 20, Espinosa reached the San Marcos River and the Blanco in the afternoon, having traveled about 23 miles. As in 1709, he thought the San Marcos was the Colorado River. Espinosa reported that he remained at the Blanco on May 21; that evening, he witnessed a comet or some other phenomenon in the sky. The padre continued to follow the route he had found with his Indian guides in 1709, passing the spring and creek that he said he had earlier named San Isidro (the Blanco) and camping on the Garrapatas (Onion Creek), also named by him in 1709. On the same day, the captain separately proceeded another 24 miles northeast. This movement permitted Ramón to reach the Colorado River after traveling only 8 miles on May 22. It was not until the next day that Espinosa caught up with the captain on the Colorado, which they both confused with the Brazos, calling the river the "Espíritu Santo or Colorado." Espinosa had exhibited the same confusion on his 1709 expedition. The Frenchman Saint-Denis was not in the area, as he admittedly became lost soon after he separated himself from the main camp to serve as an advance guard.

Ramón's party crossed the Colorado on May 24, but it took another two days to ferry the goats across and to send scouts out to search for Indian guides and a path. Ramón mentioned specifically that they had not been beyond the Colorado River before and needed a guide. Espinosa gave an imprecise reading of the sun near the Colorado of 30° "and some minutes." The crossing probably occurred near 30°10' latitude. Their movement on the first day beyond the Colorado reflected this uncertainty: according to Ramón, they moved 8 miles southeast and then switched directions to march the same distance northeast.

On May 28, the party again moved northeast, following a Payaya guide to cross Arroyo Animas, a name given to present Brushy Creek by Espinosa that continued to be used for the stream on later expeditions. Espinosa's reading of his position on Brushy Creek was 30°40' (again within 10 minutes, which is the equivalent of about 12 miles of his location as measured on contemporary maps).[14] Espinosa named the modern San Gabriel River the San Francisco Xavier four days later, but he did not proceed farther north to the Little River. Herbert E. Bolton agrees that Ramón and Espinosa in 1716 referred to modern Brushy Creek as Arroyo Animas and the San Gabriel as "San Xavier," correctly adding that Ramón was not following "the Old San Antonio Road" of later days.[15]

From the San Gabriel or Xavier, the party veered southeast with the assistance of two new Indian guides (one was a Mescal and the second an Ervipiame) into the Monte Grande and toward the crossing of the Brazos near its junction with the Little Brazos River. The Mescal and Ervipiame were encountered near the Rio Grande on earlier expeditions. The general direction taken by Ramón and Espinosa was called the Xavier Road by the Marqués de Rubí in 1767. Moving southeast on June 3, Espinosa noted that the party recrossed Arroyo Animas; they were traveling in the same direction as the Brazos flows. The party received the aid of more Indians, who helped direct the way south-southeast toward their villages on the Brazos. A prominent cross of heavy timber was constructed to mark the way.

The woods were so dense that "there were not enough hatchets and knives to open a passage and consequently the cargo was damaged." Two soldiers who became lost reported seeing wild cattle and turkeys in the wooded area as they found their way back to the main camp.

Additional guides, including a Tejas Indian, assisted Espinosa's movement first to the southeast and then east through the more open areas or corridor within the Monte Grande in central Burleson County and escorted the convoy to an Indian community near the junction of the Brazos and the Little Brazos River. Before Espinosa reached the crossing, Saint-Denis safely found his way back to the main party; Espinosa exclaimed that they thanked God that they had not suffered the hardships in the woods that Saint-Denis had endured.

Espinosa confirmed the location of the party at that time, reporting that they crossed the Brazos (which he called Río Trinidad) at a ford above where "General Alonso de León crossed." Espinosa correctly acknowledged that De León earlier had followed a different route to arrive at the ford he used farther downstream. On the same day (June 15), Ramón also reported that he crossed the Brazos (which he, too, mistakenly referred to as the Trinidad) and soon thereafter crossed a second stream (the Little Brazos River) that the Indian guide told him was a branch of the same river.[16] The accounts given in the two diaries show that they crossed the Brazos near the junction of the Little Brazos, at a point about 20 miles below the Little River junction in Milam County and above the ford used by De León near the junction with the Navasota.

Before reaching the Brazos crossing, Ramón and Espinosa reported finding a very large village or group of encampments of approximately 2,000 (according to Ramón) Ervipiame, Mesquite, Pamaya, Payaya, Xarame, Sijame, Cantona, and Mescal Indians. This was the fourth gathering estimated to number 2,000 or more Indians reported on an expedition. The eight tribes were all familiar to Espinosa and Ramón.

This congregation of several tribes (sometimes referred to as Ranchería Grande) was probably the same large Indian gathering that the Mesquite messenger had reported to Ramón several weeks earlier when they met him near the Frio. The Indians used buffalo hides and softer tanned animal skins to barter with Ramón's troops. The captain said that it was with great pleasure that he was able to authorize these exchanges with the Indians, which would otherwise be unlawful.

The Indians also helped Ramón complete the crossing with minimal loss of goats and damage to cargo. The captain reciprocated by protecting the Indian swimmers from the numerous alligators (which the natives greatly feared) and by serving them a barbecued steer and two goats.

After crossing the Brazos, Espinosa turned northeast and moved into more open country along the present-day Robertson-Brazos County line. He was guided along the way by a number of Tejas. In the more open corridor in the center of the Monte Grande, buffalo were plentiful to kill for meat or to capture for a bullfight. Wild cattle were also available for food. Later expeditions replenished their supply of meat from buffalo herds that roamed in the same open prairie corridor within the thickly wooded area northeast of the Brazos crossing, which is clearly seen on large-scale topographical maps. If the Brazos crossing had occurred at the junction of the Little River and the Brazos as suggested by some Texas historians,[17] the party would have been in the deep and heavily wooded Monte Grande, not in the open corridor that was found then and is found today running northeast from the junction of the Brazos and Little Brazos rivers.

On the second day (June 18) along the route beyond the Brazos crossing, Ramón reported meeting "in the middle of the road" a number of Tejas buffalo hunters. The four men and two women escorted Ramón's party to a creek, which Espinosa named Corpus Christi. Because this named creek and campsite, about 9 leagues northeast of the Brazos crossing, was visited two years later by Alarcón, and later by Rivera (1727), Rubí (1767), and Solís (1768), the location of the principal road between the Brazos and the Navasota in the early and middle eighteenth century can be confirmed. The creek named Corpus Christi, which runs across the open corridor about 20 miles northeast of the Little Brazos junction, is called Cedar Creek on contemporary government maps,[18] but it retained the name Corpus Christi as identified as late as 1830 on Stephen F. Austin's published map of the customary travel routes at that time between the Colorado and the Red River.[19]

On the next day, Espinosa reported that the party followed an open pathway about 10 miles through scattered oaks to a creek he called San Buenaventura (the Navasota River) and on to a nearby lake that they named Santa Ana. Ramón added that they continued moving north with the aid of the Tejas as guides. The river called San Buenaventura and the nearby lake called Santa Ana, located a few leagues northeast of Corpus Christi, were landmarks that were identified repeatedly on subsequent expeditions.

Santa Clara, located about halfway between the Navasota and Trinity, was the campsite on June 21 according to both Ramón and Espinosa. The party traveled two days, approximately 26 miles to the east-northeast, to reach the camp, which was located 10 leagues southwest of the Trinity crossing. Santa Clara, near present Centerville in Leon County, was also repeatedly cited on later expeditions. Between the Navasota and Santa Clara, the party visited a community of over twenty Tejas, who treated the Spaniards to a refreshing light meal of green ears of corn and melons. The Tejas farming community in western Leon County was located substantially farther west than the principal Tejas villages near the Neches. Later, Aguayo also saw Tejas farming communities west of the Trinity.[20] Some species of game bird (*pavo*)—perhaps wild turkey—was locally available, but no bison were seen.

On June 23, Espinosa and Ramón realized the confusion in the names of the rivers they had used when they reached the Trinity, which they had both incorrectly reported crossing a week earlier when they forded the Brazos. The impressive Trinity River was bordered with a heavy growth of trees—oak, walnut or hickory, live oak with grapevine, and pine.

Santa Efigenia was the creek campsite about 10 miles east of the Trinity. By June 28, the party had reached two large lakes along San Pedro Creek, the former site of the earlier mission, San Francisco de Tejas, about 34 miles east of the Trinity crossing.

Near the Indian village that De León had named San Francisco de Tejas in 1690, the leaders of the Tejas rejoiced at the return of the Spaniards. The deep distrust and anger that had spurred the Tejas to chase Massanet and his fellow padres from the area twenty-three years earlier had dissipated. The Spaniards' return was an occasion to celebrate. It is not clear from the diary accounts whether it was the anticipated benefits of trade between the French and Spanish that changed the distrust felt earlier by the Tejas or whether other unstated factors led to the reversal.

The celebration included the solemn ceremony of smoking a pipe. This was no ordinary pipe—it was 3 feet long and heavily adorned with white feathers. And the manner of smoking it was no less ceremonial. It was puffed first by the Tejas chieftain, who then with deliberation blew a small cloud toward the heavens, then clouds toward the east, the west, the north, the south, and finally toward the earth. The pipe, filled with tobacco locally grown, was passed to the captain for him to follow suit and then to everyone in attendance—"even to the women," added the captain.

Espinosa noted on July 2 that the Tejas delegation included "a learned Indian woman who had been reared in Coahuila and served as an interpreter." Most likely this talented woman was the prominent Indian female leader called Angelina on subsequent expeditions, for whom the present-day Angelina River was named. The meal prepared by the Indians (served on earthenware) included corn, melons, tamales, and cooked beans mixed with corn and nuts. In his *Crónica*, Espinosa later noted that the Tejas also grew sunflowers (*girasoles*) and mixed the sunflower seed with corn to eat.[21]

On June 30, 3 leagues east of the former mission site, Ramón established the first presidio in East Texas, Nuestra Señora de los Dolores de los Tejas, near the Neches River. That fall, the presidio was moved from the west side to the east side of the river.

During the following ten days, three new Queretaran mission sites were selected—Nuestro Padre San Francisco de los Tejas was founded 5 miles east of the Neches, Mission Purísima Concepción was established near the present Angelina River, and San José was established farther east among the Nazoni Indians. Near present-day Nacogdoches, the first Zacatecan mission was established, Nuestra Señora de Guadalupe. That area was described as having heavy stands of oak, live oak, pine, perhaps cottonwood (*álamo*), and walnut or hickory (*nogal*) (see Appendix II entries on "Cottonwood" and "Pecan"). The following year, Father Margil proceeded across the Sabine to establish the mission of San Miguel among the Adaes Indians a few miles west of the Red River.[22]

Regardless of the confusion in the names given to the rivers crossed, the full entourage—soldiers, priests, farm animals and all—had settled at their destination in East Texas by mid-July 1716, according to the diary of Captain Ramón. Unlike earlier expeditions, which were led by a governor and designed primarily to explore the province and return to Coahuila, this one was directed by a military captain who was under orders to remain in East Texas as commanding officer for the new presidio. Therefore, Ramón's diary account of the expedition closes shortly after his arrival in

East Texas. Espinosa also remained in East Texas, and his diary account also closes without any reference to a return trip. However, two years later, the padre and captain both returned to San Antonio de Béxar to meet Governor Alarcón and escort him to the presidio and mission field.

Soon after the Spaniards became settled in East Texas, Saint-Denis renewed his drive to establish a trade route between Louisiana and New Spain, via San Juan Bautista. In the fall of 1716, Saint-Denis and his business partner, Sieur Derbanne, decided to take goods to the Rio Grande. This time they were escorted by Ramón's troops back along the road through the San Antonio area that Espinosa and Ramón had taken earlier from San Juan Bautista to East Texas. This route, as noted, was different from the more southern route closer to the bay used earlier when Saint-Denis and his Tejas Indian escorts encountered the coastal Indians.

Derbanne's party left the community of Natchitoches in present Louisiana on November 22, 1716. At that time the village of Natchitoche Indians, an eastern tribe of the Caddo Confederacy, was near the present city that carries the same name. About 140 miles to the west and southwest, the party reached the Spanish presidio and mission among the Tejas Indians on the Angelina and upper Neches rivers. The French merchant Derbanne was not only received warmly at the Spanish presidio, but was given a mule train and an armed escort composed of Captain Ramón's men to guide and protect the caravan to the Rio Grande. His diary account of the trip gives the direction and distance traveled on most days and notes the names of the rivers crossed and campsites.[23]

The captain's men escorting Saint-Denis and Derbanne knew the way and used the Spanish names given to rivers by Espinosa, thereby confusing the names of some rivers crossed. Ramón's troops would escort the commercial caravan along the same route that they followed northeast the previous spring and summer. A review of Derbanne's journey southwest, escorted by Ramón's troops, affords a means of verifying Ramón's original line of march northeast.

On March 22, 1717, Derbanne reported leaving the area near Ramón's new presidio on the Neches. Apparently the French party had spent several months in East Texas, since they left Natchitoches in Louisiana in late November the year before. The Trinity was crossed on March 24 as the party moved southwest. During the following four days, the party covered about 30 leagues (78 miles), following Espinosa's route through open prairies, which provided pasture for wild cattle and buffalo, to the Brazos crossing near the junction with the Little Brazos. The Indian village near the junction visited the year before by Ramón's troops was still there. Derbanne described the river (the Brazos) as having two forks—one to the north (the Little Brazos River) and the second to the west-northwest (the Brazos River). Derbanne stated that the two forks joined a short distance below the crossing.

Confirmation that the crossing of the Brazos occurred at the ford used by Espinosa the year before can be found in the direction and distance recorded by Derbanne during the four days when the party moved from the Brazos crossing toward the Colorado crossing near Onion Creek. From the Brazos Derbanne recorded traveling northwest for 30 miles through "very dense woods" (the Monte Grande) to emerge on the open prairie (northeast of Austin in western Milam County) on April 4. Pine trees whose branches "grow to the ground" obstructed the progress of the caravan through the woods. (A comparable move northwest from a projected Little River crossing would place the party north of the Little River and closer to present Temple in Bell County, between Austin and Waco.) After a delay to wait for the Spanish troops to search for some of their mounts, Derbanne proceeded southeast to the Colorado River and crossed it on April 8.

Shortly after crossing the Colorado, the caravan was attacked near Onion Creek by a band of sixty mounted Apache.[24] After Ramón's soldiers resisted the attack, the Apache satisfied themselves with capturing twenty-three unloaded mules and an unprotected Spanish mulatto woman who was serving as mule driver, bringing up the rear.

Ten miles beyond Onion Creek, a friendly encampment of Payaya greeted the harassed trading party. They exchanged buffalo hides with the Spaniards for some unidentified goods. When permitted, many Indian tribes were apparently ready and eager to trade surplus hides and other items. Again, this propensity to exchange was appreciated and encouraged by the French but not by the Spaniards. The caravan reached the San Marcos River on April 11; the following day, they crossed both the Guadalupe and Comal rivers. After traveling 34 miles farther, crossing both the San Antonio River and the Medina, the party halted. On April 14, 1717, Derbanne commented that the Spaniards planned to establish a settlement on the San Antonio River, a full year before Governor Alarcón arrived to fulfill the prophecy.

The mule train proceeded from the Medina 15 miles due south to a campsite on the stream Derbanne said the Spanish called Peitre, the same location called Pita on Ramón's and Espinosa's eastward trek. Derbanne's route continued to track the path taken from the Rio Grande by Espinosa in 1709 and by Ramón and Espinosa in 1716.

During the following three days, the party covered 65 miles to the Nueces, but no direction was given in Derbanne's notes. However, the location of the Nueces crossing is clear from the identification of the campsites on each side of the river. The evening before reaching the Nueces, the party camped on a little lake (Turtle Pond, which was the first camp on the movement northeast from the Nueces). The next day they crossed the Nueces and camped at "the Spring" (Ojo de Agua) after marching 6 leagues (about 15 miles). The year before, Espinosa had reported moving in the opposite direction 6 leagues from the Ojo de Agua campsite to Turtle Pond, crossing the Nueces between the campsites.

Derbanne camped the following night on Cuervo Creek, the customary campground about 10 miles north of the Rio Grande ford. On April 21, he crossed the Rio Grande and came to the presidio after marching another 10 miles. It should be noted that some accounts suggest that Saint-Denis reached the presidio before Derbanne.[25]

After visiting Presidio San Juan Bautista and the two associated local missions, Derbanne offered some interesting observations. He correctly noted that Governor Alarcón and several local priests were prepared to embark on a substantial expedition which would include Matagorda Bay. He also said that the Spanish had reported to him that some French families from La Salle's colony were still living among the Indians near the bay. The reference may have been to some Frenchmen or French families who left the colony to live with local Indians.

Derbanne headed back to Louisiana on September 1, 1717, and was back on Dauphin Island on October 26. The arrest of Saint-Denis at the presidio may have prompted Derbanne's early return to Mobile.[26] With Derbanne's announcement, the stage was set for Governor Alarcón's expedition.

TABLE 6
Captain Domingo Ramón's 1716 Expedition

Date	Distance Leagues (Miles)	Direction	Campsite (COUNTY)
4/27	5 (13)	NW, W	Paso Diego Ramón (Rio Grande crossing, MAVERICK) [1]
4/28	5 (13)	NE	Cueva del León (Cueva Creek, MAVERICK) [1]
4/29	5 (13)	E, NE	Caramanchel (Comanche Creek, MAVERICK) [2]
4/30	3 (7.8)	—	Carrizo (tributary of Comanche Creek, DIMMIT) [2]
5/1	2 (5.2)	E	Ojo de Agua (tributary of Comanche Creek, DIMMIT) [2]
5/2	7 (18.2)	ENE	Río Nueces (Nueces River, ZAPATA) [1]
5/3	—	—	(Rested in camp)
5/4	2 (5.2)	ENE, NE	Tortuga or Ranas (Tortuga Creek, ZAVALA) [1]
5/5	—	—	(Remained in camp for wedding)
5/6	5 (13)	ENE	Río Frío (Leona River, ZAVALA) [1]
5/7	4 (10.4)	ENE	San Lorenzo (east of Leona crossing, FRIO) [1]
5/8	4 (10.4)	ENE	Saint Michael (west of Frio River crossing, FRIO) [1]
5/9	—	—	(Remained in camp)
5/10	4 (10.4)	ENE	Arroyo Hondo (Frio River, FRIO) [1]
5/11	2 (5.2)	ENE	Santa Isabel (probably on San Miguel Creek, FRIO) [1]
5/12	2 (5.2)	ENE	Pita (San Miguel tributary, MEDINA) [1]
5/13*	10 (26)	NNE	Río Medina (Medina River, BEXAR) [1]
5/14	7 (18.2)	ENE, NE	Río San Antonio (San Antonio River, BEXAR) [1]
5/15	—	—	(Remained in camp to worship)
5/16	2 (5.2)	NE	Arroyo Salado (Salado Creek, BEXAR) [1]
5/17	5 (13)	ENE	San Xavier (Cibolo Creek, BEXAR) [1]
5/18	7 (18.2)	NE	Río Guadalupe (Comal River, COMAL) [1]
5/19	0.5 (1.3)	NE	Río San Juan (Guadalupe River, COMAL) [1]
5/20	9 (23.4)	NE	Arroyo San Rafael (Blanco River, HAYS) [1]
5/21	—	—	(Remained in camp to worship)
5/22	8 (20.8)	NE	Arroyo Garrapatas (Onion Creek, TRAVIS) [1]
5/23	3 (7.8)	NNE	Río Espíritu Santo or Colorado (Colorado River, TRAVIS) [1]

[On May 24–26, the party crossed the Colorado River and searched for an Indian guide.]

5/27	6 (15.6)	SE, NE	(Unnamed creek east of Colorado River, TRAVIS) [2]
5/28	6 (15.6)	—	Arroyo Animas (Brushy Creek, WILLIAMSON) [1]
5/29	—	—	(Delayed to dry bison meat)
5/30	3 (7.8)	NNE	(Unnamed camp, WILLIAMSON) [2]
5/31	3 (7.8)	NE	Arroyo San Diego (tributary of Brushy Creek, WILLIAMSON) [2]
6/1	2 (5.2)	NE	San Francisco Xavier (San Gabriel River, MILAM) [1]
6/2	—	—	(Rested in camp)
6/3	4 (10.4)	SE	Arroyo Animas (Brushy Creek, MILAM) [1]

Date	Distance Leagues (Miles)	Direction	Campsite (COUNTY)
6/4	—	—	(Remained to search for missing man)
6/5	—	—	(Continued search)
6/6	5 (13)	NE, SE	Soledad (MILAM) [2]
6/7	—	—	(Remained near camp to clear pathway)
6/8	4 (10.4)	ESE	Arroyo San Juan (unknown creek, BURLESON) [2]
6/9	3 (7.8)	S, SE	Santa María de Buenavista (BURLESON) [2]
6/10	—	—	(Met with Indians)
6/11	—	—	(Erected cross)
6/12	7 (18.2)	E	(Large Indian village, BURLESON) [2]
6/13	—	—	(Met with Indians)
6/14	1 (2.6)	—	Río Trinidad (Brazos River, BURLESON) [1]
6/15	1.5 (3.9)	—	Río Trinidad (Brazos River, BRAZOS) [1]
6/16	4 (10.4)	E	(Unnamed camp, BRAZOS) [1]
6/17	—	—	(Waited in camp to search for missing animals)
6/18	5 (13)	NNE	Arroyo Corpus Christi (Cedar Creek, BRAZOS) [1]
6/19	4 (10.4)	NE	Lago Santa Ana (MADISON) [1]
6/20	5 (13)	ENE	(Unnamed camp, MADISON) [1]
6/21	5 (13)	ENE	Santa Clara (near Boggy Creek, LEON) [1]
6/22	10 (26)	ENE	Santa Rosa de Viterbo (west of Trinity, LEON) [1]
6/23	0.5 (1.3)	—	Río San Juan Bautista (Trinity River, LEON) [1]
6/24	—	—	(Waited to cross river)
6/25	—	—	(Received Tejas Indians)
6/26	4 (10.4)	NE	Santa Efigenia (HOUSTON) [1]
6/27	—	—	(Met Tejas Indians)
6/28	9 (23.4)	NE	(Camped near San Pedro Creek, HOUSTON) [1]
6/29	—	—	(Remained in camp)
6/30	3 (7.8)	NE	(Neches River, CHEROKEE) [1]

[On July 1–5, Ramón remained near the new site of the presidio.]

7/6	8 (20.8)	NE	Misión Concepción (near Angelina River, CHEROKEE) [1]
7/7	—	—	(Remained near camp)
7/8	—	—	(Remained near camp)
7/9	7 (18.2)	NE	Misión Guadalupe (near Nacogdoches, NACOGDOCHES) [2]
7/10	—	—	(Visited new site for mission, NACOGDOCHES) [2]

[Espinosa concluded his diary account on July 10, stating that three missions had been founded and noting only that he returned to Mission Concepción. Ramón's diary closes with an entry on July 11 indicating that he was in camp.]

---

*Ramón's diary omits the entry for May 13.

FIGURE 8
Alarcón's men parley with suspicious coastal Indians at Carancahua Bay.

EIGHT

A WAY STATION AT SAN ANTONIO

Governor Martín de Alarcón's 1718 Expedition

Martín de Alarcón, named governor of the Province of Texas in December 1716, was appointed to lead the next expedition into Texas in April 1718. His goal was to establish a mission and presidio on the San Antonio River and then to deliver supplies to the East Texas missions. His instructions specifically directed that he use the best-traveled roads, have at least four Indian guides at all times, and maintain scouts in advance of the company.

Seldom did the governor follow any of these instructions. Although he carefully tracked Fray Espinosa's 1709 route from the Rio Grande to San Antonio from campsite to campsite, Alarcón attempted to find new routes beyond San Antonio and frequently became lost. As a result, the new routes he undertook were never followed by later expedition leaders. His frequent predicament at the close of a day on the road was described on September 29, 1718, east of the Colorado River, where the usually supportive diarist Fray Francisco de Céliz reported that "the saint [San Miguel] had been invoked to afford us water and a campsite, since no one knew which way we were going."

The formal instructions required that a diary be kept for the entire expedition, and this obligation was satisfied by Fray Céliz.[1] A second diarist, Fray Pedro Pérez de Mezquía, also maintained a daily account of the early part of Alarcón's trip from the Rio Grande to San Antonio and of his short round-trip from San Antonio to the junction

---

This chapter is based on two diary accounts prepared by padres who accompanied Governor Alarcón. There is no record of any diary written by Alarcón. The account of Fray Francisco Céliz, which covers the entire period of the expedition, has been translated into English by Fritz Leo Hoffmann: Diary of the Alarcón Expedition into Texas, 1718–1719. *The account by Fray Pedro Pérez de Mezquía, which covers only the period February–June 1718, has also been translated by Hoffmann:* "The Mezquía Diary of the Alarcón Expedition into Texas, 1718," Southwestern Historical Quarterly *41 (April 1938), 312–323. A typescript copy of the Mezquía diary is held in the Manuscript Division of the Library of Congress.*

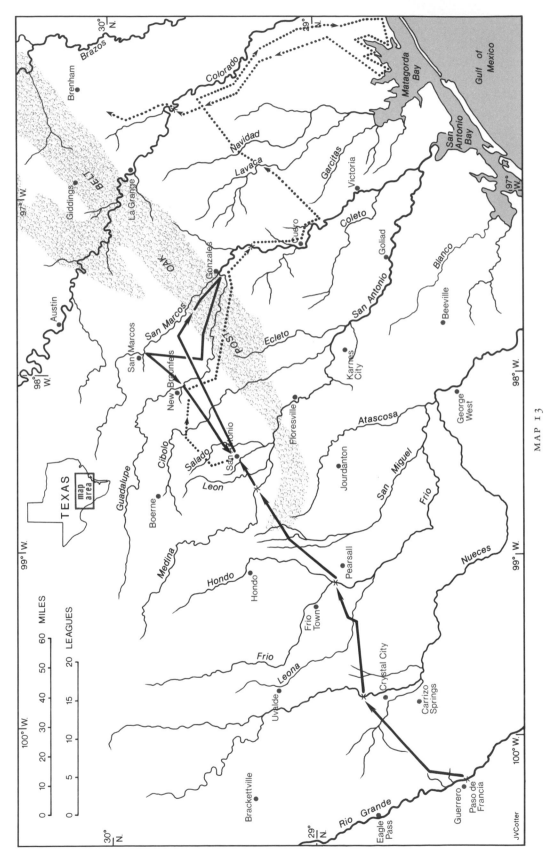

MAP 13

Governor Martín de Alarcón's 1718 Expedition, Part 1

TEXAS

map area

MILES
LEAGUES

JVCotter

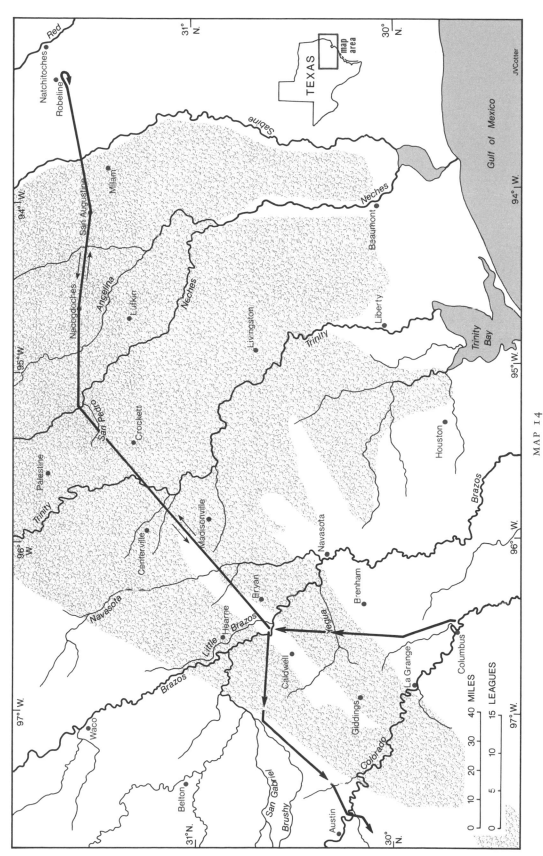

MAP 14

Governor Martín de Alarcón's 1718 Expedition, Part 2

of the San Marcos and Guadalupe rivers.[2] Mezquía's diary adds significantly to the account, with extensive supplementary information on the flora and fauna as well as comments on water control. Céliz complained throughout the tour of excessive rains, as both Ramón and Espinosa had complained of the oppressive heat during the spring and summer two years earlier.

The governor was instructed to select a site for one or two missions, in consultation with the missionaries, especially Father Antonio de Olivares. This he did. Supplies such as food, cattle, and tools were to be left at the new mission sites, as well as ten soldiers as guards. After a mission and colony (of not less than thirty inhabitants) were established on the banks of the San Antonio, Alarcón was directed to "explore carefully the San Antonio, Guadalupe, and San Marcos [Colorado] Rivers, observe how far they may be navigable, and select sites for two strong colonies to be established later for the purpose of repelling all foreign invasion or commerce." As illustrated by these instructions, the specter of La Salle still haunted Spanish policymakers in Mexico City.

Governor Alarcón crossed the Rio Grande on April 9, 1718, with a group of seventy-two, which included seven families, soldiers, and craftsmen such as weavers, master carpenters, stonemasons, blacksmiths, and stock handlers. The expedition also took cattle, sheep, goats, chickens, more than five hundred horses, and six droves of mules laden with sugar, salt, and other necessities. The horses, cattle, sheep, chickens, and pack mules probably required other individuals to drive and tend the herd. The group was comparable in size and composition to Ramón's party.

Pérez de Mezquía reported that the expedition crossed the Rio Grande on February 16 and waited until April 8 to leave the river, with the governor following the next day. The padre added that the area immediately north of the Rio Grande was covered with many wildflowers, cacti, small bushes called *rosas de San Juan,* live oaks, mesquites, and some *magueyes.* Water was available in pools in the creeks, but Mezquía commented that the quantity was insufficient for successful irrigation.

The first day, the governor followed a hilly and rough road to Real del Cuervo and camped at Las Rosas de San Juan, about 18 miles from Mission San Juan Bautista. Although the diary generally omitted a note on the direction traveled, the number of leagues reportedly traveled to the next named campsite is sufficient to mark the governor's route to San Antonio as he moved along the same road used by Espinosa in 1709, by Ramón traveling east in 1716, and by Derbanne's party going west the next year. By 1718, the road was well on its way to becoming the Camino Real that Herbert E. Bolton marked on a map compiled in 1915, entitled "Map of Texas and Adjacent Regions in the Eighteenth Century."[3]

The next day, Alarcón marched another 18 miles to El Carrizo (a spring circled with reeds) and remained there for a day to recover strayed stock. He covered only 8 miles the following day, reaching Caramanchel Creek, a rest-stop that all other expeditions had used. The spelling of the name of the creek, probably meaning a cantina in Spanish, was altered by Fritz L. Hoffmann, the translator of Céliz's diary, who substitutes a totally different word—Carabanchel—which he says is the name of a municipality 4 kilometers from Madrid, Spain. Hoffmann's annotation suggests that he was unaware that De León had given the name Caramanchel to the creek in 1690 and that the stream had been identified by the identical name by successive expedition diarists for twenty-eight years.[4] Alarcón's party camped at Caramanchel until April 14, when they proceeded 8 more miles to Los Charcos de los Encinos (Ponds of the Live Oaks).

Near these ponds, some Pacuache Indians visited to receive gifts. Governor Salinas and Espinosa had reported meeting some members of the same friendly tribe in the same general area. Nine of the Indians agreed to accompany the expedition to herd the goats, according to Mezquía. After traveling only about 2 or 3 miles the following morning, the governor crossed the Nueces River and moved on to the nearby *paraje* El Charco de Ranas, where Captain Ramón and Espinosa had camped two years earlier. The company covered a total of 10 miles that day. The total number of miles traveled by Alarcón between San Juan Bautista and the Nueces crossing was 49, about the same distance traveled between the same two points by Governor de León. Mezquía, who was an exceptionally sharp observer of the flora, noted that live oaks, willows, elms, pecans, and mulberry trees grew along the river. Map 13 places the crossing about 8 miles upstream from present Crystal City.

The next day, the party moved on another 16 miles to a small creek which the governor said had not been named earlier. He named it La Resurrección. Most likely it was a small tributary of the Leona. During the afternoon, several more Pacuache Indians appeared, and two soldiers arrived from the Rio Grande with a message from the viceroy. The governor's orders had been changed, requiring Alarcón to visit the Bay of Espíritu Santo (Matagorda) before going to the Tejas.

The governor traveled a total of 21 miles on April 17, toward La Hedionda, named for the water's foul smell. That morning, 6 miles beyond La Resurrección, the party crossed a dry Leona River near the customary crossing and moved along a level road to the overnight camp location. Both diarists call the present-day Leona the Río Frío, as did Massanet earlier.

Alarcón crossed the Frio River (still referred to by both diarists as the Hondo) the following day, after traveling only about 6 miles from Hedionda.[5] The area was described as wooded, with live oak, pecan, elm, cottonwood, and hackberry trees, some draped with large grapevines. Deer and turkeys were plentiful. The place called El Tulillo, a pond about 12 miles from the Frio crossing campsite the previous evening, was their destination on April 19.

During the next two days, the party traveled only 16 miles. They marched 8 miles on the first day, bringing the governor to Los Charcos de la Pita, and traveled 8 more miles the next day to arrive at the creek called Los Payayas. Pita was a familiar campground on the upper San Miguel used by Ramón in 1716 and by every expedition thereafter. The second creek was probably named for the local Payaya Indians. There the party rested a full day.

The expedition reached the Medina River on April 23, after marching more than 15 miles over a level road that wound among groves of oak trees. The following day, the party crossed the Medina with some difficulties, caused by flooding. However, only one cargo of sugar and salt was lost in the swift water. The thickly overgrown riverbanks were shaded with cottonwoods, elms, mulberries, hackberries, and cypresses. Before reaching the San Antonio the next day, the party crossed "the *cañón* which they call De

León" at a point about an equal distance between the two rivers.[6] Fray Espinosa had named the creek in 1709.

Céliz reported that the party found a good spring (San Pedro Springs) near the place called San Antonio on a creek about 2 miles from the river. After checking upstream and downstream for several miles, the governor determined that this spring was the best source of water in the area. It was near there that the Villa de Béjar and the Presidio de San Antonio were established on May 5. Mission San Antonio de Valero was founded about 2 miles down the creek, according to Céliz.

Padre Mezquía continued his commentary on local irrigation opportunities on the rivers crossed. The San Antonio River was swift, and the water easy to extract. Near the spring, about a half mile upstream from the crossing, the entire river could be diverted with ease. The water rose to the surface and could be directed simply by the use of a plow (*sale al pelo de la tierra y es toda obra arado*). The padre added that nearby Cibolo Creek (Arroyo del Cíbolo) already had a large area that held water.

On May 6, Governor Alarcón and the two diarists, with a party of twenty-five men and two nervous Indian guides, commenced a limited reconnaissance to find Matagorda Bay, as directed by the viceroy. The plan of the expedition was well conceived. Alarcón apparently intended to follow the route taken to the bay in 1691 by Governor Terán and Captain Martínez, traveling from San Antonio east to the Colorado River and then following it south downstream to the bay.[7] As both Espinosa (1709) and Captain Ramón with Espinosa (1716), according to their diary reports, had crossed the Colorado, a few leagues east of the Guadalupe crossing near New Braunfels, Alarcón expected no difficulty in locating the Colorado. He apparently did not know at that time that Espinosa had confused the location and names of the San Marcos, Colorado, and Brazos rivers.

Alarcón's party traveled from the new villa to the Guadalupe River, arriving on the evening of May 7. Céliz and Mezquía both noted that they crossed the brackish waters of El Salado (Salado Creek). They described the creek as thickly overgrown with poplars, live oaks, many grapevines, and blackberry bushes and noted that wild herbs also grew along its banks. Between the Salado and the Arroyo del Cíbolo, the path was overgrown with mesquites and other bushes so tall that men on horseback could hardly be seen. The party camped on the left bank of the Cibolo the night of May 6.

The trip continued the next morning to "the first river of the Guadalupe" (present Comal River), which had beautiful crystal water. Continuing another 2 or 3 miles, the travelers found the ford on the "second river of Guadalupe" (present Guadalupe River). Both diarists said that the crossing was about 5 miles above the junction of the Comal and Guadalupe rivers. Mezquía observed that here the riverbed was so deep that the water could not be extracted for irrigation.

Mass was celebrated on the morning of May 8; and in the name of his majesty, the king of Spain, Governor Alarcón performed a ceremony, by "fixing the royal standard on the location . . . [thereby taking] possession of the two rivers of Guadalupe."

The sky was overcast on May 8 as the party traveled east along a ravine toward the San Marcos River (which they thought was the present-day Colorado River). Their two local guides, fearful of the coastal Indians, disappeared into the woods, leaving the group dependent on a compass for guidance. This violation of orders to proceed with no less than four Indian guides at all times proved costly. Crossing present Guadalupe County, the expedition traveled over open, level ground, passing through mesquite thickets and live oak mottes with grapevines and dewberries. They first reported seeing many bison tracks, but later Mezquía corrected the earlier report and noted that the tracks were made by wild cattle not bison. The party camped near a creek that Alarcón named Salsipuedes (Get Out If You Can). The creek was probably a boggy branch of present Brushy Creek in Guadalupe County.

The next day (May 9), the party crossed the Gonzales County line and by noon arrived at a river they thought was the Colorado. From the distance and direction traveled and the description of the landscape given in the two diaries, it is possible to place the travelers on the San Marcos River in the vicinity of present Palmetto State Park. Fray Pérez de Mezquía reported an unusual spectacle: "There are some round pieces of white soil which rise about a foot and one-half; these move when we ride near them on horseback and even discharge some water." He thus gave the earliest known written description of the phenomenal quaking bogs or mud boils, sometimes called mud volcanoes, found in the park area.

Fray Pérez de Mezquía wrote of seeing "some poles cut with axes in this forest, and we do not know from where they might have come." He also noted seeing a large Indian village with more than 120 huts or houses. The cut poles might suggest that additional housing was under construction for the village residents; huts were typically built with arched poles and covered with hides or mats.

A short distance from the vacant Indian encampment Mezquía observed a large plain that he reported was under irrigation (*la llanada cogerá como una legua y está debajo de riego*). It is unfortunate that the padre's comments on possible Indian water control practices on the San Marcos River were not more fully developed.

On May 10, Alarcón and his party, to their great surprise, found the confluence of the San Marcos and Guadalupe rivers. Both priests described being "baffled," for it had always been believed that these two rivers, the Colorado (which they thought they were following) and the Guadalupe, "entered the sea in different places and several leagues apart." Mezquía described the area, known locally today as the forks, as "beautiful, because three plains present themselves, each consisting of about a league of level land, which reach to the river."

While exploring the area near the junction, Governor Alarcón and three men went in search of a ford on the Guadalupe. During the search, they spotted two Indians walking in the woods with loads on their backs. When Alarcón's troops called out, the Indians fled into the brush. To show the Indians that the Spaniards had come in peace, Alarcón and his men placed some crosses made from sticks with strips of tobacco leaves on trees.

Traveling upstream away from the forks, the company camped near a small lake. Early the next morning (May 11), two soldiers were sent back downriver to see if the Indians had found the tobacco; the soldiers later reported that it was gone. The party camped that night on the left bank across the river from where Capote Creek flows into the Guadalupe from the west. Mezquía listed the trees along the Guadalupe—elm, pecan, oak, mulberry, and wild plum.

On the afternoon of May 12, as the party continued upstream, Fray Céliz was surprised to see a wild black Castilian bull. He noted that the numerous tracks seen earlier were made by cattle left by De León. (These Castilian cattle were the ancestors of the wild cattle found in the area and hunted as game over a century later by the Anglo settlers.) Later that day, the party located another creek, probably Geronimo Creek, and the Guadalupe River crossing which is identified as Vado del Gerónimo on Mascaró's ca. 1807 map. Alarcón stopped to camp near the present city of Seguin.

The next morning, Alarcón apparently switched direction, away from the Guadalupe toward the north. After marching about 20 miles, the party arrived near the ford on the San Marcos River that had been used by Espinosa and Ramón. Fray Céliz recognized the crossing and the road as the one "that leads to the Tejas Indians." When he reached this ford, Alarcón realized that the river they had followed to its junction with the Guadalupe was not the Colorado. Céliz described the ford (on the present San Marcos) as wide with woods at its entrance. Without crossing the ford, the party turned around and followed the "road" back toward Villa de Béjar, traveling 10 miles southwest before a drenching rain stopped them for the night.

The travelers reached the Guadalupe River at about midday on May 14, going 10 miles over the old road thick with mud. They had crossed the same fording place on the Guadalupe safely just a week before, but it was now covered by a swift overflow. Because of the previous night's heavy rains, the river was a rushing torrent, too deep and dangerous to cross. The following day was spent attempting to locate another crossing 7 miles upstream. Finding the rocky hills too rough on both the men and horses, the party returned downstream to the old crossing above the Comal junction and set up camp for the night near the present community of Gruene.

Alarcón did not rest well that night: a premonition of doom swept over him. Céliz wrote that "the melancholy and sadness . . . was so great in [the governor's] heart, he felt . . . that the last days of his life had arrived." Alarcón thought his time was near because twenty-four buzzards had passed overhead earlier in the day.

The next morning, the river was lower, and they decided to cross. First, some soldiers with pack animals safely swam the swift stream. Then Governor Alarcón, on the strongest horse available, with a sergeant mounted behind him, entered the river. The horse carried both riders to the other side without mishap. Just as they reached the opposite bank, however, Alarcón reined the horse back, and the current swept the horse and riders downstream. With both riders still holding tight, the horse surfaced, submerged, and resurfaced. During the misadventure, Alarcón lost the buttons off his pants. Alarcón and the sergeant were sucked underwater twice. They finally grabbed cypress branches and held on until they could be rescued with ropes.

Both diarists agreed that the governor's survival was a miracle. When Alarcón's pants fell down around his feet beneath the water, a silver box containing a rosary and prayerbook did not even get wet! As reflected on Mascaró's ca. 1807 map, the upper reaches of the Guadalupe were called Alarcón for a number of years after the accident. It should also be noted that Alarcón's mishap occurred near present New Braunfels, not at Vado del Gobernador as suggested by Carlos Castañeda.[8]

After this "miraculous" event, the company continued toward Villa de Béjar, traveling about 15 miles to a high hill where they made camp near the Cibolo. On May 17, after traveling about 23 miles, they returned to the settlement at San Antonio de Béjar.

During the following month, the governor organized activities around the new presidio. Gardens were planted as well as fields of maize. The corn was lost, however, for lack of rain, and the gardens produced little because of an infestation of mice. According to Fray Céliz, the farmer/soldiers who had been especially selected for the expedition reported that irrigation there was almost impossible. This discouraging report conflicted with the earlier, more positive observations made by Father Mezquía.

Alarcón sent scouting parties out in all directions to look for Indian guides, as required for the expedition to the Tejas in East Texas. But no guides volunteered, and the local Indians refused service. In mid-June, the governor decided to return to the Rio Grande for guides and additional supplies, but no diary account of this trip is known.

Alarcón arrived back at the presidio on the Rio Grande on June 21; by late August, he had returned to San Antonio. Shortly after the governor returned, Fray Espinosa and Captain Domingo Ramón arrived in San Antonio from East Texas with Tejas guides to escort Alarcón back to their missions and the presidio among the Tejas.

On September 5, Governor Alarcón and all present took part in a formal ceremony in which an Indian called El Cuilón was given the Spanish name Juan Rodríguez and the authority as captain and governor of all the Indian nations on the road to the Tejas. Rodríguez was presented the customary baton of command. In 1721, he would act as Governor Aguayo's principal guide to East Texas from San Antonio. Soon after this ceremony, Alarcón's party began the journey to the Bay of Espíritu Santo (Matagorda Bay).

Alarcón's entourage included Captain Domingo Ramón, the governor's twenty-nine troops, an eighteen-member clerical group led by Fray Espinosa, and three Tejas Indian guides. This excursion would be the first to the bay for the veterans Ramón and Espinosa, who had pioneered the more northern route to the Colorado from San Antonio that Céliz consistently called "the road to the Tejas." For support, there were 219 horses and a total of 28 pack mules, 12 carrying provisions specifically designated for distribution among the coastal Indians. This additional support suggests that an extensive exploration of the coastal area was anticipated.

On September 5, the party traveled about 3 miles to the spring where the San Antonio River rises (San Pedro Springs); they traveled more than 15 miles farther northeast to Cibolo Creek on the following day. After marching 8 miles from the Cibolo, the party turned away from the road "which goes to Tejas," heading due east to the Guadalupe River. Captain Ramón scouted the area in advance. The governor's plan for this second attempt to find the bay was different from the first, when he became lost. This time he was to follow the right bank of the Guadalupe southeast to a point beyond its junction with the San Marcos (which he had visited earlier), cross the river below the San Marcos junction, and continue along the left bank of the Guadalupe to the open coastal prairie country. He would then turn east to the Colorado. There he planned to leave his main camp while he and a small group followed the Colorado downstream to the bay.

On September 8, Alarcón led his party east down the Guadalupe's right bank, through woods so thick that they had to use axes to open a path to lead the mules one by one. Two Indian guides immediately escaped, taking their horses. Both were local Indians, one a Muruam and the other a Payaya from San Antonio. No explanation is given this time for the guides' desertion. Apparently, the Tejas guides were unafraid, although they considered the coastal Karankawa Indians their enemy.

The next morning, while he was inspecting a waterfall, Governor Alarcón's horse fell with him. This was probably the distinctive waterfall near Seguin. After the governor recovered his horse and composure, the party continued through mesquite and prickly pear another 10 miles, seeing more wild Castilian cattle and turkeys.

The next day travelers passed some high rocky hills, probably Capote Hills, as they pushed through dense mottes of live oak, cypress, and pecan. The river was judged to be navigable, although two low falls were noted. The following day, it was necessary to use axes again to open paths as they slowly made their way downstream to camp near the junction of the San Marcos and the Guadalupe across the river from present-day Gonzales. At the crest of a small hill below Gonzales, the governor's party constructed a pedestal of rock on which they placed a cross. About two weeks later, a group of several thousand Indians found near the Colorado River asked the governor to establish a mission for them at this spot on the Guadalupe. There is no indication, however, that the location was later considered as a mission site. The party continued downstream until evening, camping at a site Alarcón named Real del Santísimo Nombre de María. Earlier in the day, the diarist had an opportunity to taste the ripe wild plums that are still found along the river south of Gonzales.

At this spot on the Guadalupe River, not far from the present DeWitt-Gonzales County line, the party spent the entire day of September 13 fording the river. First, it was necessary to open a path through the thick growth on both sides of the stream. The men then constructed rafts of logs to transfer the smaller animals that could not swim, as well as dry goods such as clothing, salt, tobacco, and other gifts for the Indians. On the evening of September 13, after the crossing was completed, the troops established camp on the left bank of the river. Alarcón named this site Real de la Exaltación de la Santísima Cruz. The governor considered this crossing of the Guadalupe and the two campsites so significant that, in addition to naming the sites, he marked the ford by carving a large cross into the trunk of a tree on each side of the river.

On September 14, the group continued downstream after crossing two creeks (McCoy Creek and Cuero Creek) to camp near the present city of Cuero. The next day, Alarcón continued to follow the Guadalupe, passing several small streams, ponds, and sloughs. He came out of the thick woods and swampy river bottom with heavy reeds to higher, open ground and camped near the DeWitt-Victoria County line.[9]

The expedition sharply changed direction the following day (September 16) to veer northeast toward the Colorado River. They traveled 21 miles over extensive, fertile plains, crossing three creeks to camp on the Lavaca River. The next day, they continued through Lavaca County 13 miles east-northeast and camped on the Navidad. The following evening, the party arrived at the Colorado River at a location below Columbus.

The governor directed the main camp to remain on the Colorado while he and seventeen men, three priests, and a Tejas Indian guide traveled to the bay.[10] The first evening the camp for Alarcón's group was near El Campo, in central Wharton County. Along the trail the next day, prairie chickens were everywhere, and they killed two buffalo before pitching camp on the right bank of the Colorado, below the Wharton-Matagorda County line. Cottonwoods and more wild plum trees were also seen along the river.

The party proceeded southeast and then veered south to Tres Palacios Bay. Near the bay the small party found more mesquite and prickly pear with some oaks and small palms. During their noon siesta, a second event occurred that was "almost a miracle," according to Céliz. While taking his nap, the governor rested on a large snake which neither moved nor bit him.

Alarcón traveled another 31 miles on September 23, going around both present Tres Palacios Bay and Turtle Bay to the shore east of present Carancahua Bay, where the party spotted two Indians. Although the Tejas guide signaled that no harm was intended, the two Indians dove into the bay and quickly crossed the half-mile-wide cove. The governor, on his brief bay tour, explored only several inlets between the Colorado River and present Carancahua Bay. Although the area had not been explored by either De León or Terán, this effort was far short of the major exploration accredited to Alarcón by Carlos Castañeda. The party camped on the evening of September 23 between Turtle Bay and Carancahua Bay.

The next morning, the party heard voices from a cove to the west. When Alarcón, the Tejas Indian guide who had conducted them to the bay, and two soldiers neared the cove, they saw first a canoe carrying several Indians and later two more Indians on shore. Alarcón's Tejas guide approached the Indians, identified by the diarist as "Caocose," making signs of peace. As they signaled for the Spaniards to leave, the Indians moved even closer to the small Spanish party. The Tejas Indian spoke in a language which the local Indians apparently understood. They seemed perturbed but nevertheless embraced Alarcón. Then more of Alarcón's party arrived at the shore to join in mutual hugs while showing other customary signs of peace. In the name of the Crown, Alarcón presented clothing and tobacco to the Indians on the shore and asked them to call those still in the canoe.

The craft was no ordinary small canoe; it held four men, four women, and eight children. When the Indians came ashore, they also were given clothing and tobacco. The Indians in turn gave the Spaniards dried fish. The Indians incorrectly thought the Spaniards intended to settle on the bay and informed them that La Salle's former fort was to the west. Soon after Alarcón took official possession of the bay, he departed, turning back northeast toward his base-camp on the Colorado.[11]

On September 26, the troops continued up the right bank of the Colorado for another 47 miles, returning to the main body of the expedition, which had moved about 10 miles upstream from the first campground. There Alarcón found what the diarist Céliz refers to as the nation of Aname Indians, who had come in search of the governor. The diarist reported that the Indians were too numerous to count. They were very proud because they had refused peace with the Spaniards on other occasions. Alarcón appointed the eldest of the Indians as governor. The Indians requested that a mission be founded for them near the former "settlement of the French." This request was indirectly granted a few years later, in 1722, by Governor Alarcón's successor, San Miguel de Aguayo.

On September 28, Alarcón crossed the Colorado near Columbus, moving north and northeast over heavily timbered hills. He halted near a stream, probably Cummins Creek, which was named San Miguel. On the following day, the governor encountered one of the largest gatherings of Indian groups reported on any expedition. The congregation consisted of six Indian nations—the Sana, Emet, Toho, Mayeye, Huyugan, and Curmicai.[12] Normally, these six tribes did not live together, although they were probably friendly. All were usually seen on the west side of the Colorado, closer to the Guadalupe, not the east side of the river. They asked Alarcón to help them return home to the Guadalupe, near the point, says Céliz, where the governor had erected the pedestal and cross and where there was a good spring, according to the Indians. They, like the displaced Aname several days earlier, asked Spanish protection to return home. But from what did they need protection? They did not say. We know only that some Indians living near the Rio Grande had earlier migrated into Central Texas to escape either the Spaniards or the Apache.

After assuring the Indians of his intention to consider the establishment of a mission at a location somewhere between present Gonzales and Hochheim, the governor traveled rapidly northeast. This movement toward the East Texas missions and presidio from the Colorado was guided by Captain Ramón, Fray Espinosa, and the Tejas guides. Céliz recorded moving 26 leagues during the next three days to the crossing of the Brazos. The trip was through dense woods of oak, plum trees, *tejocotes,* and other fruit trees, but the heavy rains continued.

During the three days (October 1 to 3) that they marched north and northeast, the party stopped at unnamed camps each evening. Alarcón continued, Céliz says, toward "the customary road which is used today for Tejas." The day before the party reached the road and crossing, they passed through several Indian camps (probably associated with the Ranchería Grande Indians who occasionally resided in the area) and found the cross that Espinosa and Ramón had erected a few leagues east of the Brazos River two years earlier.

Captain Ramón, Fray Espinosa, and the Tejas guides led Alarcón's party to the roadway near the junction of the Brazos River and the Little Brazos River. This ford and pathway east were first used on an expedition by Ramón and Espinosa in 1716. Céliz graphically describes the difficulties encountered in crossing the two branches of the Brazos, which were separated by only about 4 miles of thick mulberries, pecans, sycamores, cottonwoods, and grapevines.

Hoffmann, the translator and annotator of Céliz's diary, makes the mistake of projecting Alarcón's crossing of the Brazos at the junction of the Little River in Milam County rather than at the junction of the Little Brazos in Burleson County. The same error, made earlier by Herbert E. Bolton, was recently repeated by Elizabeth A. Robbins, who prepared the route projections for the 1991 Texas Highway Department study of Alarcón's route.[13]

After leaving the Brazos, the Tejas Indians guided Alarcón's party into a more open area where buffalo were plentiful, along a northeast route past the camp called Los

Angeles. On October 7, they moved 4 leagues to the creek called Corpus Christi, and another 5 leagues to the Buenaventura (Navasota) River and on to Lake Santa Ana. These are similar to the distances and directions that Ramón and Espinosa recorded when they named these creeks or *parajes* along the same movement east-northeast of the Brazos and Little Brazos crossing in 1716.

The next evening, they camped at the spring at Santa Clara, also used by Espinosa, where the soldiers cut many crosses on the trees. (The camp was later called Las Cruces.) The party continued along the route called *el camino* taken by Espinosa and Ramón, using the same campsites past San Luis Obispo and Santa Rosa to the Trinity.

Beyond the Trinity, the party continued east through *castaño* and pine toward the next extended rest-stop at Mission La Purísima Concepción on October 15. En route, Alarcón stopped at a frequently used *paraje* near Santa Coleta creek and traveled past the 1690 location of the Mission San Francisco de los Tejas. The pathway beyond the old mission site had been extended by Ramón across the Neches River to the new presidio location in 1716 and to Mission Nuestra Señora de San Francisco. Near the presidio, the local Tejas Indians joyously welcomed the governor, smoked their pipe of peace with him, and decorated him with a feather headdress.

Between October 16 and November 3, the governor remained in the mission area, meeting local Indian leaders, including representatives of the Bidai nation, who lived closer to the coast along a pathway that ran toward the junction of Bedias Creek and the Trinity. During the two-week period, the governor dispensed colorful clothing to the Indians and smoked other peace pipes. He met Indians armed with more muskets (acquired from the French) than his soldiers possessed; the locals had exchanged horses and skins for the weapons. He also met an Indian woman interpreter (probably Angelina), who, at the governor's insistence, moved near his encampment.

By November 4, Alarcón was ready to proceed to Los Adaes near the Red River. He accomplished this movement in a week. The Spaniards visited Nuestra Señora de Guadalupe on the first day, reached Mission Dolores on November 6, crossed the Sabine River three days later, and arrived at San Miguel de los Adaes on November 10.[14] An advance guard was sent farther east to visit the small French settlement of Natchitoches, but the sergeant reported finding only twenty inhabitants. However, the governor noted two Frenchmen among the local Indians near Los Adaes. The Frenchmen, according to Céliz, facilitated the exchange of local young Indian slaves for French-made muskets, powder, bullets, and clothing. This report of trafficking in Indian slaves by the French was noted with disdain but not with shock.

The governor remained in the Adaes and East Texas area until November 28, but Céliz gives no diary account of the exact locations visited or revisited. A diary entry for November 29 indicates that the party returned to the San Pedro Creek area in present Houston County, where De León had established the Tejas mission in 1690.

No diary account of Alarcón's return trip to San Antonio is known, and Céliz's account gives only highlights. In reporting the names of the rivers crossed on the return trip, the diarist used the original names given by De León rather than those used in 1709 and 1716 by Espinosa when he confused the names of the rivers.

At a place called San Pedro de los Navitochos, the governor's soldiers uncovered the church bell that the Spaniards had hidden when they left earlier. Shortly thereafter, the governor suffered an unfortunate accident in crossing the swollen Trinity. A raft sank, carrying the governor's African-American cook, kitchen, clothing, and silver service under the water. Only the cook was rescued. The incident gives us a glimpse of the lifestyle of governors who pioneered the early Texas trails.

Alarcón's party crossed the Brazos River (which Céliz, correctly at that time, called the Colorado) and moved through the Monte Grande. The diarist commented that the name for the densely wooded thicket was appropriate since "it is necessary to bring a guide in order to go through it, because it is so wooded and entangled." Céliz made no mention that the party followed any road. To the contrary, he described the Monte Grande as an area so heavily forested that any pathway cut on an expedition would likely be overgrown before any following expeditionary party could arrive.

The expedition left the woods, crossed Brushy Creek (Las Animas), and approached the Colorado River (called San Marcos). Apparently, Alarcón had followed the route that Rubí later referred to as the Xavier Road, although Alarcón does not refer to it by name. Immediately after crossing the Colorado, Alarcón found the Garrapatas (Onion Creek), which means that the party crossed the Colorado at the customary ford crossing a few miles below Austin, rather than downstream near Bastrop or La Grange. He then crossed the Blanco (called San Rafael) and the San Marcos. Céliz said that the river that the Blanco runs into was formerly called the San Marcos (the name used by Espinosa and Alarcón, mistakenly thinking they were on the current Colorado), but that Alarcón renamed it Los Inocentes. Next was the Alarcón (present upper Guadalupe) River, where the diarist said the governor sighted the cypress branch that had saved his life when he almost drowned on May 16. The party crossed the present Comal and shortly thereafter returned to the Mission of San Antonio de Valero. Céliz noted that nearby there were many Xarame, Payaya, and Pamaya who had been brought to the mission by an officer serving the governor. No exact date of return to New Spain is given, but the diary notes suggest that it was early January 1719. Céliz's diary closes at this point.

Alarcón returned to Mexico later in 1719. He was thanked by the Crown and relieved from office in November of that year.[15]

TABLE 7
Governor Martín Alarcón's 1718 Expedition

Date	Distance Leagues (Miles)	Direction	Campsite (COUNTY)
4/9	7 (18.2)	—	Las Rosas de San Juan (MAVERICK) [1]
4/10	7 (18.2)	—	El Carrizo (DIMMIT) [1]
4/11	—	—	(Remained in camp to recover stock)
4/12	3 (7.8)	—	Arroyo Caramanchel (Comanche Creek, ZAVALA) [1]
4/13	—	—	(Remained because of rain)
4/14	3 (7.8)	—	Los Charcos de los Encinos (ZAVALA) [1]
4/15	4 (10.4)	—	El Charco de Ranas (Tortuga Creek, ZAVALA) [1]
4/16	6 (15.6)	—	La Resurrección (Leona River, FRIO) [1]
4/17	8 (20.8)	—	La Hedionda (near Frio River, FRIO) [1]
4/18	2.5 (6.5)	—	Arroyo Hondo (Frio River, FRIO) [1]
4/19	4.5 (11.7)	—	El Tulillo (FRIO) [1]
4/20	3 (7.8)	—	Los Charcos de la Pita (near Frio-Medina County line) [1]
4/21	3 (7.8)	—	Arroyo los Payayas (MEDINA) [1]
4/22	—	—	(Rain delay)
4/23	6 (15.6)	—	Río Medina (Medina River) [1]
4/24	—	—	Río Medina (Medina River) [1]
4/25	6 (15.6)	—	Río San Antonio (San Antonio River, BEXAR) [1]

[Governor Alarcón remained near San Antonio until May 6.]

Date	Distance Leagues (Miles)	Direction	Campsite (COUNTY)
5/6	8 (20.8)	—	Arroyo Cíbolo (Cibolo Creek, Bexar-Guadalupe County line) [1]
5/7	7 (18.2)	—	Río Guadalupe (Guadalupe River, COMAL) [1]
5/8	10 (26)	E	Arroyo Salsipuedes (GUADALUPE) [2]
5/9	10 (26)	—	Arroyo Entraaverlo (near San Marcos River, Gonzales-Caldwell-Guadalupe County line) [2]
5/10	6 (15.6)	—	Río Guadalupe (Guadalupe River, GONZALES) [1]
5/11	10 (26)	—	Río Guadalupe (Guadalupe River, GONZALES) [2]
5/12	12 (31.2)	—	(Guadalupe River, GUADALUPE) [3]
5/13	13 (33.8)	—	(Comal-Hays County line) [2]
5/14	4 (10.4)	—	Río Guadalupe (about 5 miles above New Braunfels) [1]
5/15	6 (15.6)	—	(Returned to May 14 location) [1]
5/16	6 (15.6)	—	(Near Comal-Guadalupe County line) [1]
5/17	9 (23.4)	—	Río San Antonio (San Antonio River, BEXAR) [1]

[Between May 17 and September 5, the governor returned to the Rio Grande for Indian guides and supplies, but no daily diary account is given.]

Date	Distance Leagues (Miles)	Direction	Campsite (COUNTY)
9/5	1 (2.6)	—	Río San Antonio (San Antonio River, BEXAR) [1]
9/6	6 (15.6)	—	Arroyo Cíbolo (Cibolo Creek) [1]
9/7	8 (20.8)	E	Río Guadalupe (Guadalupe River, COMAL) [1]
9/8	5 (13)	E	Río Guadalupe (Guadalupe River, GUADALUPE) [1]
9/9	4 (10.4)	E	Río Guadalupe (Guadalupe River, GUADALUPE) [1]
9/10	6 (15.6)	—	Río Guadalupe (Guadalupe River, GUADALUPE) [1]
9/11	7 (18.2)	E	Río Guadalupe (Guadalupe River, GONZALES) [1]
9/12	6 (15.6)	E	Real del Santísimo Nombre de María (Guadalupe River near Gonzales-DeWitt County line) [1]
9/13	—	—	Real de la Exaltación de la Santísima Cruz (Guadalupe River near Gonzales-DeWitt County line) [1]
9/14	5 (13)	—	(Near Cuero, DEWITT) [1]
9/15	7 (18.2)	—	(Near Thompson, DeWitt-Victoria County line) [1]
9/16	8 (20.8)	NE	(Lavaca River, LAVACA) [2]
9/17	5 (13)	—	(Navidad River, LAVACA) [2]
9/18	10 (26)	ENE	Río San Marcos (Colorado River, south of Columbus, COLORADO) [1]
9/19	11 (28.6)	ESE	(West of Colorado River, WHARTON) [2]
9/20	6 (15.6)	ESE	Río San Marcos (Colorado River, WHARTON) [2]
9/21	10 (26)	ESE	(Near Colorado River, MATAGORDA) [2]
9/22	12 (31.2)	SE	(Near Tres Palacios Bay, MATAGORDA) [2]
9/23	12 (31.2)	—	Bahía Espíritu Santo (Matagorda Bay, JACKSON) [2]
9/24	10 (26)	NE	(JACKSON) [2]
9/25	16 (41.6)	N	Río San Marcos (Colorado River near Wharton-Colorado County line) [2]
9/26	18 (46.8)	N, NW	Río San Marcos (Colorado River near Columbus) [2]
9/27	—	—	(Camp prepared for continuation of expedition)
9/28	4 (10.4)	NE	(Near Cummins Creek, COLORADO) [2]
9/29	8 (20.8)	N	Arroyo San Gerónimo (near Cummins Creek, COLORADO) [2]
9/30	3 (7.8)	—	(Indian camp near Cummins Creek, COLORADO) [2]
10/1	10 (26)	NE	(Unnamed camp, WASHINGTON) [2]
10/2	8 (20.8)	N	(Unnamed camp, BURLESON) [2]
10/3	8 (20.8)	N	San Francisco (near Brazos junction with Little Brazos, BURLESON) [1]
10/4	—	—	(Cleared roadway)
10/5	7 (18.2)	ENE	Río Colorado y Los Angeles (Little Brazos River camp, east of crossing, BRAZOS) [1]
10/6	1 (2.6)	—	(Delayed by rain)
10/7	9 (23.4)	ENE	Lago Santa Ana (lake east of Navasota River, MADISON) [1]
10/8	10 (26)	ENE	Santa Clara or Las Cruces (near Centerville, LEON) [1]
10/9	7 (18.2)	ENE	Arroyo Santa Rosa (creek near Trinity, LEON) [1]
10/10	5 (13)	ENE	Río Trinidad (Trinity River, LEON) [1]

Date	Distance Leagues (Miles)	Direction	Campsite (COUNTY)
10/11	—	—	(Crossed Trinity River)
10/12	—	—	(Crossed Trinity River)
10/13	12 (31.2)	NE	Arroyo Santa Coleta (near Crockett, HOUSTON) [1]
10/14	12 (31.2)	NE	Nuestro Padre San Francisco (about 5 miles east of Neches River, NACOGDOCHES) [1]
10/15	8 (20.8)	ENE	Misión La Purísima Concepción (near Angelina River, HOUSTON) [1]

[Alarcón remained in the Mission Concepción general area between October 16 and November 3.]

Date	Distance Leagues (Miles)	Direction	Campsite (COUNTY)
11/4	10 (26)	NE	Nuestra Señora de Guadalupe (near Nacodoches, NACOGDOCHES) [1]
11/5	15 (39)	NE	Río Todos Santos (identity of creek uncertain) [2]
11/6	6 (15.6)	—	Misión Dolores (Mission Nuestra Señora de los Ais, near San Augustine, AUGUSTINE) [1]
11/7	—	—	(Remained in camp to confess)
11/8	14 (36.4)	ENE	(Unnamed creek, west of Sabine River, SABINE) [2]
11/9	13 (33.8)	ENE	(Unnamed camp east of Sabine River) [2]
11/10	15 (39)	ENE	San Miguel de los Adaes (near Robeline, Louisiana) [1]

[Governor Alarcón remained in the area between the Red River and the Trinity until November 28, when he commenced his return journey to San Antonio. No daily diary account of the return route is given.]

FIGURE 9
*Aguayo takes formal possession of the site of La Salle's former fort on Garcitas Creek,
where he erected the first Presidio La Bahía in 1722.*

NINE

BACK TO THE BAY

Governor Marqués de San Miguel de Aguayo's
1721–1722 Expedition

Governor Marqués de San Miguel de Aguayo was directed by the Crown in 1720 to lead a large *entrada* to Texas to reassert Spanish dominion over the province. Four years earlier, Captain Ramón and Fray Espinosa had established a limited presence in East Texas by constructing a presidio and missions there, and Governor Alarcón had resupplied and augmented that effort in 1718. But that presence was hastily withdrawn when the lightly armed Frenchman Commandant Philippe Blondel approached the Spanish establishments in 1719, shortly after war was declared between Spain and France.[1] After that, the Spaniards restricted their presence on the northeastern frontier to San Antonio. Now things were about to change again. Aguayo would reassert the Spanish claim by carrying the flag back to East Texas and planting it beside several new missions and a presidio at Adaes.

Aguayo was the appropriate man to defend the honor of Spain and reclaim the northeastern part of the Province of Texas that France had so boldly occupied. He was a recognized leader in northeastern New Spain and owned a large part of it. His family holdings extended from the area near Parral in Vizcaya 300 miles northeast to an area near Saltillo.[2]

In October 1720, while awaiting supplies and additional troops in Monclova, the governor was notified that a treaty had resolved the immediate differences between France and Spain. However, the French still held East Texas. So, according to plan, Aguayo's troops marched northeast toward Texas on November 16.

This chapter is based on two English translations of Padre Juan Antonio de la Peña's diary of the expedition. There is no record of a diary account written by Governor Aguayo or other member of the expedition. The first translation is Peter P. Forrestal, "Peña's Diary of the Aguayo Expedition," Preliminary Studies of the Texas Catholic Historical Society *2, no. 7 (January 1935), 3–68. The second translation (richly annotated) is Richard G. Santos,* Aguayo Expedition into Texas, 1721: An Annotated Translation of the Five Versions of the Diary Kept by Br. Juan Antonio de la Peña. *A sixth manuscript copy of Peña's diary not considered by Santos (but adding little) held in the Manuscript Division of the Library of Congress was also consulted.*

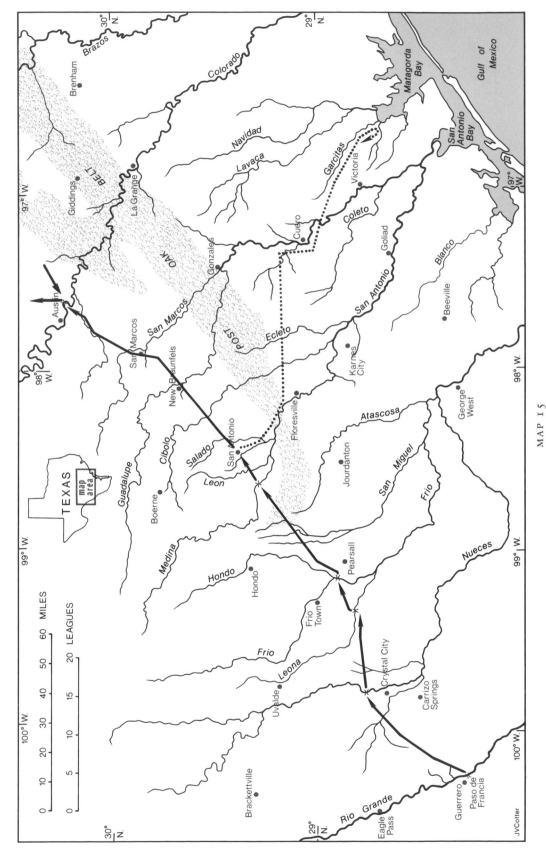

MAP 15

Governor Marqués de San Miguel de Aguayo's 1721–1722 Expedition, Part 1

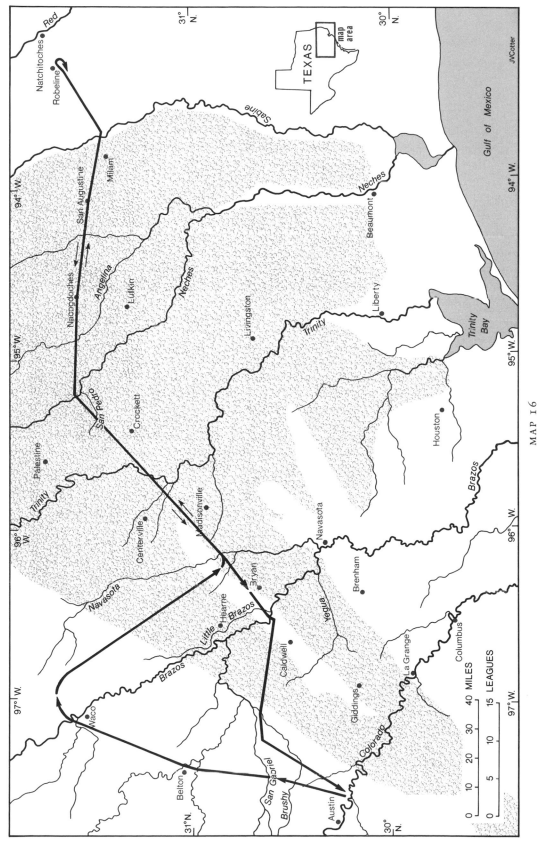

MAP 16

Governor Marqués de San Miguel de Aguayo's 1721–1722 Expedition, Part 2

The expedition traveled over the customary route (now called the Camino Real) from Monclova to the Rio Grande near San Juan Bautista, where the ecclesiastical delegation, including Juan Antonio de la Peña, was met. Peña, as diarist for the expedition,[3] noted that there was no need to give a daily account of the itinerary between Monclova and San Juan Bautista because the route called the Camino Real was well known. He did comment that the actual distance traveled from Monclova to the Sabinas River was 25 leagues and that the same distance was covered between the Sabinas and the Rio Grande. These distances are within a few leagues of those reported between the same two points by Salinas.

The group of padres who joined the expedition at the river included the remarkable Fray Espinosa. Espinosa was president of the Texas missions and the ranking clerical official; this was his third *entrada*. He could help guide the expedition because the plan was to follow the route that the padre had established from the Rio Grande to San Antonio and on to the Colorado and then (after circling modern Waco) pick up his route again in Brazos County near the Navasota River crossing to East Texas.

The crossing of the Rio Grande was accomplished in stages, with the fording of the baggage and animals occurring between January and March 1721. Snow and heavy frosts delayed the crossing effort; brandy, supplied by the governor, braced the fifty "Nadadores" who took turns swimming the barges across.[4] Peña's account of the crossing does not include the exact dates on which snow fell on the Rio Grande, but it appears to have occurred intermittently during January and February. Although snow and prolonged freezing conditions along the lower Rio Grande are rare today, the climate during the Little Ice Age was cooler and damper. Alonso de León (the elder) described the winter in Nuevo León as bitter cold in the mid-1600s. He said that it froze in November, snowed in December and January, and froze harder in February and March, adding that in the countryside snow covered the trees for a day and in the mountains it lasted for more than two months.[5]

During the crossing in early February, the marqués received word from the captain of the presidio in San Antonio that some friendly Sana Indian scouts had reported that Saint-Denis and other Frenchmen were near the Brazos above the Camino de Tejas, meeting with the Indians of the Ranchería Grande and other local Indians. In response to this report, the governor dispatched two companies (a total of 116 men) to San Antonio to protect the community.

On March 24, the leaders and eight companies moved north of the Rio Grande, each company having 350 horses, 600 head of cattle, and 800 sheep. The party first traveled through mesquite brush and good pasture a short distance along the road to Cuervo and finally camped at Las Rosas de San Juan. For the next two days, Aguayo remained at the campsite to regroup and recover some lost horses.

On Thursday, March 27, the camp proceeded about 23 miles northeast to a location called Ojo de Agua de San Diego. This campsite had been used by Ramón and Espinosa on May 1, 1716, on their trip from the Rio Grande to the San Antonio area and East Texas. Aguayo's entourage reached Caramanchel (Comanche Creek) on Friday, after marching another 13 miles to the northeast.[6] Peña, who was an avid reporter of wild game, saw near the creek wild turkeys (*guajolotes*), quail (*codornices*), jackrabbits, and cottontails.

A short move the next day brought the troops to the Nueces crossing. The 50-mile journey northeast between the Rio Grande and the Nueces was approximately the same distance and direction traveled by earlier explorers on previous occasions. The crossing is identified on Map 15 about 8 miles north of Crystal City.

After crossing the Nueces, Aguayo moved 8 miles northeast to La Tortuga.[7] This campsite near the headquarters of the present-day Tortuga Creek in central Zavala County had also been used on other expeditions, including the one led by his immediate predecessor, Governor Alarcón. Turkeys, quail, and another bird called an Indian turkey (*pavo de las Indias*, probably wild turkey or prairie chicken) were reported in the flat pasture near Tortuga. On Sunday, Aguayo marched another 16 miles east-northeast to Las Encinas del Río Frío. (Map 15 shows that the camp was located on present Leona River near the Zavala-Frio County line.) The diarist added that the river (the Leona) was also called the River of the Dead (Río de los Muertos).

On March 31, the party turned east-southeast along the Leona, and Governor Aguayo found a crossing about 7 miles downstream.[8] After crossing the Leona, the party continued along its left bank to a location he called Los Gatos, a camp not mentioned on prior expeditions. They traveled a total of 16 miles that day and spotted more deer, turkeys, quail, and rabbits along the way.

On Tuesday, April 1, the governor left the Leona River, traveling east-northeast, and reached the customary Frio (called Hondo) River crossing west of present-day Pearsall after a short march of only 7 miles. April wildflowers were in bloom, wildlife was plentiful, and heavy rains commenced that fell intermittently until June. Deer, antelope, wild goats (*cabras montesas*), turkeys, cottontail rabbits (*conejos*), and quail were seen repeatedly that day. The diarist made no further comment on the wild goats, which were not reported on any other expedition.

From this crossing area (used by De León and every expedition other than Terán's), the party changed direction from east-northeast to north-northeast, following Fray Espinosa's road to San Antonio. The party passed a previously unreported place, Las Cruces, and passed the campground El Tulillo along the San Miguel, after traveling northeast a total of 18 miles. On Wednesday, they moved only 8 miles northeast to El Charco de la Pita, a *paraje* named by Espinosa and Ramón in 1716.

The troops reached the Medina River the following day (April 3), after marching 23 miles north-northeast. As a careful observer, Peña also noted large grapevines with clusters of green grapes along the path; one vine reportedly measured 3 feet (*una vara*) in circumference, matching the size of the vine that Espinosa measured and recorded in the same area in the spring of 1716. The highlight of this day, however, was a roundup of over 300 deer and antelope (*venados y berrendos*);[9] the mounted soldiers captured two deer, having driven them into their own "spooked" horse herd. The men also saw many turkeys and quail in the area.

While camped on the north bank of the Medina, the diarist noted that the *entrada* was entering the Province of the Tejas Indians, which was separated from the Province of Coahuila to the south by the Medina River. The party marched 8 miles to Leon Creek, then 8 more to the Villa and Presidio of San Antonio de Béjar and the nearby Mission of San Antonio de Valero.[10]

During his trip from the Rio Grande, the governor had ordered the dispatch of forty soldiers, stationed at Béjar under Captain José Domingo Ramón, to secure the Espíritu Santo Bay area. The captain had retreated with his troops to Béjar from East Texas in 1719. The Ramón detachment had left San Antonio on March 10 for the bay, but the governor had received no word from the unit by the time he reached San Antonio on April 4. On April 18, however, an officer and four soldiers, dispatched from the bay by Captain Ramón, arrived in San Antonio to report that the bay was secured. The delay in sending word had been caused, the officer said, by two unidentified swollen rivers; Ramón's trip to the bay had therefore taken over a month to complete.

The four-week trip may have been required, in part, because the captain had led his troops along the route to the bay that Alarcón had followed in 1718: first southeast, encountering high water on the Guadalupe and Lavaca rivers, before he reached the right bank of the Colorado River and then followed that river downstream south to the bay. Ramón's officer, however, had shortened this long, roundabout route on his return to San Antonio. It had taken him only five days to return from the bay, which he reported with accuracy as only about 150 miles from San Antonio. With the assurance that Matagorda Bay was secure, Governor Aguayo decided to resupply the *entrada* by ship from Veracruz to the bay. This marine resupply operation had proved successful for Terán in 1691, thirty years earlier.

While Captain Ramón commenced his work at the bay, Aguayo initiated a march to East Texas on May 13, following the route from San Antonio taken first by Espinosa (1709) then by Espinosa and Captain Ramón (1716): north-northeast to the Colorado crossing below Austin. If there was a road to the Tejas between San Antonio and the Colorado, it had to be the one traveled by the expeditions led by Espinosa (1709), Ramón (1716), and now Aguayo—with Rivera to follow in 1727—all four crossing the Colorado near Onion Creek a few miles below Austin. This early road to the Tejas crossed the Colorado over 30 miles upstream from the Bastrop crossing of the Old San Antonio Road marked by Stephen F. Austin on his map for the Anglo colonists in the nineteenth century. Espinosa, who had pioneered the route with Indian guides from San Antonio in 1709, was available again to serve as a guide to Aguayo along with the Indian guides.

The statement made by Eleanor C. Buckley (and later by Charles W. Hackett) that the Camino Real in 1721 ran from San Marcos east toward or below Bastrop is quite inaccurate.[11] The suggestion that in the 1720s there was even a continuous corridor between San Antonio and East Texas that extended through the present-day Bastrop area and then crossed the Brazos River above the Little River junction is unsubstantiated by expedition diaries, as Peña's diary and Aguayo's route illustrate.[12] Peña directly addressed the question and stated that Aguayo had been advised by a trusted Indian friend, Captain Juan Rodríguez of the Ranchería Grande, that he should not attempt to follow the earlier expeditions beyond the Colorado because of the Monte Grande, through which, the captain said, there was no road for 50 miles.

Captain Rodríguez and some of his men from the Ranchería Grande agreed to serve as guides to Aguayo, marching north and bypassing the Monte Grande between the Colorado and the Brazos. Despite repeated statements in the expedition diaries that there was no identifiable and marked road through the 50-mile stretch of the Monte Grande between the Colorado and the Brazos in the early eighteenth century, Texas historians often prefer to speak of an early Camino Real running from East Texas to San Antonio and the Rio Grande. By 1720, there was a well-recognized and frequently used route (called the Camino Real by Peña) from Monclova to the Rio Grande and on to San Antonio. There was also a known road from the Brazos crossing at the junction of the Little Brazos River to East Texas. But during this period there was only an uncertain route between the Colorado crossing and the Brazos crossing that went northeast through open prairie and mixed woods from the Colorado to the San Gabriel (Arroyo Xavier) and then southeast through an unmarked area in the dense Monte Grande to the Brazos crossing in Burleson County. This middle link in the Texas road system used between 1716 and the 1730s was called the Xavier Road by Rubí, who added in 1767 that the road had been closed by Indian raids.

At each overnight camp as the party moved northeast from San Antonio, the troops and the padres constructed a cross to proclaim their return and give notice to the Apache. Peña reported, before reaching the Salado, mature grapevines that appeared to him to have been planted by hand (*donde hay muchas cepas, como si las hubieran plantado a mano*). This report, although fragmentary, was the second account of grapevines apparently planted by hand in the area near the Salado. Between the Guadalupe and San Marcos, the party saw their first wild cattle, along with numerous deer and turkeys, and passed several dense brushy areas with mesquites, cedars, cottonwoods, pecans, and mulberries. Bison were not seen until the Colorado was crossed.

On May 19, near the Blanco River, Aguayo met a squadron of mounted Sana scouts. The Indians were dressed in the garb given them earlier in San Antonio and were armed with bows and arrows and spears.[13] They were of the same loyal tribe that sent word to the governor on the Rio Grande that the French were meeting with the Ranchería Grande Indians near the Brazos.[14]

Although Aguayo's party crossed the Colorado at the customary crossing in Travis County on May 23, the party remained near the river for another three days, waiting for the heavy rains to end. During the delay, some unidentified member of Aguayo's party estimated, and Peña reported, that their camp was located at 30° latitude, a reading that missed the mark by only a few minutes. The location according to the current USGS topographical map is about 30°10' to 15'.[15] As noted, the flooded condition of the Brazos and the size of the convoy prevented the governor from traveling east to the ford at the junction of the Brazos and the Little Brazos River, the crossing used by Ramón and Alarcón. Moreover, Peña explained that the governor's convoy, including baggage, was so massive that it was impossible for the expedition to cross the Monte Grande. He added that the passage was difficult even for Indians, "who carried little" and were acquainted with the area.

Aguayo, therefore, marched slowly north from the Colorado into the more open prairie, well above the swollen rivers and far west and north of the Monte Grande. Peña warned that travel in this open prairie was very dangerous because it bordered on the Lomería Grande, the hill country northwest of present-day Austin that was controlled by the Apache. Within twenty years, the threat from the Apache and other Indian tribes would close this northern route. Each day, as the large and well-armed convoy moved slowly across the prairie, troops were detached to hunt buffalo and wild cattle.

On May 27, Aguayo's party proceeded through the continuing rain past Las Animas creek (Brushy Creek) to camp on the San Gabriel River. Continuing to move north on May 31, they reached the Little River, which the diarist correctly called Espíritu Santo or a branch of the Brazos. A sudden thunderstorm struck the camp and lightning cracked the flagpole, barely missing a soldier and his wife and two children. This was the diarist's first reference to a family in the convoy.

In the entry for the same day (May 31), Peña compared their crossing location on the Little River with the customary crossing location on the Brazos used along "the old road" to the Tejas. The other crossing was below the junction of the San Xavier and the Animas with the Brazos, which made it impassable most of the year due to autumn and winter rains.

The location of the crossing of the Little River in Bell County used by Aguayo can be identified with some accuracy, as it was close to the point where the river divides into three branches near present Temple. The streams were still rising, so the crossing was delayed until June 5. The size of the *entrada* made fording each creek a major operation and often slowed the daily movements to no more than 8 to 10 miles. Frequent buffalo hunts for sport or food to serve the large contingent also caused delays.

Beyond the Little River, the convoy continued north about 40 miles, still regularly reporting mesquite brush, to near present Waco, where the party crossed the Brazos on June 18. Peña referred to the river as the Espíritu Santo, the name given it by De León, and noted that it was also called the Brazos de Dios.

The party veered first northeast then southeast after crossing the Brazos and entered the dense woods between the Brazos and the Navasota on June 24. Several days before entering the heavily wooded area, the expedition party encountered its last herds of bison and killed a large number. The governor killed four during the three hunts he joined; the loss for the Spaniards was one horse killed, two wounded.

The party moved southeast to reach the ford of the Navasota (Arroyo San Buenaventura) on July 4.[16] A further delay was required to construct a bridge across this large stream. After the crossing, the party veered back to the northeast and marched to Lake Santa Ana, the *paraje* first used and named by Ramón and Espinosa in 1716 and used later by Alarcón traveling northeast from the junction of the Brazos and Little Brazos rivers. Peña recorded that their party had finally reached "the road to Texas ordinarily traveled."

Near the crossing of the Navasota, the soldiers found two young jaguar or *tigre* cubs (with their eyes still closed). Since young mountain lion cubs have spots that remain for several months after birth, it is not certain whether the troops had captured two young jaguars or two mountain lion cubs. In any case, the diarist said that they were beautiful little animals.

About 21 miles east-northeast, past Santa Ana Lake, Aguayo stopped at the customary camp called Santa Clara or Las Cruces. (Governor Alarcón's troops in 1718 and perhaps other travelers had carved so many crosses on the trees at Santa Clara that Peña thought the name was appropriate.) Two days later, on July 10, Aguayo's troops reached the Trinity River a short distance after passing Santa Rosa Creek. Espinosa had followed this same route from the Brazos to the Trinity with several identically named camps and streams passed on at least two earlier journeys: to East Texas from the junction of the Brazos and the Little Brazos in 1716 (and probably back to San Antonio to meet Governor Alarcón in 1718) and to East Texas with Alarcón in late 1718 (and again probably back to San Antonio after the French attack on the East Texas presidio and missions in 1719). Aguayo's expedition is the third one in which a diary account used the same names for the creeks and the *parajes* to a crossing of the Trinity at a point north of the ford used by De León and Salinas earlier.

Before crossing the Trinity, Aguayo turned south off the Camino Real and found some fields cultivated by the Tejas and nearby a large congregation of Indians identified as those of the Ranchería Grande, plus Indians of the Viday and Agdoca tribes who had been living near the Brazos de Dios junction. Juan Rodríguez, who was the captain of the Ranchería Grande Indians and was traveling with Aguayo as his principal guide, was happily received by his Indian friends and followers. As Aguayo and Captain Juan watched, the Indian soldiers marched forth carrying a white and blue silk flag with a *fleur-de-lis*, given them by the French. The governor, who may have been temporarily surprised at this apparent display of Indian allegiance to the French, simply ordered their banner to be lowered to a height beneath the Spanish flag, and everyone was happy. The 200 Indians—men, women, and children—filed past the mounted governor to have him place his hand on their head as a sign of their intended obedience (or at least neutrality). Aguayo promised to establish a mission for them at San Antonio when he returned there, and the Ranchería Grande Indians agreed to move out of Tejas country and back to their former location on the Brazos.

A two-week delay was required for the convoy to cross the Trinity. The first barges constructed by the troops and the local Indians proved unseaworthy. Finally, a very large canoe, crafted and used at the time of the Spanish retreat from East Texas, was secured for the successful crossing of personnel.

During this delay, a delegation of friendly Tejas Indians (and some Ygodosa) met Aguayo and Espinosa. Peña reported that the Tejas delegation, which included eight captains and four women, was delighted at the prospect of the Spaniards returning to East Texas and reestablishing their presidios and missions. One of the women who received the governor was called Angelina, whom Peña identified as having been reared on the Rio Grande and in Coahuila. Angelina again functioned as the interpreter, being fluent in Spanish and the language of the Tejas.[17]

Continuing to follow the customary route, Espinosa and the Tejas guided the governor east through forests dotted with pines, hickories, oaks, and *castaños* past Santa Efigenia Creek and Santa Clara (both familiar *parajes*) to San Pedro Creek where the first mission had been established by De León in 1690. This mission was 13 leagues (about 34 miles) east-northeast of the Trinity crossing and about 8–10 miles west of the Neches River, according to Peña's notes. In 1690, De León had reported a somewhat longer distance to reach the same mission area, perhaps because he crossed the Trinity a few leagues downstream, near or below Boggy Creek.

When Aguayo first reached the home of the Tejas, he was warmly received as a friend in an informal manner with a luncheon that included tamales, just as De León had been in 1690. The governor later was accorded the same formal greeting and welcome that Ramón had received when he and Espinosa first returned in 1716—a ceremonial smoking of the peace pipe, circulating it to everyone in attendance. This represented more than a private pact between the two leaders; it was a communal commitment to peace.

While Aguayo rested at the location of the old mission near San Pedro Creek, the Indians continued to demonstrate their gratitude by bringing presents of flowers, watermelons, and more beans. The usual custom of smoking the peace pipe was repeated, and, the diarist added, they all used the same pipe after mixing their tobacco with that of the Spaniards.

Captain Louis Saint-Denis from French-held Natchitoches near the Red River visited the governor on July 31. The purpose of his visit was to advise the governor that the French garrison intended to honor the truce between France and Spain but wished to determine the intent of such a large Spanish expedition. The governor told Saint-Denis that he must abandon Los Adaes and return with all his troops beyond the Red River to Natchitoches. Saint-Denis, however, returned to the Red River without giving any clear response to the ultimatum.

During the following four weeks, August 1 to 29, the governor and his troops reestablished a number of missions, including Mission San Francisco de los Neches (August 5), Mission Nuestra Señora de la Concepción (August 6), Mission San Joseph de los Nazonis, and Mission Nuestra Señora de Guadalupe de los Nacogdoches (August 16). At each mission location, the governor with all solemnity granted possession to a local Indian leader and the church representatives. During the dedication, the local potential congregation would gather—100 Indians gathered near Nacono on July 30, 400 on August 11, 300 Nazoni near their mission, and 390 at Our Lady of Guadalupe. The governor dressed each tribal leader in proper Spanish attire, gave clothing to other tribal members, and bestowed upon the chieftain a silver-tipped cane signifying formal Spanish recognition. In turn the Indians brought corn, squash, watermelons (*sandías*), and tamales, with a sincere pledge of friendship (not service).

The party moved along the general pathway that had been followed earlier by Alarcón, using the named *parajes* and crossing the same named creeks. They crossed the Sabine near Lake San Luis, traveled through pines, walnuts, oaks, and *castaños,* and, on August 29, reached the old site of San Miguel de los Adaes. No one was at the location. The French forces at the small garrison at Natchitoches, 7 leagues (about 18 miles) on the Camino Real east of Los Adaes, remained on their island in the Red River, as Aguayo's troops rebuilt the presidio near the roadway.

On September 1, the governor was visited by the chieftain of the Adaes Indians and about 400 of his followers. The chief welcomed the return of the Spaniards and sadly reported that when the French and the Natchitoches Indians invaded the area, the French took some of their men, women, and children captive. The Adaes had abandoned the area and now wished to return.

During the period in which the governor and his party reconstructed the Spanish presidios and missions in East Texas, a joint marine and overland supply route was reestablished via Veracruz and Espíritu Santo (Matagorda) Bay. Peña reported the news of the arrival of the chartered supply ship at the bay in mid-October and said there was a local celebration of the "discovery of so important a new route." Actually, Terán had used a marine route to bring supplies and troops by ship to Matagorda Bay to reinforce his expedition about thirty years earlier, in 1691.

About one month after receiving the good news about the resupply ship, the governor commenced his return trip to San Antonio. At the presidio he left six cannons and one hundred soldiers, thirty-one of whom had brought their families. The return trip was not described by Padre Peña with a daily itinerary because he said it "was over a route already known." Aguayo's party, reduced by its substantial delivery of personnel and goods throughout East Texas, followed "the old road through the Monte Grande," well south of his earlier route east.

This "old road" probably was along part of the route taken east by Ramón and Espinosa from the Brazos in 1716; by Derbanne, who traveled west in 1717; and by Alarcón (with Ramón and Espinosa), traveling from the Brazos to East Texas in 1718. Aguayo was told that the "Brazos de Dios offered a good crossing." With an Indian guide, Aguayo's troops marched only 3 to 8 miles each day, through rainstorms and sometimes ice, toward the Colorado. An Indian guide led the governor's party along "the 17-league journey" through the Monte Grande, confirming that there was no marked road to follow; on each trip through the dense forest, a different way was cut. Toward the end of the return trip, the officers and finally even the governor had to march on foot because the mounts were exhausted. At El Encadenado, 10 miles from the Colorado east of Austin, Aguayo was met by a resupply convoy headed toward East Texas.

On January 23, 1722, Aguayo's expedition returned to the presidio at San Antonio. No soldiers had been lost on the return trip, but the weather and wear had hit the horse and mule remuda hard. Out of 5,000 horses, only 50 returned; out of 800 mules, there remained only 100.

The governor was occupied during the next several months with organizing the efforts to strengthen the local presidio and mission facilities. On March 10, he granted possession of the new mission to Fray José Gonzales and to Juan Rodríguez, the Indian captain of the Ranchería Grande, who had served faithfully as his guide. The new mission, San Francisco Xavier de Nájera, was located between the missions of San Antonio de Valero (1718) and San José, which had been founded on February 23, 1720.

In compliance with orders, the governor planned next to construct a Spanish fort on the site of the former French settlement near Matagorda Bay. When a resupply of horses from the Rio Grande arrived, he dispatched Captain Gabriel Costales and fifty soldiers as an advance party to the bay. The governor followed with a company of forty men on March 16. The diarist Peña recorded the trip. Aguayo moved a few miles south to Mission San José and then a few more southwest to camp that night on Salado Creek.

The following two days, the party continued south to Aguila and Cibolo Creek. Aguayo covered 23 miles during the next two days (March 19 and 20); however, the second day was interrupted by a thunderstorm. Many turkeys were reported in the area. The abundance and availability of wild game in Central Texas at the time must have been impressive. Peña reported earlier that Aguayo personally had killed bison on the plains between Temple and Waco. The party camped that evening on a tributary of present Sandies Creek in eastern Wilson County.

On March 21, the party rode about 23 miles east to camp several miles north of the mouth of Sandies Creek on the Guadalupe River in northern DeWitt County. Aguayo's party set out initially the next morning toward the south along the west bank of the Guadalupe and then followed the river's course around the bend (across the river from present Cuero) and east for the final 10 miles "along the banks of the Guadalupe."

According to Padre Peña, they crossed where the riverbed was wide and covered with large stones, through about 3 feet of water, to camp on the "south side of the river." Map 15 locates the crossing on the only stretch of the Guadalupe that moves west (rather than the normal flow toward the southeast) and thereby permits a crossing to "the south side of the river" from the right bank. The crossing took place a few miles above the DeWitt-Victoria County line.[18]

After traveling the next morning only about a mile through thick woods, the party suddenly entered the open and treeless Chicolete Prairie. Peña's diary note describes this distinctive coastal area when he first reached it. Anyone who has traveled for days in heavy woods and through bush is struck by the quick change to a flat, treeless prairie. After riding across the prairie about 15 miles, the party established camp that evening near the upper Garcitas Creek.

Peña reported that the group reached the presidio Nuestra Señora de Loreto at Espíritu Santo Bay on March 24, which suggests that Captain Ramón had been hard at work constructing some facilities. The day's march of 23 miles was initially east downstream along the banks of Garcitas Creek (called Río de San José), crossing two streams (*arroyos*), probably present-day Casa Blanca and Marcado creeks. Since there has been considerable disagreement among authorities as to whether the first site of Presidio La Bahía was on the Lavaca or on the Garcitas, it is significant that the streams were described by the diarist as full (*bastante*), not as "rather deep" as translated by Peter P. Forrestal. The party then veered east-southeast toward the bay.

The governor, who had been traveling steadily since he left the Rio Grande a year before, rested here for eight days. On April 6, he drew the lines for the presidio on the former site of La Salle's colony in the shape of an octagon with a moat and tower. The king had directed that the new presidio sit on top of the site of La Salle's former settlement, and the diarist confirmed that nails, pieces of gun locks, and fragments of other things used by the French were found in digging the ditch for the foundation of the fort. Misión Nuestra Señora del Espíritu Santo de Zúñiga was also founded nearby.

Although the Spanish plan was to locate the presidio at Matagorda Bay on the site of La Salle's old settlement, the exact location of the presidio has been the subject of speculation for decades, in part because an early authority on Aguayo's trip, Eleanor C. Buckley, expressed the opinion that the presidio was located on the Lavaca River, rather than on Garcitas Creek.[19]

Some uncertainty as to the presidio's location near the bay has persisted despite Professor Herbert E. Bolton's strong effort to clear the record over seventy years ago by definitely showing that the post was on the Garcitas. More recently, Robert S. Weddle has added his convincing opinion supporting Bolton's position.[20] A careful review of Peña's diary record of Aguayo's route and the diary accounts of earlier expedition leaders confirms the assessment of Bolton and Weddle that the presidio and La Salle's settlement were on the Garcitas.

Governor Aguayo's route (as traced on Map 15) to the crossing of the Guadalupe near the Victoria-DeWitt County line is generally consistent with that drawn on Buckley's route map. From the Guadalupe crossing, however, the difference in route between Buckley's map and Map 15 is significant. Buckley's study does not provide a detailed daily account of the number of leagues and direction traveled by Aguayo during the next three days (March 22–24), shown in Table 8. A faithful tracking of the route described by Peña for the entire expedition and for these three days confirms that he was accurate in measuring distances and that a location 3 to 4 miles up the Lavaca River (as projected by Buckley) could not have been reached with the number of leagues and direction that Peña reported traveling. Whereas Buckley identifies the two creeks that Governor Aguayo crossed to reach the presidio as the Garcitas and the Arenosa, two other tributaries of Garcitas Creek (Casa Blanca and Marcado creeks) more closely fit the description.

It must be added, for confirmation, that a careful review of the diary accounts of De León, Terán, and Captain Martínez, all of whom reported visiting the Fort Saint-Louis site on one or more occasions, precludes any serious consideration of La Salle's colony or the La Bahía presidio being located on the Lavaca River. The distances and directions given by De León for his route of march from the Guadalupe crossing at Vado del Gobernador to La Salle's settlement in 1689 and 1690 are consistent only with a location of the French fort on lower Garcitas Creek, not on the Lavaca. Never did De León (or Massanet) mention crossing a large creek or creeks the size of Garcitas and Arenosa on his five trips between the two locations.

Moreover, in moving from the Colorado in Fayette County southwest to rescue the Talon children on San Antonio Bay in 1690, De León crossed the Lavaca River and the Garcitas before reaching "the old fort" on the right bank of the creek (Map 4). In 1691, Captain Martínez, on his way from the Colorado in Fayette County southwest to recover two more children, crossed the River of Canes (presently known as the Lavaca River) before reaching the old French fort on the west side of Garcitas Creek ("the creek of the Frenchmen"). Terán, later in 1691 and again in 1692, when approaching the bay from camps near the Guadalupe, made his camp near the old French fort without crossing either the Garcitas or the Arenosa, as indicated on Map 6.

Governor Aguayo departed the bay and returned to San Antonio on April 26 along the route he had followed to the coast. He left San Antonio for Monclova on May 5, arriving there twenty days later. There is no known daily diary record describing his return route. However, Peña noted that the governor's horses stampeded two days out of San Antonio at the Pita camp, indicating that he was following the same old route (the Pita Road) south from San Antonio to the Rio Grande followed first by Salinas moving south in 1693 and then by Espinosa moving north in 1709.

Although the dispute about the location of La Salle's fort and the first location of Presidio La Bahía may continue, it is clear that the presidio and mission did not remain there for long, probably only four years, 1722–1726. The removal was precipitated by a Karankawa uprising, the same type of incident that had devastated La Salle's colony, although this attack may have been more openly provoked.[21]

In 1726, the presidio and the mission near the bay were moved inland about 10 leagues to a location on the Guadalupe River. While the ruins of the La Bahía mission on the Guadalupe a few miles southeast of present Mission Valley in northern Victoria County are still standing and have been officially marked by the state, the former location of Presidio La Bahía on the Guadalupe remains uncertain. This uncertainty is seen in Father Pichardo's commentary and compilation of documents concerning the history of Texas, in which the author diligently sifts through relevant materials in search of the presidio's true location, including the question of which side of the Guadalupe the presidio occupied.[22]

Mascaró's map (ca. 1807) again proves to be helpful in resolving this uncertainty, just as it is useful in determining other locations and routes associated with crossings of the Guadalupe River. Mascaró's map identifies a Guadalupe River crossing named Vado del Tío Benítez as being located immediately below Vado del Piélago (where Rubí crossed) and well above Vado del Presidio Viejo (Ford of the Old Presidio) that served as a natural crossing between the mission on the west bank and Presidio La Bahía on the east bank of the Guadalupe. Chapter 10, which discusses the inspection of Presidio La Bahía by Brigadier Rivera in 1727, further examines the location and condition of the presidio after it was moved to the Guadalupe River in 1726.

TABLE 8
Governor Marqués de San Miguel de Aguayo's 1721–1722 Expedition

Date	Distance Leagues (Miles)	Direction	Campsite (COUNTY)
3/24	5 (13)	—	Las Rosas de San Juan (MAVERICK) [1]
3/25	—	—	(Remained in camp for Mass)
3/26	—	—	(Remained in camp to recover horses)
3/27	9 (23.4)	NE	El Ojo de Agua de San Diego (Comanche Creek, ZAVALA) [1]
3/28	5 (13)	NE, E	Arroyo Caramanchel (Comanche Creek, ZAVALA) [1]
3/29	5 (13)	NE	La Tortuga (Tortuga Creek, ZAVALA) [1]
3/30	6 (15.6)	ENE	Las Encinas del Río Frío (Leona River, FRIO) [1]
3/31	6 (15.6)	ESE	Los Gatos (Frio River, FRIO) [1]
4/1	7 (18.2)	ENE	El Tulillo (San Miguel Creek, FRIO) [2]
4/2	3 (7.8)	NE	El Charco de la Pita (San Miguel Creek, MEDINA) [1]
4/3	9 (23.4)	NNE	Río de Medina (Medina River, BEXAR) [1]
4/4	6 (15.6)	—	Río San Antonio (San Antonio River, BEXAR) [1]

[Governor Aguayo remained near San Antonio until May 13.]

Date	Distance Leagues (Miles)	Direction	Campsite (COUNTY)
5/13	4 (10.4)	NE	Arroyo Salado (Salado Creek, BEXAR) [1]
5/14	—	—	(Remained in camp to recover horses) [1]
5/15	5 (13)	NE	Arroyo Cíbolo (Cibolo Creek, BEXAR) [1]
5/16	—	—	(Remained in camp to recover soldiers) [1]
5/17	8 (20.8)	NE	Río Guadalupe y Río San Ybón (Guadalupe River and Comal River, COMAL) [1]
5/18	4 (10.4)	NE	(Unidentified camp, COMAL) [1]
5/19	5 (13)	—	Río Inocentes (San Marcos River, HAYS) [1]
5/20	6 (15.6)	NE	Arroyo San Bernardino (probably Plum Creek, HAYS) [1]
5/21	1 (2.6)	—	Río Las Garrapatas (Onion Creek, TRAVIS) [1]
5/22	—	—	(Remained in camp to observe the feast of the Ascension)
5/23	3 (7.8)	NE	Río San Marcos (Colorado River, TRAVIS) [1]
5/24	4 (10.4)	—	Arroyo San Francisco (Probably Wilbarger Creek, TRAVIS) [1]
5/25	—	—	(Delayed for buffalo hunt)
5/26	—	—	(Rain delay)
5/27	5 (13)	NE	Río San Xavier (San Gabriel River, WILLIAMSON) [1]
5/28	4 (10.4)	NNE	Arroyo San Ignacio (Unidentified creek, WILLIAMSON) [2]
5/29	—	—	(Remained near camp to hunt buffalo)
5/30	5 (13)	NNE	Arroyo San Fernando (Unidentified creek, BELL) [2]
5/31	4 (10.4)	NNE	Espíritu Santo y Brazos de Dios (Little River, BELL) [1]
6/1–3	—	—	(Waited for river to recede)
6/4	2 (5.2)	NW	(Probably Lampasas Creek, BELL) [2]
6/5	—	—	(Waited for creek to recede)
6/6	2 (5.2)	NE	Arroyo San Norberto (Probably Leon River, BELL) [1]

Date	Distance Leagues (Miles)	Direction	Campsite (COUNTY)

[Governor Aguayo waited near Temple from June 7 to 13 for scouting reports.]

Date	Distance Leagues (Miles)	Direction	Campsite (COUNTY)
6/14	5 (13)	NE	San Antonio de Padua (unidentified location, BELL) [2]
6/15	7 (18.2)	N	San José de los Apaches (unidentified location, MCLENNAN) [2]
6/16	7 (18.2)	NNE	San Joaquín y Santa Ana (Brazos River, MCLENNAN) [1]
6/17	—	—	(Hunted buffalo)
6/18	—	—	(Prepared to cross Brazos River)
6/19	2 (5.2)	N, ENE	Santa María (unidentified location, MCLENNAN) [1]
6/20	3 (7.8)	ENE	San Silverio Papa (MCLENNAN) [1]
6/21	5 (13)	SE	San Jorge (LIMESTONE) [2]
6/22	4 (10.4)	SE	San Juan de los Jumanes (FALLS) [2]
6/23	—	—	(Search for lost soldier)
6/24	6 (15.6)	—	El Real del Patrocinio de Nuestra Señora (ROBERTSON) [2]
6/25	7 (18.2)	SE	El Angel de la Guarda (ROBERTSON) [2]
6/26	3 (7.8)	ESE	Nuestra Señora del Camino (ROBERTSON) [2]
6/27	4 (10.4)	ENE	Nuestra Señora de Guía (ROBERTSON) [2]
6/28	—	—	(Rain delay)
6/29	4 (10.4)	E, ENE	San Pedro y San Pablo (ROBERTSON) [2]
6/30	—	—	(Awaited scout reports)
7/1	5 (13)	E	Nuestra Señora de la Estrella (BRAZOS) [2]
7/2	9 (23.4)	SE	Visitación de Nuestra Señora (BRAZOS) [2]
7/3	—	—	(Waited for slower units in convoy)
7/4	—	—	Arroyo San Buenaventura (Navasota River, BRAZOS) [1]
7/5	—	—	(Constructed bridge)
7/6	4 (10.4)	NE	Laguna Santa Ana (lagoon associated with Navasota River, MADISON) [1]
7/7	8 (20.8)	ENE	Santa Clara or Las Cruces (LEON) [1]
7/8	6 (15.6)	—	Nuestra Señora del Buen Suceso (LEON) [1]
7/9	5 (13)	—	Near Río Trinidad (Trinity River, LEON) [1]
7/10	1 (2.6)	—	Río Trinidad (Trinity River, LEON) [1]

[Aguayo delayed two weeks preparing to cross the Trinity River.]

Date	Distance Leagues (Miles)	Direction	Campsite (COUNTY)
7/26	4 (10.4)	NE	Arroyo Santa Efigenia (HOUSTON) [1]
7/27	7 (18.2)	ENE	Santa Coleta (HOUSTON) [1]
7/28	3 (7.8)	ENE	San Pedro (San Pedro Creek area, HOUSTON) [1]
7/29	4 (10.4)	NE	Río Neches (Neches River, CHEROKEE) [1]
7/30–8/2	—	—	(Met local Indians and Captain Louis Saint-Denis)
8/3	2 (5.2)	ENE	Misión San Francisco (CHEROKEE) [1]
8/4	—	—	(Remained in camp)
8/5	4 (10.4)	—	Arroyo Señora de las Nieves (CHEROKEE) [1]
8/6	5 (13)	—	Nuestra Señora de la Concepción (near Angelina River, NACOGDOCHES) [1]

Date	Distance Leagues (Miles)	Direction	Campsite (COUNTY)

[Governor Aguayo remained near Mission Concepción from August 1 to 14.]

8/15	4 (10.4)	ENE	Arroyo La Asunción de Nuestra Señora (Unidentified creek, NACOGDOCHES) [1]
8/16	4 (10.4)	ENE	Misión Nuestra Señora de Guadalupe (NACOGDOCHES) [1]
8/17–8/18	—	—	(Reconstructed mission)
8/19	6 (15.6)	ENE	San Bernardo (NACOGDOCHES) [2]
8/20	8 (20.8)	—	Todos Santos (AUGUSTINE) [2]
8/21	6 (15.6)	—	Misión de Nuestra Señora de los Dolores de los Adays [sic] (AUGUSTINE) [1]
8/22–8/23	—	—	(Reconstructed mission)
8/24	5 (13)	E	San Bartolomé (SABINE) [2]
8/25	7 (18.2)	ENE	Río Sabinas (Sabine River, SABINE) [1]
8/26	3 (7.8)	ENE	Arroyo San Nicolás Tolentino (Sabine Parish, Louisiana) [2]
8/27	6 (15.6)	ENE	Arroyo Santa Rosa de Lima (Sabine Parish, Louisiana) [2]
8/28	8 (20.8)	ENE	Arroyo San Augustino (Sabine Parish, Louisiana) [2]
8/29	3 (7.8)	ENE	Misión de San Miguel de los Adaes (near Robeline, Natchitoches Parish line, Louisiana) [1]

[From August 30 to October 12, Aguayo remained at Los Adaes to rebuild the presidio near the road leading to French Natchitoches, 7 lgs. east, and to dedicate the presidio. The governor commenced his return trip to San Antonio on November 17 and arrived at San Antonio on January 23, 1722. Peña gave no diary account of the return trip. On March 17, 1722, the governor continued his expedition, marching to Matagorda Bay.]

3/16	4 (10.4)	S, SE	Río Salado (Salado Creek, BEXAR) [1]
3/17	4 (10.4)	SSE	Aguila (WILSON) [1]
3/18	8 (20.8)	S, E	Río Cíbolo (Cibolo Creek, WILSON) [1]
3/19	7 (18.2)	ESE	Arroyo San Cleto (Ecleto Creek, WILSON) [1]
3/20	2 (5.2)	E	Arroyo San Joaquín (Sandies Creek tributary, GONZALES) [2]
3/21	9 (23.4)	E	Arroyo San Benito (Sandies Creek tributary, DEWITT) [2]
3/22	9 (23.4)	W, E	Río Guadalupe (Guadalupe River, DEWITT) [1]
3/23	7 (18.2)	E	Río San José (Garcitas Creek, VICTORIA) [1]
3/24	9 (23.4)	E, ESE	Presidio Nuestra Señora del Loreto (La Bahía Presidio, VICTORIA) [1]

[Governor Aguayo left Matagorda Bay and arrived at San Antonio on April 26, 1722, and returned to Monclova, Coahuila, on May 25. No diary is known for the return from the bay to San Antonio or from San Antonio to Monclova.]

FIGURE 10

When Rivera inspected Presidio La Bahía in 1727, it had
recently been moved to the Guadalupe River near present Mission Valley.

TEN

THE PRESIDIOS REVIEWED

Brigadier Pedro de Rivera's 1727 Inspection Tour

In late 1727, Brigadier General Pedro de Rivera y Villalón began an inspection tour of the presidios in the provinces of Coahuila and Texas as part of his more extensive assignment from the Spanish Crown to report recommendations on the management and adequacy of the military establishments throughout northern New Spain.[1] He was accompanied by Don Francisco Alvarez Barreiro, an accomplished surveyor and engineer, who contributed to the accuracy of Rivera's diary account and supplied his own maps and reports on the expedition. Rivera's personal diary of the expedition is exceptional: it was evidently written several years after the expedition and first appeared in printed (not manuscript) form.[2] The expedition itself was exceptional in that the leader's principal aide was a professional engineer rather than a representative of the church. This was a more secular tour with no rest days to celebrate religious holidays, as on the earlier expeditions, including Aguayo's.

The military inspection tour of the northern provinces in 1727 focused on a reassessment of the location, organization, and need for each presidio. However, the official viceregal orders (Article 24 of Rivera's instructions) also required an assessment of the entire royal asset—demanding a full description of the land, terrain, climate, vegetation, wildlife, and native population. Earlier expedition diarists reported with some diligence on Indian tribes and the wildlife and vegetation seen along the route, but province-wide assessments were not sought.

More significantly, broad contemporaneous assessments of the Indians and the forest and wildlife resources of the neighboring provinces—particularly Coahuila, Nuevo León, and Nueva Vizcaya (modern Chihuahua)—were not found in earlier expedition diaries and associated reports. This type of information adds perspective by examining the relationship between Texas and adjoining provinces. With contributing comments

---

This chapter is based on the Spanish version of Rivera's diary account of the trip; no English translation of the diary is presently available. The Spanish version used is his diary account published in 1945: Diario y derrotero de lo caminado, visto y obcervado . . . D. Pedro de Rivera.

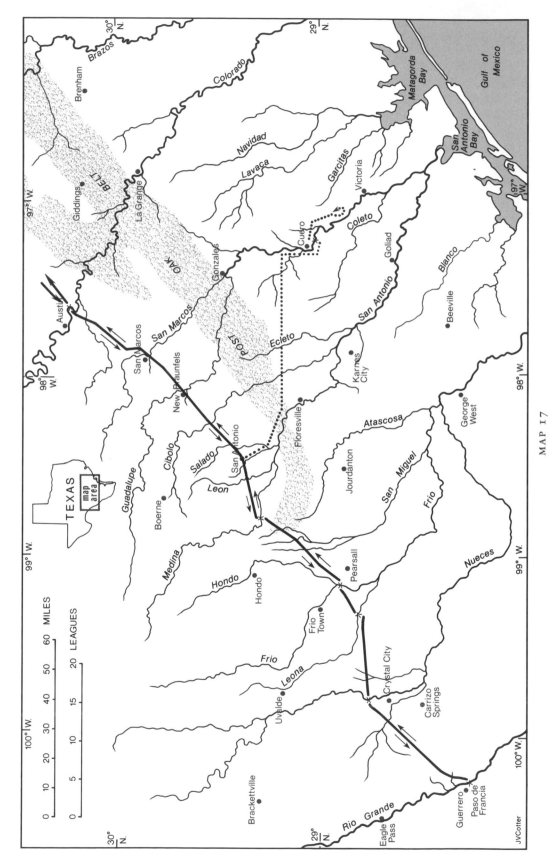

MAP 17

Brigadier Pedro de Rivera's 1727 Inspection Tour, Part I

TEXAS

map area

MILES

LEAGUES

Gulf of Mexico

Matagorda Bay

San Antonio Bay

Brazos

Colorado

Brenham

Giddings

La Grange

OAK BELT

Navidad

Lavaca

Garcitas

Victoria

Cuero

Coleto

San Marcos

Gonzales

San Antonio

Goliad

Blanco

POST OAK BELT

Ecleto

Beeville

Austin

San Marcos

New Braunfels

San Antonio

Salado

Leon

Floresville

Karnes City

Atascosa

George West

Guadalupe

Cibolo

Boerne

Medina

Hondo

Hondo

Jourdanton

San Miguel

Frio

Pearsall

Nueces

Frio Town

Frio

Leona

Uvalde

Crystal City

Carrizo Springs

Brackettville

Guerrero

Paso de Francia

Eagle Pass

Rio Grande

30° N.

29° N.

100° W.

99° W.

98° W.

97° W.

30° N.

29° N.

100° W.

99° W.

98° W.

97° W.

JVCotter

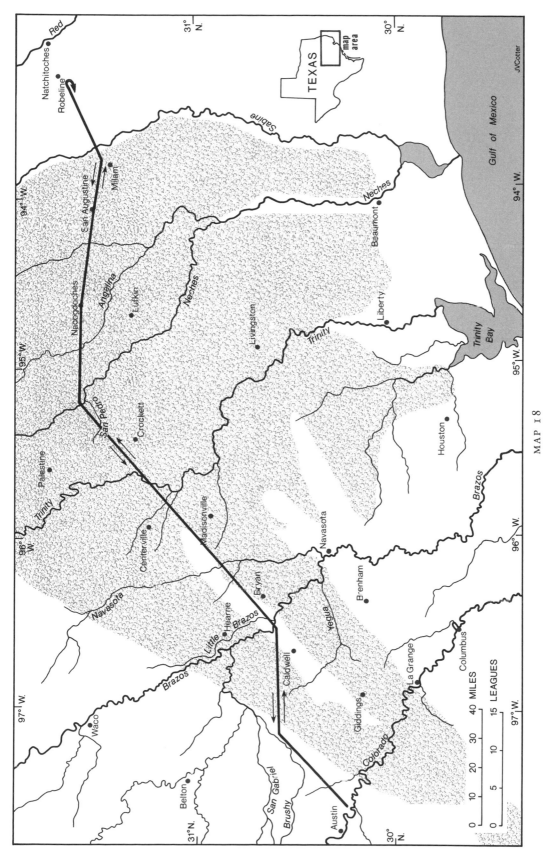

MAP 18

Brigadier Pedro de Rivera's 1727 Inspection Tour, Part 2

from his engineer Barreiro, Rivera provides one of the most exhaustive and systematic assessments of the Indian population and the vegetation and wildlife in the Province of Texas and adjoining provinces in the 1720s.

Rivera initiated his three-year, 7,000-mile inspection tour from Mexico City in November 1724. The inspection moved generally from the center of the country west to the Sea of Cortez and then east; by early July 1727, the inspection party had completed the military reviews of posts in New Mexico and Vizcaya. Moving north from Saltillo toward Texas, the party reported passing through a countryside dotted with mesquite brush to arrive at the Monclova presidio in the Province of Coahuila on July 24, 1727.[3] In Monclova, Rivera rested his horses for three days.

A small community (pueblo) of Tlaxcaltecan and Obayo Indians lived over a small hill a short distance beyond the town of Monclova. A village of over 700 Tlaxcaltecans had been reported two weeks earlier near Saltillo. (In 1692, Terán had used a guide from this same tribe to lead his expedition from deep East Texas back southwest to the Colorado.) As required by his orders from the viceroy, Rivera identified in his diary twenty-one tribes residing at the missions in the province of Coahuila. But no more than 815 Indians of all ages resided at the missions.[4] He added that some of these Indians only helped at the mission during certain seasons; when they left mission life, they went to their preferred village and "mix[ed] with an infinite number of un-Christianized Indian nations that live in the Province."

Many of the tribes named on the Rivera inspection list, such as the Pacpul, Ocane, Hape, Cibolo, Toboso, and Cacquite, had been reported by earlier expedition diarists along the Rio Grande and in present-day Texas. A Pacpul leader had served as a guide on De León's expeditions in both 1689 and 1690–1691 and on Terán's expedition in 1691–1692. The Ocane and Hape had met De León near the Rio Grande on his trips; Terán had encountered some visiting Cibolo near San Marcos in 1691. Salinas was apparently threatened by some Toboso in DeWitt County on his resupply mission to East Texas in 1693, and later Salinas secured a Spanish-speaking guide from the Saquita (or Cacquite) on his return trip from Fayette County through San Antonio. Rivera also listed the Cibolo in Nueva Vizcaya, the mineral-rich province west of Coahuila where 52,000 Indians were reported living in pueblos.

On July 17, the party marched north following downstream the Coahuila River (the present-day Monclova River), which soon merged with the Nadadores River. During the next two days, the party passed the distinct cliffs called Baluartes and camped at the old cottonwood tree (El Alamo) noted by earlier expeditions. Along the route the terrain was flat but thick with mesquite, huisache, and prickly pear. Rivera followed a route slightly west of the one taken by De León, crossing the Sabinas River upstream from the junction with the Nadadores, and continued north through the flat 50-mile stretch between the Sabinas and the Rio Grande. The last few miles of the trek were across level land covered with tall grass and a few mesquites and oaks.

The line of march taken by Rivera was about 20 to 30 miles west of the route followed by De León, Terán, and Salinas in the 1690s and did not require crossing Juan the Frenchman's Creek or Amole Creek. Rivera arrived at the Presidio San Juan Bautista about 5 miles from the Rio Grande on August 1. Near the presidio, he reported, were the two missions of San Juan Bautista and San Bernardo and an associated Indian village. The brigadier noted that most of the local Indians were nomadic.

Rivera simply noted in his diary account that there were all kinds of animals and birds in Coahuila, but Barreiro gave a much more informative account in his separately prepared description of the provinces, listing the wildlife in the provinces of Nueva Vizcaya, Nueva León, and Coahuila by name. He recorded *tigres* (jaguars), *leones* (mountain lions or panthers), javelinas, deer, antelope, lynxes, bears, wild cats, raccoons, coyotes, wolves, foxes, badgers, squirrels, cottontail rabbits, and jackrabbits. Espinosa's description of the wildlife found in Coahuila in the early 1700s includes many of the animals that Barreiro named, but also skunks, otters, and armadillos. Espinosa noted that earlier (pre-1700s) there had been large bison herds in the province but, in a critical observation, added that many of the animals had been slaughtered for just their tongue and tallow by the local Spanish residents.[5]

Rivera's expedition from San Juan Bautista to San Antonio followed closely the route taken earlier by Espinosa, Ramón, Alarcón, and Aguayo, and from San Antonio he followed the customary route to the Colorado River crossing below Austin. This was the fifth Spanish expedition along the same 300-mile route during an eighteen-year span. Some authorities, following the practice of Governor Aguayo's diarist, Padre Peña, have called the route to San Antonio the eighteenth-century Camino Real, often ignoring the earlier Spanish trail across Texas from the same crossing of the Rio Grande to East Texas pioneered by De León and Salinas late in the seventeenth century. Rivera gave no name to the route he took.

The first Spanish road, established by De León in 1689–1690, crossed the present San Antonio River near Falls City in Karnes County, the Guadalupe at the Governor's Ford near Cuero in DeWitt County, the Colorado near La Grange in Fayette County, the Brazos near the Navasota junction, and the Trinity near Boggy Creek. The road (*camino*) used by Rivera followed De León's route across the Nueces near Crystal City and the Frio near Pearsall, but then turned not east but northeast to San Antonio, New Braunfels, and San Marcos, stopping at the Colorado crossing below Austin and above Onion Creek. There was no marked road from the Colorado crossing through the Monte Grande to the crossing of the Brazos at the junction of the Little Brazos River, where the customary road—called Camino Real by Peña—east of the Brazos began.

After visiting the Presidio San Juan Bautista from August 2 to 7, Rivera's party proceeded toward San Antonio, moving first 5 miles to the east, to ford the Rio Grande by canoe at Pacuache crossing rather than at the customary Francia crossing.[6] Rivera then marched 13 miles northeast, passed an uninhabited area around Cuervo Creek, and arrived at the Rosas de San Juan campsite. From the river, Rivera was tracking the same general path followed by De León and each subsequent expedition since 1689. At the camp the next evening, "an intolerable swarm of poisonous mosquitos" awaited the troops at the water holes along present Comanche Creek (called Caramanchelito). The party tracked De León's route northeast the next day, crossing the Nueces about 8 miles above modern Crystal City and continuing 8 miles east to camp at Tortuga Creek, the same campsite used by Ramón, Alarcón, and Aguayo.

At this point, De León's earlier route had veered more to the north, above present

Tortuga Creek to the Leona River several miles west of the Zavala-Frio County line, and then northeast to near present-day Frio Town. The lower route—taken first by Espinosa and followed by each subsequent expedition including Rivera's—stopped at Charcos de la Tortuga (Turtle Ponds, also referred to as El Charco de Ranas or Frog Pond) after moving east from the Nueces crossing. This lower route crossed the Leona near the Zavala-Frio County line and then crossed the Frio River a few miles below its junction with Hondo Creek, close to or at the Frio crossing used by De León and Salinas.

Following this route from Tortuga, Rivera's party crossed the Leona to camp on the north side of the stream ("the small Frío River") on August 10. The party reached the Frio River (called Arroyo Hondo) the next day, about 13 miles northeast of the camp on the Leona. Heavy rain fell during the movement between the Leona and the Frio, an area in which the party found tall grass and numerous oaks, including live oaks.

After pausing for a day, Rivera continued marching north past Tulillo to camp at the ponds called Pita along San Miguel Creek. The brigadier was still following the path of Espinosa (1709) and Ramón (1716). Eleven years earlier, after crossing the Frio near the same ford, Ramón had moved north to camp at Pita, and both Alarcón and Aguayo also had passed Tulillo to camp at El Charco de la Pita as they moved north toward San Antonio.

The next day, Rivera passed the stream called Payayas, named for the local resident Indian tribe, after marching 15 miles, and camped on the southwest or right bank of the Medina River that evening. Two days later, Rivera camped near Presidio San Antonio de Béjar. He reported that along the river were two small Indian pueblos of Mesquite, Payaya, and Aguastaya. The Payaya, a local tribe, had been recorded as living in the San Antonio area as early as 1691 by both Terán and Massanet, the first Spanish expedition visitors to the area. Salinas in 1693 and Espinosa on his first visit to the San Antonio area in 1709 saw the friendly Payaya, who also served the padre as guides. Mesquite Indians had been reported in Texas by Ramón and Espinosa in 1716 in Frio County and in Brazos County, and Barreiro reported that they were living in Nueva Vizcaya. This was the first report of any Aguastaya by a Spanish expedition diarist.

After resting at San Antonio only one day, August 17, to prepare for the next leg of the journey to Presidio Nuestra Señora del Pilar de los Adaes, Rivera directed his party toward the customary Colorado River crossing at that time, below Austin near the mouth of present Onion Creek. The trip between the Presidio de Béjar and the Colorado River took Rivera six days. Near Cibolo Creek the brigadier noted mesquites, sycamores, wild plum trees, and blackberries. No bison were reported until the party reached the San Marcos River area; near the river a herd of 500 was seen grazing among the oak trees and mesquite brush. Rivera crossed the Colorado on August 23, near the fording area first used by Espinosa in 1709 and later by Ramón and Aguayo.

A comparison of the South Texas rivers and creeks crossed by Rivera confirms that the names of most had not changed during the 38-year period between De León's expedition in 1689 and Rivera's inspection tour in 1727. The present Rio Grande was called Río Bravo by De León in 1689 but Río Grande del Norte or just Río Grande by later explorers. Cuervo Creek was called the same; Comanche Creek was called Caramanchel; the names of the Nueces River and Tortuga Creek were unchanged; the

Leona was called the Frío; the Frio was the Hondo; and the Medina was unchanged. Continuing beyond the Medina, Rivera followed a route first taken by Espinosa to San Antonio and on to the Colorado River crossing near Onion Creek. (Terán had crossed farther south below Bastrop.) Along the route beyond the Medina, the brigadier crossed the León (Leon), the San Antonio River, Salado Creek, the Cíbolo, the Guadalupe, the Ynocentes (the San Marcos River) named by Alarcón, the Blanco, the Garrapatas (Onion Creek), and finally the San Marcos (Colorado River).

The brigadier crossed the Colorado on August 23 and marched 12 miles northeast to Encadenado, a creek and camp that had been used by Aguayo on his return from East Texas to San Antonio in January 1722. The party continued northeast through an open and sparsely wooded area with some large herds of several hundred bison for the next two days, passing first upper Animas Creek (present Brushy Creek) and then Animas de Abajo (lower Brushy Creek) before veering southeast and entering the dense woods called Monte Grande. The brigadier did not cross either San Xavier (San Gabriel) Creek or the more northerly Little River before turning southeast toward the Brazos crossing. Travel through the dense forest of oak, walnut, and live oak was hampered by numerous deep stream beds and the choking and intertwining grapevines and *cocolmecates*.

Rivera's party found a friendly village of Mayeye Indians between Brushy Creek and the Brazos de Dios crossing and distributed the customary gifts of tobacco, blankets, beadwork, and food. Four days after leaving the Brushy Creek camp and entering the Monte Grande (August 27–30) and after traveling an unmarked course of about 70 miles, circling southeast and finally again to the east, Rivera reached the *paraje* called Los Angeles near the crossing of the Brazos at the junction of the Little Brazos River "a short distance above the junction of the two streams." (The *paraje* had first been called Angeles by Alarcón.) Rivera's four-day trek from Brushy Creek and the San Xavier (San Gabriel Creek) area and then southeast through the Monte Grande to the Brazos crossing apparently did not trace closely the route of Ramón and Espinosa eleven years earlier—the daily directions, distances, and campsites are all dissimilar. The density of the woods assured that a path cut one day would soon be overgrown and disappear. However, the approach to the Brazos was through the same 20-league wooded area and was sufficiently known to be identified forty years later by Rubí as the San Xavier Road (not the Camino Real).

Over the next two days, Rivera's party traveled 36 miles northeast, through mottes of oak, live oak, and walnut trees, past Corpus Christi Creek and beyond to the lagoon called Santa Ana (both named by Espinosa on the 1716 expedition). Along the route to the customary Trinity River crossing, Rivera moved through more woods of oak, walnut, elm, and pine trees and passed the *paraje* Santa Clara and the lake of San Luis Obispo, as had Alarcón and Aguayo.

The evidence is overwhelming that Espinosa and Ramón in 1716, and all expeditions after them (except Aguayo's), crossed the Brazos at the same ford and proceeded northeast in relatively open terrain past a series of named campsites to the Trinity. The established route east of the Brazos followed an open corridor in the center of the Monte Grande that is shown on contemporary topographic maps (see *Austin,* NH14-6). Rivera's diary is significant, in part because his entries confirm that the location of the

Brazos crossing was at the junction of the Brazos and the Little Brazos, not at the junction of the Little River as projected by Herbert E. Bolton, most later Texas historians, and the 1991 Texas Highway Department study, *A Texas Legacy*.[7]

Rivera continued to follow the route of the earlier expeditions beyond the Trinity to the Neches River, passing creeks and camps used by Espinosa in 1716 and Aguayo in 1721—Efigenia and Coleta Creek—to camp at San Pedro Creek, near the 1690 mission site. On the day Rivera arrived at the San Pedro Creek area (September 5), over fifty Necha Indians arrived, armed with French rifles, flasks of gunpowder, and bags of bullets.

From the Neches, Rivera traveled east, visiting Presidio de Nuestra Señora de los Dolores (which Rivera noted was usually called Los Tejas) and arriving at the Presidio Nuestra Señora del Pilar de los Adaes on September 15. Eleven days later, on September 26, Rivera completed his inspection at Los Adaes and commenced his return west to the Presidio de Los Tejas, arriving on October 5.[8]

The brigadier described the Presidio de Los Tejas as consisting of a few insubstantial huts of sticks and grass and the Presidio Los Adaes as maintaining an excessive number of soldiers. He concluded that the former should be abolished and the latter reduced in size from one hundred men to sixty. He also noted that the French firearms (used by local Indians) were effective at long range, while the Spanish arquebuses had only a short-range capability. Eight tribes were reported living in the area near the posts—the Adaes, Aes, Nacodoche, Aynay, Nazone, Neche, Naconome, and Nabidacho. All had been noted by earlier expedition diarists except the Aynay, which may have been a variant for Asinay.

By early November, the party had completed the East Texas inspection and had returned to the San Antonio presidio. Rivera explained that the return route simply retraced the pathway they had taken east, and no daily account was maintained. The principal military impact of the inspections in East Texas was to eliminate the Presidio Dolores (Los Tejas) and reduce the troop strength of the Presidio Adaes.

Rivera next visited the Presidio La Bahía, which had been moved from its original site on Garcitas Creek near Matagorda Bay inland about 26 miles (10 leagues) west to the Guadalupe River, away from the hostile Karankawa Indians. The location of the presidio on the Guadalupe has been in dispute for decades, but the brigadier's diary account of the route he traveled to reach the fort from San Antonio is helpful in locating its site.[9] For the first several days of travel, Rivera followed Aguayo's route from San Antonio to Matagorda Bay five years earlier, and thus the brigadier's movements can be rather easily tracked (see Map 17).

On November 3, Rivera's party departed the Presidio of San Antonio de Béjar and traveled southeast 23 miles, passing Salado Creek, to a campground called Aguila (Eagle), the same camp used by the Spanish military inspector Marqués de Rubí forty years later on his trek from San Antonio south to the Guadalupe crossing. Rivera crossed the "Síbulo" (Cibolo Creek) and Cleto (Ecleto Creek) moving east the next two days through grass-covered hills with occasional live oak, pecan, and mesquite. The inspector traveled 26 miles southeast the next day to a creek he called Mezquite, a tributary of present Sandies Creek near the DeWitt-Gonzales County line. On November 7, the party continued in the same direction and struck the Guadalupe after marching about

12 miles. There they turned southeast downstream, following the "west side" of the river to camp on Robalo Creek (present Sandies Creek).

The inspector did not suggest that this camp at Sandies Creek or any other camp used on his journey from San Antonio (with the exception of Aguila) was an established campground. Parts of present-day Sandies Creek, which Rivera called the Robalo, were referred to by several different names during the early Spanish period, including Nogales and Cuchillo, probably as a result of its complex network and the size of its drainage area, which includes parts of five counties.[10] The word *robalo* refers to a species of rather large (up to 24 inches) edible fish, probably a bass found in many of the rivers and larger creeks of South Texas.[11]

The next morning, the party continued on the west side (right bank) of the Guadalupe about 8 miles downstream east-southeast to a known ford (Vado del Tío Benítez), where Rivera crossed to the east side. This crossing is identified by the name Tío Benítez (Uncle Benítez) on Mascaró's ca. 1807 map as being between Vado del Piélago (upstream) and Vado del Presidio Viejo (downstream). Rivera then followed the left bank about 15 miles (6 leagues) to the presidio. This distance places the Spanish fort across the Guadalupe from the existing ruins of Mission La Bahía (1726–1749), as marked by the State of Texas in 1938, and near the crossing Vado del Presidio Viejo, which is also identified on Mascaró's map.

The brigadier remained at the presidio from November 8 to 27, the longest period he spent at any single presidio stop. During this time, he prepared a lengthy report on the improvements to be made at the presidio's new location. He directed that the local troops, then numbering ninety, clear the river downstream for the movement of cargo by supply vessels from Veracruz and expand the cleared area upriver on both sides, where crops could be irrigated and large rocks were available for constructing more permanent presidio facilities.

Whether any of Rivera's bold recommendations were followed is unknown, but the military base and related community appears very sizable, successful, and active in the report given by its commander in 1748, one year before it was moved to its present location on the San Antonio River near Goliad.

The report, cited in Charles W. Ramsdell II's study of La Bahía presidio, is from Captain Orobio Basterra's description of a fiesta held in honor of the accession of Ferdinand VI to the Spanish throne.[12] On February 4, 1748, a formal ceremony was observed, with the fathers of "the pueblo of Espíritu Santo" and the governor present, to mourn the death of the former king. The *túmulo* was appropriately covered with wreaths, fifty candles of virgin wax were burned on the altar, drums rolled, and firearms cracked. The celebration apparently occurred in the presidial chapel, not at the mission across the river.[13] On the following day, a parade took place around the plaza with cannon volleys and drums. The royal standard was raised above the officers' quarters. With ninety soldiers, their families, and the pueblo nearby, Presidio La Bahía on the Guadalupe in 1748 was the largest Spanish military establishment in Texas.

Rivera's *proyecto,* composed after the party had departed the province, made several comments regarding Indians in the area surrounding the post on the Guadalupe. The Coco, Karankawa, Coapite, Cujane, and Copane, he said, were cowards and would cause no problem. The Tacame, Aranama, Mayeye, Pampopa, Pastia, and other nations in the area lived in isolated, but not established, settlements; they were also considered cowardly and no threat to Spanish arms.[14]

According to his diary notes, the brigadier returned to the San Antonio presidio on December 2, using the same route of 54 leagues or about 140 miles. By December 18, Rivera's party was back at San Juan Bautista, after traveling another 62 leagues or about 161 miles, following the same road and using the same campsites as on the journey between the Rio Grande and San Antonio. No daily account of the return route has been found.

Rivera offered a number of interesting comments on the Province of Texas at the close of his diary entries. He first described the boundary of the province as running between 26° and 34° latitude, as measured from the mouth of the San Antonio River where it entered the Gulf of Mexico upriver to the "Hills of the Apache" (probably referring to the hill country in present day Bandera and Kerr counties). The province extended east to the Red River.

Rivera observed bison, deer, bears (which provided fat to flavor food), rabbits, mice (which, he said, resembled small rabbits), turkeys, and fish. The catfish (*bagre*) was the most important, serving as food for the Indians most of the year.

At San Antonio, which Rivera thought had the best prospects for colonization, there were about 250 "Christian" Payaya, Mesquite, and Aguastaya Indians who lived in two mission communities (pueblos). Most of the other Indians he described as nomads who wore only a few pieces of deer or buffalo skin. The brigadier's final diary note on the Indians in the province included a list of twenty-nine Indian tribes (those "he could remember"). They were apparently listed by region, starting with tribes in East Texas and concluding with those living along the San Antonio River from San Antonio to the coast.[15] Rivera's list offers no surprises; the tribes had been identified earlier in the daily entries or reports of other expeditions.

After completing the inspection of the Presidio de San Juan Bautista on the Rio Grande in early January 1728, Rivera returned 50 leagues to Monclova and then traveled southeast to visit posts in Nuevo León. After a journey past the mining district of San Pedro de Boca de Leones and through some flat terrain with yuccas, mesquites, huisaches, and anacuas, Rivera's party arrived in "Monte Rey," the capital of Nuevo León, on February 13, 1728.[16] From Monterrey it was a short trip back to Saltillo and then south to San Luis Potosí and the post at the villa of Valles to inspect the officers and men stationed there. This was the final inspection in a three-and-a-half year tour that covered about 7,000 miles. Shortly after returning to Mexico, in August 1728, Rivera was hard at work again—this time composing his *proyecto* and then a draft of the new regulations for presidios.

Near the close of the *reglamento* of 1729, which implemented Rivera's recommendations, several significant observations and directives were included in the six articles regarding the native population. First, no officer would be permitted in the future to capture Indians during a military campaign and keep them as his own, as slaves, or give the Indian captives to others. The captives were to be sent to Mexico City and controlled pursuant to the orders of the Crown. Moreover, captured women and children should be returned to their respective parents or spouses. Requests for peace made by members of an enemy camp should be granted.[17] The effect of these orders is questionable, because similar orders (or pleas) were issued again at the close of Rubí's expedition forty years later.[18]

Rivera's expedition closed out an exceptionally active period in which Spanish expeditions were sent into Texas beginning in the early eighteenth century with Espinosa. Rivera's expedition was the last of the significant expeditions from northern New Spain that entered Texas between 1709 and 1727, but it should be emphasized that Spanish movement over many of the same Spanish trails continued.

Robert S. Weddle and Carlos Castañeda have described the march of the Canary Islanders from Veracruz, through Saltillo, to San Juan Bautista. From the Rio Grande, the captain of the presidio was directed to escort the colonists to San Antonio along the designated road that all eighteenth-century expeditions had followed—by way of Las Rosas de San Juan, Caramanchel, Charcos de la Tortuga, the Frio, the Hondo, Charco de la Pita, and the Arroyo de las Payayas to the Medina and San Antonio de Béjar.[19] However, several decades later, in 1777, Fray Juan Agustín de Morfí described a different line of march between San Juan Bautista and San Antonio that he and Comandante Croix followed. According to Morfí, Croix's party traveled east of the route followed by Rivera to stop at the *aguaje* San Lorenzo, the Ponds of Barrera, the Nueces crossing (probably in eastern Dimmit County), Las Encinas, San Miguelito (the present San Miguel Creek), Arroyo El Atascosa (the present Atascosa River) and on more northward to San Antonio de Béjar.[20]

Although five major expeditions took place from northeastern New Spain to Texas during the brief period from 1709 to 1727, according to Herbert E. Bolton, there were no Spanish expeditions from New Spain across Texas for the next forty years.[21] In 1767, however, another inspector, the Marqués de Rubí, crossed Texas to report on military conditions. Rubí's route reflected the changes that occurred in mid-eighteenth century Texas, principally the increasingly dominant role played by the Apache and Comanche Indians. The more docile and depopulated local Indian tribes, including immigrants from Coahuila—and the Spaniards—were being crowded into an increasingly narrow belt along the Rio Grande and the coast.

The numerous Apache and Comanche—comparatively healthy, well-equipped, and mounted—made the crossing near Austin dangerous and forced the reopening of De León's Road, the more protected southern route, as noted in a report by Governor Tomás Felipe Winthuysen describing the customary road used in 1744 from San Antonio to Los Adaes.[22] Carlos Castañeda also suggested that the lower route from San Antonio to Los Adaes that ran southeast of San Antonio and crossed the Colorado in Fayette County was the preferred route by the mid-1730s.[23]

This southern route from San Antonio that crossed the Guadalupe in DeWitt County near Cuero, not at present-day New Braunfels and San Marcos, and crossed the Colorado at La Grange rather than below Austin was called the Camino Real. Both Governor Francisco García Larios and Captain Joachín de Orobio Basterra, who commanded Presidio La Bahía, repeatedly referred to this lower route as the Camino Real in their correspondence.[24] This protected southern route was followed by the next two expedition leaders, who also came to inspect, not expand, the presidio and mission facilities in Texas.

TABLE 9
Brigadier Pedro de Rivera's 1727 Inspection Tour

Date	Distance Leagues (Miles)	Direction	Campsite (COUNTY)
8/7	7 (18.2)	NE	Rosas de San Juan (Comanche Creek, MAVERICK) [1]
8/8	10 (26)	ENE	Caramanchelito (tributary of Comanche Creek) [1]
8/9	6 (15.6)	NE	Los Charcos de Tortuga (Turtle Pond, ZAVALA) [1]
8/10	8 (20.8)	NE	Río Frío (Leona River, FRIO) [1]
8/11	5 (13)	NE	Río Hondo (Frio River, MEDINA) [1]
8/12	—	—	(Remained at camp, poor weather) [1]
8/13	6 (15.6)	N	Charcos de la Pita (near San Miguel Creek, MEDINA) [1]
8/14	12 (31.2)	E, NE	Medina (Medina River, BEXAR) [1]
8/15	—	—	(Crossed river)
8/16	8 (20.8)	E, NE	Presidio San Antonio de Béjar, (San Antonio, BEXAR) [1]
8/17	—	—	(Remained in camp to prepare for continuation of tour)
8/18	8 (20.8)	ENE	Arroyo Cíbolo (Cibolo Creek GUADUALUPE) [1]
8/19	7 (18.2)	ENE	Río Guadalupe (Guadalupe River, COMAL) [1]
8/20	6 (15.6)	NE	Pinitos (COMAL) [2]
8/21	6 (15.6)	NE	Arroyo Blanco (Blanco River, HAYS) [1]
8/22	9 (23.4)	ENE	Arroyo de Garrapatas (Onion Creek, TRAVIS) [1]
8/23	8 (20.8)	NE	Arroyo Encadenado (probably Wilbarger Creek, TRAVIS) [1]
8/24	8 (20.8)	NE	Arroyo Animas de Arriba (Upper Brushy Creek, WILLIAMSON) [1]
8/25	—	—	(Remained to cure buffalo meat)
8/26	8 (20.8)	ENE	Arroyo Animas de Abajo (lower Brushy Creek, WILLIAMSON) [1]
8/27	8 (20.8)	ESE	Arroyo San Agustín (MILAM) [2]
8/28	9 (23.4)	ENE	Buenavista (BURLESON) [2]
8/29	6 (15.6)	ESE	Arroyo Nuncio (BURLESON) [2]
8/30	8 (20.8)	E	Paraje Angeles (BRAZOS) [1]
8/31	8 (20.8)	NE	Arroyo Corpus Christi (BRAZOS) [1]
9/1	6 (15.6)	NE	Santa Ana (MADISON) [1]
9/2	11 (28.6)	NE	San Luis (LEON) [1]
9/3	8 (20.8)	ENE	Arroyo San Juan (east of the Trinity River, HOUSTON) [1]
9/4	7 (18.2)	ENE	Castaño (HOUSTON) [1]
9/5	7 (18.2)	ENE	San Pedro de los Nabidachos (HOUSTON) [1]
9/6	6 (15.6)	ENE	Misión San Francisco de Nechas (NACOGDOCHES) [1]
9/7	10 (26)	ESE	Presidio Nuestra Señora de los Dolores (NACOGDOCHES) [1]
9/8	—	—	(Rested horses)
9/9	9 (23.4)	E	Paraje Nacogdoches (NACOGDOCHES) [1]
9/10	8 (20.8)	ESE	Tinajita (NACOGDOCHES) [2]
9/11	11 (28.6)	E	Paraje Aes (SAN AUGUSTINE) [1]

Date	Distance Leagues (Miles)	Direction	Campsite (COUNTY)
9/12	7 (18.2)	ENE	Arroyo Patrón (SABINE) [2]
9/13	7 (18.2)	ENE	Río San Francisco de las Sabinas (Louisiana) [1]
9/14	8 (20.8)	ENE	*Paraje* Cavallada (Louisiana) [2]
9/15	11 (28.6)	ESE	Presidio Nuestra Señora del Pilar de los Adaes (near Robeline, Louisiana) [1]

[Rivera visited the presidio until September 26, when he commenced his return trip "along the same road and *parajes* as on the way in," arriving at Presidio San Antonio de Béjar on October 31. After resting the horses for two days, the brigadier departed San Antonio for Presidio Loreto de la Bahía on the lower Guadalupe River.]

Date	Distance Leagues (Miles)	Direction	Campsite (COUNTY)
11/3	9 (23.4)	SE	Aguila (on Aguila Creek, WILSON) [1]
11/4	9 (23.4)	ESE	Arroyo Cíbolo (Cibolo Creek, WILSON) [1]
11/5	6 (15.6)	E	Arroyo Cleto (Ecleto Creek near GONZALES) [1]
11/6	10 (26)	SE, E	Arroyo Mezquite (tributary of Sandies Creek, GONZALES) [2]
11/7	11 (28.6)	SE, E	Arroyo Robalo (Sandies Creek, DEWITT) [1]
11/8	9 (23.4)	W, SE	Presidio de Nuestra Señora de Loreto (near Mission Valley, VICTORIA) [1]

[From November 8 to 26, Rivera inspected the presidio. On November 27, he left for the San Antonio presidio, arriving on December 2. He was back on the Rio Grande at San Juan Bautista on December 18. Rivera kept no diary record of his trip between La Bahía and San Juan Bautista.]

FIGURE 11
*A salute welcomes the Marqués de Rubí to Presidio La Bahía, which was at its present site
(Goliad) by 1767.*

ELEVEN

THE FRENCH THREAT FADES

The Marqués de Rubí's 1767 Inspection Tour

The Marqués de Rubí was directed by the Spanish Crown to visit the presidios in northern New Spain, from the Gulf of California to Texas, and to recommend changes in the location, strength, and operation of the posts needed as a result of the peace accord in Paris in 1763, at the close of the Seven Years' War in Europe. The reshuffling of international boundaries that resulted from the peace treaty granted Spain control over territory west of the Mississippi that had been French Louisiana and thereby relieved the threat (or perceived threat) from the French presence along the Texas-Louisiana border that had shaped Spanish colonial policy during the first half of the eighteenth century.[1]

This full-scale review occurred forty years after Brigadier Rivera had completed his comprehensive military inspection tour. There had been no expedition from New Spain across the Province of Texas since Rivera. In 1727, the brigadier had been accompanied, at least periodically, by his engineer, Francisco Alvarez Barreiro, whose reports, comments, and maps greatly augmented the work of the inspector. The Marqués de Rubí also had with him (at all times rather than periodically) two excellent engineers on his inspection: Nicolás de Lafora, who maintained a diary account of Rubí's tour, and Joseph de Urrutia, who was responsible for preparing maps and plans for the expedition.

Until recently Lafora's diary, which was very competently translated into English by Lawrence Kinnaird in 1958, has been the primary source of firsthand information on Rubí's day-to-day activities on his inspection tour. However, Rubí's own manuscript diary has recently become available. This account of Rubí's inspection tour is based

---

This chapter is based primarily on Nicolás de Lafora's diary of the trip, translated by Lawrence Kinnaird, The Frontiers of New Spain: Nicolás de Lafora's Description 1766– 1768. *The manuscript of Lafora's diary in the Thorn Family Spanish Colonial Documents Collection in the Barker Texas History Center at the University of Texas, Austin, was also consulted. Additions and corrections in Rubí's expedition route and the Indians, flora, and fauna described by Lafora were made after consulting a newly acquired untranslated manuscript of the Marqués de Rubí's diary of the expedition, which is also held in the Thorn Family Spanish Colonial Documents Collection at the Barker Texas History Center.*

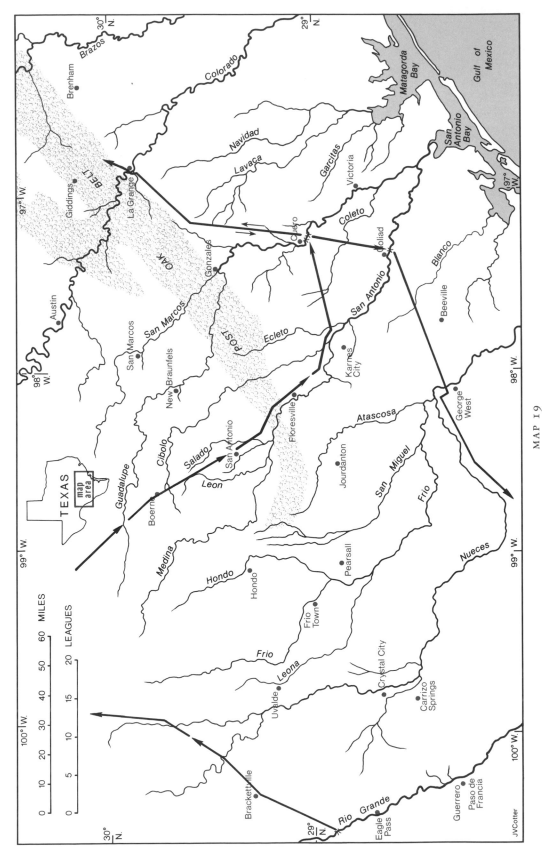

MAP 19

The Marqués de Rubí's 1767 Inspection Tour, Part 1

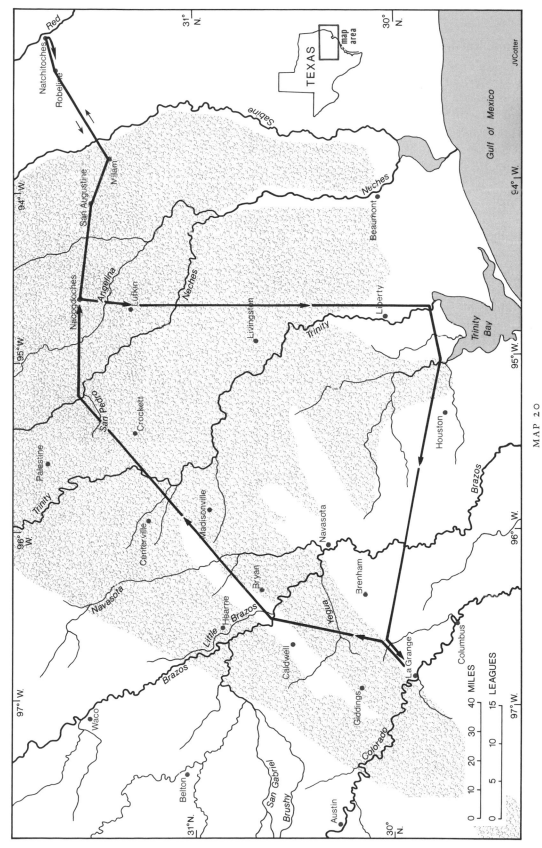

MAP 20

The Marqués de Rubí's 1767 Inspection Tour, Part 2

primarily on Lafora's diary supplemented by Rubí's unpublished and untranslated diary.[2] My use of Rubí's diary is intentionally restricted principally to his account of the route and the Indians and wildlife reported in northeastern New Spain.[3]

Rubí and Lafora occasionally report traveling different distances on the same day, but they usually differ by only 1 or 2 leagues. Rubí does, however, correct several lapses in reporting by Lafora: days on which there were travel delays or side trips (for example, Rubí's trip from Adaes to Natchitoches). The fact that the two diarists frequently refer to the same camp or stream by slightly different names and confuse the sequential order in which named streams or creeks were passed or crossed tends to confirm that the diaries were not written in consultation.

Much had changed during the forty-year period after Rivera's inspection tour, including a shift and consolidation of Spanish military presence toward the lower Rio Grande and Texas coastal area, partially in response to increased Indian hostility from western and northern Texas. The military shift in the Spanish defensive posture along the coastline and the lower Rio Grande had prompted the establishment of the Presidio San Agustín de Ahumada a few miles north of Trinity Bay in present-day Chambers County in May 1756. Thus, a new military outpost in the eastern Texas Gulf area required inspection. A mission for the Orcoquiza Indians was established nearby.

During the forty-year period between the visits of Rivera and Rubí, Presidio La Bahía was relocated for a second time, from the Guadalupe, near the present-day small community of Mission Valley a few miles south of the DeWitt-Victoria County line, to present-day Goliad on the San Antonio River. This consolidation was intended to bring the presidio into closer line with Spanish colonization efforts along the lower Rio Grande valley initiated in 1746 when the king commissioned José de Escandón to colonize the area. The formal establishment of several towns along the lower Rio Grande in turn resulted in shifting some attention from San Juan Bautista to Laredo, over 80 miles downstream.

In response to the continued, and at times even expanding, threat from the Comanche and Norteños in North-Central Texas, the Spaniards established a presidio and associated mission near the present-day city of Menard in Menard County one year after inaugurating the new fort near the coast. This San Sabá post, called Presidio San Luis de las Amarillas, was erected to protect Mission Santa Cruz and the Apache Indians associated with the mission. This protective measure did not work; the Comanche, with help from the Norteños, sacked the mission the following year (1758). By the time Rubí was scheduled to make his inspection, the presidio of San Sabá was still standing but was of questionable use for military purposes.[4]

Rubí and Lafora included in their diaries and associated reports extensive firsthand notes on the flora and fauna of the areas visited. In the introduction, Rubí wrote that one objective of his account was to record the exact location of fixed natural landmarks, watering holes, springs, and deep ravines and to identify the native population and describe their strength and "cunning" behavior. Rubí and Lafora therefore made numerous diary comments on the type of terrain and vegetation the party passed, the wildlife found, and the living conditions of the Indians who were seen or known to have been living in the area visited.

These rich diary comments and reports were made for each leg of the journey as the party moved through northern New Spain generally from the west coast toward the east. The party had left New Mexico and proceeded south and then east, arriving in Saltillo on June 6, 1767. The trip from Saltillo to Monclova took five days, the party arriving at the capital of the Province of Coahuila on June 15.

On June 28, Rubí's party left Monclova and headed north-northeast first to inspect the presidio at Santa Rosa near the Sabinas River and then on to the Rio Grande at a crossing above Eagle Pass rather than below the city near San Juan Bautista. The route that Rubí took to the Sabinas from Monclova followed De León's road along the Nadadores River and through the Baluartes Pass. From there the inspector crossed the Nadadores and moved west, away from De León's route. On June 30, the party passed Santa Cruz and camped at a spring called Sauz (Willow) south of the Sabinas River. The trail Rubí followed north from the Sabinas to San Fernando and from there to the Rio Grande is easily tracked because most of the rivers and streams carry the same names today as they did in Rubí's day—Río Escondido (a few leagues south of the village), Río de San Antonio, and Río de San Rodrigo (near the Rio Grande camp). At the Rio Grande crossing Rubí recorded the presence of Apache; here the Indians had a large encampment and areas that had been under cultivation.

After the difficult Rio Grande crossing at a ford about 15 miles upstream from Eagle Pass was completed on July 17, the convoy proceeded 14 leagues north-northeast through mesquite, cactus, a few wild plum trees, and sagebrush. About midday, the party passed a deserted village of Apache where some stubble remained from the previous year's crop. Rubí said that the party used a prominent peak (present Las Moras Mountain, elevation 1,366 feet), as a marker toward which they marched (see *Del Rio*, NH14-7). Camp that evening was at the base of the peak near a tank (*tanque*) called Cabacera de las Moras, which was filled with water. The nearby mountain and the local stream are both identified today by the name Moras and are found near modern Brackettville.

Rubí's party traveled another 14 leagues north-northeast the next day (July 18) to camp near the abandoned mission of Candelaria on the upper Nueces (called Cañón) near the Uvalde-Edwards County line.[5] Thick stands of pecan and cottonwood lined the stream. Rubí explained that this river (the Nueces) emptied into the Gulf of Mexico above the Rio Grande and added that it was believed that the British had occupied Isla Blanca (Padre Island) along the coast at that time.

The marqués continued the next day northeast (in the vicinity of present-day Camp Wood) 4 leagues to the Mission San Lorenzo to inspect the detachment of one officer and twenty men stationed there from Presidio San Sabá. No Indians were present at the mission; the Comanche had driven the Apache away earlier that year. The inspection was completed and the party was again underway on July 21.

During the next five days, the party recorded traveling 48 leagues (about 125 miles) north to the Presidio of San Luis or San Sabá. Along the canyon streams, the party identified more pecans, either blackberry or dewberry bushes (*zarzamoras*), cypresses, and many cedars. The Llano (called the Río de los Janes or Chanes) was repeatedly forded on the second day in present Kimble County (see Appendix IV entry on "Chane"). On July 23, the marqués marched northeast upriver to a campsite near the present Kimble-Mason County line, requiring a movement the next morning back north-northwest, following the Arroyo Abuela (Las Moras Creek) downstream to the San Saba River near the presidio. Near the post the party first saw bison and killed two for much-needed food.

Rubí wrote that during the nine days it took to complete the inspection his party was in constant danger from the Comanche, who sent smoke signals to their Indian friends informing them of Rubí's arrival.

After Rubí and his engineers Lafora and Urrutia completed their inspection of the presidio at San Sabá, the team traveled about 175 miles south and east in five days to the largest settlement in Texas at that time, San Antonio de Béjar. The party departed San Sabá on August 4 and traveled 13 leagues that day south-southeast through mesquite and live oak to the Llano, where they stopped near the campsite used on July 23. Along the way local wildlife was plentiful—four bison were taken from numerous herds, a bear was roped and taken alive, and three wild turkeys were killed.

Rubí forded the Pedernales (Los Pedernales), lined with tall live oaks, the second day in Gillespie County near the headwaters of the river. The inspector again found large herds of bison (taking another two), with deer and other unidentified large game animals. When he crossed the Guadalupe River near the Kerr-Kendall County line on August 7, Rubí said the stream was more properly called the Río de Alarcón (referring to the name given to the upper Guadalupe by Governor Alarcón in 1718). Pecans, cypresses, cottonwoods, live oaks, many fruit trees (including plum), and grapevines were seen along the river.

Camp that evening was a few miles south near Boerne on Balcones Creek. The next day (August 8), Rubí moved 31 miles southeast near the upper Leon springs and creek area and through Puerto del Viejo a few miles north-northwest of the city of San Antonio.

At the Presidio San Antonio de Béjar, Lafora counted a company of only twenty-two men, including a captain and a sergeant. The engineer reported that along an 8-mile stretch of the San Antonio River were five Franciscan missions—San Antonio de Valero, La Purísima Concepción, San José de Aguayo, San Juan Capistrano, and San Francisco de la Espada. Three of the five missions had been moved from East Texas and refounded at San Antonio. After Presidio Los Tejas was closed in 1729, as recommended by Rivera, the three Queretaran missions were moved and established as the new missions of San Francisco de la Espada, La Purísima Concepción de Acuña, and San Juan Capistrano.[6]

Without identifying which of the fifteen Indian tribes were associated with each mission, Lafora reported that the missions were inhabited by 809 Indians, including Payaya, Sarame, Chane, Coco, Pajalate, Tecamo, Pampopa, Mesquite, Aguastaya, Pamaca, Chayopine, Pacao, Venado, Borrado, Patas de Perro, and others.

The Payaya, Aguastaya, and Pampopa were local residents; some Payaya were found living near San Antonio by Terán and Massanet in 1691 and by Salinas in 1693. Earlier in the tour, Lafora had identified the Pampopa as residents of the missions in the Province of Coahuila. The Chane had been noted earlier as Rubí moved north along the Llano River. The Mesquite and Chayopine probably were from the area south and west of San Antonio, usually ranging near and north of the Rio Grande in the mid-eighteenth century. Tecamo may be a variant of Tacame.

The Sarame, Pajalate, Venado, and Borrado are considered by some authorities to be more recent immigrants. Thomas N. Campbell says that the Sarame may have moved northeast, out of Coahuila and away from the Rio Grande, partly because of Apache and Spanish local pressure during the preceding decades. Rubí added that the Borrado were brought from the Gulf Coast. The Pajalate and Borrado had also been found in Coahuila, indicating that all members of the tribes had not moved. The Pacao had been noted by Rivera. The Pamaca and the Patas de Perro were not identified on any other expedition, at least by those names.

The identification of the Coco living with the other tribes is significant because they are usually considered to be within the larger Karankawan group, as noted by T. N. Campbell and W. W. Newcomb, Jr.[7] This classification, however, may be subject to qualification. A number of reports on earlier expeditions suggest that the Coco had a closer connection with tribes other than Karankawa. In 1690, a Coco village was identified by De León over 50 miles from the central Gulf Coast and between two close neighboring tribes of Toho and either Aranama or Aname. Thereafter, expeditions continued to report Coco living near and associating with tribes other than the three traditionally recognized Karankawan coastal tribes. As Rubí proceeded on his inspection tour, the evidence of the close association of the Coco with tribes other than the Karankawa continued to build, suggesting a reconsideration of the nature of the linkage between the Coco and the Karankawa.

Rubí completed his assessment of the San Antonio presidio and was ready in late August 1767 to commence his journey to the presidio at Los Adaes. At this time, the "road to the Tejas" from San Antonio to the Colorado—which had been followed by Spanish expeditions for eleven years between 1716 and 1727, crossing the Guadalupe at New Braunfels and the Colorado River below Austin—was no longer the customary route to East Texas. The safer (meaning less vulnerable to Indian attack) and preferred road was along a lower route that followed the Camino Real from San Antonio southeast along the left bank of the San Antonio River to Cibolo Creek near Falls City in Karnes County and then east along De León's old road to the Guadalupe and north-northeast to the Colorado River crossing at La Grange and on to East Texas.

It is uncertain when the more northern route that crossed the Colorado at a point a few miles below Austin and continued to the modern San Gabriel and then on to the Brazos crossing in Burleson County became less popular; however, as early as 1744, about seventeen years after the upper route was followed by Rivera, the governor of the Province, Tomás Felipe Winthuysen, reported that the customary road from the presidio at San Antonio to the presidio at Los Adaes was southeast from San Antonio "about 60 leagues" to Presidio La Bahía on the Guadalupe (this report was filed five years before the presidio was moved from the Guadalupe to the San Antonio River) and then east-northeast "about 40 to 50 leagues" to the Brazos de Dios.[8] From the Brazos crossing, the land was open, the governor reported, but was protected from the Apache because of the nearby woods and the Tejas Indians, who were the principal enemies of the Apache. Apparently, the deep animosity between the Tejas and the Apache reported by Father Massanet in 1690 had not abated.

The comments by Governor Winthuysen suggest that the Brazos crossing used in the mid-1740s was near the junction of the Little Brazos River where the "road to the Tejas" inaugurated by Espinosa and Ramón ran northeast to the Trinity crossing. The distance between the presidio on the Guadalupe and the junction of the Brazos and the Little Brazos River is approximately 50 leagues, the land beyond to the northeast is relatively open, and the Tejas were frequently found hunting in the open corridor northeast of the Brazos crossing. It would therefore appear that the Espinosa-Ramón road from San Antonio to the Colorado and the diverse paths taken from the Colorado crossing in Travis County to the Brazos may have been the preferred route to the Tejas for only a few years—certainly from 1716 to 1727, and perhaps into the mid-1730s, as suggested by Carlos Castañeda, but not as late as 1744.

On August 25, 1767, Rubí and his party left San Antonio and traveled east-southeast 31 miles, first following the left bank of the San Antonio River to its junction with the Salado, then on through mesquite, pecan, elm, and live oak groves to Aguila Creek at Calaveras. They made camp that evening at Los Chayopines, above present Floresville. On August 26, they marched 39 miles—a long day—moving downstream through red grasslands along the left bank of the river, across Marcelino Creek to the *rancho* San Bartolo at Cibolo Creek. Lafora added that the ranches near the Cibolo had not been harassed by the Indians. Despite this assertion, Rubí subsequently recommended that a small fort or post be placed on the Cibolo to protect the ranchers and travelers along the Bahía Road to San Antonio.[9] Toward the end of the long summer day, the convoy continued to a camp near the mouth of the Cleto (present Ecleto Creek). Deer and wild turkeys were thick between the Cibolo and Cleto.

On the morning of August 27, the marqués turned sharply east-northeast from the river. At this point, probably by intention, Rubí picked up De León's 1689 and 1690 route from the San Antonio River to the Guadalupe crossing and on to the Colorado. The party proceeded about 16 miles to present Coleto Creek, which he called El Cuchillo, near modern Yorktown in western DeWitt County, and continued another 21 miles to a ford that the diarist Lafora called Vado del Gobernador on the Guadalupe River. This is the first specific diary entry identifying by name the location of the Governor's Ford.[10] The crossing is identified by this name on the ca. 1807 Mascaró map.[11] Governor De León twice earlier used the ford, in both 1689 and 1690, and Governor Salinas crossed there in 1693.[12]

According to Lafora, the ford was located where the river flowed south-southeast and the river channel ran narrow and swift, as high as a horse's belly. The party set up camp outside the wooded left bank near present-day Cuero, in the river valley that Lafora accurately observed would surely flood after heavy rains. Rubí, in his own diary account, offered the observation that near the ford the Guadalupe joined or became the Alarcón River, referring again to the name given by Governor Alarcón in 1718 to the river farther upstream near New Braunfels and Kerrville (Mascaró's map also gives the name Alarcón to the upper Guadalupe).

The following day, Rubí proceeded north-northeast toward the Colorado River along the pathway that he called the Adaes Road (also called the Camino Real) to the Colorado crossing at La Grange. One road began at La Bahía presidio and mission on the San Antonio river near present Goliad and then ran north-northeast to the

Guadalupe, where three crossings were available—Vado del Gobernador, Vado del Piélago, and Vado del Tío Benítez, each within a few miles of the adjacent ford. This first leg of the road across Goliad and DeWitt counties (later called the Bahía Road) had been laid out after La Bahía mission and presidio had been moved from the Guadalupe to the San Antonio River in 1749.

From the Guadalupe River near present Cuero to the Colorado crossing near La Grange, the Camino Real followed the old Indian trade route used by De León in 1689 and again in 1690, by Terán south on his return trips in 1691–1692, and by Salinas moving north in 1693. It should be noted that the route followed across Texas by the earlier expedition leaders led to the Tejas country, the destination of expeditions in the early 1700s, and was therefore referred to as to "road to the Tejas." In the middle 1700s, the destination of the expedition leaders was Los Adaes, the capital of the Province of Texas, and the name of the road reflects the new destination.

The locations and creeks noted by Rubí and Lafora along the route east of the Guadalupe all had been named before the inspection team passed that way: El Cuero Arroyo (present-day Cuero Creek), El Rosal (probably the present upper Big Brushy Creek area near the DeWitt-Lavaca County line), the pond of Padre Campa on the upper Lavaca River, Los Ramitos Creek, and, finally, San Esteban Creek, another small Lavaca-headwater creek, where they camped on the evening of August 28. Rubí added that on that day and on the movement between the San Antonio River and the Guadalupe, they passed innumerable herds of deer and flocks of wild turkeys.

The next day, the party continued following the Camino Real to the north-northeast past other locations familiar to their guides: La Vaca Creek, a *paraje* called Breviario, La Navidad (a large tributary of the present Navidad River), and then northeast to Los Cedritos (probably Buckner's Creek), which ran about 3 miles from the Colorado River near La Grange.[13] The marqués said that they were following the principal horse and mule-train pathway and were stopping at the regular roadside campsites normally used by the military and commercial convoys.

Lafora complained that the Camino Real near the river crossing was reduced to a narrow path that led beneath tree limbs which they had to dodge. His comments confirm that the party was following an established and identifiable road then called the Camino Real (although it may not have been cleared) and that the river crossing was a short distance beyond the large creek (Buckner's Creek) that they had crossed. Rubí referred to the Colorado River by its present name, rather than calling it the San Marcos as was the practice on earlier expeditions. The marqués also understood correctly that the San Saba and Llano (called Chanes or Janes) flowed into the Colorado farther to the north, upstream. When crossing a major river, Rubí frequently related the stream to its headwater creeks (by name) and to the bay into which it drained. In contrast, Lafora seldom gave this helpful information, which reflected the accuracy or inaccuracy of the Spaniards' picture of the Texas river system in the middle eighteenth century.

Rubí's route to East Texas from the Colorado was north-northeast about 33 leagues (86 miles) to the crossing of the Brazos called Brazos de Dios. This is approximately the measured distance between La Grange and the junction of the Brazos and the Little Brazos and is substantially less than the distance from the Colorado to the junction of the Little River and the Brazos. The measurements of distance and the direction noted by both Rubí and Lafora continued to be very similar and reasonably accurate, including those measurements given from San Antonio to the Colorado and beyond.

Rubí and his party traveled three days (August 30, 31, and September 1) to reach the Brazos ford. Unlike Lafora, who called the road the Camino Real, Rubí usually referred to the road as *el camino*. The first day, Rubí noted that their party traveled 12 leagues and passed the regular named watering locations or campsites called Azúcar, Peltonte, Soledad, and Juana Rosa, where, he said, the road forked—one road led east to the Presidio Orcoquisac. The party camped at the Arroyo Bernabé, 3 leagues beyond the forks. Lafora wrote that they traveled 14 leagues that day, adding a camp called La Sandía that Rubí omitted. The second day the party traveled 13 leagues according to both Rubí and Lafora, passing Las Cruces, Don Carlos, and Quita-Calzones. They camped that evening at a dry creek called La Plazeta. Rubí added that the summer months had been so dry that moss (*pastle*) was used to feed the animals, but some trees, such as the wild plum, provided very tasty fruit for the troops.

Near the crossing of the Brazos reached on the third day, Lafora warned that "the pagan Aranama" lived in the area and that one had to be cautious when traveling near this tribe. He said that these were renegade Indians, former residents of La Bahía mission, who had rejected mission life. The same well-known band threatened Padre Solís near the Colorado ford the following year.

Rubí described the crossing as near the junction of two branches of the river, one large branch flowing from west to east (the Brazos) and the second moving from northwest to southeast (the Little Brazos). This description of the directional flow of the Brazos and the Little Brazos River a few miles above the junction matches the riverbed as drawn on contemporary government maps, on which the Brazos runs due east for 4 to 5 miles above the junction and the Little Brazos runs southeast (see *Austin*, NH14-6).

Rubí commented that the "old San Xavier Road," which he described as running by way of the San Marcos River (the one, he said, that joined the Guadalupe River), also crossed the Brazos near the same fording area. The fact that this old road from San Antonio to Adaes was not in use was confirmed again in Rubí's 1768 *dictamen*, paragraph 17, in which he asserted that the San Xavier road was then impassable.

The diary description not only of the crossing of the Brazos but also of the country seen immediately after the crossing confirms that the ford was near the junction of the Brazos and the Little Brazos. The party forded the first branch of the river and about four miles farther crossed the "second arm at a short distance above its junction." Carlos E. Castañeda mistakenly places the crossing downstream in the vicinity of Washington-on-the-Brazos.[14]

After crossing both branches of the Brazos de Dios, the party camped at a location called El País, about 5 miles east of the ford. The next day, the inspection party moved along the "road" north-northeast through open pasture, "crossed by belts of live oaks." After traveling 8 leagues, the group crossed Corpus Christi Creek. Although Rubí saw no Indians, he said that the Coco, Mayeye, and Aranama from the coast usually were found hunting together in the nearby area. The Navasoto (called a creek) was forded 4 leagues beyond Corpus Christi and the party camped on the Navasoto lagoon.

Had the crossing of the Brazos been made 20 miles farther north, at the junction of the Little River in Milam County, rather than the junction of the Little Brazos, the direction taken toward Los Adaes would have been east, not north-northeast, and the party would have been in the heart of the Monte Grande, not in a relatively open corridor as is found to the northeast of the Little Brazos junction.

In 1716, Captain Ramón's party had crossed the Brazos at the same ford a few miles above the Little Brazos junction and had marched a reported 9 leagues north-northeast to a creek he named Corpus Christi. The campsite was probably on present-day Cedar Creek.[15] Rubí passed Corpus Christi, moved northeast another 4 leagues to ford the Navasota, and camped at an associated lagoon. This distance and direction again match those of Ramón and Espinosa, who had traveled 4 leagues northeast from Corpus Christi to reach the creek San Buenaventura (the Navasota River) and the associated lake or lagoon they called Santa Ana.

Between the Navasota camp and the Trinity, Rubí recorded traveling 21 leagues in one day. Lafora reported that "the road" they were following passed Arroyo El Carrizo (about midway). This reference may have been to the springs called Santa Clara by Espinosa and by other expedition leaders that followed him, probably associated with the springs that feed present-day Boggy Creek. Two lagoons were also passed about midday: first the French Lagoon and then a few miles beyond the Alligator Lagoon, named for the "amphibians" that occupied the place according to Rubí. He reached the Trinity later that day, September 3, at a crossing southeast of the present city of Crockett.

The camps and creeks passed by Rubí between the Trinity and the Neches (called the San Pedro River) were also the same as those named by Ramón and Espinosa fifty-one years earlier and Alarcón two years later: Efigenia (about 4 leagues northeast of the Trinity crossing), Coleta (about 12–14 leagues northeast of the Trinity), and San Pedro (about 3 leagues west of the Neches crossing). The road led through thick growths of pine, castaño, oak, and walnut draped with grapevines. Near the Neches crossing (1 league beyond, on the crest of a hill along the route), Lafora reported finding a mound which appeared to be artificial (this reference was to the Caddoan mounds that have been identified by the state in southwestern Cherokee County).[16]

From the Neches, the party continued to the Angelina River, where Rubí began seeing distinct villages of Tejas Indians living in very large huts. Inside the dwellings the space was divided into room areas by the use of woven grass curtains and the sleeping area was made comfortable by elevated beds. The Tejas also had large granaries and cultivated corn, beans, squash, melons, and nuts. Rubí added that because the mission Indians once had their property taken by the church, the Tejas had little interest in going to the mission. The Indians were called Nacodoche, Rubí said, and the Indians at San Pedro were referred to as the Navidacho. The mission near Nacogdoches had only one friar, two soldiers, and no Indian converts.

At Nacogdoches, the diary accounts of Rubí and Lafora diverge for a day. Rubí wrote that it was necessary to halt for a day (September 7) and also the following morning in order to rest the horses and to gather needed provisions before continuing the journey on September 8. Lafora made no reference to any delay, and their daily entries are one day apart until the day after they reach the presidio at Adaes. Beyond Nacogdoches, Rubí and Lafora followed the road that ran toward present San Augustine and Milam. On September 9, Rubí recorded that the party camped beyond the creek called Aes, or Ais according to Lafora, which was close to Mission Dolores, but the two priests hid themselves upon his arrival.

During the next two days, Rubí said his party continued to follow the Camino Real that they had taken from the beginning of the journey; they were now moving through tall forests of *castaños,* pines, and oaks to the Río Sabino (Sabine River) and on to the Adaes presidio. Because Lafora had failed to note the one-day delay en route, his diary account indicates that the party arrived at the presidio on September 10 rather than September 11 as correctly noted by Rubí.

Although Lafora did not mention Rubí's side trip, the marqués briefly described his journey (of 7 leagues) to the presidio of San Juan Bautista de Natchitoche, which he pointed out was still protected by a garrison of French troops. The route along the Camino Real that Rubí had followed from San Antonio was the same one that Athanase de Mézières called the Camino Real and followed in 1778 and that Pedro (Pierre) Vial traveled in 1787.[17]

Rubí and Lafora both wrote that they remained near the Los Adaes post until September 28, when the party returned west 46 leagues, arriving at Nacogdoches on October 1. Between October 2 and 9, Rubí proceeded south along a pathway, crossing the Angelina and Neches and then following the Trinity River downstream, a few miles east of the riverbank, to Presidio Orcoquisac.

This route south from Nacogdoches to the Trinity Bay area was along an old Indian pathway used by the Bidai and others as a trade route connecting the more coastal tribes to the friendly Tejas Indians in East Texas. The Indian path had been used earlier by the former captain of the Bahía presidio, Joachín de Orobio y Basterra, when he led a search party in 1746 from Nacogdoches south to the coastal area to investigate a report of foreign infiltration. The captain acknowledged that he was following an Indian trade route that had earlier flourished.[18]

Between Nacogdoches and the Angelina, the caravan moved 13 miles along the pathway through dense woods of pines, oaks, walnuts, and persimmon trees on October 2. A deserted village of Bidai Indians was found the next day between the Angelina and the Neches near modern Lufkin. Here the empty huts contained furniture of woven cane and palm fiber constructed with excellent workmanship. The road followed during that next three days was named Purgatory by Rubí; the rains made the bogs and swamps almost impassable. The entire road at times was submerged. The movement was halted for a full day on October 6 because of the constant rain.

On October 7, the party proceeded 8 leagues south-southeast past a known *paraje* called La Tinaja (jug or canteen), so named for the deep stone cistern (*aljibe*) near the camp that reportedly captured excellent clear rainwater. The entry suggests (but does not make clear) that the cistern was made by hand. About five weeks later, Rubí called attention to another roadside stone cistern that he again called an *aljibe* near the Bee–Live Oak County line, suggesting a possible pattern of stone cisterns constructed along some of the Spanish roadways during this period. Lafora omits any reference to passing the *paraje* named La Tinaja or to the cistern noted by Rubí. The possibility of identifying Spanish roadside campsites by the location of stone-lined cisterns may warrant further consideration. That evening, the party camped on a creek called Santa Gertrudis, which Rubí said ran into the Trinity (probably near the Polk–Hardin–San Jacinto County line).

The day before reaching the presidio, below *rancho* El Atascoso, the party camped on a plain that had "extraordinary features." These unusual objects were described by Lafora as a large number of natural, flat-topped mounds, from 12 to 18 feet in diameter, rising 3 to 6 feet above the water table. Passage through the swampy area, the engineer said, would be impossible without the aid of these dry mounds, which served as resting places.

The conditions at Presidio Orcoquisac were similar to those at Adaes: there was a small cavalry company (this one composed of thirty-one men) with no Indian converts residing at the nearby mission. Lafora identified the associated mission as Nuestra Señora de la Luz and added that the two Franciscan friars there administered to the troops. No Indians, he reported, had been converted during the nine years that the mission had been active. Rubí added that the captain of the Orcoquiza Indians regularly visited the presidio and mission, but only to receive gifts of food and other items.

Lafora described the local Indians as being lazy, content to eat nuts and fruits and never troubling themselves to hunt the larger game animals such as deer or bear, both of which were available. The engineer added that the Indians did harpoon fish in the lagoons and play with alligators, which they caught by the snout and dragged ashore to kill—a rather dangerous and strenuous activity for "lazy" people.

After inspecting the presidio and the immediate Gulf area, Rubí proceeded northwest on October 16 from the Orcoquisac presidio toward the Colorado, following a dim pathway until they struck the Camino Real taken northeastward earlier by their party, at the junction about 30 miles from the Colorado River crossing at La Grange. The one-week trip (October 16–23) along the irregular route through the woods and swamp covered a reported 65 leagues or about 170 miles; the straight-line distance is about 120 miles. This route followed by Rubí was along the pathway that Captain Orobio y Basterra had used when he returned from the Trinity Bay area to La Bahía in 1746. The captain said that he had also intersected the Camino Real on his line of march near the *paraje* called Bernabé.[19]

On October 17, the party crossed the San Jacinto River on a raft after moving from one swamp or bog to another all day. The following day, they passed two deep creeks: the first (Arroyo del Gallo) was crossed on an existing bridge, the second (Cypress Creek) over a large log. *Castaños,* pines, live oaks, and other oaks were all along the route.

When they forded the Brazos on October 20, Lafora again warned of the dangers of the Aranama Indians, who would slip unnoticed out of the heavy brush and weeds to steal the horses of careless travelers. On the same day, Rubí reported that in that area, as well as elsewhere along the road, the party killed both bears and deer.

The junction with the Camino Real was located two days later, about a league before reaching Juana Rosa and Bernabé, which the party had crossed and reported on August 30 on the trip northeast to Adaes. The party camped here before turning southwest and marching 9 leagues on October 23 back to the banks of the Colorado. This reported distance of about 23 miles is consistent with that reported earlier between the Colorado and the junction with the road to Orcoquisac, placing the junction near the present-day city of Round Top in the area of the Austin-Washington-Fayette County junction. The fording of the Colorado was difficult because of the continued heavy rains, but Rubí was able to cross on October 24 after repairing an old canoe that was found near shore.

From the Colorado crossing at La Grange, Rubí proceeded southwest (on the route he had used earlier moving northeast) about 34 miles along the Camino Real back to El Breviario for the first night; El Rosal was the campground the next night. Rubí mentioned that the majority of his escort became very ill with fever because of the constant dampness and the fact that they became drenched crossing the Colorado river. Rubí called these people his *familiares,* but did not disclose more details about their relationship. The inspector also mentioned receiving a relief shipment of food from Presidio La Bahía.

Rubí again reached Vado del Gobernador 26 miles south of El Rosal, but the Guadalupe, like the Colorado, was at flood stage. Because of the rising water Rubí did not recross the river at Gobernador but moved 5 miles downstream to another ford at a place that Lafora called El Piélago. The Spanish word *piélago* refers to a slough or low backwater area, often a river bottom where the old riverbed was located. The engineer commented further that at the ford near Piélago the river made a distinct semicircle, as it does today. Rubí also noted that the river almost made a circular turn. Vado del Piélago is a crossing identified on Mascaró's ca. 1807 map of the Guadalupe River a short distance downstream from Gobernador. The *piélago* and the semicircular bend are also clearly marked on the 1860 map of DeWitt County compiled by the Texas General Land Office and on contemporary topographical maps.[20]

On October 29, Rubí crossed the Guadalupe at Vado del Piélago. Lafora described an awkward and comical crossing in two vessels, a combination of canoes and rafts. One canoe was small, having been constructed by La Bahía soldiers for Rubí's use a few days before the crossing. The small craft was so unstable that the marqués had tree trunks tied to each side of the canoe for support. The second canoe was a larger one cut by Rubí's men, who worked through the night. When the canoes were launched at eleven the following morning, the large one began to sink. The tree trunk selected for the canoe was green, and the canoe was too heavy. The crossing was delayed another day so that further refinements in the water crafts could be made. Finally the crossing was accomplished, using the two insecure but apparently serviceable canoes with stabilizing rafts attached to each side. Rubí noted that the horse herd was moved across the river at a better location a short distance downstream, which may have been a reference to Vado Tío Benítez, used by Rivera.

The inspector's small party proceeded toward La Bahía after the river crossing, moving south about 26 miles along the lower stretch of the Bahía Road. That day, Lafora recorded crossing four creeks: Las Moharras, El Bagre, Las Cruces (probably Coleto Creek), and finally "La Cabecera, the source of El Perdido," a tributary of present-day Coleto Creek that arises in northern Goliad County. On the same day, Rubí wrote of crossing six creeks, with an equal distance between each: La Rositas de San

Juan, El Sanquillo, Les Masarritas, El Bagre, Las Cruces, and El Perdido. The two diarists obviously did not confer in composing their respective diary entries on this day. The marqués added that these creeks all flowed into the large Animas (Coleto) Creek before it met the Guadalupe River (which he incorrectly had flowing into Espíritu Santo Bay or Matagorda Bay, rather than into San Antonio Bay).

After a trip of only 10 miles, Rubí reached Presidio La Bahía on October 31. A short distance before coming to the presidio, Rubí crossed a creek and passed a nearby small motte of trees that he called La Monahuilla. The term is very similar to the word *monaquía* used by Fray Solís the following year to identify what was apparently a homosexual Karankawa Indian community associated with the same creek area.[21] Rubí forded the San Antonio River (called the San Antonio and Medina River) near the mission.

According to Lafora, a cavalry company of fifty men, including three officers, was at the post. Near the presidio there was a settlement of forty-six residents, and Mission Espíritu Santo contained ninety-three Aranama and Tamique Indians. At Rosario, 5 miles upstream on the right bank, there were seventy-one baptized Cojane, Guapite (or Coapite), and Karankawa along with thirty "savages."

Rubí's diary comments about the La Bahía presidio and its environment differed from Lafora's to some extent and expanded upon the engineer's entry. He said that there were twenty-five families of Coco, Aranama, Karankawa, and Cujane at the Mission Espíritu Santo, which possessed land and livestock "sufficient to support all of Mexico City." The number of Indians at the nearby Mission Rosario was uncertain, he added, because the Indians frequently deserted the mission and fled to the coast, only to be retrieved by local presidio forces, who sometimes returned with other Indians as well. The marqués thought that "the presidio population has been oppressed by the enormous extension of lands that the missions have taken. . . ."

On November 12, the inspection party completed work at La Bahía and proceeded west toward San Juan Bautista by way of Laredo. This 75-league journey from present-day Goliad to Laredo took a week (November 12–19). The first day, Rubí's party moved up the San Antonio River a short distance (2 leagues) to Mission Rosario and on to its ranch, which was teeming with cattle and horses belonging to the mission (or perhaps some herds belonged to the former presidio captain and some settlers). Camp that evening was made on Arroyo de Cunillo, probably present-day Blanco Creek.

The Nueces River in Live Oak County was the campsite on the following day (November 13). Rubí recorded the location of another stone cistern (or *aljibe*) 8 leagues before reaching the river, near a location named Agua Dulce (probably near Medio Creek in Bee County north of present-day Beeville).

A thick stand of trees lined the Nueces bank, and some dead tree trunks and dry logs were gathered to make the raft used to cross the river the next day. The stream was too deep to ford because of high water. The troops and Indian escorts also made rafts using cowhides to carry the baggage across the narrow stream, which was "only 14 to 16 *toesas*" (a total distance of about 90–102 feet) wide. The horses and mules swam across.

Rubí's party continued southwest the following day through heavy mesquite brush, huisaches, small yuccas, prickly pears, and catclaws. Cottonwood trees were seen only around the occasional water holes where the pack trains regularly stopped. The party followed along the right (or southeast) side of the Nueces.

The caravan continued heading southwest on November 16 along the riverbank until the point at which the Nueces veered first west and then northwest. At the first turn, near the intersection of the corners of La Salle, Webb, Duval, and McMullen counties, the party left the river and continued along the road southwest to intersect or follow several creeks: San Casimiro (present-day San Casimiro Creek), El Carrizo (Carrizitos Creek), and El Saladito (Salado Creek).

On November 17, the party reached the mule train stop called El Pato, where the road intersected the San Antonio to Laredo road, only 12 leagues (one day's travel) from Laredo. They followed the present-day San Ygnacio Creek (also called San Ygnacio by Rubí) into town. Lafora said there was nothing special to report that day other than the prodigious multitude of rattlesnakes that occupied the country.

The caravan reached Laredo on November 18, after passing several horse and mule ranches. According to Rubí, the town (*villa*) had only twelve huts on the left bank made of branches and leaves, and another group of shacks on the right side. Lafora counted sixty huts situated on both sides and said these were armed settlers commanded by a local militia captain. Rubí added that upriver and downriver from Laredo were three additional settlements: Revilla, Camargo, and Miera (Mier). All had been founded on the right bank of the Rio Grande between 1749 and 1752.

Once the Rio Grande was crossed (by canoe), Rubí proceeded upriver along the right bank for 32 leagues to inspect the Presidio San Juan Bautista del Río Grande and then on to Monterrey, the capital of Nuevo León. By February of the following year (1768), Rubí was back in Mexico City ready to complete his *dictamen*.

At the close of his *dictamen*, Rubí made a number of interesting comments on Indians, as Rivera had included recommendations on Indian relations in his *reglamento* of 1727. The marqués recommended that when Indians were needed on expeditions as guides, spies, and scouts, they should be provided daily rations (like the troops) and that the Indian guides and scouts (up to eight or ten in number) should always be with the troops at the post on a permanent basis. In closing the inspector also protested strongly (as a violation against humanity and the Indians' rights as a people) against the existing practice of disposing of captured Indians by selling them as slaves, making their return by the government impossible. Apparently Rivera's earlier recommendation had not been followed in practice. In northern New Spain the Spaniards rounded up and held Indians as slaves, and the practice proved difficult to stop.

At the end of Lafora's diary, a very negative summary description is given of the province of Texas. Both the substantive comments and tone of the remarks seem designed to discourage any further investment in or development of Texas. Lafora's assessment, like Rubí's later recommendations (*dictamen*), called for a sharp retrenchment by the military, just as Brigadier Rivera's report or *proyecto* had suggested forty years earlier.

Lafora followed Rivera's and Barreiro's practice of formally listing all the Indian tribes in the several provinces at the time of the visit, without identifying where each tribe lived within the province.[22] The engineer also related, as evidence of the lack of Spanish influence over the Indians, a story about a Spanish girl being held as a slave of the Tejas Indians in the San Pedro village near the Neches. The inspection party had sought her release, he said, both by requesting the aid of local Indian leaders and by offering money to purchase her liberation, but to no avail. The captors preferred to keep her as their slave and did. Lafora's outrage was evident, but Rubí did not mention the incident.

In support of his negative general comments, Lafora made the following additional observations. There were so many fleas, ticks, horseflies, mites, and other insects that the Province of Texas was uninhabitable. According to the diarist, conditions in Texas were so deplorable that the women became sterile, which Lafora said had been reported when Presidio La Bahía was on the Guadalupe River. Lafora did not connect the reports of sterility with the smallpox epidemics that occurred at the former French settlement and elsewhere in Texas, but sterility is credited as one if not the major contributor to the depopulation of native tribes.[23]

In winter, only bears, coyotes, deer, and bison inhabited the country between San Antonio and Nacogdoches, Lafora continued. The cry of the hoot owl suited perfectly the sad nature of the country, and the unending forest made the place even more dismal. This discouraging report on the living conditions and landscape of Texas (much of which was in the area recommended to be abandoned) was followed by Fray Solís's entertaining and lively account of the province the following year.

TABLE 10
Marqués de Rubí's 1767 Inspection Tour

Date	Distance Leagues (Miles)	Direction	Campsite (COUNTY)
7/17	14 (36.4)	NNE	Cabecera de las Moras (MAVERICK) [1]
7/18	14 (36.4)	NNE	Misión Candelaria (REAL) [1]
7/19	4 (10.4)	NNW	Misión San Lorenzo (EDWARDS) [1]
7/20	—	—	(Remained for inspection)
7/21	12 (31.2)	N	El Cedral (REAL) [1]
7/22	13 (33.8)	N	El Ojo (EDWARD) [1]
7/23	10 (26)	NE	Arroyo de las Trancas (KIMBLE) [1]
7/24	11 (28.6)	NNW	Arroyo de Abuela (MENARD) [1]
7/25	2 (5.2)	N	Presidio San Sabá (MENARD) [1]

[The party remained until August 4 to inspect the post.]

Date	Distance Leagues (Miles)	Direction	Campsite (COUNTY)
8/4	13 (33.8)	SSE	Río de Janes (KIMBLE) [1]
8/5	15 (39)	ESE	Los Pedernales (GILLESPIE) [1]
8/6	16 (41.6)	SSE	Río de Alarcón (KERR) [1]
8/7	11 (28.6)	ESE	Arroyo de los Balcones (KENDALL) [1]
8/8	12 (31.2)	SE	Presidio de Béjar (BEXAR) [1]

[The party remained until August 25 to inspect the presidio.]

Date	Distance Leagues (Miles)	Direction	Campsite (COUNTY)
8/25	12 (31.2)	SE	Los Chayopines (San Antonio River, WILSON) [1]
8/26	15 (39)	ESE	Arroyo de Cleto (Ecleto Creek, KARNES) [1]
8/27	14 (36.4)	ENE	Vado del Gobernador (Guadalupe River, DEWITT) [1]
8/28	14 (36.4)	NNE	Arroyo San Esteban (tributary of Lavaca River, LAVACA) [1]
8/29	18 (46.8)	NNE	Río Colorado (Colorado River, FAYETTE) [1]
8/30	12 (31.2)	NNE	Arroyo de Bernabé (FAYETTE) [1]
8/31	13 (33.8)	NNE	Arroyo La Plazeta (BURLESON) [1]
9/1	10 (26)	N	El País (BRAZOS) [1]
9/2	14 (36.4)	NNE	Arroyo de Navasota (Navasota River, MADISON) [1]
9/3	21 (54.6)	NE	Río Trinidad (Trinity River, LEON) [1]
9/4	8 (20.8)	NE	Arroyo Las Peñitas (HOUSTON) [1]
9/5	15 (39)	NE	Arroyo Alazán (east of Neches River, CHEROKEE) [1]
9/6	14 (36.4)	ENE	Misión de Nacogdoches (NACOGDOCHES) [1]
9/7	—	—	(Delayed to rest horses)
9/8	3 (7.8)	ESE	Arroyo Atascoso (NACOGDOCHES) [2]
9/9	16 (41.6)	E	El Ojo de Agua del Palo Gacho (SAN AUGUSTINE) [2]
9/10	17 (44.2)	ENE	Las Cabezas (Sabine Parish, Louisiana) [1]
9/11	10 (26)	ENE	Presidio Nuestra Señora del Pilar de los Adaes (near Robeline, Natchitoches Parish, Louisiana) [1]

[The party remained near Los Adaes until September 28, when Rubí returned to Nacogdoches, arriving on October 1. No daily diary entries were given for this trip.]

Date	Distance Leagues (Miles)	Direction	Campsite (COUNTY)
10/2	5 (13)	S	Rio de Angelina (Angelina River, NACOGDOCHES) [1]
10/3	14 (36.4)	SSW	Río de Nechas (camped on left bank of Neches River, ANGELINA) [1]
10/4	10 (26)	SSW	San Francisco (POLK) [2]
10/5	11 (28.6)	SW	Purgatory (POLK) [?]
10/6	—	—	(Delayed by rain)
10/7	8 (20.8)	SSE	Santa Gertrudis (LIBERTY) [2]
10/8	14 (36.4)	SSE	El Atascoso (LIBERTY) [2]
10/9	10 (26)	S	Presidio San Agustín de Ahumada or Orcoquizac (near mouth of Trinity River, CHAMBERS) [1]

[Rubí inspected the presidio and surrounding area, visiting the bay area, until October 16, when he continued the journey to the Colorado River.]

Date	Distance Leagues (Miles)	Direction	Campsite (COUNTY)
10/16	5 (13)	NW	(CHAMBERS) [2]
10/17	8 (20.8)	WNW	Río San Jacinto (San Jacinto Creek, HARRIS) [2]
10/18	9 (23.4)	W	Arroyo Sabinos (HARRIS) [2]
10/19	13 (33.8)	WNW	Arroyo San Ysidro (WALLER) [2]
10/20	12 (31.2)	W	Viperina (AUSTIN) [2]
10/21	8 (20.8)	WNW	La Zorrilla (AUSTIN) [2]
10/22	10 (26)	WSW	Arroyo Juana Rosa (FAYETTE) [1]
10/23	9 (23.4)	SW	Río Colorado (Colorado River, FAYETTE) [1]
10/24	—	—	(Began river crossing)
10/25	—	—	(Completed river crossing)
10/26	13 (33.8)		El Breviario (Navidad River, FAYETTE) [2]
10/27	11 (28.6)	—	El Rosal (Lavaca River, LAVACA) [2]
10/28	10 (26)	—	El Piélago (Guadalupe River, DEWITT) [1]
10/29	—	—	(Crossed Guadalupe River)
10/30	10 (26)	S	Arroyo del Perdido (Perdido Creek, GOLIAD) [1]
10/31	4 (10.4)	SW	Presidio La Bahía (near Goliad, GOLIAD) [1]

[Rubí's party remained at the presidio from October 31 to November 12. From La Bahía, Rubí proceeded southwest to Laredo.]

Date	Distance Leagues (Miles)	Direction	Campsite (COUNTY)
11/12	12 (31.2)	W	Arroyo Cunillo (Blanco Creek, BEE) [2]
11/13	10 (26)	SW	Río Nueces (LIVE OAK) [1]
11/14	1 (2.6)	WNW	(Crossed river)
11/15	13 (33.8)	SW	Arroyo del Olmito (tributaries of Nueces River, MCMULLEN) [2]
11/16	14 (36.4)	SW	Unnamed pond (WEBB) [2]
11/17	13 (33.8)	SW	El Pato (WEBB) [1]
11/18	12 (31.2)	SW	Laredo (Laredo, WEBB) [1]
11/19	4 (10.4)	NW	Arroyo de Carrizo (right bank of Rio Grande) [2]
11/20	16 (41.6)	NW	El Toro (right bank of Rio Grande) [2]
11/21	11 (28.6)	NW	Arroyo Agostadero (right bank of Rio Grande) [2]
11/22	5 (13)	NW	Presidio San Juan Bautista (Rio Grande) [1]

FIGURE 12
Fray Solís is impressed by the progress his brethren have made with the Indian children in the Zacatecan missions of Texas.

TWELVE

REVIEW OF THE ZACATECAN
MISSIONS IN TEXAS

Fray Gaspar José de Solís's 1768 Inspection Tour

In the fall of 1767, when Rubí was returning south to San Juan Bautista from his military tour of the presidios in the Province of Texas, the Council of the College of Our Lady of Guadalupe near the city of Zacatecas sent Fray Gaspar José de Solís north to Texas to inspect the Franciscan missions there.[1] The scope of his ecclesiastical charge was limited to the missions in Texas, whereas Rubí's royal charter required the inspection of all presidios in northern New Spain. Solís's assignment was different not only in scope, but also in character, because it required an assessment of the need for the missions and a review of all aspects of mission life with the Indians. By contrast, Rubí was concerned with military security and organization, and his observations were slanted toward minimizing the significance of missions. Rubí described Texas as uninhabitable and the local Indians as disinterested in the Catholic faith and as lazy cowards. Solís, serving as his own diarist for the journey, visited many of the same camp locations, presidios, and missions that Rubí had toured and gave a far different account. One striking similarity however, is the extraordinary attention both men gave in their diary accounts to the Indians and to the abundant and diverse wildlife and flora they saw.

As a result of the padre's more narrow charge, Solís's inspection route differed from that of Rubí. Rubí left Monclova and crossed the Rio Grande above modern Eagle Pass to inspect the troops at San Lorenzo and the Presidio San Sabá in Menard County. From San Sabá, Rubí traveled southeast to San Antonio and then followed the Camino Real

This chapter is based on two translations into English of the diary of Fray Gaspar José de Solís. The first translation is by Margaret Kenney Kress, "Diary of a Visit of Inspection of the Texas Missions Made by Fray Gaspar José de Solís in the Year 1767–68," Southwestern Historical Quarterly 35, no. 1 (1931–1932), 28–76. The second translation is by Peter P. Forrestal, "The Solís Diary of 1767," Preliminary Studies of the Texas Catholic Historical Society 1, no. 6 (March 1931), 3–42. Several manuscript copies of Solís's diary were consulted, including a copy in the Manuscript Division of the Library of Congress and two copies at the Barker Texas History Center (one in Documents, History, Texas Archives of Mexico, 248–298, and the second in the Thorn Family Spanish Colonial Documents Collection).

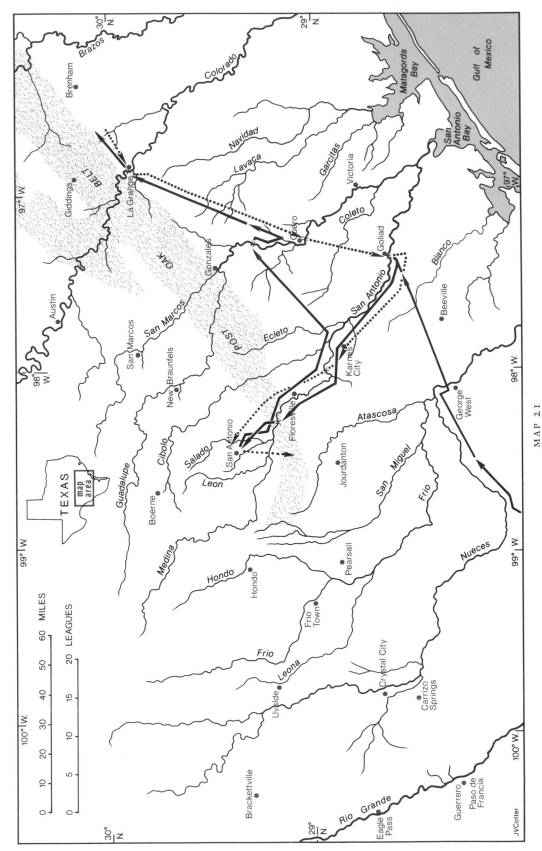

MAP 21

Fray Gaspar José de Solís's 1768 Inspection Tour, Part 1

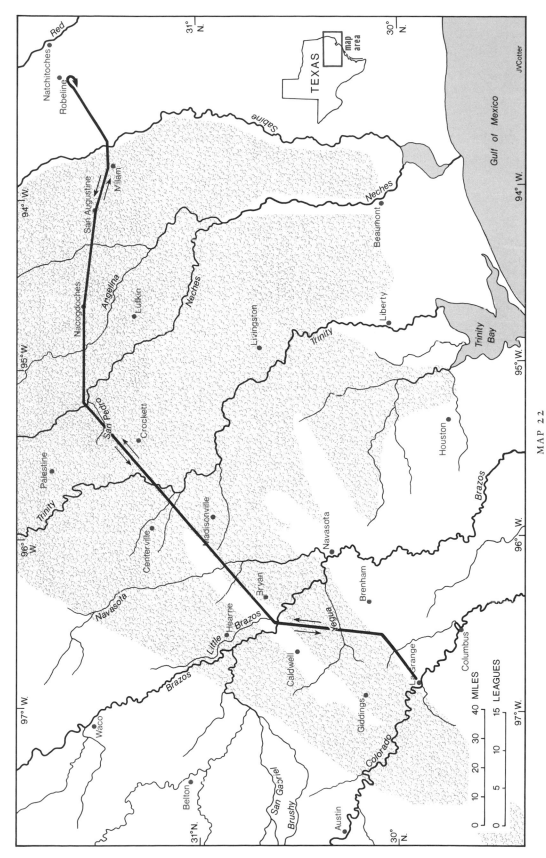

MAP 22

Fray Gaspar José de Solís's 1768 Inspection Tour, Part 2

(also called the Adaes Road) to the crossing of the Guadalupe near present-day Cuero and the Colorado near La Grange. After crossing the Brazos near the junction with the Little Brazos, the marqués continued on the Camino Real to Adaes and returned via the Trinity Bay area to the same Guadalupe crossing before moving southeast to La Bahía. Rubí went to San Juan Bautista via Laredo and then on to Monterrey and Saltillo before returning to Mexico City. From Zacatecas Solís both entered and left present-day Texas through the gateway town of Laredo. His orders took him to East Texas and Los Adaes, but did not require him to visit either San Sabá or Trinity Bay. In contrast to Rubí and Lafora, who called their route from San Antonio to Adaes the Camino Real, Solís had no name for the same route.

As Solís approached the Rio Grande from the south on February 12, 1768, he saw herds of wild mustangs and reported moving through woods of live oak, mesquite, huisache, chaparral, ebony, catclaw, yucca, and cactus. During his short stay on the Rio Grande, Solís gave a comprehensive account of the plants and wildlife along his route north from Zacatecas to the Rio Grande. There were deer, wolves, coyotes, rabbits, and squirrels between Boca de Leones and Lampazos, an area 60 to 100 miles south of the river. There were also many birds—quail, doves, hawks, crows, owls, small parrots, and macaws.

Shortly before reaching the Rio Grande, the padre passed several camps of Carrizo Indians;[2] he baptized one baby who was dying. Several of the older children were not baptized, as they had not been instructed in the faith. The Carrizo nation, the padre added, ran half wild and existed by eating snakes, small rodents, rabbits, and other wild animals.

Apparently, Solís sailed across the Rio Grande near Laredo (*en que pasé en un vote muy bueno con su vela latina*). On earlier expeditions, which crossed about 80 miles upstream near San Juan Bautista, the leaders swam with their horses or were barged across. Solís was the first expedition leader to cross on a sailboat. Near the shore an escort of eight soldiers from the Presidio of San Antonio de Béjar and four armed Indians from Mission San Juan met the padre. Solís was pleased to have the escort because he knew there was danger from Indian attacks above the Rio Grande.

Solís's itinerary was to move first directly from the Laredo area to the missions Espíritu Santo and Rosario on the San Antonio River, a movement that took him in the reverse direction (northeast) over the same pack-train route Rubí had followed southwest from La Bahía to Laredo three months earlier. The road from Laredo to La Bahía was not new; the route had been described with each rest-stop and creek crossing named in a report on Rancho de Laredo filed ten years earlier (1757) by Agustín Lopez de la Cámara Alta. Lopez's report said the way led through Pato, Salado, San Joseph, El Mesquite, Paso del Río de las Nueces, and Agua Dulce to Presidio de la Bahía del Espíritu Santo.[3]

From the Rio Grande, Solís's party moved north into present-day Texas about 44 miles in two days to a *paraje* and creek called Salado, one of the stops named by Alta. Although the woods were not thick, there were oaks, huisaches, and mesquites, as in the region to the south. From Salado, Solís said, one entered the land of the Apache, which extended northeast to the Nueces. In that stretch of land near the Nueces there were more oaks and large huisaches, along with numerous javelinas, just as there are today.

The mid-February weather was cold, and a norther brought snow on February 18 and 19 to Webb County, in the area about 20 to 30 miles south of the Nueces. Although measurable snow has not been reported in this century in Cameron County (about 100 miles south and east) according to the records of the National Oceanic and Atmospheric Administration, Solís passed through the country during the Little Ice Age. Fray Espinosa described the area about 60 miles southwest of Laredo, near Lampazos, in the early 1700s as a frigid region in the winter with ice and snow each year.[4]

After passing the creeks called Salado and San Casimiro (which are identified on the contemporary USGS map *Laredo*, NG14-2), Solís was guided on February 19 to a place called Señor San Joseph, another stop noted by Alta in his 1757 report. The party was kept at the camp for two days (February 20 and 21) by a snowstorm. During the next two days, the party passed Tablitas and Arroyo Blanco to camp on the Nueces.

The crossing of the Nueces apparently occurred between the modern cities of Three Rivers and George West in Live Oak County. On the first day beyond the Nueces (February 24), past a stream called Leona, the party was greeted first by six armed men led by Padre Escovar and later in the day by the captain and ten soldiers from Presidio La Bahía. Solís mentions that he found some very good sweet water (*agua dulce, muy buena agua*) near their camp (probably Agua Dulce) that evening after marching 12 leagues. This encampment places the padre near the cistern or *aljibe* that Rubí said was located about 8 leagues east of the Nueces on November 13, 1767. Without referring to any cistern, Lafora had called the location Agua Dulce. The difference between the number of leagues recorded between the Nueces crossing and Agua Dulce by Rubí and by Solís is typical of the differences found all along the route. The padre was not precise in measuring distances traveled and rather consistently overstated the number of leagues traveled by 20 to 30 percent.

On February 25, the party traveled an estimated 30–35 miles and had only a short march to the Rosario mission ranch on the San Antonio River (no longer called the Medina) the next day. Between February 26 and March 14, Solís inspected both missions and visited Presidio La Bahía. Before commencing his inspection, Solís presented to the local officials his authorization for the visit (*patente de visita*).

His diary entries include details on the size of the two missions and their property. Rosario had two droves of burros, forty horses, thirty mules, five thousand head of cattle, two hundred milk cows, and seven hundred sheep and goats. This extensive animal herd supported an undisclosed number of Coxane (Cujane), Guapite (or Coapite), Karankawa, and Copano at Rosario, most of whom had left mission life and returned to live at liberty in the nearby woods or on the coast.

The four Indian tribes named by Solís as residents of Rosario included four of the five tribes traditionally identified as part of the larger Karankawan group.[5] In addition to the four identified by Solís, W. W. Newcomb, Jr., adds a fifth Indian tribe, the Capoque (most frequently referred to by the Spanish as Coco). It should be noted that Solís did not find any Coco among the Karankawa at Rosario and that Rubí earlier (1767) had identified the Coco among the other non-Karankawan tribes in the missions of San Antonio.

In describing the local Karankawa at Rosario, Solís first emphasized the difficulty of keeping the Indians in line at the mission. He reported that they would escape, preferring liberty rather than the protection of the mission. One reason given by the padre for this difficulty was the failure of the presidio troops to force the Indians to congregate at the missions; when they ran away, the soldiers did not round up the escapees and punish them so severely that they would be afraid to escape again. Solís held the presidio responsible for the weak condition of the missions, thereby acknowledging that faith alone was not adequate to attract the Indians.

In contrast, Massanet had earlier blamed the military for offending and mistreating the Indians and had rejected any substantial force of troops at the East Texas mission in the early 1690s. The view that the church alone would congregate and hold the loyalty of Texas tribes had changed to one that acknowledged the church's dependence on severe punishment by the military for "escapees." Carlos E. Castañeda denies that force was used to keep the Indians under mission control.[6]

Solís paused in his diary account to describe in detail the social life of the Karankawa, including an account of the several techniques coastal Indians used to cook (or at least warm) and eat other Indians (or "the priests and Spaniards if they catch any"). He described four basic ceremonial techniques for the preparation and consumption of captives. In the first, the victim was tethered to a stake near a large bonfire. The men, each with a long sharp knife, danced about the captive, occasionally cutting flesh from his body to roast on the nearby fire and eat, until the victim perished and his body was devoured. The second technique involved stringing the captives up by their feet, presumably under a tree limb, and roasting them above a large fire. A third approach involved the use of long, one-inch-thick cedar poles set afire, first to torture then to roast the victim. The last technique that Solís described was significantly less ritualistic, for no fires, dances, or knives were required: the captive was simply torn to pieces and eaten raw by the Karankawa, who used only their teeth.

Although the victim may not have cared much about the technicality, some historians and anthropologists have noted that this practice is characterized as ritual cannibalism. As noted, Alonso de León (the elder) said that the Indians living about 80 miles southwest of Rio Grande City (Starr County) were so casual that they ate friend and foe. De León told of a personal experience in which the Indians who accompanied his military company into hostile Indian country took with them half-roasted and ground-up human bones mixed with *mezquitamal* to munch along the road. De León concluded that this was a common practice among all the Indians in the area.[7]

Solís argued, unpersuasively, that despite the appearance of being brave, the Indians were actually cowards—a characterization that both Rivera and Rubí had earlier advanced. The padre said that the Indians boasted of being tough and valiant just because they went naked in the most burning sun, broke the ice with their bodies at early dawn to bathe in streams in the winter, and when wounded in battle were were able to continue fighting because they quickly stuffed the wound with a special grass that stopped the flow of blood. This rather impressive account of human determination and prowess did not impress the padre, who saw in the Indians a more fundamental weakness—their preference for independence, freedom, and liberty over the protective security of the Catholic church.

As further evidence of the barbaric nature of the local Indians, Solís added that they even ate and enjoyed the foul-smelling polecat or skunk. This disquieting thought, however, should be balanced against a later report made in 1828 by the urbane European botanist Jean Louis Berlandier, who noted that during one of his scientific journeys near San Antonio he had dined with Mexican soldiers from Béjar who were having skunk (*zorrillo*) for dinner, which he considered a great meal, like eating a "suckling pig."[8]

Solís also told of the Karankawa custom of exchanging wives and trading slaves and of the presence of Karankawa "hermaphrodites" or homosexuals. He stated that the Karankawa Indian nation "abounds" with homosexuals called *monaguia* (*abundan en estas Nationes los emanfroditos a quienes llamas monaguia*). Solís said the homosexuals or berdaches (as referenced in the literature on American Indians) took part in military engagements or campaigns, but their role was limited to serving those engaged in the fight and acting as herdsmen, who drove any horses or mules stolen by the combatants back to their village.

The report of a homosexual community within the Karankawa group is not surprising. Texas anthropologists, including W. W. Newcomb, Jr., report that berdaches also were found among the Coahuiltecans and other Texas Indian tribes.[9] Alonso de León (the elder) wrote about the Indian men near Monterrey who served as women and dressed in women's clothing. The historian added two observations about the homosexuals or transvestites: first, he said that other men did not affront them and women did not despise them; second, he concluded that one should not blame the "savages" since in the advanced nations (Spain) parents sent their sons to schools to be educated in a formal manner and instead the boys learned the same "sins."[10] Berdaches, who often dressed, spoke, and acted like women, were well recognized and widely reported among many North American Indian tribes, including the Plains Indians.[11]

One of the earliest written accounts of "hermaphrodites" or homosexuals among Texas Indians is found in an account of La Salle's journey from Matagorda Bay to the Tejas in East Texas in 1687. Father Douay said their party found among an Indian tribe living northeast of the French settlement about sixty homosexuals, who were further described only as going naked after sunset.[12]

The 300 Indians at Mission La Bahía del Espíritu Santo were not members of the Karankawan group of tribes who inhabited Rosario. At Espíritu Santo there were Aranama, Tamique, Piguique, and Manos de Perro, more peaceful tribes, some of whom had supported the mission when it was on the Guadalupe (1726–1749) and moved with the mission to the San Antonio River. These were the same Indians that Rubí reported at the mission the year before, with the exception of the Manos de Perro and the Piguique, two coastal tribes from the more open areas farther south.[13] Although the padre found the Indians at Espíritu Santo more civilized than the Karankawa, he said they had the same customs, inclinations, and vices as the Indians at Rosario—which may suggest that he thought that these other Indians also participated in ritualistic cannibalism, had homosexual groups, and perhaps ate skunks.

Solís recorded that the Espíritu Santo mission owned one hundred horses, seventy mules, fifteen hundred sheep and goats, and two hundred yoke of oxen as well as large fields for planting corn, cotton, watermelons, cantaloupes, and both sweet potatoes and Irish potatoes. The mission also maintained orchards of several varieties of peach and fig trees. The padre was apparently proud of the 623 baptisms that had occurred at the mission since the year it was founded, which he mistakenly reported as 1717 (rather than 1722).

Before leaving the San Antonio River near present-day Goliad, Solís gave an account of the wildlife in the local area: there were many deer and bison as well as numerous bears, antelopes, javelinas (perhaps also referring to wild boars), jack rabbits, cotton-tails, and occasional jaguars and mountain lions. He added to his list snakes (some poisonous), wild turkeys, geese, ducks, quail, and prairie chickens.

On March 15, Solís left the La Bahía area accompanied by eight soldiers from the presidio and six armed Indians from Mission Espíritu Santo. The party moved 31 miles up the right bank of the San Antonio River along the Bahía Road to Béjar and camped at the creek called La Escondida. The campsite was probably on the stream identified by the same name on contemporary government maps (see *Beeville*, NH14-12). The next day, Solís passed through La Parrita and the ranches of El Capote and La Mora and arrived at Rancho de Labor del Padre Cardenas on the San Antonio River. On March 17, he crossed the river near the corral of San Juan Capistrano, after having passed La Mota and Arroyo del Padre Mariano, a reported total of about 42 miles. The following day, Solís passed the Salado River at its junction with the San Antonio River near Mission San Juan Capistrano and continued for a total of about 18 miles to Mission San José, where the governor of Texas, Don Hugo Oconor, greeted him.

Along the route from La Bahía to San Antonio, the diarist recorded large herds of cattle and horses and a wide range of wild animals and birds in Goliad, Karnes, and Wilson counties. The padre noted deer, wolves, coyotes, rabbits, a few cougars, wildcats, javelinas, ducks, geese, turkeys, quail, and some prairie chickens, as well as crows, hawks, eagles, and owls. He identified both mesquite and huisache along the road to San Antonio. The fact that the padre found huisache all along his route from Laredo to Wilson County (a few miles south of San Antonio) suggests that the views of the Texas naturalist Roy Bedichek on huisache may be subject to review. Bedichek says huisache was brought to Texas in the nineteenth century, by wagon trains with mules (presumably with huisache beans in their digestive tracks) driven north from Mexico.[14]

Between March 21 and April 7, Solís inspected the missions near San Antonio. On April 1, he visited Concepción and later returned to San José, where he reported extensive fenced farms with fields of corn, brown beans, lentils, melons, sweet and Irish potatoes, and sugarcane. Like the Espíritu Santo mission, San José had extensive orchards of fruit trees, especially peaches. The mission ranch El Atascoso consisted of about fifty thousand acres where horses, burros, fifteen hundred yoke of oxen, and five thousand head of sheep and goats were pastured. The Indians were well trained, the padre added, to care for the fields and herds without supervision.

The Indians that resided at the San Antonio mission of San Miguel de Aguayo y San José were the Pampopa, Mesquite, Pastia, Camama, Cacama, Cano, Aguastaya, and Xauna. The Pampopa, Mesquite, and Aguastaya had been reported in the San Antonio mission the year before by Lafora. Forty years earlier, Rivera had also reported that the

Pastia lived in the province. In these tribes there were about three hundred and fifty adult males, of whom sixty-five were armed with bows, arrows, and lances and forty-five carried guns. The Indians spoke Spanish, played the guitar or other instruments, worked diligently at their assigned tasks, and lived comfortably in enclosed houses with beds of buffalo hide mattresses and cotton or wool blankets. Solís expressed pride in the 1,054 baptisms performed since the mission was established, as the padre reported, in "either 1716 or 1717."[15]

On April 7, Solís's party left the mission of San José headed for East Texas and Los Adaes. The small group moved a short distance south by the mission of San Juan de Capistrano and crossed the Salado Creek to camp on the edge of the heavily wooded Monte Grande, which the padre called Monte del Diablo (the Devil's Woods). This belt of trees and thick brush today, as in the 1700s, stretches from northern Atascosa County south of San Antonio to the east, forming a 20-mile-wide forested area between San Antonio and Floresville. The thickly wooded area widens farther east across northern Wilson, Gonzales, and Fayette counties, and through most of Bastrop County to the Colorado River. The Devil's Woods or Monte Grande continues east of the Colorado River within an area south of the Travis-Bastrop County line and north of a line that extends from La Grange to the Brazos River near the present-day city of Navasota.

An appreciation of the impenetrable nature of this thick woods that divides the state running southwest to northeast is essential for an understanding of the early Texas road system. For example, during the study period there were only two routes from the San Antonio area to East Texas—the northern route that went north of Monte Grande, crossing the Colorado below Austin in Travis County, and the southern route that followed the Camino Real south of the heavy woods and crossed the Colorado at La Grange in Fayette County. Not until the nineteenth century did a third route emerge that crossed the Colorado at Bastrop (in the heart at the Monte Grande), which has become celebrated as the Old San Antonio Road.

Solís remained in camp near the Salado on April 8 because of foul weather; a bitter norther brought snow. The padre was joined in camp by about 100 individuals (probably mostly Adaesaños), with a military escort, who were going to Presidio Los Adaes.[16]

The large entourage, which included both Solís's party and the Adaesaños group, continued their journey on April 9 along the left bank of the San Antonio River through woods of oak. They passed Calaveras and camped near the Chayopines crossing of the river in Wilson County. The next day, they continued downstream (not crossing at the Chayopines to the opposite side), through La Patanya and Los Pájaritos to Marcelino (present-day Marcelinas) Creek. Solís reported that the road was dotted with many and varied flowers—yellow, red, purple, blue, and white—that unfolded into colored carpets across the plains and low hills.

The following day, Solís continued downstream, passing the ranch of San Bartolo, the ranch of Guerra, and Amoladeras Creek, and camped at the ranch of Corralitos de Reyes, which belonged to Mission Espíritu Santo.[17]

On April 12, the party changed direction, turning away from the river toward the northeast. They passed La Sinfonía, "Arroyo Cleto" (modern Ecleto Creek), and camped at Arroyo Cuchillo (Sandies Creek), which was not the same Arroyo del Cuchillo (Coleto Creek) crossed by Rubí the year before soon after leaving the San Antonio River. Rubí had turned northeast away from the river at a point a few miles farther south to cross at Vado del Gobernador. Solís's military escorted party planned to cross the Guadalupe about 20 miles above Gobernador, at a crossing called Vado de Adaesaños. The distance Solís traveled suggests that the route followed generally the DeWitt-Gonzales County line (see *Seguin*, NH14-9).

At this camp, Solís was joined again by armed Indians from Mission Espíritu Santo who came to guide and accompany him. He was traveling through ranch country that belonged to the mission, so the appearance of these armed native escorts is not surprising. These Indians knew the local area well; they also were the cowboys for the huge (million-acre) mission spread. They could, with credibility, confirm local place-names for Solís.

Another norther, complete with snow, again delayed the movement. Although a heavy snow and ice storm in the DeWitt County area in mid-April is improbable today (there is no account of one in the records of the U.S. National Oceanic and Atmospheric Administration), a similar prolonged February snowstorm repeatedly struck Captain Orobio y Basterra's 1747 expedition about 40 miles south of Solís's line of march.[18]

On April 13, Solís's party marched only 10 miles through more oak to a known campsite called Adaesaños near a creek with heavy thickets. The name of the camp is associated with the inhabitants of the presidio and mission at Los Adaes in East Texas, suggesting that the residents of Los Adaes who traveled to San Antonio frequently used this protected campsite and its nearby ford on the Guadalupe River. The crossing is identified by the name Vado de Adaesaños on Mascaró's ca. 1807 map.

Solís's party, with the convoy of Adaysaños and their escort, made their way to the Guadalupe and crossed during the following two days. They forded where the river was wide and swift, probably below present Hochheim. Solís went across on a raft and made note of the large willows, cottonwoods, pecan trees, cypresses, and oaks along the banks. Grapevines climbed to the top of many trees.

While waiting for the large Adaesaños convoy to pass, Solís received several letters. The padre did not explain where the letters came from, but perhaps they were delivered by an early service between San Antonio and Los Adaes. The mail delivery suggests that Solís's party was apparently on the established route. In addition, an early Spanish casualty of poison ivy was reported: Brother Antonio Casai, who had joined Solís at the Espíritu Santo mission, was sent back to the mission to be cured.

On April 17, the small group, probably following behind the convoy, moved downstream to camp that evening at a site that Solís called Cuero, which means rawhide in Spanish. Along the path that day, the party passed two large creeks (probably McCoy's Creek and Cuero Creek) and arrived at a bend on the bank of the Guadalupe. The campsite called Cuero was probably identified by name by the local Indian escorts from La Bahía and was within a few miles of the present-day city of the same name.

The following day, Solís turned north along the pathway Rubí had also called the Camino Real to East Texas. They passed El Rosal and camped at the *paraje* La Mota del Padre Campa, both of which Lafora had mentioned the year before. El Rosal was probably the crossing of Big Brushy Creek a few miles north of Yoakum; Mota del Padre Campa was likely a crossing of Mustang Creek between modern Yoakum and Shiner. Solís reported seeing green and pleasant open lands with oak mottes and many deer, turkeys, and prairie chickens.

On April 19, the party continued to follow the road north, past Los Ramitos, La Cabeza, and La Vaca, and camped at the frequently used Breviario campsite. These places or stream crossings are the same or similar to those visited by Rubí. Los Ramitos was probably the crossing of present Rocky Creek near Shiner; La Cabeza was the crossing of present Boggy Creek, north of Shiner; La Vaca was the crossing of the present Lavaca River near Moulton; and Breviario was on one of the numerous small tributaries of the Navidad near Flatonia (see *Seguin*, NH14-9).

The next day, the party continued the march about 31 miles, seeing elms, cottonwoods, and pecans, to a camp near the Colorado River. They passed La Lamedita and La Navidad and camped at a creek location that Solís called "Los Creditos." This identification (found in three manuscript copies of Solís's diary) was probably a mistake by Solís: both Rubí and Lafora called a creek in the same area Cedritos (cedar trees) and Solís mentioned, for the first time along the southern route, the presence of cedars among the oaks, elms, and cottonwoods. He added that the entire region along the road north from the Guadalupe was inhabited by Aranama Indians, who were rebellious former members of Mission Espíritu Santo. These Indians had been caught and returned by force to the mission on several occasions for worship and work; consequently, they were vengeful and considered "very dangerous." Given their earlier treatment, the Indians' disposition is not surprising.

Solís reported that the "barbarous" Coco tribe also lived on the nearby banks of the Colorado. He was probably referring not only to the area toward the coast where De León (in 1690) had found some Coco living on Sandy Creek in Colorado County, but also to the open area northeast toward the Brazos. Along the river the party also identified willows, cypresses, pecans, and different species of oak.

Solís's party continued on April 21 along the road that Rubí had followed the year before, fording the Colorado near La Grange. Immediately beyond the Colorado the road was open, leading through rolling prairie and then past two creeks that Rubí had mentioned, La Sandía and Pilmonte. The next day, Solís noted again that they were passing through Coco country and that they saw the junction of the road to the presidio and mission of Orcoquisac on the right side. Solís also recorded seeing bison among the herds of wild Spanish cattle. He attributed the presence of the cattle herds to the farsightedness of De León, who (according to Solís) intentionally left a cow, a bull, a horse, and a mare in this area. The truth is that most expeditions had abandoned stock along the route, some of which were runaways or were left because they were in poor condition. They camped at Bernabé Creek, where Rubí had stopped on August 30, 1767.[19]

On April 23, the party finally entered the Monte Grande called El Diablo, passed Quita Calzones, and camped at Don Carlos. Solís was still tracking Rubí's earlier route and noting the same named camps. The name El Diablo referred to the northern extension of the thick woods of the Monte Grande that Solís earlier called Diablo southeast of San Antonio. The party continued to follow the road, but at times had to cut their way and move single file. In the limited but open prairie areas in the woods there were numerous wild bulls, cows, calves, bison, and deer. Sassafras, persimmon, laurel, and *granaditas de China* (see Appendix II entry on "Pomegranate") were among the smaller trees in the deep woods. On April 24, the party arrived at El Encadenada, an encampment that Solís said was famous for the faithless Indian found there, near the junction of the Brazos River and the Little Brazos.

The next day, Solís crossed both the Brazos and the Little Brazos at a point where the two rivers were about 8 miles apart. The men used a raft made of logs to cross the "first Brazos de Dios," which was the larger river, and then waded across the smaller "second Brazos de Dios" (the Little Brazos). It is significant that the first branch was reported to be so much larger than the second branch. If the ford had been at the junction of the Little River and the Brazos, as some historians have projected, the first branch (the Little River) would have been smaller, not larger, as Solís reported.[20]

Solís continued a short distance beyond the crossing to El Paes, the camp for the night. Rubí had camped at the same location (called País) on September 1 the year before. A number of tribes lived near the junction of the two rivers, according to Solís, including the "Coco, Mayeye, Jojuane, Tancagueye, and many others." Each tribe, Solís wrote, could be distinguished easily by the different stripes they painted on their bodies and how they cut their hair. Some had their heads shaved like the padres, while others just shaved near the forehead, allowing most of the hair to grow down their necks or leaving a long lock of hair on the crown of the head.

The presence of the Coco in this immediate area with the other named tribes is significant because their customary classification as Karankawan suggests that they would more likely be found elsewhere, with coastal Karankawan tribes.

The two nations identified as the "Jojuane" and the "Tancagueye" may have been the Yojuane and the Tonkawa. The assumption that several tribes native to the area between the central Guadalupe and Colorado (the Sana, Cava, Toho, and Emet, for example) were linguistically and perhaps otherwise associated with the Tonkawa has recently been disputed by Texas anthropologists LeRoy Johnson and T. N. Campbell. These authorities have carefully examined the documentary evidence, found primarily in the records of Mission San Antonio de Valero, and concluded that the Sana, Toho, Cava, Sijame, and perhaps the Mesquite and Emet Indians spoke a Sanan language,[21] not the Tonkawa language as suggested much earlier by the historians Herbert E. Bolton and John R. Swanson of the Bureau of American Ethnology. This conclusion that Tonkawa Indians did not appear in lower Central Texas until the middle or later eighteenth century is supported by the fact that Solís makes the first reference to the Tonkawa by any expedition diarist. By the time the Anglo settlers arrived in the 1820s and 1830s, the Tonkawa were widely spread through Central Texas, as reported by Berlandier.[22]

The padre added the comment that the Indians who gathered near the Brazos did not congregate and live near each other because they were linguistically related and, in fact, they were not. The different tribes did not speak to each other to communicate, but used a sign language which, Solís said, permitted them to "chat" for hours or "for entire days." The padre explained that one of the first tasks of a new priest in Texas was to learn Indian signs. At the time of first European contact, Native Americans used sign language from the plains to the Caribbean. The signs recognized and used by Americans with a hearing impairment today (American Sign Language) are in many instances identical to Indian sign language recorded by experts who studied the subject and published works illustrating Indian signs over 150 years ago or within about fifty-five years after Solís's diary report.[23]

On April 26, the party moved 12 leagues northeast to camp at Corpus Christi, the *paraje* named by Ramón and Espinosa in 1716 and noted by Rubí the year before as the first camp northeast of the Brazos crossing.[24] Solís's party saw deer, bison, turkeys, and quail in the open corridor within the thick line of woods. Again, had the crossing occurred farther north, at the junction of the Little River and the Brazos in Milam County, the direction taken by the party would have been east toward the Trinity crossing, not north-northeast. In addition, the area immediately beyond the crossing— if that crossing had occurred at Little River—would have been in the heart of the Monte Grande, where there is no open prairie to support the large herds of buffalo and deer reported by Solís.

The following day, the padre reported crossing the Navasoto, a stream that was "not very large." Rubí had also mentioned Navasoto Creek and Navasoto Lagoon when he traveled through the same area north-northeast of the Brazos crossing. Earlier expeditions had mentioned a Santa Ana Lake or Lagoon in the area, which also may have been associated with the Navasota River. On April 27, the evening before Solís reached the Trinity, the creek named El Carrizo was his campsite. Rubí had crossed the same named creek on September 3 the year before.

The party suffered no delay in crossing the Trinity, which was full, but they waded across on a bed of fine flint rock. The dense canebrakes along the river banks gave protection for the large alligators. According to Solís, many "barbarous Indians" also lived near the Trinity: the "Taguacane, Quichuixe, Asinai, Vidai, Deadose, and many others." The Deadose frequently lived near the Trinity during the middle eighteenth century. The "Taguacane" were most likely the Tawakoni, a Wichita tribe that moved near the Trinity from the Red River area in the mid-eighteenth century. The "Vidai" were probably the local Bidai Indians. The "Quichuixe" cannot be further identified with certainty.

Near the Trinity crossing, the "mailman" stopped again, delivering letters addressed to Solís from associates at the College of Guadalupe and from several other correspondents. The mail delivery reported on the Guadalupe two weeks earlier had included letters from some of the same individuals, who apparently were writing to the padre from New Spain. These two episodes may suggest that by 1768 a rather frequent mail service from northern New Spain to the capital city of Los Adaes had been established.

Solís continued to follow the Camino Real northeast from the Trinity to the familiar *paraje* Efigenia the following day and proceeded to Santa Coleta and the San Pedro Creek area. The padre noted that beyond the Trinity there were a few deer and no bison, but the bear population increased. He wrote that the Tejas Indians he met near the creek were white, rather than reddish-tan, the color normally attributed to the Indians. The

Tejas were well built, with light-colored hair. The men were naked, except for a breechcloth; the women, who were fair and pretty, wore deerskin dresses, bordered with colored beads, and bone earrings. The Tejas raised corn (two crops each year), chickens, and turkeys and had orchards of peach, plum, persimmon, and fig trees. Their grass houses were rounded like domes and roofed from the ground. Their hammock beds were made of buffalo hides, which were tanned on both sides. The abundance of food, including domesticated stock, and their own domestic stability were factors that made any effort to regroup these Indians into new church communities within the traditional mission system rather fruitless.

The Tejas were different from the Indians reported on earlier expeditions in another respect. One Tejas leader, called Santa Adiva, was female. Solís described her as a queen, who had five husbands. Santa Adiva lived in a very large house with many male and female servants, and Solís added that she received gifts from other members of the tribe.

The padre also emphasized that the Indians here were armed with French guns (which Rubí had noted were more accurate at a longer range than the Spanish weapons) and rarely used a bow and arrow, the weapons available to most of the Indians in San Antonio to fight the Apache, who were also well armed. The musket, he added, was so significant to the Tejas that they were buried in a sitting position with their guns, powder, and balls near at hand along with their meat, jug of water, and traditional feathers and beads.[25]

Beyond the Neches, the party proceeded to the Angelina River (reached on May 1), where they encountered "the Tejas, Asinay, and Navidacho, all friendly." Solís added that the local Indians made a jam of figs and persimmons to trade to the Spaniards and French; they kept long-nose dogs (*jubines*) that were a cross between a dog and a coyote or wolf. The next day, they reached Mission Guadalupe near present-day Nacogdoches. Solís's group visited Mission Ayes (Ais) on May 5, but then continued the following morning through woods of pine, cedar, sassafras, *castaño,* and persimmon toward the Sabine River, which they reached on May 7. Solís could not wade across, as he had crossed the Navasota and Trinity; he used a raft instead.

The padre gave no direction or distance traveled each day from the Sabine to Los Adaes, but the diary does disclose that he met with a number of Indian leaders, called captains, along the route to the Sabine and beyond. Near the Angelina, Captain Vigotes of the Navidacho and Captain Gorgoritos of the Bidai welcomed the party. At Mission Nacogdoches, Captain Sanchez met and ate with the padre. Later, Captain Urjataña of the Ays nation and Captain Antonio Abad of the Bidai also greeted Solís.

Governor Hugo Oconor was present at the party's arrival at the capital on May 8. The padre's report on the mission was discouraging: the only item found in abundance was whiskey, provided by French traders, who were located 18 miles east. There was no Indian congregation. The church was old, reduced, and almost destroyed; church ornaments were badly abused. The weather, particularly in the winter, was difficult: violent northers brought snow for many days, covering the country with more than a foot and a half of powder that quickly froze.

Immediately after the inspection of the mission at Los Adaes was completed, Solís returned west via the route taken earlier. He noted in his diary that a daily itinerary would not be kept on the return march because it would be essentially a duplication of the notes made earlier on the trip northeast.

When Solís arrived near present San Augustine on May 27, he did note that he met with the Indians of the Ais nation. This tribe was the worst in the province, he wrote, showing open disrespect to the church and the local padres by physically abusing churchmen and making jokes about them. The padre, however, made a curious report of an inspection visit to the Zacatecan Mission Orcoquisac with Father Santa María, who was its minister. The year before, Rubí had reported on conditions at the mission far to the south, where it was established a few miles north of Trinity Bay.[26]

The only serious delay on the return occurred at the mission near Nacogdoches, where the padre was detained waiting for an escort of soldiers from the governor. While visiting near Nacogdoches, Solís wrote about the many diseases suffered by the local Indian population, including smallpox, measles, typhoid fever, blisters, and *onanahuiates*, all of which were induced, according to the padre's diagnosis, by the excessive drinking of whiskey and sugarcane wine. The correct translation of the word *onanahuiates* cannot be given with certainty. One literal interpretation would be an addiction to masturbation, but Solís may have been referring to venereal diseases, as suggested by translator Peter P. Forrestal.[27]

After fruitlessly waiting for twelve days (from June 7 to 19) for an official escort, Solís joined a mule train with some other passengers and proceeded down the road back toward the Trinity, which he crossed by raft one week later. The Brazos de Dios crossing took Solís two days (July 2 and 3), and he found the second branch (the Brazos) more flooded and difficult to cross than the Little Brazos. He reached the Colorado River on July 9. Because of high water, Solís had to wait four days for the river to recede and then crossed in a canoe that had been used the year before by Rubí. The horses and baggage followed the next day.

On July 14, the party left the Colorado River and camped at Breviario, where Solís was met by Padre Martínez from Mission Espíritu Santo. (Rubí had also camped at this *paraje* on his return trip.) At Breviario, two Indian guards from the mission, identified as "Pedro and Ramón," protected Solís by holding off a threatening advance by the Aranama. These Indians were members of the same party of apostates mentioned as dangerous earlier by both Solís and Rubí. After a two-day march, camping the first evening at Piélago del Rosal, Solís arrived at the Guadalupe and was met by a military guard from Presidio La Bahía. The padre pointed out, in a sharply negative comment, that the troops were sent not to offer protection but to inspect his party for French contraband. His diary does not identify which of the three available Guadalupe fords was used.

On July 17, the party continued south, crossing Las Animas Creek (noted by Rubí) and camping on the Piélago de las Cruces. The next day, they arrived at the La Bahía presidio and mission after crossing Monaguía Creek. As Solís mentioned earlier, there were numerous homosexuals called *monaguía* among the Karankawan group. The relationship between the creek and this segment of the Indian population is unknown. Rubí earlier reported the creek named Monaguilla at the same location. Although the names of creeks crossed along the road from the Guadalupe to the San Antonio River near Goliad have all changed from the Spanish names used in the 1760s, the creek Solís called Monaguía is called Manahuilla today (see *Seguin,* NH14-9).

Solís remained at Mission Espíritu Santo to bathe and rest. On July 28, he visited the neighboring mission of Rosario on his way north toward San Antonio. The party then proceeded up the right bank of the San Antonio River to La Escondida (present Escondido Creek) and then forded the river near the Conquista crossing used by De León and Salinas. Following the left bank of the river, the party reached the ranches San Francisco and Chayopines. Solís arrived at Mission San José on August 1, which means that he recrossed the river via the road network that connected the San Antonio missions.

After bathing and resting for another two weeks, Solís began his return trip from San Antonio to Zacatecas by way of Laredo. The padre recorded neither the distance nor the direction covered daily after he left San Antonio on August 16 headed toward Laredo. He traveled with an escort that included one sergeant, a corporal, and eight troopers. The party moved south to cross the San Miguel and camped near the Nueces. Solís said that care was taken along the full length of the trail to detect any sign of Apache or Comanche who came to the area looking for the Apache. Before reaching Laredo, they camped at the watering hole called El Pato, where Rubí said the road north from Laredo forked into two trails—one to La Bahía and the second to San Antonio.

Solís reached Laredo on August 24 and arrived at the College of Our Lady of Guadalupe near Zacatecas on October 1. Although no formal directives resulted from Solís's visit to Texas, as they did from Rubí's inspection trip, the padre's diary remains one of the treasures of the Spanish colonial period, containing richly detailed observations and comments on Texas and its native people and environment in the late 1760s.

TABLE 11
Fray Gaspar José de Solís's 1768 Inspection Tour

Date	Distance Leagues (Miles)	Direction	Campsite (COUNTY)
2/15	2 (5.2)	—	Río Grande (WEBB) [2]
2/16	5 (13)	—	Rosario (WEBB) [2]
2/17	12 (31.2)	—	Salado (WEBB) [2]
2/18	12 (31.2)	—	San Casimiro (DUVAL) [2]
2/19	—	—	Senor San Joseph (DUVAL) [2]
2/20	—	—	(Delayed by snow)
2/21	—	—	(Delayed by snow)
2/22	8 (20.8)	—	Tablitas (JIM WELLS) [2]
2/23	12 (31.2)	—	Río Nueces (Nueces River, LIVE OAK) [1]
2/24	12 (31.2)	—	Agua Dulce (BEE) [2]
2/25	—	—	Río San Antonio (GOLIAD) [1]
2/26	3 (7.8)	—	Misión Rosario (Mission Rosario, GOLIAD)

[Solís remained in the mission area until March 15, when he proceeded northwest to San Antonio.]

Date	Distance Leagues (Miles)	Direction	Campsite (COUNTY)
3/15	12 (31.2)	—	La Escondida (Escondido Creek, KARNES) [1]
3/16	—	—	Rancho de Labor (San Antonio River, WILSON) [1]
3/17	16 (41.6)	—	San Juan de Capistrano (below Salado Creek, WILSON) [1]
3/18	7 (18.2)	—	Misión San Joseph (Mission San José, San Antonio River, BEXAR) [1]

[Solís remained in the San Antonio area until April 7, when he proceeded to Los Adaes.]

Date	Distance Leagues (Miles)	Direction	Campsite (COUNTY)
4/7	—	—	Arroyo Salado (Salado Creek, BEXAR) [1]
4/8	—	—	(Remained in camp because of snow) [1]
4/9	7 (18.2)		Chayopines (above Floresville, WILSON) [1]
4/10	16 (41.6)		Arroyo Marcelino (Marcelinas Creek, WILSON) [1]
4/11	11 (28.6)		Corralitos de Reyes (Cibolo Creek, WILSON) [1]
4/12	17 (44.2)	NE	Arroyo Cuchillo (Sandies Creek, Gonzales-DeWitt County line) [1]
4/13	4 (10.4)	—	Adaesaños (Fulcher Creek, near Gonzales-DeWitt County line) [1]
4/14	—	—	(Remained in camp because of snow) [1]
4/15	4 (10.4)	—	Río Guadalupe (Guadalupe River, DEWITT) [1]
4/16	—	—	(Remained in camp to rest)
4/17	5 (13)	—	Cuero (near modern Cuero, DEWITT) [1]
4/18	8 (20.8)	N	La Mota del Padre Campa (near Yoakum, LAVACA) [1]
4/19	16 (41.6)	—	Breviario (headwater creek, Navidad River, FAYETTE) [1]

Date	Distance Leagues (Miles)	Direction	Campsite (COUNTY)
4/20	12 (31.2)	—	Creditos (near Buckner's Creek, FAYETTE) [1]
4/21	18 (46.8)	NE	Arroyo El Pilmonte (FAYETTE) [1]
4/22	16 (41.6)	NNE	Arroyo Bernabé (FAYETTE) [1]
4/23	12 (31.2)	NNE	La Pulsera (WASHINGTON) [2]
4/24	12 (31.2)	NNE	El Encadenado (BURLESON) [2]
4/25	8 (20.8)	E	El Paes (junction of Little Brazos and Brazos) [1]
4/26	12 (31.2)	NNE	Corpus Christi (BRAZOS) [1]
4/27	12 (31.2)	NE	El Carrizo (MADISON) [1]
4/28	16 (41.6)	NE	San Juan (HOUSTON) [1]
4/29	16 (41.6)	NE	Peñitas (HOUSTON) [2]
4/30	16 (41.6)	NE	Río de Nechas (Neches River, CHEROKEE) [1]
5/1	12 (31.2)	NE	Río Angelina (Angelina River, NACOGDOCHES) [1]
5/2	8 (20.8)	NE	Misión Nuestra Señora de Guadalupe de Nacogdoches (NACOGDOCHES) [1]
5/3	—	—	(Remained in camp to worship)
5/4	12 (31.2)	E	Río Atollague (SAN AUGUSTINE) [2]
5/5	8 (20.8)	E	Misión Ayes (SAN AUGUSTINE) [1]
5/6	—	E	Arroyo Gonzalitos (Louisiana) [1]
5/7	12 (31.2)	E	Arroyo Puerto de Las Cavaszas (Louisiana) [2]
5/8	—	E	Misión Adays (near Robeline, Louisiana) [1]

[Solís inspected the mission, met with Governor Don Hugo Oconor, and visited the Indians in the area. Without giving the distance and direction traveled, the padre described his return journey, which followed the same route as the one taken east. From the Brazos, Solís moved southwest, camping at the *parajes* used earlier, until he reached the Colorado crossing at the La Grange on July 13.]

Date	Distance Leagues (Miles)	Direction	Campsite (COUNTY)
7/14	—	—	Breviario (Navidad River, FAYETTE) [1]
7/15	—	—	Piélago del Rosal (Lavaca River, LAVACA) [1]
7/16	—	—	Río Guadalupe (Guadalupe River, DEWITT) [1]
7/17	—	—	Piélago de las Cruces (Coleto Creek, DEWITT) [1]

[Solís remained near Goliad until July 28.]

Date	Distance Leagues (Miles)	Direction	Campsite (COUNTY)
7/28	—	—	Misión Rosario (GOLIAD) [1]
7/29	—	—	La Escondida (Escondido Creek, KARNES) [1]
7/30	—	—	Rancho San Francisco (left bank of San Antonio river, WILSON) [1]
7/31	—	—	Rancho Chayopines (WILSON) [1]
8/1	—	—	Misión San José (BEXAR) [1]

[On August 16, Solís left San Antonio, traveling south toward Laredo. The diary includes no daily notation of the number of leagues traveled or direction taken beyond San Antonio.]

FIGURE 13
*Disillusioned with life at the Texas missions, some Indians returned to their old ways
below the Rio Grande.*

THIRTEEN

CONCLUSION

A careful study of the diaries of the eleven Spanish expeditions into Texas from northeastern New Spain from 1689 to 1768 leads to the conclusion that Alonso de León's 1689–1690 route from Monclova to East Texas was the first Spanish trail (*camino*) across Texas and that De León followed existing Indian trade routes that had been in use for decades, perhaps longer (see Map 1). Every Spanish expedition that crossed the Rio Grande between 1691 and 1768 followed all or part of De León's road. Major segments of his route continued to be used throughout the eighteenth century, when the Camino Real was one of the principal routes connecting northeastern New Spain to East Texas and Louisiana (see Map 2).

The expedition diaries record that De León did not blaze his first trail through Texas; rather, he followed local Indian guides who directed him along their own well-known trade routes to his destination. From Monclova to the Guadalupe, the governor was guided by two Indians from northern Coahuila. One was a Quem Indian who had visited La Salle's settlement near Matagorda Bay a short time before agreeing to lead De León to the French fort. The second Indian guide, called Juan (or Juanillo), was a leader of the Pacpul Indians. The same two guides also served on De León's second journey and then later on Terán's expedition of 1691–1692. In addition to the Indian guides, De León had the services of the old Frenchman Jean Géry, who reported that the trail was marked from near the Rio Grande to La Salle's bay. De León's party found that the known pathway was an old Indian trade route marked years earlier by inscriptions at a critical location on the present Frio River in northwestern Frio County and by a cairn or stone pile marker a few miles east of Cibolo Creek in Karnes County.

The first clear indication that De León was following a marked Indian trade route is found in the governor's diary entry for April 6, 1689. According to De León's account, near the Río Hondo (present Frio River) the expedition found some large white rocks near the pathway, with carved crosses and other figures that had been cut with great skill many years before. The following day, as the party continued 4 leagues down the right bank of the Frio, De León noted that all along the line of march the party had seen Indian paths made long ago. One week later, the governor commented that in a motte of oaks about half a league east of Cibolo Creek the party found a small pile of stones placed by hand. These three references by De León in 1689, indicating that he was following a marked Indian route, show that there was at least one known and used Indian trade route out of northeast Mexico leading across South and Central Texas to the Tejas Indians in East Texas in the late seventeenth century.

Beyond the Guadalupe River, De León depended on other Indian tribes (Toho, Emet, and Sana), whom he first encountered in present DeWitt County, to lead him along a connecting Indian roadway through relatively open country north to the Colorado River crossing near La Grange in Fayette County. This prominent crossing was marked by the high hill later called Buenavista (the present-day Monument Hill) on the right bank of the Colorado and was located at the southern border of the dense woods called the Monte Grande. In 1689, these local Indians also escorted De León from the Guadalupe to Matagorda Bay; the same tribes assisted him near the Colorado River crossing near La Grange when he returned in 1690.

Recently, LeRoy Johnson and Thomas N. Campbell have concluded that some of these tribes that guided De León had their own language (Sanan) and were not associated at that time with the Tonkawa, as suggested by earlier authorities including Herbert E. Bolton. These tribes that lived principally between the Guadalupe and the Colorado were also familiar with the Indian trade route that led beyond the Colorado to East Texas, as evidenced by the Emet Indian messenger who, in 1689, delivered De León's letter to the Frenchmen living in a Tejas village near the Neches River and then returned the next week with their written reply to De León at Matagorda Bay.

In 1690, when De León moved east from the Colorado on his journey to visit the Tejas, he was led by Tejas guides who (according to Massanet) "showed us the way until we met the Tejas governor." Along the same Indian pathway, De León was also guided by two young Frenchmen (Pierre Talon and Pierre Meunier) who had lived with the Tejas and knew well the Indian pathway that crossed the Trinity near Brushy Creek in Leon County and led to the Tejas villages in the present-day San Pedro Creek valley in Houston County a few miles west of the Neches. Thus, this series of connecting pathways from the Rio Grande to the Neches that had served as an Indian trade route for decades, perhaps centuries, became De León's road and the first Spanish trail across Texas.

After De León established the first Spanish road to East Texas, the Spaniards continued to use his route on the two later expeditions in the 1690s. Terán, using Tejas and Cantona Indian guides, followed De León's route from the Colorado to East Texas on his second journey to the mission field in the fall of 1691 and on his return trip to Matagorda Bay in the winter of 1692. On Terán's first trip to East Texas in the spring and summer of 1691, he had taken De León's road from Monclova to the Frio River, but then followed his own Indian guides through the modern San Antonio area to a Colorado River encampment below present-day Bastrop. While a unit from Terán's company visited the Matagorda Bay area to the south, Terán moved his camp farther downstream along the left bank closer to modern La Grange. From that camp Terán, Massanet, and their Tejas guides moved along a route to East Texas that was north and west of De León's road. Finally, Salinas tracked the full stretch of De León's road, campsite to campsite, on his resupply mission from Monclova to East Texas in the spring and summer of 1693.

The strongest evidence that there was at least one Indian trade route out of northeastern New Spain into South Texas in the late seventeenth century is found in the repeated reports of Indian tribes from modern northeastern Mexico and West Texas camping, hunting, or trading with tribes that lived in Central Texas on the west (never east) side of the Colorado River crossing at La Grange in Fayette County or on the west side of the Colorado crossing near San Marcos.

The first report by Spanish diarists that the tribes met along the expedition route in Central Texas were actually visitors from below the Rio Grande was by Terán and Massanet in the summer of 1691. The two diarists noted that near San Marcos their expedition party encountered a large Indian encampment (2,000 to 3,000) composed of Jumano, Cibolo, Catqueza (perhaps Cacquite), Caynaaya, and Chalome who were meeting with a local tribe, the Cantona. Massanet confirmed that these tribes (and possibly others) annually traveled from West Texas and from Coahuila and Chihuahua below the Rio Grande to hunt and trade with Indians who lived between the Guadalupe and the Colorado and with the Tejas and other Caddo Indians in East Texas. Elizabeth A. H. John and other historians have suggested that these Indians had visited Tejas trade fairs for decades.

The expedition of Governor Salinas adds substantial evidence that De León's route, which Salinas followed with his own Indian guides, tracked an early Indian trade route. Shortly after crossing the Rio Grande, Salinas was warned that some Jumano and Toboso Indians from below the Rio Grande intended to attack his supply column near the traditional Colorado crossing in present Fayette County. This warning was taken seriously because all the parties, Indians as well as Spaniards, knew the same route and used the same Colorado crossing near La Grange. As warned, about 90 miles south of the Colorado crossing, a large armed and angry Jumano party threatened Salinas near the creek De León had named Salado in western DeWitt county. Farther along the same trail, between the Guadalupe and the Colorado, Salinas reported several gatherings of local Indians with tribes from Coahuila and others from East Texas. The area, it seems, was used as something of a "rendezvous," as described by William R. Swagerty. La Salle had also met some mounted tribes, with saddles and spurs, from west of the Rio Grande on one of his journeys between the lower Guadalupe and Colorado.

West of the Colorado crossing, the Simaoma and Mescal from northern Coahuila were meeting with some local Tohaha Indians; some Cacaxtle Indians from below the Rio Grande were also gathered near the La Grange crossing. Later, in the same area, Salinas met some Jumano from West Texas and Chihuahua with a group of Asinai (Tejas) from East Texas and a second group of Tejas who were meeting with the local Cantona. Nearby, other Simaoma from Coahuila were meeting with members of another gathering of East Texas Asinai. The Saquita (or Cacquite), probably members of the tribe from Coahuila that Terán had met two years earlier while visiting San Marcos, were also encountered along the route in Lavaca County near a local Sana Indian encampment. The Saquita or Cacquite supplied a knowledgeable Spanish-speaking guide to lead Salinas along an Indian trail to a destination he had not previously visited (the San Antonio area) and south to the familiar crossing of the Frio below Hondo Creek.

The Spaniards' repeated use of the same Indian route extending over 500 miles was made possible, in part, by the presence of several of the same expedition officials, senior members, and Indian guides on successive journeys. Captain Martínez, who was with De León in 1689 and again in 1690, was an officer on Terán's expedition in 1691–1692. Captain Salinas accompanied De León in 1690 and therefore could also help guide Terán between Matagorda Bay and East Texas in 1691–1692 and was well qualified to lead his own expedition along De León's road in 1693. Fray Massanet and the Quem and Pacpul Indian guides traveled with De León in both 1689 and 1690 and assisted Terán in 1691–1692. Pierre Talon, who served as a guide to De León in 1690, was used as a guide again by Terán in 1691–1692. This continuity of experienced personnel (military, ecclesiastical, French captives, and Indian guides) on subsequent expeditions substantially strengthened the Spanish use of the same trail. De León's route was the only Spanish road used on successive expeditions in the seventeenth century. This route was not identified at the time by any name (such as the Camino Real), but was simply called *el camino*.

In the early eighteenth century, when the Spaniards decided to reestablish a presence in East Texas by building a presidio and several new missions there, they sought a new road that ran through the San Antonio area. Both Terán and Salinas had visited the San Antonio area in the 1690s, but they had traveled through San Antonio moving in opposite directions and following different routes. The Spaniard principally responsible for establishing this new road through San Antonio to the Colorado crossing south of Austin and on to the Brazos crossing in Burleson County and to East Texas in the eighteenth century was Fray Isidro Félix de Espinosa. In 1709, Espinosa, Fray Olivares, and Captain Aguirre left San Juan Bautista on the Rio Grande (near the Rio Grande crossing used by De León) and generally followed De León's road to the Frio crossing a few miles west of present-day Pearsall. Fray Espinosa then turned north to the Medina and the San Antonio area, rather than continuing east as De León had toward the bay. Espinosa followed north from the Frio to the Medina the pathway that Salinas with his Saquita (or Cacquite) guide had first taken south when returning to Monclova from East Texas in 1693.

Espinosa named the river at San Antonio Río de San Antonio de Padua (Massanet and Terán, in 1691, had called the location itself San Antonio de Padua) and found some visiting Siupam, Chalome, and Sijame from below the Rio Grande to lead him to the Colorado. These Indians guided Espinosa's small caravan northeast, past modern New Braunfels and San Marcos, through relatively open areas to a crossing of the Colorado a few miles above the present Onion Creek junction and a few miles below Austin in Travis County. Espinosa's crossing of the Colorado was north of the heavy timber belt called the Monte Grande; De León's crossing at La Grange was a few miles south of the same wooded area. On this first journey (in 1709), Espinosa ventured only a few miles east of the Colorado near the present-day Travis-Bastrop County line and then returned to the Rio Grande. Espinosa's route from San Antonio to the Colorado crossing (not Terán's 1691 route, which first crossed about 30 miles south and then moved downstream) was called "the road to the Tejas" by one diarist on Governor Alarcón's expeditions.

In 1716, Espinosa and Captain Domingo Ramón returned northeast from the Rio Grande along Espinosa's route through San Antonio to the same crossing on the Colorado below Austin, intending to extend the road to East Texas, where a presidio and missions were to be established. Although neither the padre nor the captain (nor any immediately available guide) knew of a trail beyond the upper Colorado crossing, the party searched and found near the Arroyo de San Xavier (present-day San Gabriel River) several Indians, including some Mescal and Ervipiame, to serve as guides. These Indians led the party southeast from the San Gabriel about 50 miles mostly through the dense woods called the Monte Grande to their cluster of villages known later as Ranchería Grande near the junction of the Brazos and the Little Brazos River in Burleson County. Texas historians beginning with Herbert E. Bolton have incorrectly placed this crossing, later called the Brazos de Dios ford, at a location near the junction of the Brazos and the Little River in Milam County. The Marqués de Rubí later called this route from San Antonio to San Marcos and the Colorado and on via the San Xavier (San Gabriel) to the Brazos the Xavier Road.

Espinosa's 1716 party, led by Tejas guides, moved beyond the Brazos into a relatively open corridor that runs through the surrounding Monte Grande along the present Robertson-Brazos County line and continued northeast into present Leon and Madison counties. This significant narrow but open corridor is easily identified on contemporary government topographical maps that indicate the more heavily wooded areas (see *Austin*, NH14-6).

Espinosa named the first major creek and campsite that he found, 9 leagues northeast of the Brazos crossing, Corpus Christi. This creek (present-day Cedar Creek) and camp continued to be used along the same route and to be identified by the same name for over 100 years. On his return from the Trinity to San Antonio, Jean Louis Berlandier passed the same camp and creek named Corpus Christi about 3 leagues west of the Navasota River on June 1, 1828. Stephen F. Austin also referenced the creek and roadway on his *Map of Texas* published in Philadelphia in 1830, which shows the principal route between the Red River and the Colorado.

The Navasota River, about 3 leagues east of Corpus Christi, was called the Buenaventura by Espinosa, and the next stop, a few miles east of the Navasota, was the lake or lagoon that Espinosa named Santa Ana. These may have been the lakes or ponds Terán noted on his first journey from the Colorado to East Texas in 1691 and visited again on his return that summer to Matagorda Bay. Before the party and their Tejas guides reached the Trinity, Espinosa named several other creeks, valleys, or springs: Santa Clara, San Cristobal, San Fernando, Linares, San Luis Obispo, and Santa Rosa de Viterbo. These locations were repeatedly cited on subsequent expeditions.

Espinosa's route crossed the Trinity at a point southwest of the present-day city of Crockett in Houston County, above the ford used by De León. Beyond the Trinity, Espinosa gave the name Efigenia to a creek that he crossed before he reached the lakes in the San Pedro Creek area where De León and Massanet established the first mission. With local guides, Ramón and Espinosa continued beyond the Neches and the Angelina (without naming the rivers) to the present-day Nacogdoches area.

The old Indian pathway beyond the Brazos crossing became Espinosa's (and to some measure, Ramón's) new road. It was called the customary road to the Tejas by Fray Céliz and the Camino Real by Peña. It served as the principal route for expeditions moving east of the Brazos during the following decades. Thus, to Espinosa, not Terán, is due the credit for the upper route to East Texas from San Antonio, the eastern leg of which in time became known as the Camino Real and later the Old San Antonio Road.

During the ten-year period from 1718 to 1727, three more expeditions from northeastern New Spain marched across Texas, following parts of De León's lower road to the Frio and parts of Espinosa's upper road through San Antonio. Only one (Rivera's) followed Espinosa's way between the Colorado crossing and the Brazos de Dios junction (later called the Xavier Road), but all followed his route (called the Camino Real by Peña) beyond the Navasota to the Neches. In 1718, after Alarcón had journeyed from San Juan Bautista to San Antonio, he was under orders to proceed to the bay before visiting the presidio and missions in East Texas and in present-day Louisiana. At the same time, both Espinosa and Ramón returned from East Texas to San Antonio with their own Tejas guides to escort Alarcón to the crossing of the Brazos at the junction of the Little Brazos that they had pioneered two years earlier. At the river junction, Alarcón's party picked up Espinosa's route, citing many of the same campsites and creeks that Espinosa had previously named along the route to Nacogdoches. Alarcón went on beyond Nacogdoches to the mission at Los Adaes, 7 leagues west of the Red River near the present-day city of Robeline, in Natchitoches Parish, Louisiana.

The location of the mid-eighteenth-century Spanish road through the villages of the closely related Caddoan tribes is relatively clear and noncontroversial compared to the location of expedition routes between the Rio Grande and the Trinity. The Spanish road in East Texas followed more well-worn and familiar Caddoan trails connecting related nearby Indian communities. The principal route ran from San Pedro Creek in northeastern Houston County, across southern Cherokee County east to Nacogdoches, and then east-southeast toward the modern city of San Augustine, through Sabine County, across the Sabine River, and then east-northeast across Sabine Parish to near present-day Robeline, Louisiana. Although expedition leaders over the years varied the road used to reflect the changed locations of presidios and missions, the East Texas route remained reasonably clear compared to the badly misinterpreted South Texas routes.

When the Marqués de Aguayo marched from the Rio Grande with his large expedition to reestablish a Spanish presence in East Texas after the French "invasion" of 1719, Espinosa accompanied the new governor. Aguayo followed the same road that Espinosa and Ramón had taken in 1716 through San Antonio to the Colorado, crossing below Austin. Aguayo's diarist Peña called the route to San Antonio the Camino Real. From the Colorado, Aguayo's large convoy veered from the Camino Real north to avoid the Monte Grande and crossed the Brazos near present-day Waco. Then he marched southeast, between the Brazos and Navasota, to pick up the Camino Real near Espinosa's crossing of the Navasota River. Since Espinosa was with Aguayo (Captain Domingo Ramón had been dispatched from San Antonio to secure the bay), the expeditionary party could easily follow Espinosa's earlier route, citing creeks and campsites named by Espinosa to the Neches and on to Los Adaes, where Aguayo constructed a presidio and reestablished the mission there.

In 1727, Brigadier Pedro de Rivera performed, in certain respects, the same service for Espinosa's road that Salinas had performed for De León's road. He journeyed along the full course of the roadway, referring to it only as *el camino* and confirming the distance and direction between named campsites soon after the road had been established. Rivera left Monclova and rode directly 600 miles to Los Adaes along De León's road to the Frio and then Espinosa's road through San Antonio to the Colorado crossing in Travis County. Then he found his own way through the 50-mile stretch of the Monte Grande from the San Gabriel River (Arroyo de San Xavier) to the Little Brazos River junction. The route from San Antonio through San Marcos to the Brazos de Dios crossing would later be called the Xavier Road. Beyond the Brazos he followed the customary road to Los Adaes. Rivera's journey confirmed the identifiable route with connecting campsites, except that no recognizable or marked road with established campsites existed between the Colorado and the Brazos crossing in Burleson County.

No major expeditions into Texas originated from New Spain during the forty-year period between 1727 and 1767. Sometime before 1744, probably in the mid-1730s, the customary route from San Antonio to Los Adaes shifted from Espinosa's road that ran northeast from San Antonio north of the Monte Grande and into Apache country to a more secure southern road south of the Monte Grande that followed the San Antonio River downstream southeast to pick up De León's road above the mouth of the Cibolo and then ran east to the Guadalupe crossing at either Vado del Adaesaños or Vado del Gobernador and then north to the Colorado crossing in Fayette County and northeast to the Brazos crossing in Brazos County. This southern route that Rubí and Lafora called the Camino Real was the way that both Rubí (1767) and Solís (1768) traveled to East Texas. The accounts of the journeys of Athanase de Mézières in 1778 and Pedro Vial in 1787 between Nacogdoches and San Antonio convinced Herbert E. Bolton that the lower route called the Camino Real continued to be used into the 1780s.

At no time during the Spanish expeditionary period (1689–1768) was there any San Antonio Road or Camino Real that crossed the Bastrop area in the heart of the Monte Grande, as did the Old San Antonio Road in the nineteenth century. The Camino Real, as identified by the Rubí and Lafora expedition and by other local Spanish officials in Texas, ran south from San Antonio (not northeast) to cross the Colorado below the Monte Grande at La Grange (not in Travis or Bastrop County).

The Camino Real from San Antonio to East Texas and Louisiana followed the left bank of the San Antonio River downstream to the area between Cibolo and Ecleto creeks in Karnes County and then turned east across DeWitt County to the Guadalupe. Rubí and his relatively small group crossed the Guadalupe at Vado del Gobernador near Cuero, but Solís, who had joined a large military-escorted convoy of over 100 persons destined for Los Adaes, crossed the Guadalupe the next year about 20 miles upstream from the Governor's Ford, near a campsite called Adaesaños located a few miles from a crossing called Vado de Los Adaesaños. The names of the campsite and crossing on the Guadalupe strongly suggest that Solís was following the route used by military convoys, public officials, and other travelers regularly moving between Los Adaes and San Antonio at the time. The fact that Solís was following a large military convoy and received mail twice along the route also supports this conclusion.

After fording the Guadalupe, both Rubí and Solís crossed Cuero Creek, about 6 leagues east of the Guadalupe, and proceeded along De León's 1689–1690 route, which Rubí and Lafora called the Camino Real, past many of the same named creeks and *parajes* through Lavaca and Fayette counties to the Colorado. From the Colorado, Rubí and Solís moved northeast through several of the same named campsites and creeks in Burleson County to the ford above the junction of the Brazos and the Little Brazos. De León had crossed the Brazos farther south near the present-day city of Navasota. At the time he crossed the Brazos, Rubí commented that the Xavier Road, which came to the Brazos from the northwest via the Colorado crossing in Travis County, was no longer usable. Espinosa's 1716 road that picked up at the Brazos de Dios crossing was then followed by both Rubí and Solís through Brazos, Madison, and Leon counties into East Texas.

Whereas the first nine expeditions into Texas entered and departed present-day Texas through the Rio Grande crossing near San Juan Bautista, Rubí's military inspection in 1767 and Solís's mission inspection in 1768 used Laredo as a gateway. After completing his inspection, Rubí left the province from Presidio La Bahía and proceeded south to Laredo. A few months later, in early 1768, Solís entered present Texas from Laredo and headed north to the two missions near La Bahía along the same military road that Rubí had used moving south. This road, the lower Bahía Road to Laredo, was a truly Spanish military trail of about 150 miles, not a converted former Indian trail or trade route. The lower Bahía Road was described in detail in formal reports filed ten years before Rubí and Solís followed the route. Here the points of origin and destination were Spanish; La Bahía on the San Antonio River and the *villa* of Laredo were established in response to Spanish needs and were independent of any Indian trade patterns. This is in contrast to the points of origin and destination of De León's first road—the old Indian crossing of the Rio Grande called Francia along the Indian trade route to the Colorado crossing near La Grange and the Tejas communities on San Pedro Creek in Houston County.

This detailed delineation of the routes of the eleven Spanish expeditions from New Spain was developed primarily through a multiexpeditionary approach and a close sequential comparison of the directions and distances recorded and the named rivers, creeks, and campsites cited in the diary entries. The projections were confirmed by the use of contemporary topographic maps and by direct on-site observation by air and on the ground. Manuel Agustín Mascaró's ca. 1807 map, which locates and identifies by name over twenty crossings of the Guadalupe River, provided a valuable additional means of checking and verifying the route projections. Mascaró's map, held in the Bibliothèque Nationale in Paris, was not widely available for study in the United States until the *Southwestern Historical Quarterly* published an article by Jack Jackson on the maps of Father José María de Jesús Puelles in 1988.

Although many of the significant historical documents relating to the early Spanish period in Texas were copied (often by typescript) or otherwise obtained from European and Mexican archives many decades ago, there remain in these same archives numerous maps that could not have been conveniently reproduced at that time and thus were not copied. Now, however, the technology exists and they should be reproduced and made accessible for research in the United States. Mascaró's map is just one example of how critical the information on a map may be. It demonstrates the benefits that could be expected from an active program to secure copies of other manuscript maps in foreign archives relating to Texas and the Gulf Coast.

The chronological review and rigorous cross-document analysis of the Spanish expedition diaries not only show the development of the early Spanish road system in Texas, but also trace the history of the names applied to Texas rivers and creeks. Some stream names used today are the same as the names given the rivers and creeks in the late seventeenth or early eighteenth centuries. Most of the names for major streams, however, have changed over the past 200 years or have even switched from one river to another.

The three principal Texas rivers whose names have not changed in the last 300 years are the Nueces, the Guadalupe, and the Trinity; the first two were named by De León in 1689, the latter in 1690. The river De León called the Medina in 1689 is the present-day San Antonio River, but the stretch of the river course above its junction with the San Antonio River has kept its original name, Medina.

The names of most other Texan rivers, however, have changed over the last several hundred years. The fact that Texas rivers have been called by different names at different times has seriously confused some historians who have translated, annotated, or studied the diaries and related materials on the routes of early expeditions. One example of this confusing switch is found in the several names that have been given the present-day Leona River in Frio, Zavala, and Uvalde counties. The river was named the Sarco by De León in 1689, but Massanet mentioned that the local Indians called the river by a name that meant the equivalent of cold (*frío*). Most later expedition leaders, including Salinas (1693), called the present Leona the Río Frío. The confusion concerning the name of the present-day Leona was compounded by De León naming the present-day Frio the Hondo.

Serious confusion was also caused by the naming of the present-day Colorado River. De León first called it the San Marcos in 1690, thinking he was on the upper stretch of the Lavaca River, which he had named the San Marcos the year before near Lavaca Bay. Expeditionary leaders continued to call the present-day Colorado the San Marcos until the mid-eighteenth century. By the 1760s, Rubí and Solís, however, both referred to the river by its present name.

The uncertainty over the name of the present-day Colorado was aggravated by the different early names given to the Brazos River. De León first called it the Colorado and then renamed it the Espíritu Santo. Massanet also reported that the local Indian name for the same river was the Spanish equivalent of red, *colorado*. Many early expeditionary leaders after De León called the Brazos the Colorado, but later expeditions in the eighteenth century (starting with Aguayo) referred to the present-day Brazos as the Brazos de Dios (Arms of God). Many authorities have also confused the crossing of the Brazos de Dios (first made on an expedition by Ramón and Espinosa in 1716) with a crossing location either farther north at the junction of the Little River or farther south at the junction of the Navasota.

The Navasota River also changed names several times. In 1690, De León called it the San Juan. Espinosa, Ramón, and Aguayo referred to it as the Buenaventura. Rivera,

Rubí, and Solís called it by its present name. The Neches and Angelina were not named by the seventeenth-century Spanish expeditionary leaders, but apparently Alarcón named the Sabine (Sabinas) in 1718. Rubí and Lafora called the present-day Llano River the Janes or Chanes, the present San Saba by the same name used today, and the modern Pedernales Los Pedernales.

Although the names of many of the Texas rivers have been altered over the past 300 years, it appears from the diary accounts that the principal courses of the riverbeds have not changed materially. The description of the location of the rivers, creeks, and associated landscape noted in the diaries is strikingly similar to the physical features of the same streams today. Small gravel or rock beds or islands seen at specific river crossings 300 years ago can often be found today. The steep riverbanks, horseshoe bends, and related sloughs (piélagos) can usually be identified.

Of course, the observation that the course of the rivers has not changed significantly in the past few centuries does not imply that the volume of water, water quality, or abundance of fish and other aquatic life in the streams has remained the same. The same can be said of the Gulf breezes which still blow; the air quality may not be the same as 300 years ago. Moreover, many smaller creeks have shriveled from the loss of flow, making diary accounts of the headwaters of streams extending miles beyond the present-day headwaters appear unrealistic. As noted, the diary accounts were written during the Little Ice Age, when precipitation in the form of sleet and snow was higher than today. Other former creekbeds have been lost and riverbeds drowned by high water, held by dams at devastating depths.

The Monte Grande, the thick post oak belt that stretched then—and stretches now—from an area south and southeast of San Antonio northeast across the Colorado and beyond the Brazos, was mentioned on expeditions as one of the most geographically significant features encountered. It is shown distinctly on topographic maps depicting heavily wooded areas such as the map produced in 1988 by the Texas General Land Office entitled Natural Heritage of Texas. The sophisticated current USGS topographic maps are extremely helpful in confirming projections of expeditionary routes. Even the boundaries of the dense woods of the Monte Grande have remained remarkably stable, allowing the reader of an expedition diary to see on a contemporary map that 300 years ago, as today, the thick woods commenced about the same distance beyond a named creek or that a relatively open corridor, enveloped by the Monte Grande, still runs northeast from the junction of the Brazos River and Little Brazos, just as it did when the Tejas Indians led Espinosa through open lands in the middle of the otherwise dense woods toward the Trinity in 1716.

Where De León reported (in 1689) that the coastal prairie abruptly ended, giving him and the recovered Talon children wooded shelter (near the present DeWitt-Victoria County line), the open prairie still stops suddenly today. The coastal plains near the headwaters of Garcitas Creek appear just as flat and treeless today as when De León and Massanet first described the coastal area on their initial trip to the bay. The ducks, geese, and cranes are still there, although perhaps not in the same number.

The numerous references in the Spanish expeditionary diaries to the flora and fauna seldom surprise a reader familiar with the Texas woods today. Diarists identified about fifty different species of trees, bushes, cacti, woody vines, ferns, mosses, and grasses (see Appendix II). The rivers and creeks in South Texas are described in the diaries as being lined with large pecan, cypress, and live oak trees, which have a life expectancy of several hundred years. Some of these tall trees that shaded the expedition troops may still be alive and well, representing some of the last of the living that witnessed the Spaniards' arrival.

The more open grassy areas between the rivers were dotted with the lower mesquite brush, yucca, and prickly pear. These scenes are not surprising; nor is the description of trees draped with Spanish moss and grapevines, dewberry, wild plum, and persimmon trees near the Colorado, and tall pine trees and chinquapins in the northeast. However, the early report of huisache and mesquite north of the Nueces and along the upper San Antonio River may surprise readers who have been told by some Texas naturalists that they were brought to Central Texas from Mexico in the last century. Wild animals and mules on pack trains may have carried in their stomachs as many huisache and mesquite beans to areas south of the Rio Grande as later moved north of the river on cattle drives.

In the diary descriptions of the vegetation 300 years ago we find a familiarity that suggests a land determined to preserve itself—and to return if temporarily altered by human intervention. The country seems to know what it is supposed to be and, if respected, will endure.

But there are some surprises in the diary descriptions, especially scenes of wildlife that will not be seen again. Appendix I identifies where and when forty species of wild animals were seen by expedition diarists. Many of the animals are still with us today—the wolf, coyote, bobcat, deer, javelina, owl, goose, duck, quail, and dove. Some are hunted regularly. The armadillo, which was reported only on the south side of the Rio Grande, has expanded its range to include not only the north side of the Rio Grande but also the east side of the Mississippi. The eagle, hawk, sandhill and whooping crane, osprey, parrot, crow, mockingbird, cardinal, and hummingbird are still with us, but the huge flocks of prairie chickens and wild turkeys have been seriously reduced. There appears to be no shortage today of the rattlesnakes, cottonmouths, copperheads, and coral snakes that were also recorded.

Alligators have left the middle Guadalupe, the San Marcos, and the middle Brazos and Trinity, but they are surviving in some coastal areas of Central Texas. Bears are seldom sighted. The antelope that roamed in large herds even into deep South Texas (Webb County) and north to the area southwest of San Antonio (Medina County) have been reduced and today are restricted to the open range west of the Pecos. In contrast, the antelope's running and browsing companion, the white-tail deer, has flourished even within city limits.

The range of the panther and jaguar is severely restricted to the southwest closer to the Rio Grande. But the marvelous herds of 3,000 to 4,000 bison, grazing on the endless unfenced rolling prairie that stretched from West and Central Texas into northeast Mexico, are gone forever. Espinosa graphically described how the Spanish settlers decimated the large bison herds in northeastern Mexico in the latter seventeenth century. By the late nineteenth century, American bison hunters, encouraged by public policy and money, essentially eliminated the remaining herd in Texas. The large wild horse and cattle herds that grew from the tired stock and strays left by the Spaniards and thundered on the open range with the bison are gone too.

Expedition diarists did not give regular daily weather reports. Only if the diarist considered the weather conditions exceptionally harsh was a comment included in the daily entry. The most frequent weather account noted heavy spring and summer rains or flooding. Although daily accumulations of rainfall were not measured, the moisture apparently was sufficient to assure a water flow that could sustain a variety of large fish in creeks that frequently run dry today and to support pasturage for large bison herds on both sides of the Rio Grande and into northern Coahuila and Nuevo León. Today grass is thin in many parts of these regions; some experts say the loss of vegetation results from overgrazing. But the green grassland in South Texas and northeastern Mexico that was so frequently reported as good pasturage by the diarists may have dried up at the close of the earlier cooler and wetter period called the Little Ice Age.

Most expeditions were conducted in, or at least planned for, the spring and summer months. Only two expeditions covered by this study crossed the Rio Grande during the winter; a third winter crossing of the Rio Grande was described in 1777 by the diarist Padre Juan Agustín de Morfí. But these weather reports from South Texas are uniform and surprising. Aguayo's diarist, Padre Peña, reported that several days of ice and snow hampered their party when crossing the Rio Grande at San Juan Bautista, 35 miles south of Eagle Pass in the winter of 1720–1721. The second winter crossing of the Rio Grande occurred in February 1768, when Solís repeatedly encountered snowstorms soon after crossing the river at Laredo and as he moved into the San Antonio area that spring. In mid-April, Solís's military convoy was again delayed for a day by a severe snowstorm in DeWitt County, 60 miles east-southeast of San Antonio. As diarist for the Spanish inspector Teodoro de Croix, Padre Morfí reported snow on December 31, 1777, about 20 miles south of San Antonio and said the heavy snow and icy conditions continued in San Antonio until he returned to the Rio Grande after his two-week visit.

These diary weather reports—plus comments by Alonso de León (the elder), Espinosa, and Chapa on the winter weather in northeastern Mexico suggesting a cooler period 200 to 300 years ago—are consistent with Professor David J. Weber's observation that Spanish expeditions were undertaken during the Little Ice Age, which ended in the mid-nineteeth century. The heavier precipitation along the lower Rio Grande in the seventeenth and eighteenth centuries apparently watered the rich and extensive grasslands which then served as forage for the large deer, antelope, and bison herds, which in turn could support a substantially larger Indian population. The Little Ice Age may have resulted in only marginal climatic change in areas where precipitation was adequate to support a rich environment of flora and fauna, but cooler and wetter weather may have made a significant difference in the semiarid areas of South Texas and northeastern Mexico. The impact of these changing climatic factors on the flora that supported the animal life that in turn affected the population, distribution, and movement of the Indian tribes in northeastern New Spain is a subject worthy of further study.

The most dramatic change over the last 300 years, however, is not any serious alteration of the landscape or weather or even any change in the number or kinds of wild animals or birds, but rather the change in the people who lived on the land. These people, the Indians—whose ancestors arrived in the Southwest from Asia over 10,000 years ago—have gone, as the Spanish chronicler Juan Bautista Chapa predicted in the late 1600s. Based on the 200-year Spanish experience in the New World, Chapa expected that the exposed Indian population in New Spain would be annihilated principally by aggression and highly contagious European diseases. Experts today estimate that, by 1690, epidemics of smallpox and other diseases of European origin had struck hard and spread widely in northeastern New Spain, across South and Central Texas, and among the Caddo including the Tejas Indians, whose number had been diminished by as much as 50 to 80 percent of the precontact level. Appendix III lists some of the major reported epidemic disease episodes that struck the native population in the study area between 1577 and 1760. The story of Spanish expansion into Texas can be understood only with a full appreciation that Juan Bautista Chapa's prophecy that all Indians would be annihilated by European introduced diseases and by occupation was coming to pass as he first rode with De León across South Texas (as our narrative commenced) and continued throughout the eighteenth century.

Appendix IV lists about 140 Indian tribes or bands that were recorded in the diaries and in documents related to the eleven expeditions. Decades earlier, before first European contact, there were undoubtedly many more. Chapa named over 160 tribes or bands that lived or had lived in Nuevo León in the 1600s. Some of the named tribes (such as the Tejas and other Caddo-related tribes) resided in established communities with a strong local agricultural base. But by the time Spanish expeditions and diarists arrived, in the late 1600s, Indians from Coahuila such as the Hape and Pacuache seem to have led a limited nomadic life, moving periodically within a known region but with no fixed agricultural base.

A substantial number of other tribes (the Jumano, Toboso, and many others) were highly mobile but were not simply nomads wandering in search of food and without a home (see Map 1). These tribes, some mounted, were seen by the diarists along their trade routes that ran hundreds of miles from the Big Bend area and south of the Rio Grande deep into Coahuila and Chihuahua to the rich bison hunting grounds of Central Texas and trade fairs west of the Colorado.

The Jumano, Cibolo, Cacquite, Pacpul, Quem, Simaoma, Mescal, Salinero, Sijame, Cacaxtle, Chalome, Mesquite, Caynaaya, Toboso, Timamare, Tlaxcalan, and other nonresident tribes were seen and used as guides on more than one expedition into Central Texas. Some of these tribes may have been immigrating, as has been suggested by T. N. Campbell, but the colonial historic record is sufficient to suggest that many of the Indians journeyed several hundred miles over well-recognized trade routes to Central Texas as hunters and traders and then returned home.

Espinosa described how the bison in Coahuila and western Nuevo León had been depleted by the end of the seventeenth century, but the herds in South Texas were still bountiful. This critical animal resource, which furnished nourishment, clothing, and trade items, attracted Indian hunters, traders, and immigrants to Texas from below the Rio Grande, where the herds had been depleted.

The exchange of goods by these Indians from northeastern New Spain required the accumulation of some form of capital—hides, horses, slaves, plants, or other items of potential value to a distant trading partner in Texas. Experts believe that corn and beans were introduced from Mexico to northern North America, while sunflower seeds moved in the opposite direction. At a minimum, an informal territorial agreement would be expected between the hunting and trading tribes. These exchanges necessitated a means of communication among tribes that spoke many different languages. As Solís and other diarists noted, bartering and other communication between tribes was accomplished by an Indian sign language, a communication technique seldom if ever used between Europeans in the New World at that time. Studies of Indian sign language suggest that many signs used by the Indians were very similar (and sometimes identical) to the officially recognized signs illustrated in manuals of American Sign Language.

As fully documented in the diaries, these Native Americans were not of limited intellect or spirit or fitness. Some were amazing and startled the Spanish diarists who recorded their abilities and lifestyles. The Indians were described as proud, sagacious, competent, athletic, competitive, and hearty. A notable example of their fitness was the Emet Indian runner who raced round trip over 500 miles in ten days to deliver De León's written message to the Frenchmen in East Texas and returned with their written reply to Matagorda Bay. Solís, who was one of the most astute observers of daily Indian life, was more than surprised when he was greeted in East Texas by a female Indian leader escorted by her five husbands and when he learned how members of a male homosexual community in Central Texas made their contribution during campaigns against the enemy.

Indian camps in Central Texas were found near streams, where the Indians could conveniently take their customary morning baths. The Spaniards later used the same locations as watering holes for their horses and stock. Indian tribes traveled hundreds of miles to visit, trade, or plunder, just as Europeans did. They captured, sold, or exchanged slaves, as did the Europeans. The Indians exhibited emotional reactions that ranged from joyous love to bitter hatred, and they used torture techniques that challenged the ingenuity of the methods of the Spanish Inquisition and the British penal code (which at the time included the use of the rack). Cannibalism (of the ritual type) among the Karankawa did shock some Spaniards, but De León (the elder) had earlier reported cannibalism (of the type in which deceased family members were eaten) among the tribes living in Nuevo León.

The Indians, as recorded in the diaries, were adaptable in some respects, such as quickly learning how to use horses and guns, but were resistant in other matters, such as switching religions. By the close of the period of expeditions from New Spain in the late 1760s, Indian power—particularly Comanche power—was ascending. The Spaniards, who subdued the Indians in Coahuila and Chihuahua and then backed the French out of East Texas in the early 1720s, faced the more numerous and frequently better armed and mounted Apache, Comanche, and Norteños fifty years later. This unprecedented mounted Indian power, fueled by French and English trade in hides for firepower, led Rubí to relinquish the defense of all of Texas north of the San Antonio River at the end of the expeditionary period. Rubí decided to seek alliances with the Comanche and Norteños against the Apache, their common enemy.

At that time, the Spaniards had no plan or capability to extinguish the Indian population or drive them from all Spanish-claimed lands. The Spaniards could not occupy all the land or dominate the Indians fully; they sought recognition and a minimum of respect. An uncertain accommodation was being reached, and the question after the French threat faded was whether the Spaniards or Indians would dominate in any particular area of Texas. In 1768, neither seemed to require the total extermination or absence of the other. Present-day Texas was Indian country when De León entered in 1689, and when Rubí completed his inspection, eighty years later, "Spanish Texas" was still Indian country.

The last Spanish episode of the Texas drama unfolded during the following decades, from the 1770s to the 1820s. New Spanish exploration, initiated from within Texas, extended trails into the undiscovered areas of the province and into West Texas, the Panhandle, and Southeast Texas. Later, Anglo colonization brought new people with new ideas about frontier life, wanting the largest space they could grab and the least interference by a distant government. The ideas that sparked the revolution in the 1770s and 1780s on the east coast of the United States (which the Spaniards in Texas aided) spread first to New Spain and then to Texas.

Some Indians, along with Mexican families, migrated or were driven into northern Mexico by the Anglo surge. Many Indians melted into the Mexican population and survived. Today they are a part of the Mexican resurgence back across the Río Grande del Norte to a land their tribal ancestors knew well.

WILDLIFE RECORDED ON SPANISH EXPEDITIONS INTO TEXAS, 1689–1768

This appendix was designed primarily to illustrate the variety of wildlife recorded in Spanish expedition diaries and associated colonial period documents. To achieve this limited objective, it was not necessary to include every reference to wildlife in northeastern New Spain found in the diaries. Because each entry notes the data and location of the sighting, some entries include a sufficient number of sightings to indicate the range and migratory pattern of the animal. Some reports include estimates of the number of animals seen, which are useful to historical demographers in assessing the Indian population in the area.

The appendix is based primarily on information found in the expedition diaries, but also includes relevant notes about wildlife found in the journals kept by La Salle's colonists and in the histories or *crónicas* of Alonso de León (the elder), Juan Bautista Chapa, Fray Juan Agustín de Morfí, and Fray Isidro Félix de Espinosa, as well as clarifying comments on wildlife made by Jean Louis Berlandier in his *Journey to Mexico* during the years 1826 to 1834. Comments on the present-day population and location of several animals are based on recent studies, including Robin W. Doughty, *Wildlife and Man in Texas;* Robin W. Doughty and Barbara M. Parmenter, *Endangered Species;* and Edward A. Kutac and S. Christopher Caran, *Birds and Other Wildlife of South Central Texas.* The short references cited in the text give only the names of the authors or translators (or diary editors) and the appropriate pages. Full citations are found in the Bibliography.

I hope this information will give general readers, biologists, historical demographers, and other scientists an indication of the extensive wildlife data available in early Spanish diaries and other colonial documents.

I. ALLIGATOR (*cocodrilo, caimán*)

Expedition diarists used the Spanish words *cocodrilo* or *caimán* to identify alligators, found not only in the Gulf coastal regions but also in the rivers of Central Texas. The reptiles were seen at river crossings near the present-day cities of San Antonio, New Braunfels, and San Marcos, on the Brazos and Little Brazos west of Bryan in Brazos County, at the crossing on the Navasota River in western Leon County, and near the Trinity crossing in western Houston County.

Along the Gulf Coast, alligators were reported near Lavaca Bay in Victoria and Calhoun counties by De León in 1689 (West, 398); he thought that alligators had eaten many of the bodies of the massacred French settlers near the French settlement. In the mid-1680s, Henri Joutel confirmed that numerous alligators were found near the French community on Matagorda Bay (Cox, vol. 2, 80–81). Massanet (with Terán) reported alligators near San Antonio in 1691 (Hatcher, 55). In 1716, according to Ramón, his troops captured one near the San Gabriel River in Milam County (Foik, 15). Espinosa (in 1709 and 1716) and Ramón (in 1716) reported *caimanes* in several locations: Espinosa found alligators near the city of San Antonio in 1716 (Tous, 10) and along the Guadalupe River near New Braunfels in 1709 (Tous, 6); both Espinosa and Ramón saw them near the Brazos River crossing in Burleson County in 1716 (Tous, 16; Foik, 17).

The reptiles were so prominent in the area near Boggy Creek, about 25 miles east of the Trinity River crossing in Leon County, that Lafora said a lagoon (Laguna del Caimán) was named for them (Kinnaird, 164). Lafora later saw them on the lower Trinity in 1767 (Kinnaird, 172). Solís also reported alligators on the Trinity (Kress, 59). Lafora said the local Orcoquiza Indians captured the reptiles in the shallow lagoons associated with the lower Trinity River in Chambers County.

In the 1830s, Berlandier reported there were no alligators south of the Nueces River in Texas, but a different species was found in Mexico (*Journey to Mexico,* 337). However, Espinosa reported that *caimanes* were found in the Río San Isidro in Coahuila (*Crónica,* 769); at least, he saw the skull of an alligator that had been recovered near the river.

Although in recent years the range of alligators (*Alligator mississippiensis*) in Texas has been narrowed to the coastal area, recent population estimates suggest that 250,000 alligators inhabited the wetlands of the state in 1986 (Doughty and Parmenter, *Endangered Species,* 48).

2. ARMADILLO (*armadillo*)

Alonso de León (the elder) wrote that armadillos (meaning little armored ones in Spanish) were found in present-day Nuevo León and Coahuila in the middle 1600s (*Historia,* 82). In his summary of the wildlife in northeastern Coahuila in the early 1700s, Fray Espinosa also said that there were many armadillos in the two provinces below the Rio Grande (*Crónica,* 769). No expedition diarist, however, noted the presence of armadillos north of the Rio Grande during the period 1689 to 1768.

A recent comprehensive study of the twenty-one species of armadillos, including the nine-banded species found in Texas (*Dasypus novemcinctus*), identifies the range of the armadillo from northern Argentina east of the Andes north to northern Mexico and the United States, with a permanent population first having been established in Texas in the 1850s. Its present range includes all Gulf coastal states east of Texas to Florida (Larry L. Smith and Robin W. Doughty, *The Amazing Armadillo: Geography of a Folk Critter* [Austin: University of Texas Press, 1984], 2–20).

The reports by De León and Espinosa that armadillos were plentiful in Nuevo León and Coahuila during the seventeenth and eighteenth centuries and the conclusion by

Smith and Doughty that they were not established north of the Rio Grande until the 1850s suggest that armadillos required a minimum of 200 years to cross the Rio Grande. However, it has taken the armadillos much less time to cross the Mississippi and reach Florida, as the adventuresome critters continue their exploration of the North American continent.

3. BEAR (oso)

In his 1709 diary description of the wildlife in Texas, Fray Espinosa listed bears among the animals found between San Antonio and Austin (Tous, 11). The padre reported bears in Nuevo León and Coahuila in the early 1700s (Crónica, 764) and added that during the same period he saw many bears in East Texas near the mission field (690).

Aguayo's party (1721) reported bears near Adaes in western Louisiana (Santos, 72) In 1727, Rivera's engineer, Alvarez Barreiro, said that bears were found in the present states of Chihuahua, Nuevo León, and Coahuila (Naylor and Polzer, 214, 222), which then included areas to the west and south of present-day San Antonio.

In 1767, Lafora reported that he and Rubí saw bears between the Llano River and the Pedernales in Gillespie County (Kinnaird, 152); in the manuscript copy of his diary, on August 4, 1768, Rubí added that one bear was lassoed and captured by his escort troops. Lafora later reported that numerous bears were found in the area around the presidio San Agustín de Ahumada (Orcoquisac) on the lower Trinity in the Houston-Chamber-Liberty County area (172). On October 20, Rubí reported bears in the Harris and Waller County area near the Brazos River.

Fray Solís (1768) added that bears were found in several locations along his inspection route: near the San Antonio River between Goliad and San Antonio (Kress, 43, 47), in the area approaching the Brazos River crossing in Washington and Burleson counties (56, 57), near the Navasota (59), and in the Trinity River area in Leon and Houston counties (60).

The black bear (Ursus americanus) in Texas was reduced in population by 1900; only a limited number roamed the remote area of East Texas and the southern Edwards Plateau. Today a few may be found in the mountains of the Trans-Pecos, but essentially the bear has moved west or south to Mexico (Doughty and Parmenter, Endangered Species, 23).

4. BADGER (tejón)

Alonso de León (the elder) reported badgers (Taxidea taxus) in both Nuevo León and Coahuila in the mid-1600s (Historia, 82). A similar report was made by Espinosa for the early 1700s (Crónica, 764). Alvarez Barreiro said that badgers were found in Nuevo León, Vizcaya, and Coahuila in 1727 (Naylor and Polzer, 214, 222). At that time, Coahuila included the area of South Texas to the west and south of San Antonio.

5. BIRDS (aves)

The diarists recorded seeing a number of songbirds and other birds in the expedition areas; these birds were also cited in related documents prepared by expedition leaders. Espinosa gives a list of birds found in Coahuila and Nuevo León in the early 1700s, including the mockingbird (*zenzontle*), cardinal (*cardenal*), sparrow (*gorrión*), thrush (*tordo*), pelican (*alcatraz*), and osprey (*quebrantahuesos*) (*Crónica*, 767).

Fray Solís (1768) reported that the lark (*calandria*), the Mexican mockingbird, and the thrush were found along the Rio Grande near Laredo (Kress, 36).

6. BUZZARD (*busardo, aura, zopilote*)

In 1718, Fray Céliz (with Alarcón) recorded seeing a flock of twenty-four buzzards circling above the Guadalupe near New Braunfels (Hoffmann, 53). Solís (1768) reported buzzards along his route from Zacatecas to Laredo (Kress, 53). Espinosa recorded that turkey buzzards (*auras* and *zopilotes*) were found in the early 1700s in Coahuila and Nuevo León (*Crónica*, 767).

7. BEAVER (*castor*)

Solís (1768) described the behavior of beavers (*Castor canadensis*) in detail and reported that they were found near the Brazos and Navasota rivers (Kress, 58).

8. BISON OR AMERICAN BUFFALO (*cíbolo*)

Father Anastase Douay and Henri Joutel reported seeing herds of several hundred bison ("beeves") on the prairies north of Matagorda Bay (Cox, vol. 1, 224; vol. 2, 79). De León first reported seeing bison or American buffalo (*Bos bison*) in Texas south of the Guadalupe River in DeWitt County in April 1689 (Bolton, *Spanish Exploration*, 394). Earlier on the trip, when De León's party met five Indian tribes south of the Rio Grande, Juan Bautista Chapa reported that some of the tribal members were away hunting bison (*Historia*, 143). In May 1675, Fernando del Bosque reported bison in Maverick County, but none below the river (Bolton, *Spanish Exploration*, 296). In the spring of 1690, De León saw herds south of the Rio Grande near the crossing about 35 miles downstream from present-day Eagle Pass (Bolton, *Spanish Exploration*, 407). In June 1691, Terán also reported that large herds roamed south of the Rio Grande in the same area (Hatcher, 12).

One of the most reliable firsthand descriptions of bison ranging below the Rio Grande and into the northern regions of Coahuila and Nuevo León in the late seventeenth century was given by Fray Espinosa. The padre reported that large bison herds roamed the mission area near Boca Leones and modern Lampazos in northern Nuevo León and Coahuila before the turn of the seventeenth century, but that the herds had been decimated by the early Spanish settlers, who killed hundreds of the bulls daily for only their tongues and tallow, leaving the meat for the scavenger birds (*Crónica*, 764). In his description of the mission area in northeastern New Spain at the end of the seventeenth century, Espinosa also gave weather information describing how much cooler and wetter the climate was at that time (during the Little Ice Age) and detailed the richer vegetation, which was apparently sufficient to sustain sizable herds of the large animals (761, 762). (This same country probably would not be capable of supporting such herds today.) Later, in 1709, Espinosa noted that bison had not been eliminated in present Texas; he found bison near the Colorado River on his expedition across South Texas (Tous, 6, 7).

In his travel account of Texas and northeastern Mexico, the European botanist Jean Louis Berlandier gave a report of bison ranging as far south as the valleys near Monterrey when Spanish priests and settlers first entered the area at the end of the sixteenth century (*Journey to Mexico*, 454).

Terán and Massanet (June 1691) saw bison herds that spooked their horse remuda near San Antonio (Hatcher, 14), and the two expedition leaders saw a number of herds northeast of San Antonio in Guadalupe, Caldwell, Hays, and Travis counties (15). In September, Terán reported over 4,000 head on the upper Navidad River in Fayette County (22) and herds of 1,000 to 3,000 near the Lavaca and the Guadalupe rivers in Colorado, Lavaca, Victoria, DeWitt, and Jackson counties (23, 25, 46). Salinas confirmed that bison roamed near the Rio Grande; he reported his first herd moving northeast between the river and Comanche Creek in Maverick County on May 11 (Foster and Jackson, 53).

Ramón reported in May 1716 that his party traveling to East Texas first found bison east of the Colorado River crossing in Travis County (Foik, 14) and that his troops captured two calves that were used in a mock bullfight near the Brazos River in Burleson County (17).

In September 1718, Fray Céliz (with Alarcón) reported bison herds on the lower Colorado near Matagorda Bay in Wharton and Matagorda counties (Hoffmann, 63). Aguayo's diarist, Padre Peña, noted in June 1721 that their party had found bison as far north as Waco, where they captured several (Santos, 44, 45). Governor Aguayo personally killed four of the more than one hundred bison the troops had taken for food and sport, according to his diarist (45).

In August 1727, Rivera found bison on Onion Creek in Travis County and along Brushy Creek in Williamson County (Porras, 113). Lafora (with Rubí in 1767) said bison wintered in the area south of the San Saba River in the Edwards County area (Kinnaird, 148), and Rubí and Lafora found them in August on the Pedernales River in Gillespie County (152). In April 1768, Solís reported herds near Goliad (Kress, 47), in eastern Fayette County (56, 57), and near the Navasota (59), but added that they were not found east of the Trinity (60). The diaries do not support the frequently asserted view that bison were seldom found in Central Texas during the summer months.

Bison continued to roam the open plains in Central and West Texas until the herds disappeared in the 1880s (Doughty and Parmenter, *Endangered Species*, 25). Their disappearance in Texas was caused by the same wasteful slaughter that the herds had endured earlier in Coahuila, with the same disastrous impact on the Indian population.

9. CRANE (*grulla*)

Espinosa described two species of large cranes that frequented the mission area in northern Nuevo León and Coahuila about 50 to 80 miles west-southwest of Laredo: one was white (probably the whooping crane) and the second was brownish (probably the sandhill crane) (*Crónica*, 767). Espinosa said that cranes were also found in the East Texas mission field area (690). Padre Solís (1768) reported that cranes were present along the San Antonio River between present-day Goliad and San Antonio (Kress, 43).

10. COYOTE (*coyote*)

Alvarez Barreiro reported in 1727 that coyotes (*Canis latrans*) were found in Coahuila, which then included parts of South Texas (Porras, 214, 222). This account was supported by Espinosa, who wrote that coyotes were found near the mission area in northern Nuevo León and Coahuila in the early 1700s (*Crónica,* 762).

Lafora, in his 1767 summary of wildlife, mentioned that coyotes were found throughout the provinces of Nuevo León, Coahuila, and Texas (184). The next year, Solís said that they were found along his route from Zacatecas to the area near Laredo (Kress, 36) and also along the Bahía road between Goliad and San Antonio (49).

11. CROW (*cuervo*)

In April 1689, De León saw a flock of "more than 3,000 crows" about 12 miles north of the Rio Grande in Maverick County (West, 390); the governor named the campsite and nearby creek El Paraje de los Cuervos for the birds. Espinosa reported crows in northern Nuevo León and Coahuila in the early 1700s (*Crónica,* 767). Solís (1768) said that they were found along the Rio Grande near Laredo (Kress, 36).

12. DEER (*venado, ciervo*)

Alonso de León (the elder) described many large herds of deer ("up to 50") foraging throughout the region (*Historia,* 82). Referring to the deer (*Odocoileus virginianus*) as both *venados* and *ciervos,* Espinosa reported that the animals roamed in large numbers throughout northern Coahuila and Nuevo León in the early 1700s (*Crónica,* 764). The padre added that deer were plentiful in the mission area in East Texas in the 1720s and 1730s (692).

Governor Terán and Padre Massanet reported in 1691 that deer were seen along the Medina River in the San Antonio area (Hatcher, 54). Terán later said a large number of deer were seen in East Texas in the Panola-Harrison County area (31). In 1709, Espinosa said that deer and fawns (*ciervos*) were so plentiful between San Antonio and Austin that they resembled flocks of goats and were encountered at every step (Tous, 11).

Alarcón (1718), according to the diarist Fray Céliz, found deer near the Frío River crossing below Hondo Creek in Frio County (Hoffmann, 46). In 1721, Peña (with Aguayo) reported seeing them from the Leona River (in Zavala County) to the Frío River crossing (Santos, 29), in the vicinity of the San Marcos River (37), and later near Lavaca Bay (79). On April 3, Aguayo's troops captured two deer out of a mixed herd of 300–400 deer and antelope south of the Medina River in the Medina-Bexar-Atascosa County area (30).

On August 6, 1767, Rubí reported deer on the Pedernales, along Coleto Creek in Karnes County (on August 26), between the Guadalupe and Colorado rivers in DeWitt, Lavaca, and Fayette counties (August 28), and later in Harris and Waller counties (October 20). Lafora, Rubí's engineer, found deer on the lower Trinity River (Kinnaird, 172).

Solís (1768) saw large numbers of deer near the Rio Grande at Laredo (Kress, 36), again near Goliad (43), between the Brazos and Navasota rivers in Burleson, Brazos, and Madison counties (57, 59), and east of the Trinity (60).

13. DOVE (*tórtola*)

Solís (1768) reported doves along the Rio Grande near Laredo (Kress, 36), but the padre did not mention them among the gamebirds he reported farther north. Espinosa noted that doves were found in northern Coahuila in the early 1700s (*Crónica*, 767).

14. DUCK (*pato*)

Solís (1768) said that wild ducks were found on the San Antonio River between Goliad and San Antonio (49). Espinosa also reported wild *patos* of various sizes and colors in northern Coahuila in the early 1700s (767).

15. EAGLE (*águila*)

On March 20, 1768, Solís recorded in his manuscript diary that *águilas* were found near the Bahía Road between Goliad and San Antonio. Espinosa included eagles in his list of birds found in northern Coahuila and Nuevo León in the early 1700s (*Crónica*, 767).

16. FISH (*pescados*)

Spanish diarists and historians identified by name a number of different species of fish, but the English equivalent of several cannot be given with confidence. Alonso de León (the elder) provided one of the earliest listings (1650s) of fish found in Coahuila and Nuevo León, including *robalos* (bass), *bagres* (catfish), *mojarras, truchas* (trout), and *besugos* (*Historia*, 82). Espinosa adds that other aquatic animals were found in the same region of northern Coahuila and Nuevo León, including *tortugas* (turtles), *camarones* (shrimp) that are "large but not reddish-colored," *ostiones* (oysters), and *almejas* (clams), "which the Indians eat regularly" (*Crónica*, 769). De León named the present-day Atascosa River the Robalo for the bass found in that stream (Bolton, *Spanish Exploration*, 408).

In 1709, Espinosa reported that his party caught *bagres* or catfish in a stream between the Rio Grande and the Nueces River near the corner of Dimmit and Zavala counties (Tous, 3) and that the fish was found in many streams between the Medina and the Colorado (11). Rivera (1727) said that catfish were the principal fish in many streams in the Province of Texas (Porras, 124). On March 20, 1768, Solís noted in his manuscript diary that catfish were caught in the San Antonio River near Goliad along with many other species.

Espinosa (1709) listed a number of species in many streams between the Rio Grande and the Colorado: *bobos* (minnows), *moharras,* and *piltontes* (yellow catfish) (Tous, 11). Espinosa identified the *piltonte* as the large yellow catfish and described one taken from the Rio Grande that stretched to the ground when roped by its gills to the saddlehorn of a large horse (*Crónica*, 768). Solís said that the same fish was taken from the San Antonio River (49).

Solís provided a list of fish in either the Rio Grande or the San Antonio River: *bagres, piltontes, pullones,* and *mojarras* (Kress, 38, 49).

17. FOX (*zorro*)

In his 1709 diary description of wildlife in Texas (Tous, 11), Espinosa said that foxes (*Urocyon cinereoargenteus*) were found in the province, and he reported *zorrillos* in

Coahuila and Nuevo León in his *Crónica* (764). In 1727, Alvarez Barreiro listed them among the wild animals found in Vizcaya, Nuevo León, and Coahuila (Porras, 214, 222), which then included parts of present-day Texas.

18. GOOSE (*ánsar*)
Espinosa recorded wild geese in northern Coahuila and Nuevo León in the early 1700s (*Crónica,* 767). Padre Solís (1768) reported that wild geese were found on the San Antonio River in Goliad, Karnes, and Wilson counties (Kress, 49).

19. GROUND SQUIRREL (*ardilla*)
Alvarez Barreiro (1727) reported ground squirrels (*Spermophilus mexicanus*) in Vizcaya, Nuevo León, and Coahuila (Naylor and Polzer, 214, 222). Solís (1768) said that they were found near Laredo (Kress, 36).

20. HAWK (*gavilán*)
Espinosa reported hawks in Coahuila and Nuevo León (*Crónica,* 767). Solís (1768) noted the presence of hawks near Laredo (Kress, 36).

21. JAGUAR (*tigre*)
In 1709, Espinosa noted in his diary that the jaguar (*Panthera onca*), a buff-colored large cat marked with dark spots, was found in Central Texas between the Medina River and the Colorado (Tous, 11). The padre also reported that the large cat was found in northern Coahuila and Nuevo León (*Crónica,* 764). However, the only sighting of the cat was reported in 1721 by Aguayo (Santos, 49): his troops captured two cubs along the Navasota River crossing near the four corners area of Brazos, Burleson, Leon, and Madison counties. Aguayo's diarist, Peña, said that the young *tigres* still had their eyes closed and had very colorful fur.

Alvarez Barreiro reported in 1727 that *tigres* were found in the provinces of Vizcaya and Coahuila (Porras, 214, 222), which included the Rio Grande area south of El Paso to the Pecos River area and the region northeast to the San Saba River and southeast along the Medina and San Antonio rivers toward the coast.

The jaguar, unlike the cougar, has not adapted by retreating for cover to isolated mountain ranges; therefore, only a few scattered sightings in Texas have been noted during this century (Doughty and Parmenter, *Endangered Species,* 34–35).

22. JAVELINA (*jabalí, javaline*)
The word *jabalí, javalí,* or *javaline* in the Spanish diaries may refer to either a feral hog or a javelina (the collared peccary that resembles a young pig or boar). Alonso de León (the elder) noted that there were numerous javelinas (*Tayassu tajacu*) in Nuevo León in the mid-1600s (*Historia,* 82). Espinosa reported many javelinas in the mission areas of northern Coahuila and Nuevo León in the early 1700s (*Crónica,* 764).

Members of La Salle's community brought hogs to the French settlement near Matagorda Bay in the 1680s (Cox, vol. 2, 98), and the animals apparently escaped after the settlement was destroyed. However, the local Indians were not inclined to hunt or eat the animals according to testimony from Pierre and Jean-Baptiste Talon (see Weddle, *La Salle*, 233). References to *jabalís* being seen in the South Texas area (principally those noted by Solís in 1768) may have meant either javelinas or wild hogs introduced to the area from the former French settlement.

Alvarez Barreiro reported in 1727 that *javalines* were found in Vizcaya, Nuevo León, and Coahuila (Naylor and Polzer, 214, 222), which then included parts of present-day South Texas.

Solís (1768) reported *javalís* in Texas on three occasions: on March 5, when he was moving nearing the Nueces in McMullen County (Kress, 37); again near Goliad (Kress, 43); and a third time along the road between Goliad and San Antonio (49). The year before, Rubí's engineer Lafora reported *jabalís* in Coahuila and Nuevo León (Kinnaird, 214, 222).

23. LYNX (*onza*)
Alvarez Barreiro (1727) said the lynx was found in Vizcaya, Nuevo León, and Coahuila (Naylor and Polzer, 214, 222), which included parts of South Texas. Alonso de León (the elder) reported that in Nuevo León and eastern Coahuila there were large spotted cats without tails (*gatos pintados, sin cola*) that were large enough to kill a three-year old horse (*Historia*, 82).

24. MOUNTAIN LION (*león, puma*)
The cougar (also called panther or mountain lion) was noted by diarists on several expeditions. In 1689, De León found a dead mountain lion near the mouth of Cibolo Creek in Karnes County (West, 294), which he named Arroyo del León. Espinosa reported *leones* in present-day Texas in his diary in 1709 (Tous, 11) and in northern Nuevo León and Coahuila in the early 1700s (*Crónica*, 764).

In 1727, Barreiro said cougars were found in Coahuila and Vizcaya, which included or bordered parts of South and West Texas (Porras, 214, 222). Solís (1768) reported that they roamed along the San Antonio River between Goliad and San Antonio (Kress, 49).

From 1956 to 1966, between eleven and twenty-two mountain lions (*Felis concolor*) were killed annually in Texas under the Federal and Supervised Cooperative Predator Control Operation (Doughty, *Wildlife in Texas*, Table 3, 208–209).

25. MUSTANG (*caballo mesteño*)
In 1716, Ramón found large herds of mustangs or wild horses a few miles north of the Sabinas River in northern Coahuila (Foik, 7); two days later, he captured two colts from a herd found south of the Sabinas (7). On December 2, 1767, Rubí also reported several herds (*caballería mesteña*) between the Rio Grande and the Sabinas River in Coahuila. Solís (1768) saw them (*mucha caballada y mesteñada*) when he was approaching Laredo from the south (Kress, 35) and along the Camino Real in Washington County on April 22 and 24 (Forrestal, 24, 26). In December 1777, Padre Morfí (diarist on Teodoro de Croix's inspection tour) reported wild mustangs between the Francia crossing in Maverick County and Bexar County (*Viaje de Indios*, 334, 338, 340).

26. OTTER (*nutria*)

Fray Solís (1768) said otters (*Lutra canadensis*) were found throughout Central and East Texas (Kress, 58). Fray Espinosa described the appearance and behavior of the otters in the Río Candela in eastern Coahuila during the early 1700s (*Crónica*, 769).

27. OWL (*tecolote*)

In 1727, Rivera said that owls were seen throughout the Province of Texas (Porras, 124). Solís (1768) reported that owls were found along the Rio Grande near Laredo (Kress, 36). Espinosa listed the bird among those found in northern Coahuila and Nuevo León (*Crónica*, 767).

28. PARROT (*papagayo, perico*)

Padre Solís (1768) reported two species of parrots found near Laredo (Kress, 36). *Perico*, a small green parrot, and *guacamaya*, the colorful macaw, were both seen by the padre along his route from Zacatecas north through Nuevo León to the Rio Grande. Alonso de León (the elder) noted that many *papagayos* were raised in the province (*Historia*, 82).

29. PRAIRIE CHICKEN (*gallina montés* OR *perdiz*)

One of the earliest reports of prairie chickens (*gallinas monteses*) in Coahuila was given by Alonso de León (the elder) (*Historia*, 82). Espinosa reported that *perdices* were abundant in Coahuila and Nuevo León in the early 1700s (*Crónica*, 767).

In 1691, Padre Massanet (with Terán's party) saw prairie chickens along the Medina River south-southwest of the present-day city of San Antonio (Hatcher, 54) and in central Guadalupe County north of Seguin (56). In May 1716, Espinosa (with Ramón) saw a large flock of *gallos de la tierra* along the Leona River near the Zavala-Frio County line and caught two to eat (Tous, 7). Ramón later reported the birds near the San Gabriel River in Williamson County (Foik, 15).

Alarcón (1718) found very large flocks of prairie chickens near the Gulf Coast in Matagorda County (Hoffmann, 63). Solís (1768) reported *perdices* on the route along the San Antonio River between Goliad and San Antonio (Kress, 49) and again in Fayette County east of the Colorado (55). Aguayo's party (1721) also found the birds on the Nueces River in southern Zavala County (Santos, 28) and later near the modern city of San Marcos (37). In 1768, Solís reported that *gallinas* and *perdices* were seen from Goliad County northwest to San Antonio (Kress, 43, 49) and from Goliad east to the Colorado River area in Fayette County (55).

The prairie chicken (*Tympanuchus cupido*) was seriously depleted in the 1800s; today the population, found mostly in the coastal area near the Colorado River, numbers only a few thousand (Doughty and Parmenter, *Endangered Species*, 63).

30. PRONGHORN ANTELOPE (*berrendo*)

Alonso de León (the elder) reported that in the 1650s pronghorn antelope were found in Coahuila and Nuevo León (*Historia*, 82). Espinosa also said that *berrendos* were found in northern Nuevo León and Coahuila in the early 1700s (*Crónica*, 764). In his *Viaje de Indios,* Morfí listed *berrendos* among the animals found in the middle 1700s near Parras in southern Coahuila (201). Henri Joutel (with La Salle) described the prairies north and west of Matagorda Bay as being covered with "wild goats" (*antilopes*) in the mid-1680s (Cox, vol. 2, 79).

The diarist Peña (with Aguayo) reported in 1721 that antelope, along with deer (*venados*), were seen north of Pearsall in Frio County (Santos, 29). Aguayo's troops chased a large mixed herd of several hundred antelope and deer as the party approached the Medina River in Bexar County (30).

Rivera's engineer, Alvarez Barreiro, reported in 1727 that antelope were found throughout present northeastern Mexico in the provinces of Coahuila, Nuevo León, and Chihuahua (Naylor and Polzer, 214, 222), three provinces that included or bordered present-day Texas.

In the manuscript copies of his diary, Solís (1768) reported that *berrendos* were found along his route from Zacatecas in northern Nuevo León to Laredo, and later he found them along the San Antonio River between Goliad and San Antonio (Kress, 43).

In the 1830s, Berlandier noted, when moving through Fayette County near the Colorado River, that the local Indians (identified by him as Tonkawa) were dependent primarily on pronghorn antelope, not bison, for food (*Journey to Mexico*, 313).

The pronghorn antelope (*Antilocapra americana*) has been the subject of a state rehabilitation program in Texas in recent years, and the state population is estimated to be about 25,000 (Doughty and Parmenter, *Endangered Species*, 38–41; see also Doughty, *Wildlife and Man in Texas*, 52–54, 197–199).

31. QUAIL (*codorniz*)

Espinosa reported quail in Coahuila and Nuevo León in the early 1700s (*Crónica*, 767) and in the mission area in East Texas (690). Fray Peña (with Aguayo) in 1721 reported quail on Comanche Creek in Zavala County (Santos, 28); the birds were frequently sighted along the route thereafter as Aguayo's party progressed northeast to the Nueces River, the Leona, the Frio, and past San Antonio to the San Marcos River (29, 30, 37).

Fray Solís (1768) saw quail near Laredo in Webb County (Kress, 36), again in the area near Goliad County (43), and at the Brazos River crossing at the Burleson-Brazos County line (57).

32. RABBIT (*conejo, liebre*)

Two different rabbits (*Sylvilagus floridanus* and *Lepus californicus*) are noted in the expedition diaries: the smaller rabbit, probably the cottontail (*conejo*), and the larger hare or jackrabbit (*liebre*). Both were reported in Nuevo León and Coahuila by Alonso de León (the elder) in his *Historia* (82) covering the mid-1600s and by Espinosa in his *Crónica* covering the early 1700s (764).

Aguayo (1721) noted that rabbits were found near both Comanche Creek and the Nueces River in Zavala County (Santos, 28), along the Frio River in Frio County (29), and near San Marcos in Hays County (37). Alvarez Barreiro (1727) said both were found in Coahuila, Nuevo León, and Vizcaya (Porras, 214, 222). In 1768, Solís reported that *conejos* and *liebres* were found near Laredo (Kress, 36) and along the San Antonio River between present-day Goliad and San Antonio (49).

33. RACCOON (*mapache*)
Alvarez Barreiro (1727) reported raccoons (*Procyon lotor*) in Vizcaya, Nuevo León, and Coahuila, which included parts of present-day South Texas (Naylor and Polzer, 214, 222).

34. SKUNK (*zorrillo*)
Solís (1768) reported that skunks (*Mephitis mephitis*) were a favorite meat in the diet of the Karankawa Indians near Mission Rosario on the San Antonio River (Kress, 43). Earlier, Fray Espinosa said that *zorrillos* were found in Nuevo León and Coahuila in the first decades of 1700s (*Crónica*, 764).

35. SNAKES (*culebras*)
Spanish diarists identified several different snakes in Coahuila and Texas. The term *culebra* was used to refer to snakes generally; *viperinas* were poisonous snakes (such as cottonmouths and copperheads); and *víboras de cascabel* were rattlesnakes.

Lafora, Rubí's engineer, reported finding numerous rattlesnakes a few miles north of Laredo (Kinnaird, 180). Rubí noted some poisonous snake (*viperina*) on September 4, 1767, near the Trinity River.

Padre Solís reported snakes on several occasions; there were many huge poisonous snakes (*víboras*) near Laredo (Kress, 36) and along the route from Laredo to Presidio La Bahía in Goliad County (37). The padre added that both poisonous snakes (*víboras*) and other snakes (*culebras*) were found between Goliad and San Antonio (43).

Rattlesnakes and coral snakes (*coralillos*) were found in Coahuila and Nuevo León in the early 1700s, according to Espinosa. The padre described the *coralillos* as having three colors (red, white, and black) in the shape of corals around the body. He also identified a short but very thick snake (called *hocico de puerco*) that he said was the most poisonous of all snakes in the area (*Crónica*, 770).

36. TURKEY
(*guajolote, pavo de Indias, pavo silvestre, pavo de la tierra*)
Turkeys were one of the most frequently noted birds on Spanish expeditions; they were seen from the Nueces River in southern Zavala County to the Trinity River in Houston County. Espinosa said that wild turkeys (*pavos silvestres*) were plentiful in the early 1700s south of the Rio Grande near the mission area around present-day Lampazos, about 50 miles west-southwest of Laredo (*Crónica*, 767). The birds were hunted almost daily in the area. Espinosa also reported turkeys in the East Texas mission area (690). In 1709, Espinosa wrote in his diary account that wild turkeys (*guajolotes*) were found in northern Guadalupe County (Tous, 6).

Ramón (1716) also saw turkeys along the Leona River in eastern Zavala County (Foik, 11), near the Brazos River in Burleson County (17), and along the Trinity River in Leon County (18). Fray Céliz (with Alarcón in 1718) reported *guajolotes* on the Leona River near the Zavala-Frio County line and on the Frio River in Frio County (Hoffmann, 46). Aguayo's party found *pavos de Indias* in several other locations: on Comanche Creek in southern Zavala County (28), at the Nueces River crossing in central Zavala County (28), north of the campsite called Pita near the Medina-Frio County line (29), along the lower Cibolo Creek in southeastern Wilson County (77), and near Matagorda Bay in Victoria and Jackson counties (79).

Rubí (1767) reported finding turkeys all along his extensive trek across the province. He saw *guajolotes* on August 4 between the Llano and Pedernales rivers in Mason and Gillespie counties; on August 26, as he moved south from San Antonio along the San Antonio River to the Cibolo Creek area in Karnes County; and on August 28, when moving across DeWitt and Lavaca counties to the Colorado River crossing near present-day La Grange.

Solís (1768) found *guajolotes* south of the Rio Grande along his march north from Zacatecas (Kress, 36), from Goliad to San Antonio (43, 47), east from the San Antonio River to the Colorado river crossing in Fayette County (55), and between the Brazos and Trinity rivers along the Adaes Road to East Texas (56, 57, 59).

The wild turkey (*Meleagris gallopavo*) population was seriously depleted in the 1800s, but a reasonably successful restoration program in Texas has been underway for several years (Doughty and Parmenter, *Endangered Species,* 42–46).

37. WILDCAT (*gato montés*)

The term *gato montés* used by Spanish diarists may have referred to a number of cats (other than cougars and jaguars) including the jaguarundi (*Felis yaguarondi*) and the margay (*Felis wiedii*), but probably meant principally the bobcat.

In 1727, Alvarez Barreiro reported wildcats in Vizcaya, Nuevo León, and Coahuila, which then included parts of present-day South Texas (Naylor and Polzer, 214, 222). In 1768, Solís reported the animals in two areas in South Texas: between Laredo and the Nueces River (Kress, 37) and along the road to San Antonio, which included parts of Goliad, Karnes, and Wilson counties (49).

38. WILD CATTLE (*ganado salvaje*)

During the expedition period, wild cattle herds grew in part from strays and abandoned stock and were hunted for food or for their hides by the Indians and the Spaniards. Ramón (1716) found a small number of wild cattle near the Brazos crossing in Burleson County (Foik, 17). Alarcón (1718) saw several head near the San Marcos River in Gonzales County (Hoffmann, 52). Peña (with Aguayo in 1721) reported wild cattle in Travis and Williamson counties (Santos, 39).

When Solís arrived in Texas in 1768, large herds of cattle, many unbranded and semiwild, were ranging along the San Antonio River between La Bahía and San Antonio (Kress, 49) and near the Brazos crossing in Burleson County (56).

39. WILD GOAT (*cabra montés*)

In 1721, Padre Peña said wild goats were seen near the Frio River crossing in north-central Frio County (Santos, 29). The attempt to restore these animals in Texas has not been successful (Doughty and Parmenter, *Endangered Species,* 61).

40. WOLF (*lobo*)

Alvarez Barreiro (1727) noted wolves (*Canis lupus*) in Vizcaya, Nuevo León, and Coahuila (Naylor and Polzer, 214, 222). Espinosa reported *lobos* in Coahuila and Nuevo León in the early 1700s (*Crónica*, 764). Solís (1768) said that wolves were found along his route north from Zacatecas to the area near Laredo (Kress, 36) and along the San Antonio River between Goliad and San Antonio (49).

TREES, SHRUBS, BUSHES, VINES, MOSSES, AND GRASSES REPORTED ON SPANISH EXPEDITIONS INTO TEXAS, 1689–1768

This appendix lists alphabetically the plants most frequently mentioned in the diaries of the Spanish expeditions into Texas between 1689 and 1768. Some entries also include information on flora given in historical accounts of the study area by Alonso de León (the elder), Juan Bautista Chapa, Fray Juan Agustín de Morfí, and Isidro Félix de Espinosa. Information on the type, density, and range of flora in an area is of interest to historical demographers in estimating the precontact Indian population. Each entry notes by whom, when, and where the plant was reported. Not all references to flora in the diaries are included. The entry cites only the name of the author, translator, or editor of the translation or history and a page notation.

In most instances the Spanish plant identification by the diarists is considered reliable, and the English translation is reasonably certain. However, several plant references are noted as questionable. For example, diarists occasionally used a local or vernacular name to identify a plant. Some entries close with references to other Spanish and Mexican colonial documents or contemporary handbooks and encyclopedias on flora in Texas and northern Mexico. The contemporary studies of flora in Texas and northeastern Mexico most frequently consulted include Robert A. Vines, *Trees, Shrubs, and Woody Vines of the Southwest*; Del Weniger, *Cacti of Texas and Neighboring States*; Benny J. Simpson, *A Field Guide to Texas Trees*; Roland H. Wauer, *A Naturalist's Mexico*, and Nancy R. Morin, ed., *Flora of North America North of Mexico*.

1. ALDER (*aliso*)

Lafora (with Rubí in 1767) mentioned alders (*Alnus*) along the banks of the Rio Grande a few miles upstream from Eagle Pass in Maverick County (Kinnaird, 145). Alder, native to Texas, is a member of the birch family (Vines, *Trees of the Southwest*, 139–141).

2. ALFALFA (*alfalfa*)

In 1709, Espinosa reported alfalfa near the Nueces River in Zavala County (Tous, 3). The padre added that the grass was also found in northern Coahuila in the early 1700s (*Crónica*, 763).

3. ANACUA (*anaqua*)

Rivera (June 10, 1727) reported *anaquas* (*Ehretia anacua*) near Monterrey, Nuevo León (Porras, 129). This tree is a native of Nuevo León, Coahuila, and South Texas, but no diarist reported seeing the tree in Texas (Vines, *Trees of the Southwest*, 882–883).

4. ASH (*fresno*)

One of the earliest recordings of ash growing in northern Coahuila and Nuevo León was made in the early 1700s by Espinosa in his *Crónica* (763). In both 1709 (Tous, 3) and 1716 (Tous, 6), Espinosa reported ash (*Fraxinus berlandieriana*) along the Nueces River in Zavala County. Lafora noted it along the Sabinas River in Coahuila in 1767 (Kinnaird, 144). The following year, Solís recorded ash south of San Antonio in Wilson County (Kress, 53).

The species is named for the European botanist Jean Louis Berlandier, who recorded in his diary and other reports valuable information on the flora in Texas and northern Mexico in the late 1820s and early 1830s. Fresno is also a local name in Texas for ash (Vines, *Trees of the Southwest*, 862).

5. BLACKBERRY BUSH (*zarzamora*)

Spanish expedition diarists apparently used the same word, *zarzamora*, to identify both blackberry (*Rubus texanus*) and dewberry (*Rubus trivialis*) bushes. Alonso de León (the elder) noted *zarzamoras* in the province in the late 1600s (*Historia*, 83). Espinosa said that the bushes were found in northern Coahuila and Nuevo León in the early 1700s (*Crónica*, 763).

Aguayo (1721) found the bushes near the Colorado River in Travis County (Santos, 39). Rivera (1727) saw *zarzamoras* near the Salado Creek in Bexar County (Porras, 112). Rubí reported them along the headwaters of the Nueces near the Real-Edwards County line in his diary entry on July 21, 1767. Vines describes numerous species of blackberry and dewberry bushes found in Texas and northern Mexico (*Trees of the Southwest*, 448–483).

6. BLUEWOOD CONDALIA (*brasil* OR *brazil*)

In May 1716, Espinosa recorded *brasil* along the Leona River near the Zavala-Frio County line (Tous, 7). Bluewood condalia (*Condalia obovata*) is a low bush or shrub found today throughout South Texas. Alonso de León (the elder) listed *braziles* as one of the principal trees or shrubs that grew in the province in the middle 1600s (*Historia*, 81).

Brazil is today a vernacular name for bluewood condalia in Texas (Vines, *Trees of the Southwest*, 697; Tull and Miller, *A Field Guide to Wildflowers, Trees, and Shrubs of Texas*, 261). Berlandier noted that the shrub called *brasil* was used to make a red dye (*Journey to Mexico*, 495). Simpson identifies brazil or bluewood as *Condalia hooker*, a small tree that forms thickets, with bright and shiny green leaves and black berries (*Texas Trees*, 110–111).

7. CATCLAW (*uñas de gato*)

Catclaw is a thorny acacia (Vines, *Trees of the Southwest,* 497–498). Terán (1691) found this shrub or small tree (*Acacia greggii*) along his march from Monclova to the Rio Grande (Hatcher, 11) and again later on the Nueces after he crossed the river in Zavala County (12). Lafora (1767) reported finding it near San Juan Bautista in northern Coahuila (Kinnaird, 187). The next year, Solís recorded it near Laredo (Kress, 34).

8. CEDAR (*cedro*)

The diarists used the Spanish words *tascate* and *cedro* to refer to the many forms of this evergreen juniper (*Juniperus ashei*). In parts of Central Texas it is found as a small tree, often with a twisted trunk, rarely over 30 feet in height (Vines, *Trees of the Southwest,* 32–33). Terán and Massanet both reported seeing growths of *cedro* near San Antonio in 1691 (Hatcher, 14). Later on the same expedition, Terán saw the tree near the present-day city of San Marcos (15), and Massanet reported it near the Colorado in Bastrop County (61). Ramón (1716) noted some *cedros* along the Trinity River in Houston County (Foik, 19).

Lafora reported cedar trees along his route from the Sabinas River in northern Coahuila to the Rio Grande crossing a few miles above Eagle Pass (Kinnaird, 144), again on the upper Nueces in the Edwards-Real County area (148), and in Kimble and Menard counties (149).

9. CENTURY PLANT (*maguey*)

Padre Mezquía passed some "mageies" about 20 miles northeast of the Francia crossing in Maverick County (Hoffmann, 313). Solís saw the plant between Zacatecas and Laredo, but reported none north of the Rio Grande (Forrestal, 7, 8). Berlandier considered the plant native to Mexico rather than Texas and described the methods used by the Spaniards in the 1820s to prepare pulque and mezcal from the plant (*Journey to Mexico,* 75, 528–531).

10. CHINQUAPIN (*castaño*)

Alarcón found *castaños* on the Trinity River in 1718. Three years later, Aguayo reported the tree near the Trinity (Hoffmann, 72). Both Rivera (Porras, 116) and Lafora (Kinnaird, 165) identified a creek called Castaño near the Trinity. Rubí noted finding the tree in Houston County on October 8, 1767. The next year, Solís saw the tree near the Navasota River crossing in Brazos County (Kress, 59) and later near Nacogdoches (63).

The references to *castaño* by the diarists were most likely to the species of *Castanea* called chinquapin found today in East Texas. There is no known record of the American chestnut (*Castanea dentata*) growing in Texas. In Berlandier's study of flora in Texas and Mexico, he referred to the chinquapin or a chinquapin *castaño,* not to the American chestnut.

Espinosa described in some detail the *castaño,* which had a very small fruit or nut (*Crónica,* 689). This description matches the chinquapin nut but not the large spiny covering of the American chestnut. Padre Céliz made a similar comment about the *castaño* he saw in East Texas in 1718, describing the nut as "very delicious, but small" (Hoffmann, 72). The chinquapin has only one small nut, whereas the American chestnut has two or three larger nuts enclosed in a large ball.

11. COTTONWOOD (*álamo*)

Cottonwood (*Populus fremontii*) is one of the few poplars indigenous to Texas. Today alamo is used in Texas as a vernacular name for cottonwood (Vines, *Trees of the Southwest*, 87).

An exceptionally tall, lone cottonwood marked a campsite for the early expeditions along the Nadadores River in central Coahuila. De León (West, 388), Terán (Hatcher, 11), and Salinas (Foster and Jackson, 281) noted the *álamo gordo* or *álamo grande* along the river. De León (the elder) included cottonwood as one of the principal trees growing in the province in the mid-1600s (*Historia*, 82). Espinosa reported that the tree was found in Coahuila in the early 1700s (*Crónica*, 763).

Massanet (1691) found the tree along the Medina River in Bexar County (Hackett, 54) and later on the Guadalupe River in Guadalupe County (56). On July 6, 1691, when Captain Martínez traveled from the Colorado River to Matagorda Bay, he reported cottonwoods along the upper Navidad River in the Colorado-Lavaca County area. On July 2, 1963, Salinas found them on Hondo Creek in Medina County (Foster and Jackson, 307).

In 1716, Espinosa reported cottonwoods near the modern city of San Marcos (Tous, 12), along the Brazos River in Burleson County (16), and as far east as Nacogdoches County (13). Alarcón (1718) saw them on the Frio River in Frio County (Hoffmann, 46), the Medina River in Bexar County (48), and along the lower Colorado in Matagorda County (63). Lafora (1767) reported the tree in several locations, including the Sabinas River in Coahuila (Kinnaird, 144) and along the Rio Grande in northern Maverick County (145).

12. CREOSOTE BUSH (*gobernadora*)

The creosote bush (*Larrea tridentata*) is a lowlands evergreen that grows to a height of 6 to 8 feet (Wauer, *A Naturalist's Mexico*, 18–20). Solís (1768) found the bush near the Nueces River in the Webb County area (Kress, 36). Berlandier saw the creosote bush (referred to as *gobernadora*) near Laredo and said it was also found in Nuevo León and Coahuila (*Journey to Mexico*, 213, 421). Vines (*Trees of the Southwest*, 574) also equates the Spanish *gobernadora* with the creosote bush.

13. CYPRESS (*sabino, sabina, ciprés*)

The common bald cypress (*Taxodium distichum*), a deciduous juniper, was seen by Terán (1691) when he first visited the San Antonio area (Hatcher, 14). Alarcón later saw *sabinos* on the nearby Medina River (Hoffmann, 48). The low branch of a cypress tree is credited with saving the life of Governor Alarcón when he almost drowned crossing the Guadalupe near New Braunfels in May 1718 (54). Fray Solís (1768) saw cypresses along the San Antonio River (Kress, 53) and near the Brazos River in Burleson County (57).

Two prominent rivers crossed on Spanish expeditions from Monclova to Los Adaes were named for the tree—the Sabinas River, which flows from west to east across northern Coahuila, and the Sabine, which tracks part of the present Texas-Louisiana line.

The cypress found north of the Rio Grande was probably a common bald cypress; those seen below the Rio Grande may have been another variety, the evergreen Montezuma bald cypress (*Taxodium mucronatum*). The second variety is found in Nuevo León and Coahuila and is known there as *ciprés* or *sabino* (Vines, *Trees of the Southwest*, 12, 13). Berlandier discussed the huge size and age of the cypress called Ahuehuete de Moctezuma or Arbol de Moctezuma at Chapultepec near Mexico City (*Journey to Mexico*, 135).

Alonso de León (the elder) listed cypress among the prominent trees growing in Nuevo León in the middle 1600s (*Historia*, 82). On his expedition to the mouth of the Rio Grande in 1686, De León saw cypresses along the lower Rio Grande (Chapa, *Historia*, 130). Espinosa described the *sabinas* along the bank of the river in Coahuila that carried the name (*Crónica*, 761).

14. DEWBERRY BUSH (*zarzamora*)

See the entry for "Blackberry Bush."

15. EBONY (*ébano*)

Solís (1768) noted the thorny tree (*Pithecellobium flexicaule*) or large shrub (also known as Texas ebony) growing along the Rio Grande near Laredo (Kress, 34), and he later saw *ébanos* along the Nueces River in the McMullin County area (36). Berlandier also described *ébanos* near Laredo (*Journey to Mexico*, 449–450, 582–583). Alonso de León (the elder) recorded *ébanos* growing in the new province in the middle 1600s (*Historia*, 81).

16. ELM (*olmo*)

Captain Martínez saw elm trees (*Ulmus*) along the upper Navidad River in Fayette County on July 6, 1691, on his trip from Terán's base-camp on the Colorado to Matagorda Bay. In 1709, Espinosa saw the tree on both the Medina in Bexar County (Tous, 5) and Colorado River in Travis County (Tous, 7). The padre reported *olmos* in northern Coahuila in 1700 (*Crónica*, 763). Alarcón (1718) found them on the Nueces River in Zavala County (Hoffmann, 45); and Solís saw them on the Colorado in Fayette County (Kress, 56).

A species identification can not be made with certainty because several elm species are found in Texas (Vines, *Trees of the Southwest*, 208–214).

17. FLAX (*lino*)

In 1709 (Tous, 10) and again in 1716 (Tous, 9), Espinosa reported wild flax growing in the fields between San Antonio and Austin.

18. GAMMA GRASS (*zacate granilla*)

On November 21, 1767, Rubí identified gamma or some small-grain grass growing near the Rio Grande on his march up the river from Laredo to San Juan Bautista (near present-day Guerrero, Coahuila). Padre Mezquía (with Alarcón in 1718) reported a wide distribution of the grass in Maverick County (Hoffmann, 314).

19. GIANT CANE (*otate*)

On June 6, 1693, Governor Salinas identified some giant cane or *otate* (*Arundinaria gigantea*) near the Trinity River in Leon County. On an expedition to the mouth of the Rio Grande in 1686, Leon reported *otates gruesos* or giant cane along the river (Chapa, *Historia*, 130). (See Vines, *Trees of the Southwest*, 44.)

Carrizos (reeds), which Massanet found along the Rio Grande in Maverick County (Hatcher, 51) and which were recorded on other expeditions, are the much smaller plants.

20. HACKBERRY (*palo blanco*)

On June 30, 1691, Massanet carved a cross on a hackberry (*Celtis*) when he first reached the Colorado (Hatcher, 62). Padre Mezquía (with Alarcón in 1718) found hackberry near the Frio River in Frio County (Hoffmann, 315) and saw the tree again on the Medina River in Bexar County (317).

21. HAWTHORN (*tejocote*)

On October 2, 1718, Alarcón saw *tejocotes* with some wild plum and persimmon trees in central Burleson County (Hoffmann, 70). Fritz Hoffmann identified the tree as a member of the hawthorn family. Berlandier referred to present Peach Creek in eastern Gonzales County as Arroyo de los Tejocotes (*Journey to Mexico*, 306–309). Several species of hawthorn are widely distributed across Texas, including the Gonzales County area (Vines, *Trees of Central Texas*, 141–151; Simpson, *Texas Trees*, 128).

22. HEMP (*cáñamo*)

In 1709 (Tous, 10) and 1716 (Tous, 9), Espinosa recorded finding hemp in open fields in Bexar County. The padre reported that hemp was found throughout Coahuila in the early 1700s (*Crónica*, 763) and also near the modern city of San Marcos in Hayes County in 1716 (Tous, 13). Alarcón found hemp growing in eastern Zavala County (Hoffmann, 45). Solís (1768) found it in Wilson County along the San Antonio River (Kress, 53). The fibers from the plant were used to make cloth and rope.

23. HERB (*yerba*)

Rubí recognized a medicinal plant (*viperina*) in East Texas on September 4, 1767. The next year, Solís gathered some *viperina* near the Brazos and near the Trinity (Kress, 60, 63). Berlandier said the plant (*la yerba del Indio*) was used as a remedy against snake venom (*Journey to Mexico*, 458–459). Experts believe that Native Americans used more plants for medicine than they did for food (Martin, 205).

24. HICKORY (*nogal*)

See the entry on "Pecan."

25. HUISACHE (*huisache*)

Rivera (1727) reported huisache (*Acacia farnesiana*) in the Province of Vizcaya (Porras, 101) and saw it along the Nadadores River north of Monclova (107).

Lafora (1767) reported the tree north of Monclova on his trip to Texas (Kinnaird, 143) and again south of San Juan Bautista in northern Coahuila (187). Solís (1768) found the tree or shrub in northern Nuevo León (Kress, 34) and also across South Texas as he moved north along the lower Bahía Road near Laredo (36), near the Nueces River in Live Oak County (36), and along the San Antonio River in Karnes, Wilson, and Bexar counties (18, 19).

Solís's three reports of huisache in the San Antonio area in 1768 conflict with Roy Bedichek's account that the tree is a "newcomer," having arrived from south of the border during the early years of the twentieth century (*Karankaway Country*, 92–93; see also Vines, *Trees of the Southwest*, 496–497).

26. LANTANA (*orégano*)

On May 6 and 7, 1693, Salinas saw *orégano* between the Sabinas River and the Rio Grande in northern Coahuila. This reference is to types of wild verbena and lantana (Foster and Jackson, 282*n*43).

27. LAUREL (*laurel*)

The tree that the diarists referred to as *laurel* (*Sophora secundiflora*) was probably the shrub or small tree today called the Texas laurel or mescal-bean sophora, which is not a member of the laurel family (Vines, *Trees of the Southwest*, 568–569). Solís (1768) mentioned laurel on the Brazos River near the Burleson-Brazos County line (Kress, 57). Alonso de León (the elder) reported *laureles* in Nuevo León in the middle 1600s (*Historia*, 81).

28. LECHUGUILLA (*lechuguilla*)

De León in 1690 (Bolton, *Spanish Exploration*, 406) and Salinas in 1693 (Foster and Jackson, 285) mentioned seeing lechuguilla (*Agave lechuguilla*) as they moved across northern Coahuila and into Maverick County. It is a low-growing plant with a full body of spiked leaves that form a full circle to the ground. The Spanish name means little lettuce. The plant has a tall flower stalk; its root (*amole*) was used as a substitute for soap (Vines, *Trees of the Southwest*, 80–81; Wauer, *Naturalist's Mexico*, 23–25). Arroyo Amole, which enters the Rio Grande from Coahuila near the Francia crossing, was identified by Rivera in 1716 (Foik, 7).

29. LIVE OAK (*encino*)

The two Spanish words used most frequently to identify oaks were *encino*, usually meaning an evergreen live oak, and *roble*, usually referring to one of a large number of deciduous oaks. The live oak (*Quercus virginiana*) was one of the most frequently reported trees on the Spanish expeditions. It was seen from Coahuila to Houston County east of the Trinity River. Alonso de León (the elder) recorded *encinos* growing in Nuevo León in the 1650s (*Historia*, 81). Espinosa said that live oaks were found in northern Coahuila and Nuevo León in the early 1700s (*Crónica*, 689).

On his 1689 expedition, Governor De León found mottes of live oak first on the Frio River near the crossing below the junction with the Hondo in Frio County (West, 392). He reported seeing the tree all along his route east into DeWitt County (393). In 1690, De León again reported live oaks near the Guadalupe base-camp in DeWitt County (Bolton, *Spanish Exploration*, 409, 412) and as far east as the San Pedro Creek area in Houston County (415).

Terán (1691) noted live oaks near San Antonio (Hatcher, 14). Later that year, on July 3, Captain Martínez found the tree on his trip to Matagorda Bay from Terán's base-camp on the Colorado. Salinas (1693) reported live oaks on the Leona River in Zavala County and the Frio River in Frio County (Foster and Jackson, 286, 287), in central Atascosa County (289), along the Guadalupe in DeWitt County (291), and east of the Trinity in Houston County (299).

Alarcón (1718) confirmed that live oaks were found on the Nueces in Zavala County (Hoffmann, 45). Lafora (1767) saw the trees on the Llano River (Kinnaird, 149) and the Pedernales (152) and east of the Trinity River (165). Solís reported the next year that they were found below the Nueces in Webb County on his march north from Laredo (Kress, 37). (See Vines, *Trees of the Southwest*, 170–171.)

30. MESQUITE (*mezquite*)

The mesquite tree or shrub (*Prosopis juliflora*) was recorded on expeditions as the parties marched north from Monclova, Coahuila, and was repeatedly seen in areas north and east of the Colorado River. One of the earliest reports of mesquite in Nuevo León and Coahuila was by Alonso de León (the elder) who said it grew in the area in the middle 1600s (*Historia*, 81). In both 1689 and 1690, De León repeatedly reported mesquite from Maverick County to Atascosa County (West, 390, 391, 392; Bolton, *Spanish Exploration*, 406, 407).

The expedition diaries dispute Roy Bedichek's assertion that "normally, and in course of nature, this mesquite has no business here [Texas]." The naturalist mistakenly thought that the tree had invaded Texas in "the last two or three hundred years" (*Karankaway Country*, 56). Over 300 years ago, De León reported mesquite in Atascosa County 100 miles north of the Rio Grande, and over 250 years ago Padre Peña recorded mesquite as far north as Waco (Santos, 44, 45).

Terán and Massanet (1691) both noted seeing mesquite in central Coahuila below the Rio Grande (Hatcher, 49) and again in Frio County (13). In 1716, Espinosa found it east of the Colorado River on Brushy Creek in Williamson County (Tous, 14), and Padre Peña (with Aguayo five years later) recorded it not only as far north as present-day Waco and but also east to the Brazos River in Robertson County (Santos, 46). On his trip from San Antonio southeast to establish the presidio at Matagorda Bay, Aguayo found the shrub on the lower Cibolo in Karnes County (76).

Rivera (1727) saw mesquite from Vizcaya north to the Nadadores River in Coahuila

(Porras, 101, 107). Following parts of Rivera's route, Rubí (1767) reported mesquite on June 14 on his journey from Saltillo to Monclova and near the Llano river in Kimble County on July 24. The next year, Solís said mesquite was found along the Rio Grande near Laredo (Kress, 36) and on the route between Laredo and Mission Espíritu Santo near Goliad (37, 49).

Espinosa described graphically how important the mesquite bean was to the Indians in Coahuila and Nuevo León. When green, the bean was wrapped in a large green leaf and eaten or made into a drink. The Indians also sun dried the bean, ground it, and made a paste that could be kept for a year (*Crónica*, 763). (See also Vines, *Trees of the Southwest*, 515–516.)

31. MULBERRY (*mora*)

The mulberry trees reported by the expedition diarists were probably the Texas mulberry (*Morus microphylla*), which is also known in Texas by the vernacular name mora (Vines, *Trees of the Southwest*, 219–220). Alonso de León (the elder) listed *morales* as a tree found in Nuevo León in the middle 1600s (*Historia*, 83). Espinosa recorded that mulberry trees were found in Coahuila in the early 1700s (*Crónica*, 763).

Fray Massanet (1691) reported mulberries in the San Antonio area and also on the Colorado River in Bastrop County (Hatcher 54, 61). On July 1, 1693, Salinas said the tree was found in Bexar County, along the present San Antonio River (Foster and Jackson, 307). In 1709, Espinosa found it on the Medina in Bexar County (Tous, 5) and near the San Marcos River in Hayes County (6). On his 1716 expedition, Espinosa reported *morales* on the Nueces in Zavala County (Tous, 6). Alarcón (1718) saw mulberry trees on Tortuga Creek in Zavala County (Hoffmann, 45) and on the Medina River in Bexar County (48).

32. OAK (*roble*)

Spanish diarists usually did not distinguish one deciduous oak or *roble* from another. Terán reported oak trees (*Quercus*) near San Antonio (Hatcher, 14); on the same expedition (1691), Massanet saw four tall oaks on Comanche Creek near the crossing in Zavala County (52). In 1709, Espinosa reported oaks about 20 miles northeast of the Rio Grande (Tous, 3), between the Nueces and Leona (4), and up the San Miguel to the Medina River in Bexar County (5).

Alarcón (1718) confirmed that oaks were found on the Nueces in Zavala County (Hoffmann, 45). Rivera (1727) reported oaks on San Miguel Creek in Medina County (Porras, 110). The diary accounts are not sufficiently detailed to permit an identification of the species. Charles B. Heiser, Jr., notes that acorns were a significant source of food for Native Americans (199).

33. PALM (*palma, sabal*)

Chapa's *Historia* reports that De León saw *palmas* near the mouth of the Rio Grande on his 1686 expedition in search of La Salle's settlement on the lower Texas Gulf Coast (130). However, the Spanish terms *palma* and *sabal* may have been used for yucca or Spanish dagger (see the entry on "Spanish Dagger"). The dwarf palm (*sabal minor*) or trunkless palmetto was probably reported by Solís as *palmito* (Kress, 34, 36). Espinosa said *palmitos*, which looked like the top of a palm tree, were found in northern Nuevo León and Coahuila in the early 1700s (*Crónica,* 763). Diarists seldom described the plant as having fan-shaped leaves or other identifiable characteristics that would permit positive identification. (See Vines, *Trees of the Southwest,* 45–48.)

34. PECAN (*nogal*)

The Spanish diarists used the term *nogal* to refer to a number of different nut trees, including pecan (*Carya illinoensis*), hickory (*Carya ovata*), and walnut (*Juglans microcarpa*). The references to *nogal* in the expedition diaries, therefore, may have been to any one of the three trees, which were all probably found across broad areas of the state during the expedition period, as they are today. Alonso de León (the elder) reported *nogales* in Nuevo León in the middle 1600s (*Historia,* 83). Espinosa recorded *nogales* in Coahuila in the early 1700s (*Crónica,* 763).

In 1689, De León found *nogales,* probably pecan trees, along the Nueces and named the river for the nut (West, 391). He also saw the trees along the San Antonio River in Karnes County in 1690 (Bolton, *Spanish Exploration,* 393). In 1693, Salinas found *nogales* on the Nueces (Foster and Jackson, 286) and the San Antonio River (289). Alarcón saw pecans or other nut trees at the Pita campsite on the San Miguel (Hoffmann, 47) and farther east on the Trinity (71), near Nacogdoches (80), and near Los Adaes in western Louisiana (81).

Lafora reported nut trees on the Llano River (Kinnaird, 149) and on the lower Trinity north of Trinity Bay (172). On July 13, 1767, Rubí said that *nogales* were found a few miles south of Eagle Pass in Coahuila; on July 18, he saw the trees along the Nueces River.

35. PERSIMMON (*nísperos, zapote, chapote*)

Texas persimmon or chapote (*Diospyros texana*) is a small native fruit tree or shrub found in both Texas and northeastern Mexico (Tull and Miller, *A Field Guide to Wildflowers, Trees, and Shrubs of Texas,* 184). Espinosa (1709) said that the *nísperos* found along the streams in Central Texas were similar to fruit trees in Spain (Tous, 11) and that *nísperos* were also found in Coahuila in the early 1600s (*Crónica,* 763).

Rubí saw the tree growing in eastern Maverick County on July 17, 1767. Solís (1768) reported finding *nísperos* on the Brazos near the crossing in Burleson County (Kress, 57) and later near the Sabine (63). Berlandier noted near the Frio River in Frio County many bushes called *chapotes* (which the annotators identify as Texas persimmon), whose fruit "is greatly esteemed in the region" (*Journey to Mexico,* 564). (See also Vines, *Trees of the Southwest,* 838–839.)

36. PINE (*pino*)

De León (1690) reported pine trees (*Pinus*) east of the Trinity, near the mission location in Houston County (Bolton, *Spanish Exploration,* 415). According to De León, *pinos* were seen near the mouth of the Rio Grande on De León's expedition in 1686 (cited in Chapa, *Historia,* 130). Ramón (1716) wrote that the trees were found near the Trinity

(Foik, 18) and Nacogdoches (22); Aguayo (1721) also saw them along his route near the Trinity River (Santos, 52). The diary records are insufficient to permit an identification of the species of pine. (See Vines, *Trees of the Southwest*, 15–26.)

37. PLUM (*ciruela*)

Wild plum trees (*Prunus mexicana*) are native to Texas and to northeastern Mexico (Vines, *Trees of the Southwest*, 402–403). Espinosa reported plum trees in East Texas near the mission area (*Crónica*, 689). In 1718, Padre Mezquía (with Alarcón) said *ciruelas* were found in Gonzales County (Hoffmann, 320). Later, the diarist Céliz (also with Alarcón) recorded finding them near the Colorado in Fayette County (Hoffmann, 63) and the Brazos in Burleson County (70). Three years later, Aguayo saw the fruit tree farther north and east in Robertson County (Santos, 47). Rivera (1727) wrote that they were found on upper Cibolo Creek near the city of San Antonio (Porras, 112). On August 7, 1767, Rubí saw them on the upper Guadalupe River in Kendall County.

No positive identification of the species of the fruit tree or shrub can be made based on the information in the expedition diaries alone. Vines identifies numerous species of the genus *Prunus* in Texas (see wild peach [*Prunus caroliniana*], Texas almond cherry [*Prunus glandulosa*], small-flower peach-brush [*Prunus minutiflora*], and creek plum [*Prunus rivularis*], in *Trees of the Southwest*, 387-402).

38. POMEGRANATE (*granada de China*)

In April 1768, Solís found numerous pomegranate trees (*granaditas de China en abundancia*) in the woods in Burleson County near the Brazos crossing (Kress, 57). Two days later, he identified them along the Camino Real near the Brazos-Robertson County line (Kress, 58). Robert Vines says that pomegranate trees (Punicaceae) are found growing wild in the Texas woods, having escaped cultivation (*Trees of the Southwest*, 788–789).

39. PRICKLY PEAR (*nopal*)

The Spanish word *nopal* refers to a prickly pear cactus (*Opuntia lindheimeri*); *tunal* is the seasonal fruit from the cactus. Vines identifies thirty-three species of *Opuntia* in Texas (*Trees of the Southwest*, 776–777). Alonso de León (the elder) reported that *nopales* were found in the province in the middle 1600s (*Historia*, 81).

De León (1689) saw prickly pear near the Leona River in Zavala County (Bolton, *Spanish Exploration*, 392). Fray Mezquía (with Alarcón in 1718) saw them near Crystal City (Hoffmann, 313). Solís (1768) reported the cacti in northeastern Webb County (Kress, 36). (See Weniger, *Cacti of Texas and Neighboring States*, 228.)

40. SASSAFRAS (*sasafrás*)

Sassafras (*Sassafras albidum*) is a small tree, native to East Texas (Vines, *Trees of the Southwest*, 297–298). Solís (1768) saw sassafras in Burleson County near the Navasota River (Kress, 59), in the Brazos-Leon-Madison County area (59), and near the Sabine (63).

41. SCRUB OAK OR CHAPARRAL
(chaparra, chaparro de espina, cocolmecalt)

The Spanish term *chaparras* was frequently used to describe a thick, low, and usually thorny scrub, much as chaparral is used in Texas today. Vines identifies a number of small trees or scrubs that are commonly referred to in Texas as chaparral, including the catclaw acacia, the lotebush condalia or Texas buckthorn, the bluewood condalia, the downy forestieria, and the Texas mahonia or agarita bush (*Trees of the Southwest*, 499, 695, 697, 850, 273).

De León reported *chaparras* growing in northern Coahuila in 1690 (Bolton, *Spanish Exploration*, 406). On May 15, 1693, Salinas found scrub oaks between the Nueces and Frio (Foster and Jackson, 287). Espinosa (1709) found *cocolmecaltes* near the Nueces in Zavala County (Tous, 3). Alarcón (1718) saw *cocolmecates* on the San Marcos River (Hoffmann, 50) and the lower Colorado (64). Lafora (1767) found some along the Llano River in Kimble County (Kinnaird, 149) and the Pedernales in the Gillespie County area (152). Solís (1768) reported seeing them in northern Nuevo León (Kress, 75).

42. SIENE BEAN OR RATTLEBUSH *(taray)*

In 1691, Terán identified *tarayes* on the Sabina River in Coahuila (Hatcher, 11). The Spanish word *taxaya* or *taray* refers to a bush that grows with several stems from the base and has a pod with partitions between the seeds, which rattle when dry (*Diccionario de la lengua española* [Madrid: Real Academia Española, 1984], 1288). Although the identification cannot be made with certainty, based solely on the diary account, the plant reported is probably the Drummond rattlebox or siene bean (Vines, *Trees of the Southwest*, 545–555).

Solís identified *tarais* or tamarisks with some laurels and cypresses in Burleson County in 1768 (Kress, 57).

43. SPANISH DAGGER *(pita palma)*

It is difficult to identify with certainty the type of yucca, or perhaps palm, reported by diarists. The Spanish word *pita* or *pita palma* was used to identify Spanish dagger and yucca plant. In 1716, Espinosa reported that *palmitos* (perhaps dwarf palmetto palms) or fan-palms were found near the city of San Antonio (Tous, 9). Alarcón (1718) found *palmas* at the coast near Matagorda Bay in Matagorda County (Hoffmann, 65). Lafora reported them near Saltillo (Kinnaird, 194). Solís noted that palmettos were found near Laredo (Kress, 36) and later saw *montes de palma* along the Nueces near the four corners of Duval, McMullin, Webb, and LaSalle counties (37).

Berlandier described *palmas* "with flowers" in the lower Rio Grande area; the annotation probably correctly notes that he was referring to yuccas rather than to palms (*A Journey to Mexico*, 456–468).

44. SPANISH MOSS *(pastle)*

When Terán left the mission area in Houston County to visit the "Cadodacho Nation" near the Red River in November, 1691, he noted that the mules ate the moss on the trees because of lack of grass (Hatcher, 30). This report and others on later expeditions probably referred to Spanish moss (*Tillandsia usneoides*), which is a member of the flowering plant family Bromeliaceae. Spanish moss is therefore related to the pineapple and is not a moss (William Dean Reese, *Mosses of the Gulf South, from the Rio Grande to the Apalachicola* [Baton Rouge and London: Louisiana State University Press, 1984], 3).

On August 31, 1767, Rubí said that the horses and pack animals with his party ate moss because grass was scarce during the dry summer months. Berlandier described Spanish moss hanging on oak trees along the Guadalupe River and reported that the Tonkawa used moss as mattress material (*Journey to Mexico*, 312).

45. SYCAMORE (*álamo negro y blanco* OR *verde y blanco*)

It is difficult to determine from diary references alone whether the Spanish diarists saw sycamores or cottonwoods. Some diarists may have used the term *álamo* for both (see *Journey to Mexico*, 534). But it appears that Espinosa saw sycamores (*álamos verdes y blancos*) near San Antonio in 1709 (Tous, 4). In 1727, Rivera also reported *álamos blancos y negros* growing near San Antonio (Porras, 112). The description of green and white or black and white cottonwood suggests the sharp color variations seen in the trunks of sycamores, but not the trunks of cottonwoods.

46. WALNUT (*nogal*)

See the entry on "Pecan."

47. WILD GRAPEVINE (*parra*)

Wild grapevines were reported hanging from trees on San Miguel Creek in Frio County and were sighted from southwest Texas to the Trinity River in Houston County. However, the diarists did not distinguish one type of grape or grapevine from another. Two independent sightings of large grapevines, approximately 3 feet in circumference, were reported in the same area—the first by Espinosa on May 12, 1716, at the Pita campsite on San Miguel Creek near the Frio-Medina County line (Tous, 8) and the second, on April 4, 1721, by Aguayo in the same area (Santos, 30). Vines identifies over twenty species of wild grape (*Vitis*) found in Texas, including the riverbank grape (*Vitis cordifolia*), which has been recorded with a trunk girth of 5 feet (*Trees of the Southwest*, 707–731).

De León (1689) noted that grapevines were thick along the Atascosa River (West, 393). In 1691, Massanet found them on the Colorado (Hatcher, 61). Solís (1768) saw them along the Navasota (Kress, 59).

48. WILD SWEET POTATO (*camote silvestre*)

Lafora identified wild sweet potatoes growing near Trinity Bay in October 1767 (Kinnaird, 172). Solís found and ate some *camotes* in Brazos County in April 1768 (Kress, 58).

49. WILLOW (*sauz* OR *sauce*)

Alonso de León (the elder) said willows (*Salix*) were found in Nuevo León and Coahuila in the middle 1600s (*Historia,* 82). In 1686, De León saw willows near the mouth of the Rio Grande on his expedition (Chapa, *Historia,* 130). Espinosa reported the tree in Coahuila in the early 1700s (*Crónica,* 763). Terán (1691) said *sauces* were found along the Rio Grande (Hatcher, 12), San Antonio River (14), and also near the modern city of San Marcos (15). On July 1, 1693, Salinas found willows near Hondo Creek in Medina County on his return trip from East Texas (Foster and Jackson, 306).

DOCUMENTED EPIDEMIC DISEASE EPISODES IN NORTHEASTERN NEW SPAIN, 1577–1768

This appendix lists chronologically some of the major epidemic disease episodes in northeastern New Spain recorded in Spanish expedition diaries and colonial histories during the period 1577 to 1768. Many other recorded, and probably more unrecorded, epidemics occurred before 1577. For example, outbreaks of typhoid and measles associated with Cabeza de Vaca's sojourn in south Texas and northern Mexico between 1528 and 1534 are well documented, as is the spread of smallpox by the Luis de Moscoco/Hernando De Soto expedition, which reached East Texas in the 1540s. These epidemics in Texas were cited by John C. Ewers in 1973 ("The Influence of Epidemics on the Indian Population and Cultures of Texas," *Plains Anthropologist* 18 [1973], 104–115) and by P. I. Nixon in 1946 (*The Medical Story of Early Texas, 1528–1853*). Henry F. Dobyns relied heavily on the Ewers study in the preparation of his tables on epidemic episodes of diseases among Indians in North America from 1520 to 1898 (*Their Number Become Thinned,* 13–23). The impact of European diseases on the Caddo nation, including the Tejas Indians in East Texas, has recently been carefully documented by Timothy K. Perttula (*"The Caddo Nation"*).

These recent studies are part of a sometimes limited but nevertheless continuing effort initiated by such distinguished colonial historians as Juan Bautista Chapa (*Historia del Nuevo Reino de León desde 1650 hasta 1690*), Alonso de León the elder (*Historia de Nuevo León*), Fray Isidro Félix de Espinosa (*Crónica de los colegios de propaganda fide de la Nueva España*), and Fray Juan Agustín de Morfí (*Viaje de Indios y diario del Nuevo Mexico*) to record the devastating depopulation and extinction of many Indian tribes during the time the Spaniards were seeking to settle northeastern New Spain. Eugenio del Hoyo's *Historia del Nuevo Reino de León (1577–1723)* and Peter Gerhard's *The North Frontier of New Spain* have done the same.

This study has identified the Indian trade routes and the specific tribes that frequently followed the routes from Nuevo León and Coahuila to Central and East Texas carrying goods for trade, weapons to hunt, and highly contagious diseases.

Date	Disease and Location	Description and References
1. 1577–1616	Series of plagues in Vizcaya.	Gerhard refers to epidemics throughout the area in 1577, along the lower Nasas River in southern Viscaya in 1590, and in the mountains, where the Acaxee, Xixume, and Tepehuane tribes were decimated (*North Frontier of New Spain*, 169).
2. 1636–1639	Smallpox epidemic near Monterrey, Nuevo León.	Epidemic eliminated a community of Alazapa Indians and depopulated most other tribes in the area (Hoyo, *Historia*, 413, 414).
3. 1646	Smallpox epidemic near Cadereyta and Monterrey spread throughout Nuevo León.	Epidemic killed more than 500 Spaniards and Indians. Entire Indian villages were depopulated during the 14-month period (De León, *Historia*, 148).
4. 1650s	Venereal disease (syphilis?) reported to be widespread among Indian tribes in Nuevo León.	De León described a venereal disease that produced painful sores on the genitals and thighs and added that few Indians escaped the deadly disease (*Historia*, 43–46).
5. 1650s	Unidentified epidemic in Cerralvo spread through northern Coahuila, Nuevo León, and South Texas.	Deadly and highly contagious unidentified diseases decimated 161 named Indian tribes, the last 70 of which were listed as residing within 26 to 30 miles of Cerralvo near the lower Rio Grande. Chapa predicted that an additional 80 named tribes living within 100 to 130 miles of Cerralvo would soon be lost to the diseases (*Historia*, 117–120).
6. 1660–1662	Unidentified epidemic in Nuevo León.	Epidemic decimated the Tlempenienniguo, Michiaba, and Abayo tribes. The Alazapa and Quiaguixcagui tribes were reduced to no more than 3 or 4 members (Hoyo, *Historia*, 413).
7. 1674	Smallpox in northern Coahuila, 50 miles south of Rio Grande.	Epidemic affected more than 300 Bobole, Guyquechale, Tiltiqui, and Mayhuam Indians (Steck, "Forerunners of De León," 11–12).
8. 1675	Smallpox episode in Maverick County area.	Fernando del Bosque reported that a large but undisclosed number of Bibit and Jume Indians died (Bolton, *Spanish Exploration*, 298).

Date	Disease and Location	Description and References
9. 1682	Smallpox epidemic at Parras, Nuevo León.	The epidemic lasted ten years (Morfí, *Viaje de Indios*, 217, 218).
10. 1685	Unidentified highly contagious disease at La Salle's settlement at Matagorda Bay.	Father Chrétien Le Clercq reported that the diseases contracted by the troops at Santo Domingo killed 100 in a few days (Cox, *Journeys of La Salle*, vol. 1, 281).
11. 1686	Smallpox among Indians on the lower Rio Grande.	According to Jean Cavelier La Salle, local Indians reported that the area north of the lower Rio Grande was healthy except for smallpox (Cox, *Journeys of La Salle*, vol. 1, 281).
12. 1688	Smallpox epidemic at Matagorda Bay.	The epidemic in which over 100 residents of La Salle's French settlement died was recorded in the expedition diaries of De León (Bolton, *Spanish Exploration*, 395) and Chapa (*Historia*, 146, 155) and in the testimony of a former resident of the French community (Weddle, *Wilderness Manhunt*, 195*n*13).
13. 1691	Unidentified epidemic among Tejas Indians in East Texas.	Massanet twice reported that the Tejas community had suffered a severe epidemic (Hatcher, "The Expedition of Terán," 56, 57).
14. 1695	Unidentified epidemic in Nuevo León.	The epidemic eliminated the Guiniguio tribe (Hoyo, *Historia*, 414).
15. 1700	Epidemic of *cursos de sangre* in Nuevo León.	The epidemic killed 22 Pauxane Indians, based on a record in the local archive of Lampazos in northern Nuevo León (Hoyo, *Historia*, 414).
16. 1706	Smallpox epidemic at missions near Eagle Pass.	Espinosa described the impact of the epidemic on local Indians and the methods they used to control the spread of smallpox (*Crónica*, 776–777; Weddle, *San Juan Bautista*, 73–75).
17. 1737–1739	Typhus epidemic in Nueva Vizcaya, Nuevo León, and Texas.	Gerhard refers to the epidemic in his study (*North Frontier of New Spain*, 26).

Date	Disease and Location	Description and References
18. 1768	Measles, smallpox, typhoid fever, and venereal disease among tribes in East Texas.	Solís listed a number of epidemic (and other) diseases found among the "Asinay, Nazones, Nacogdoches, Navidachos, and Caddodaches" (Kress, "Diary of a Visit by Solís," 70).

INDIAN TRIBES REPORTED ON SPANISH EXPEDITIONS INTO TEXAS, 1689–1768

This appendix lists alphabetically the names of the Indian tribes or bands reported in the diaries of the eleven Spanish expeditions from northeastern New Spain into Texas between 1689 and 1768. The appendix has the narrow objective of locating as precisely as possible (usually by county) where each tribe listed was seen, the name of the expedition leader or diarist, and the date of the meeting or reference. Most references between 1689 and 1722 were encounters under native conditions, but Rivera, Rubí, and Solís usually recorded encounters at missions or compiled lists of tribes residing in a province. A short citation annotating each report gives the name of the translator or editor of the diary and the page reference in the English translation. The unpublished diaries of Martínez and Rubí are cited with only the date of the diary entry in the Spanish diary manuscript.

Indian tribes residing in the study area (parts of present-day northeastern Mexico and Texas) were exceptionally numerous and diverse during this period. The region has been described by Thomas N. Campbell in the *Handbook of North American Indians* as one of the most poorly known regions of Indian population on the North American continent (vol. 10, *Southwest,* 344). The map of North American Indian tribes in the *Handbook* labels most of the geographic area covered by this study "Poorly Known Groups of the Gulf Coastal Plains and the Interior" (ix). All other areas in Mexico, Canada, and the United States are identified in the *Handbook* map with specific Indian tribal names, but tribal identifications are not given for northeastern Mexico and Central Texas because of the complexity and diversity of the Indian population.

During most of the eighty-year period (1689–1768) covered by the study, the Province of Coahuila generally included the present-day State of Coahuila, Mexico, and the area north of the lower Rio Grande that extended into present-day Texas up to the Medina River and the upper San Antonio River. The Province of Nuevo León was immediately to the east of Coahuila, and Vizcaya (present-day Chihuahua) was to the west. Therefore, Indian tribes identified in the diaries as residents of the provinces of Vizcaya, Coahuila, or Nuevo León may also have been living in or ranging into present-day Texas.

Although recognized variants in tribal names are given in most entries, the appendix gives the tribal name as recorded by the diarist in the manuscript or translation; occasionally, therefore, there may be duplicate references to the same tribe.

For further study, some entries conclude with citations to other Spanish and Mexican colonial histories and materials and to corresponding tribal entries in *The Handbook of Texas* (HOT) and citations in the *Handbook of North American Indians* (HONAI). Thomas N. Campbell is the author of most of the corresponding entries in vol. 3 of *The Handbook of Texas*. Campbell and William W. Newcomb, Jr., contributed most of the relevant materials on Texas Indians in vol. 10, *Southwest*, of the *Handbook of North American Indians*.

1. *Adaes* (ADYES, ADÁYS)

The Adaes Indians greeted Aguayo when he arrived at Los Adaes in present-day Natchitoches Parish, Louisiana, on September 1, 1721 (Santos, 70). Rubí described the tribe as docile and peace-loving in nature in his assessment of the number of troops required to garrison the presidio at Los Adaes (Naylor and Polzer, 157). Rubí's engineer Lafora reported only that the tribe was living in the Province of Texas at the time of his inspection in 1767 (Kinnaird, 185). When Solís visited the mission at Los Adaes between May 8 and 24, 1768, he did not report meeting any members of the tribe because "there was no Indian congregation," but he did add that they lived nearby (Kress, 65). *HOT*, 1:4, 5.

2. *Agualohe*

Salinas met members of the tribe on May 10, 1693, near the Francia crossing of the Rio Grande into Maverick County (Foster and Jackson, 284). *HONAI*, 10:355.

3. *Aguapalam*

On June 10, 1691, Massanet (on Terán's expedition) reported meeting the tribe with twelve other Indian nations at the Frio River near modern Frio Town in northwestern Frio County (Hatcher, 53). *HOT*, 3:10; *HONAI*, 10:349, 355.

4. *Aguastaya* (AGUATAYO)

On August 16, 1727, Rivera reported seeing some tribal members living with the Mesquite and Payaya Indians in villages near modern San Antonio about a mile south and east of the presidio. (Porras, 111). Rubí's engineer Lafora in 1767 (Kinnaird, 160) and Solís in 1768 (Kress, 51) reported that the tribe resided at one of the five San Antonio missions at the time of their visits. *HOT*, 3:10, 11; *HONAI*, 10:349, 356.

5. *Ais* (AES, AYS, AYES)

Alarcón encountered this tribe in East Texas, about 50 miles east of Nacogdoches in San Augustine County on November 6, 1718 (Hoffmann, 81). Rivera saw the Aes on September 11, 1727, about 40 to 50 miles east of Nacogdoches (Porras, 118). On September 8, 1767, Lafora reported that they lived in East Texas near mission "Dolores" (Kinnaird, 166). Solís met with Ays and their leader, Captain Urjataña, on

May 5 and 27, 1768, at Mission Nuestra Señora de las Dolores de Bonavente (Kress, 63, 66). *HOT*, 1:19.

6. *Alachome*

On May 27, 1691, Massanet (with Terán) met this tribe, who were with five other tribes at a place called San Juanico near Juan the Frenchman's Creek (modern Arroyo Salado) about 12 miles south of the Rio Grande crossing area near modern Guerrero, Coahuila (Hatcher, 50). *HOT*, 3:14.

7. *Alasapa* (ALAZAPA)

In 1728, Rivera and Barreiro both reported that this tribe was living in the Province of Nuevo León (Porras, 132; Naylor and Polzer, 222). In 1767, Lafora reported that they were living in both Texas and Nuevo León (Kinnaird, 185, 195). *HONAI*, 10:356.

8. *Aname*

Alarcón met a large congregation of tribal members near modern-day Columbus in Colorado County on September 26, 1718 (Hoffmann, 67). Because Rivera (Porras, 125) and later Lafora (Kinnaird, 185) reported that both the Aname and the Aranama were living in the Province of Texas, the two are identified here as separate tribes. However, some authorities consider the name Aname to be a variant of Aranama. *HOT*, 1:43; 3:33, 34.

9. *Anxau* (ANNA)

In 1727, Rivera listed the Anna among the tribes that lived in the Province of Texas (Porras, 125). In 1767, Lafora also listed the tribe as residents of the Province of Texas (Kinnaird, 185). *HOT*, 3:31, 32; *HONAI*, 10:349, 356.

10. *Apache*

Apache and Apache settlements were seen and reported on Rubí's expedition when he was preparing to cross the Rio Grande into Maverick County about 15 miles upstream from Eagle Pass on July 13 and 14, 1767. Throughout the study period (1689–1768), numerous Spanish expedition diarists referred to the tribe, but no other direct Spanish encounters with the tribe were reported. However, a band of sixty mounted Apache attacked the French trader François Derbanne's convoy along its route moving west between the Colorado and the San Marcos rivers on April 8, 1717 (Bridges and De Ville, 247, 248).

Aguayo concluded that the tribe had launched an attack within 3 leagues of the presidio at San Antonio two days before he arrived in May, 1721 (Santos, 34). Shortly thereafter, Peña (with Aguayo) noted Apache in the hill country northwest of Austin (39).

Solís reported that he was passing through "Apache and Lipan country" northeast of Laredo (in Webb, Duval, and Live Oak counties) in February 1768 (Kress, 36), but none were encountered. *HOT*, 1:54–55; *HONAI*, 10:368–392.

11. *Apaysi* (APAYXAM, APASXAM)

Massanet (with Terán) reported that their party met this nation with twelve other tribes near modern Frio Town in Frio County on June 10, 1691 (Hatcher, 53). *HOT*, 3:33.

12. *Apilusa* (APILUCA)

In 1767, Lafora reported that this tribe (perhaps the Opelousa of Louisiana) was living somewhere in the Province of Texas (Kinnaird, 185).

13. *Aranama* (JARANAME, TARANAME, ARANAME, XARANAME)

In 1727, Rivera reported that members of this tribe were living in Texas (Porras, 125). On October 31, 1767, Rubí found members living near Espíritu Santo mission on the San Antonio River in Goliad County. The next year Solís reported the same (Kress, 46).

On August 30, 1767, Rubí found an abandoned Aranama hunting camp along his route near the Washington-Burleson County line and said that the Indians were hunting for bison nearby. During the next few days, Lafora also noted that the tribe lived between the Colorado and the Brazos in Burleson County and added that at times the tribe moved farther south toward the coast (Kinnaird, 164).

On September 2, 1767, Rubí wrote that the tribe frequently was found with the Coco and Mayeye between the Colorado and the Brazos hunting for meat. On October 20, on Rubí's return from East Texas moving west to La Bahía, Lafora again noted that members of the tribe resided between the Brazos and the Colorado (Kinnaird, 175).

A renegade band of the tribe who were former La Bahía mission residents lived between the Guadalupe and the Colorado, according to a comment made by Solís when he was approaching La Grange in Lavaca County on April 20, 1768 (Kress, 57). Solís was threatened by members of same tribe later that year, on July 14, near the same location along the road that Lafora had called the Camino Real the year before. *HOT*, 3:33, 34; *HONAI*, 10:331, 341, 361.

14. *Atakapa*

In 1767, Lafora reported that the tribe was living somewhere in the Province of Texas (Kinnaird, 185). *HOT*, 3:44.

15. *Atastagonie* (ATASTAGONIA)

Rivera reported that members of this tribe were living somewhere in the Province of Texas in 1727 (Porras, 125). In 1767, Lafora also reported that they were residing in the Province of Texas (Kinnaird, 185). *HOT*, 1:75.

16. *Bidai* (VIDA, BEDIA, BIDAY, VIDAY, VIDAI)

Alarcón met members of this tribe on October 27, 1718, near the Neches River in Houston County; the governor noted that the nation, which was friendly with the Tejas, lived to the south of the Tejas community toward the coast (Hoffmann, 78). Aguayo met Viday on July 8, 1721, with the Agdoca and the Indians of the Ranchería Grande near the Trinity River crossing in Leon County (Santos, 51).

On October 3, 1767, Rubí found a deserted village of Biday near the Angelina River along the Polk-Angelina County line. The same year, Lafora reported that Vidai were living somewhere in the Province of Texas (Kinnaird, 185). Solís noted on April 28, 1768, that they lived between the Navasota and the Trinity in Leon County (Kress, 59). The padre met members of the tribe and their Captain Gorgoritos on May 1 and their Captain Antonio Abad near the Navasota River in Leon County on June 29 of the same year (63, 71). *HOT,* 3:79.

17. *Bocarro* (VOCARRO)

In 1728, this tribe was listed among residents of the Province of León by Rivera (Porras, 132) and Barreiro (Naylor and Polzer, 222). Forty years later, Lafora filed the same report (Kinnaird, 195).

18. *Borrado*

On February 13, 1728, Rivera reported that he saw this tribe near Monterrey, Nuevo León (Porras, 129, 132). Barreiro also reported that they were living in the Province of León in 1728 (Kinnaird, 222). Members of the tribe were found at a San Antonio mission by Rubí between August 9 and 24, 1767, and Lafora reported that they were living in the Provinces of Coahuila and León in the same year (Kinnaird, 155, 195).

On November 12, 1767, Rubí said a few members of the tribe brought from the coast were at Mission Rosario in present-day Goliad County. On November 23, Rubí saw more tribal members at the two missions near San Juan Bautista. Near Monterrey, on December 20, Rubí said the local farmers are frequently attacked by the "Meco or Borrado Indians." *HOT,* 3:97, 98; *HONAI,* 10:329, 331, 352, 353.

19. *"Bozale"*

Espinosa saw some Indians whom he called "Bozales" on April 29, 1716, near Comanche Creek in Zavala County (Tous, 6). However, this may not have been the tribal name.

20. *Cacase*

On July 12, 1693, the Cacase (with the Hape and Mescal) helped Salinas cross the flooded Rio Grande in Maverick County on the captain's return from resupplying Massanet and the mission in East Texas (Foster and Jackson, 311). See the entry "Cacaje" in *HONAI,* 10:356.

21. *Cacaxtle* (CACASTLE, CACAXTE)

On his journey to East Texas (May 9, 1693), Salinas found this tribe with the Ocana and Piedras Blancas near the Rio Grande crossing area in Maverick County, and he met several tribal members again that year (on May 27) at the crossing of the Colorado River near La Grange in Fayette County (Foster and Jackson, 283, 294). *HOT,* 3:132; *HONAI,* 10:329–337.

22. *Cacquite* (CATQUEZA, SAQUITA)

In 1727, Rivera and his engineer Barreiro both reported that the tribe (along with the Cibolo and Toboso) was living in the Province of Coahuila (Porras, 131; Naylor and

Polzer, 222). In 1767, Lafora also listed the tribe as residing in Coahuila (Kinnaird, 154). In 1691, Terán and Massanet met Catqueza from Coahuila or Vizcaya visiting near the present-day city of San Marcos (see the entry "Catqueza" below). Two years later, Salinas met Saquita in the same area who were apparently also from a mission area south of the Rio Grande (see the entry "Saquita" below). These reports suggest that Catqueza and Saquita may be variants of Cacquite.

23. *Caddodacho* (CADODACHO)
Terán met this tribe and inspected their large village area northeast of the Tejas on November 28, 1691 (Hatcher, 32). Aguayo met members of the tribe on August 11, 1721, near Nacogdoches (Santos, 63), where they had come with their friends the Tejas Indians to greet the returning Spaniards. On June 19, 1768, Solís reported that the tribe lived near Nacogdoches (Kress, 69). See the entry "Caddo Indians" in *HOT*, 1:264–266.

24. *Caisquetebana*
The only sighting of this tribe was by De León on June 20, 1690, on the upper Arenosa Creek along the Victoria-Jackson County line (Bolton, *Spanish Exploration*, 420n4). See the entry "Caiasban Indians" by Thomas N. Campbell in *HOT*, 3:133.

25. *Camama*
On April 6, 1768, Solís reported that the Camama were living at Mission San José in San Antonio (Kress, 51). *HOT*, 3:136.

26. *Cano* (CANA, CANNA)
In 1727, Rivera reported that the Cano were living in the Province of Coahuila (Porras, 131), and Barreiro noted the same (Naylor and Polzer, 222). In 1767, Lafora repeated that they were in Coahuila (Kinnaird, 154). Solís found them at Mission San José in San Antonio in 1768 (Kress, 51). *HOT*, 3:140.

27. *Cantona* (CANTUNA)
De León met members of this tribe near the crossing of the Colorado at La Grange on June 18, 1690 (Bolton, *Spanish Exploration*, 419n5). Terán and Massanet reported seeing them with several other tribes (Jumano, Cibolo, and Catqueza) west of the modern city of San Marcos on June 19, 1691 (Hatcher 15, 57); on July 4, Massanet saw them again at the Colorado River near the Bastrop-Fayette County line (63). The captain of the Cantona was identified on October 5, 1691, as a guide for Terán on his second journey to the Tejas (26). On February 27, 1692, Terán reported meeting some members of the tribe near the Colorado crossing at La Grange on his return from his second trip to East Texas (46).

On June 23, 1693, Salinas saw them at the Colorado River crossing near La Grange meeting with some Jumano from the Rio Grande and some Asinai from East Texas (Foster and Jackson, 303). Espinosa met Captain Cantona with several Indian nations (Yojuane, Simaoma, and Tusonibi) on the Colorado near the Bastrop-Travis County line on April 19, 1709 (Tous, 8). Espinosa met them and the Mescal, Xarame, and Sijame on his expedition with Ramón near the crossing of the Brazos River on the Burleson-Brazos County line on June 13, 1716 (Tous, 17). *HOT,* 3:143.

28. *Carrizo*

In 1727, Rivera (Porras, 131) and Barreiro (Naylor and Polzer, 222) both reported that the tribe was living in the Province of Coahuila; in 1767, Lafora noted the same (Kinnaird, 155). Solís met them on February 12, 1768, about 26 miles south of Laredo in Nuevo León (Kress, 35). *HOT,* 3:146; *HONAI,* 10:341–357.

29. *Catqueza* (CASQUESA, CACQUITE, SAQUITA)

Massanet and Terán met the Casqueza and their Spanish-speaking leader, Captain Nicolás, with several other tribes from Coahuila and Chihuahua including the Jumano and Cibolo at a temporary but large camp west of the San Marcos River on June 19, 1691 (Hatcher, 15, 57). *HOT,* 3:151.

30. *Catujano* (CATAJANE)

In 1727, both Rivera (Porras, 131) and Barreiro (Naylor and Polzer, 222) reported that the Catujano were living in the Province of Coahuila. *HOT,* 3:152; *HONAI,* 10:302, 356.

31. *Cava* (CAQUA, CAUYA, LAVA)

According to Massanet, De León visited a Cava (and Emet) village on Irish Creek, DeWitt County, on April 16, 1689 (Bolton, *Spanish Exploration,* 359). De León also met them near the crossing of the Colorado River near La Grange in Fayette County on June 18, 1690 (Bolton, *Spanish Exploration,* 419n5). *HOT,* 3:153; *HONAI,* 10:349, 356.

32. *Caynaaya* (CAYNAAQUA, CHAYNAYA)

Members of this tribe were sighted only once during an expedition: Massanet saw them with several other nations west of the San Marcos River in Guadalupe County on June 19, 1691 (Hatcher, 57). He noted that they traveled each year to the San Marcos area to hunt bison and returned home south of the Rio Grande in the winter. *HOT,* 3:155.

33. *Chaguan*

Massanet, with Terán, reported meeting the nation with five other tribes on June 5, 1691, at Comanche Creek in Zavala County (Hatcher, 53). See the entry "Chaguantapam Indians" in *HOT,* 3:158.

34. *Chalome* (CHOLAME, CHAULAAME)

Massanet (with Terán) met Chalome at their hunting camp near the headwaters of the San Marcos River with several West Texas and Chihuahua Indian nations including the Cibolo and Jumano on June 18, 1691 (Hatcher, 57). He identified the tribe as residents of West Texas along with the Jumano, with whom they were traveling. On April 13, 1709, Espinosa met the Chaulaame with some Siupam and Sijame near San Pedro

Springs in Bexar County (Tous, 5). See the reference to the Cholome as well as the Jumano and Cibolo as possible Apacheans in *HONAI,* 10:368.

35. *Chane*

When he reached the headwaters of the Llano River near the Edwards-Kimble County line on July 22, 1767, Rubí identified the river as the "Río de los Janes, or Chanes, which is a nation of Indians allied with the Comanche." Lafora found members of this tribe living at one of the missions in San Antonio on August 24, 1767 (Kinnaird, 160). See the entry "Llano River" in *HOT,* 2:70–71.

36. *Chayopine*

Lafora listed the Chayopine among the Indians that Rubí saw at a mission in San Antonio in 1767 (Kinnaird, 160), but no other sighting of the tribe was reported on any expedition. *HOT,* 3:162; *HONAI,* 10:349, 356.

37. *Cibola* (CIBULA, CIBOLO, SIBULO, SIBOLA)

Terán and Massanet both reported meeting Cibula west of the San Marcos River in Guadalupe County with other Indians (Jumano, Catqueza, Cantona, and others) on June 18 or 19, 1691 (Hatcher, 15, 57). Rivera saw Sibulo in a pueblo at Mission San Bernardino de la Candela in eastern Coahuila, about 50 miles east of Monclova, on January 29, 1728 (Porras, 126). Rivera (Porras, 131) and Barreiro (Naylor and Polzer, 222) also reported that Cibolo were living in the Province of Coahuila in 1727 and 1728. In 1767, Lafora also reported that they lived in the Province of Coahuila (Kinnaird, 154). *HOT,* 3:171; *HONAI,* 9:178, 253, 481, 519; 10:368.

38. *Coapite* (GUAPITE)

This nation was reported living in the Province of Texas by Rivera in 1727 (Porras, 125). The Guapite were recorded at the Mission Rosario by Lafora on October 31, 1767, and by Solís on March 4 and 5, 1768 (Kinnaird, 178; Kress, 39). *HOT,* 3:179–180; *HONAI,* 10:360–364.

39. *Coco* (CAPOQUE, CAÓE, COAQUE)

On June 19, 1690, De León found a village of a tribe called Caóe located within a few miles of a Toho village and a large "Na aman" village on Sandy Creek, 60 miles inland from the coast near the Lavaca-Colorado County line (Bolton, *Spanish Exploration,* 420*nn*1, 2). According to Céliz, Alarcón met some friendly "Caocose" near Carancahua Bay in Matagorda County and exchanged gifts with them on September 24, 1718 (Hoffmann, 66). Rivera reported that they lived somewhere in the Province of Texas in 1727 (Porras, 125).

According to Lafora, Rubí met the tribe with some Aranama, Payaya, and other tribes at one of the San Antonio missions in Bexar County in August 1767 (Kinnaird, 160). On October 31, 1767, Lafora reported that the tribe had earlier lived near the Espíritu Santo mission at modern Goliad and warned of the dangers posed to travelers by the tribe (Kinnaird, 178).

On April 21 and 22, 1768, Solís identified the area his party was passing through (Fayette and Washington counties) as "Coco Indian country" (Kress, 56). Solís met them on April 25 with several other Indian nations (including Mayaye and Cujane) near the Brazos crossing in Burleson County (58). *HOT*, 3:181; *HONAI*, 10:359–367.

40. *Colorado*
In 1727, Rivera (Porras, 131) and Barreiro (Naylor and Polzer, 222) both reported that this tribe was living in the Province of Coahuila. Forty years later, Lafora reported the same (Kinnaird, 154). *HOT*, 3:185.

41. *Comanche*
No sighting of Comanche was reported on any expedition. On August 24, 1767, Rubí noted that the Comanche "and their allies of the north" stole horses from his expedition party at the presidio near San Sabá. He included them among the Norteños in Article 16 of his *dictamen* and said that "until now [1767] they were little known [in Central Texas]." Solís mentioned them on August 22, 1768, when he noted that his party was in Comanche country when traveling south near the Nueces through Webb, Duval, and McMullen counties. *HONAI*, 10:345–349.

42. *Conhumeno*
In 1767, Lafora wrote that this tribe (Conhumeno in the manuscript) was in the Province of Coahuila (Kinnaird, 155 [as Conhumero]).

43. *Copane* (CHUPANE, COPANO, COOPANE)
Rivera reported that Copane were residing in the Province of Texas in 1727 (Porras, 125). Lafora listed them among the tribes that were living in Texas in 1767 (Kinnaird, 185). On March 4 and 5, 1768, Solís reported that the Coopane were at Mission Rosario on the San Antonio River with the Cujane, Coapite, and Karankawa (Kress, 40). *HOT*, 3:197–198; *HONAI*, 10:360, 364.

44. *Cujane* (CUSANE, COJANE, COXANE, JOJUANE)
Rivera mentioned that the Cusane were living in the Province of Texas in 1727 (Porras, 125). Lafora included the Cujane in his 1767 list of Indians residing in Texas (Kinnaird, 185). Rubí found them near Mission Espíritu Santo during his inspection of the nearby presidio on November 1–11, 1767, and Solís also reported Coxane at Mission Rosario on March 5, 1768 (Kress, 40). *HOT*, 3:213; *HONAI*, 10:360–361.

45. *Curmicai*
The only reference to this tribe was made by Alarcón on September 30, 1718 (Hoffmann, 69), after he had visited Matagorda Bay and was moving northeast along Cummings Creek near the Colorado-Fayette County line, about 30 miles northeast of Columbus. They were with five other large Indian nations (the Sana, Emet, Toho, Mayeye, and Huyugan).

46. *Deadose* (AGDOCA, YGODOSA)

On July 8, 1721, Aguayo encountered the Agdoca tribe with some Bidai and Nasoni Indians in Leon County near the Trinity River with a large number of other Indian tribes ("tribes of the Ranchería Grande") that earlier had been living near the Brazos River crossing near the Brazos County line (Santos, 51). On July 24, 1721, Aguayo met the Ygodosa with several Tejas Indians near the Trinity River in Leon County (Forrestal, 38). On April 28, 1768, Solís reported that the Deadose lived between the Navasota and the Trinity in Houston County with some Bidai and other tribes (Kress, 59). *HOT,* 3:232–233.

47. *Emet* (EMAT)

According to Massanet, De León found a village of the tribe (with Cava) near Irish Creek, DeWitt County, on April 16, 1689 (Bolton, *Spanish Exploration,* 359), and the next day found a second village of the tribe near the present-day city of Shiner in northwestern Lavaca County (360). Alarcón encountered them on September 30, 1718, near Columbus in Colorado County with several other large tribes that asked the governor to establish a mission for them on the Guadalupe in central Gonzales County (Hoffmann, 69). *HOT,* 3:279.

48. *Ervipiame* (YEZIPIAMO, YERIPIAMO)

On May 30, 1716, Espinosa met several Yeripiamo with some Mescal near Big Brushy Creek in Williamson County (Tous, 14), and the padre found them near the Brazos crossing in Burleson County on June 10 (Tous, 16). Rivera listed them among the nations that lived in the Province of Texas in 1727 (Porras, 125). Lafora reported the same in 1767 (Kinnaird, 185). *HOT,* 3:283; *HONAI,* 10:345, 355.

49. *Hape* (APE)

On his first expedition into Central Texas in 1689, De León met the tribe on March 29 on a stream (present-day Salada Creek) in Coahuila about 15 miles south of the Francia crossing (southern Maverick County) of the Rio Grande (West, 389). Salinas received assistance from members of the tribe in crossing the Rio Grande in the same area on July 12, 1693. (Foster and Jackson, 311).

In 1727, Rivera both reported that the tribe was residing in the Province of Coahuila (Porras, 131), and he found some members at Mission of San Bernardino de la Candela in eastern Coahuila on January 29, 1728 (126). In 1767, Lafora also reported that the tribe was residing in the Province of Coahuila (Kinnaird, 154). *HOT,* 3:373–374; *HONAI,* 10:348.

50. *Hasinai* (ASINAY, ASINAI, AYNAY, AINAI, TEJAS)

De León met with a chieftain of this tribe and several tribal members on April 29 and 30, 1689, along the old Indian trade route near the crossing of the Colorado at La Grange in Fayette County (West, 402). The Tejas captain and his men then returned with León to his main camp on the Guadalupe near Cuero in DeWitt County for meetings that continued until May 2 (403). On May 4 and 5 of the following year,

De León met several members of the tribe hunting buffalo about 12 miles northeast of La Grange in Fayette County (Bolton, 411), and the governor later (May 11) recovered the young Frenchman Pierre Meunier at the same location (413). When De León then marched northeast from the Colorado, he met more tribal members near Bedias Creek in Grimes County on May 18 (414) and near present-day Crockett, Houston County, on May 20 (415). Members of the Tejas chieftain's family returned with De León to New Spain in 1690 (418).

On July 4, 1691, Massanet (with Terán) noted that several Tejas Indians were included in Terán's expedition party when it returned to East Texas (Hatcher, 63). Massanet also mentioned meeting additional tribal members near the Brazos crossing in Burleson County on July 23, 1691 (64).

On June 23, 1693, Salinas found Asinai meeting with some Jumano and Cantona on his return trip from East Texas along the old Indian trade route 8 miles southwest of La Grange in Fayette County, and he saw a party of them the following day with the Simaoma near the same location (Foster and Jackson, 303).

Espinosa reported meeting some members of the Asinai nation on June 10, 1716 near the Brazos crossing in Brazos County (Tous, 16). On the same expedition Ramón reported meeting them in Brazos and Leon counties on June 18 and 20, 1716 (Foik, 18), and in Houston County on June 27 (19). Alarcón, with Espinosa, used Tejas as guides on his expedition from San Antonio to East Texas in 1718 (Hoffmann, 59), and they served as interpreters with the Indians at Matagorda Bay (65).

On July 24, 1721, Aguayo met them near their farming areas west of the Trinity River crossing in Leon County (Santos, 51) and on August 11 in Nacogdoches County (63). In 1727, Rivera identified the tribe by the name Aynay (Naylor and Polzer, 157). On September 5, 1767, Rubí encountered them near San Pedro Creek in Houston County, and the next day he found them on the Angelina River. In 1768, Solís saw them on April 28 between the Navasota and the Trinity in Leon County (Kress, 59) and near San Pedro Creek and the Neches River in Houston County on April 30 and May 1 and 2, 1768 (60, 61, 62). *HOT*, 1:783; 3:958.

51. *Huyugan*

Alarcón met the Huyugan with several other large tribes about 30 miles northeast of Columbus in Colorado County on September 29 and 30, 1718 (Hoffmann, 69). See the entry "Huyuguan Indians" in *HOT*, 3:426.

52. *Jicarilla-Apache* (XICARILLA)

This tribe was identified in Article 14 of Rubí's *dictamen* as an Apache tribe that lived (1767) in the "Sandia Range and Pecos valley," meaning present-day southeastern New Mexico. The marqués added that they communicated regularly with the Mescalero and associated tribes living near the mouth of the Pecos River.

53. *Julimeño* (JULIME)

Barreiro reported in 1727 that the Julime were residing in the Province of Vizcaya (Naylor and Polzer, 214). In 1767, Lafora recorded that they were residing in the

Province of Coahuila (Kinnaird, 155). See the entry "San Francisco de los Julimes Mission" in *HOT*, 2:551.

54. *Jumano* (CHOMENE, CHOME, COMANE, JUMANA)

De León saw members of this tribe on his first expedition on March 29, 1689, in northern Coahuila on a stream later called Juan's Creek (modern Arroyo Salado), about 15 miles south of the Francia crossing of the Rio Grande (West, 389). Massanet reported meeting Chome at Juan's Creek on May 27, 1691 (Hatcher, 50).

Terán reported meeting Jumano or Chome with several other tribes west of San Marcos on June 18 and 19, 1691 (Hatcher, 15). Massanet wrote in his diary account at that time that Chomane and Jumano referred to the same nation and that the tribe, along with several other Chihuahua and West Texas tribes, traveled annually to the Guadalupe (the present San Marcos River) to hunt bison and to trade with the local tribes (and also with the Tejas). On July 19 of the same year, Massanet reported seeing the Jumano again near La Grange (63).

On May 11, 1693, Salinas was warned that the tribe planned to ambush his caravan near the crossing on the Colorado (Foster and Jackson, 284–285). Ten days later, Salinas encountered an aggressive band of the tribe who were painted and armed when he was moving toward the Colorado crossing along the old Indian trade route that ran between Ecleto and Salt creeks in eastern Karnes County and western DeWitt County (290). On June 23, 1693, Salinas met members of the tribe with some East Texas Asinai and local Cantona near the same Colorado River crossing in Fayette County on his return trip from East Texas (303). *HOT*, 1:933–934; *HONAI*, 10:122–137.

55. *Karankawa* (CARANCAGUAZE, CARANCAGUCA)

De León was apparently referring to this tribe, or an associated tribe, in his account of the recovery of three Talon children at the head of San Antonio Bay on June 21, 1690 (Bolton, *Spanish Exploration*, 420–421). The first reference to the tribe by name on any expedition was by Rivera in 1727, when he reported that the Carancaquaze lived in Texas (Porras, 125). Lafora listed Carancaguace living in the Province of Texas in 1767 (Kinnaird, 185). Solís reported some members at Mission Rosario on the San Antonio River in Goliad County in 1768 (Kress, 40). *HONAI*, 10:331, 359–367; *HOT*, 3:464.

56. *Lipan-Apache* (YPANDE)

From February 17 to 23, 1768, Solís reported that his party was crossing "Lipan and Apache" country between the Rio Grande and modern Three Rivers on the Nueces River in Live Oak County (Kress, 37). Rubí saw Ypande on July 11, 1767, at the Villa San Fernando de Austria located about 20–25 miles west-southwest of Eagle Pass. Three days later, on the southwest side of the Rio Grande, Rubí saw some watered areas that were cultivated by the Lipan-Apache across the river from the present-day city of Normandy in Maverick County. Near the river was a large Lipan encampment with huts made of branches. On July 17, Rubí saw a village of about 100 Apache (Lipan), where stubble remained from the previous year's crop, in the northeast corner of Maverick County. *HOT*, 1:61; *HONAI*, 10:388, 390, 450.

57. *Manos de Perro*

In 1767, Lafora reported that this tribe was living in the Province of Coahuila (Kinnaird, 155). They were reported at Espíritu Santo Mission in Goliad County by Solís in 1768 (Kress, 46). *HOT*, 3:570; *HONAI*, 10:356.

58. *Mayeye* (MALLEYE)

Alarcón saw members of this nation with Indians from several other large tribes about 30 miles northeast of Columbus in Colorado County near the Fayette-Austin-Colorado County line on September 29 and 30, 1718 (Hoffmann, 69). Rivera met them between the Colorado and Brazos rivers in Burleson County on August 28, 1727 (Porras, 114).

Members of the tribe were residents of the Province of Texas, according to Lafora in 1767 (Kinnaird, 185). On September 2, 1767, Rubí reported that the tribe frequently hunted with the Coco and Aranama between the Colorado and the Brazos. Solís met them at the Brazos crossing in Burleson County on April 25, 1768 (Kress, 58). *HOT*, 3:582.

59. *Mescal* (MEZCAL)

De León saw this tribe in northern Coahuila about 15 miles south of the Francia crossing on the Rio Grande on March 29, 1689 (West, 389). On May 28, 1691, Terán saw them near the same location (Hatcher, 12).

Salinas noted that Mescal were reported to be camped along the old Indian trade route at Tres Cruces in Fayette County about 12 miles south of the crossing of the Colorado near La Grange, according to a message he received from the Sana Indians whom he met on the upper Navidad on May 26, 1693 (Foster and Jackson, 293). On July 12, 1693, Salinas received help from the tribe in crossing the Rio Grande from Maverick County into Coahuila (311).

On May 30, 1716, Espinosa found them between the Colorado and the Brazos in Burleson County (Tous, 14) and encountered them again on June 13 (17). In 1767, Lafora reported that they were living somewhere in the Province of Coahuila (Kinnaird, 155). *HOT*, 3:592; *HONAI*, 10:349, 355–357.

60. *Mescalero-Apache*

This tribe is considered the same as the Natage Apache. See the entry "Natage-Apache" below.

61. *Mesquite* (MEZQUITE, MESQUITA)

On May 9, 1716, Espinosa met one member of this tribe about 8 miles east of the Frio River crossing below the Hondo in north-central Frio County (Tous, 8). The lone Mesquite was moving toward the Rio Grande, and Ramón was traveling in the opposite direction along the same Indian trade route. The Mesquite advised Ramón that a large number of Indians were gathered on the Brazos, and Ramón and Espinosa later met the large encampment of tribes, including some Mesquite, near the Brazos crossing (16). Rivera found some members of the tribe at the San Antonio missions on August 16, 1727

(Porras, 111). Barreiro reported that the Mesquite lived in the Province of Vizcaya (Naylor and Polzer, 214). Rubí found tribal members in San Antonio between August 14 and 23, 1767, and Solís also saw them there on April 6 of the following year (Kress, 51). *HOT,* 3:592–593; *HONAI,* 10:349, 356, 358.

62. *Momon* (MOMONE)
Terán reported on May 28, 1691, that the tribe lived with the Mescal and Odoesmade in the area near the Rio Grande crossing in northern Coahuila and southern Maverick County, but none were seen there at the time (Hatcher, 12). *HONAI,* 10:355.

63. *Muruam* (MORUAME)
The earliest noted sighting of members of this tribe on an expedition was west of the present-day city of San Marcos in June 1691, when Massanet reported that Terán traded horses for five Muruam youths who were being held by the Jumano Indians (Hatcher, 60). He said that the Muruam then lived on the Guadalupe.

Salinas engaged a large and very hostile Muruam village on June 26, 1693, along Peach Creek in eastern Gonzales County; during the confrontation, members of the aggressive tribe stole four horses from the governor's party (Foster and Jackson, 304–305). In early September 1718, Alarcón had a member of the tribe as a guide on his march to the coast from San Antonio, but the guide deserted when the expedition party reached his traditional residential area near the Guadalupe in Gonzales County (Hoffmann, 59). *HOT,* 3:621; *HONAI,* 10:353, 356.

64. *Naaman*
The only reference to a tribe with this name was made on June 19, 1690, when De León was traveling southwest from the Colorado River toward Matagorda Bay (Bolton, *Spanish Exploration,* 421n3). The exceptionally large village, reportedly numbering about 3,000, was on the lower Lavaca River in Jackson County. *HOT,* 3:629.

65. *Nabidacho* (NABEDACHE, NABIDOCHE, NAVIDACHO)
In 1727, Rivera included this tribe among the Indian nations that lived in the Province of Texas, listing them next to the Aynay, Neche, Nazone, and Naconome (Porras, 125). Rubí found the tribe on September 6, 1767, near present-day Nacogdoches. On June 19, 1768, Solís reported meeting the tribe near present-day Nacogdoches with some of the same East Texas tribes listed by Rivera (Kress, 69). See the entry "Nabedache Indians" in *HOT,* 2:255.

66. *Nacogdoche* (NACODOCHE)
Ramón saw this tribe with the Nasoni near the Neches River in Cherokee County on June 30, 1716 (Foik, 21). On September 9, 1727, Rivera camped near a *paraje* called Nacodoches where the tribe lived (Porras, 118). Lafora reported that they were in the Province of Texas in 1767 (Kinnaird, 185). *HOT,* 3:630.

67. *Nacono* (NACONOME)

Espinosa, with Ramón, met the Nacono on July 8–10, 1716, about 18 miles east of Mission Concepción near Nacogdoches (Tous, 24). Rivera reported in 1727 that the Naconome were residing in the Province of Texas (Porras, 125), and Lafora reported the same in 1767 (Kinnaird, 185). *HOT*, 3:631.

68. *"Nadadores"*

Richard Santos suggests that members of this tribe helped Aguayo's large expedition party cross the Rio Grande in February 1721 (Santos, 25). It is not clear whether the reference in Peña's diary to "Nadadores" (which was capitalized in the manuscript copy) referred to a tribe or to the activities of the Indians in the waters of the Rio Grande during the crossing (*nadadores* means swimmers). No other reference to a tribe by that name has been found.

69. *Nasoni* (NAZONE, NAZONI)

Ramón met this tribe with the Nacodoche Indians on June 30, 1716, near the Neches River in Cherokee County (Foik, 21); on July 10–11, he met them in their own villages near Mission San José de los Nasonis about 26 miles east of Nacogdoches (23). Espinosa met them 7 leagues northeast of Mission Concepción on July 8 and 9 of the same year (Tous, 23). On July 13, 1721, Aguayo met the Nazoni near "Mission San Joseph de los Nazonis" (Santos, 63). Rivera listed the Nazone next to the Naconome among the tribes living in the Province of Texas in 1727 (Porras, 125). Lafora also reported them in the Province of Texas forty years later (Kinnaird, 185). Solís met the Nazone on June 19, 1768, near Nacogdoches with the Asinai and Cadodacho (Kress, 69). *HOT*, 3:633.

70. *Natage-Apache*

In his *dictamen* (Article 14), Rubí commented that the Natage (and the Salinero) occupied a large area in Coahuila near the Rio Grande and farther west. *HONAI*, 9:392.

71. *Natchitoche*

During his stay at Los Adaes (September 1, 1721), Aguayo mentioned that the Natchitoche had assisted the French in occupying Los Adaes when the Spanish retreated (Santos, 70).

72. *Neche* (NECHA)

Rivera met the Neche on September 5, 1727, near the Neches River in Houston County (Porras, 116). Lafora reported that the tribe resided somewhere in the Province of Texas in 1767 (Kinnaird, 185). On September 5, 1767, Rubí noted that the tribe's ancient residence was 2 leagues beyond the San Pedro River (probably meaning the modern Neches River rather San Pedro Creek). *HOT*, 3:641,42.

73. *Norteños*

This reference is to a group of tribes, not to a single tribe. Rubí, in Article 16 of his *dictamen*, referred to the Norteños as several tribes that included the Comanche, Taovaya, Tawakoni, and Yscani.

74. *Obayo* (OBAYA)

Rivera met some Obaya near Monclova, Coahuila, on July 24, 1727 (Porras, 107), and Lafora reported that they resided in the Province of Coahuila in 1767 (Kinnaird, 154). *HONAI*, 10:355.

75. *Ocana* (OCANE)

Massanet (with Terán) met members of this tribe on June 5, 1691, at Comanche Creek in Zavala County (Hatcher, 52). Salinas met them on May 9, 1693, near the Rio Grande crossing into Maverick County (Foster and Jackson, 283). Rivera reported that the tribe was living in the Province of Coahuila in 1728 (Porras, 131); Lafora reported the same in 1767 (Kinnaird, 154). *HOT*, 3:666; *HONAI*, 10:345, 349, 355.

76. *Odoesmade*

On May 28, 1691, Terán said that this tribe, with the Mescal and Momon, lived in an area that included northern Coahuila and western Maverick County near the Rio Grande crossing (Hatcher, 12). *HOT*, 3:668; *HONAI*, 10:355.

77. *Orcoquiza* (ORCOQUISA)

Rubí reported on this tribe on October 9, 1767, when he inspected the Presidio San Agustín de Ahumada (or Orcoquizac) in Chambers County near Trinity Bay. The marqués said the mission was near the village of the tribe. *HOT*, 2:317.

78. *Paac*

On June 5, 1691, Massanet and Terán (Hatcher, 52) met members of this tribe with some Quem, Pachul, Ocana, and other Indians on Comanche Creek in Zavala County. *HONAI*, 10:349, 355; *HOT*, 3:681.

79. *Pacpul* (PACHUL, PACPOLE)

Massanet said that a leader of this tribe was his guide on De León's expedition in 1689 (Bolton, *Spanish Exploration*, 356), and the Pacpul was again a guide for Massanet in 1690 and 1691 (Hatcher, 64). Rivera said that the Pacpul were living in the Province of Coahuila in 1727–1728 (Porras, 131); Lafora reported that the Pacpole were residing in Coahuila in 1767 (Kinnaird, 154). *HOT*, 3:682–83; *HONAI*, 10:349, 355.

80. *Pacuache* (PACOCHE, PACHOCHE)

Salinas met the Pacuache near the Rio Grande crossing in Maverick County on May 11, 1693 (Foster and Jackson, 284–285). Ramón met them at the Comanche Creek area in southwestern Zavala County on April 29, 1716 (Porras, 10).

Rivera met the Pacoche with some Hape on January 29, 1728, at Mission of San Bernardino de la Candela in eastern Coahuila (Porras, 126), and Barreiro reported that they were living in the Province of Coahuila in 1727–1728 (Naylor and Polzer, 222). Lafora reported that they were living in Coahuila forty years later (Kinnaird, 154). *HOT*, 3:683; *HONAI*, 10:345, 349, 350, 355.

81. *Pacuasin* (PAQUASIN, PACUASIAN, PACUACHIAM)

Massanet reported seeing the Pacuachiam tribe on June 10, 1691, in Frio County (Hatcher, 53). Espinosa saw some Pacuasian on Comanche Creek in Zavala County on April 7, 1709 (Tous, 4), and the padre reported that his party met them again the following day near the Leona River (4). In 1718, Alarcón saw Pacuasin near Comanche Creek on April 13 and 14 (Hoffmann, 44) and met two members of the tribe near the Leona River in central Zavala County on April 16 (45). Rivera noted in 1727 that they lived in the Province of Coahuila (Porras, 131), and Lafora in 1767 made the same report (Kinnaird, 155).

82. *Pajalat* (PAJALAC, PAJALATAME, PAJALTO, PAXALTO)

In 1727, Rivera reported that this tribe was living in Texas (Porras, 125) and in Coahuila (131). At the same time, Barreiro listed Pajalatame and Pajalto both in Coahuila and in Nuevo León (Naylor and Polzer, 222). Rubí and Lafora saw them at one of the San Antonio missions on August 24, 1767, and Lafora reported them living in Coahuila and Nuevo León (Kinnaird, 155, 195). It is not certain whether Pajalto is a variant of Pajalat or a separate tribe. *HOT*, 3:689; *HONAI*, 10:349, 356.

83. *Pamaya* (PAMAI, PUMAYA)

Massanet reported meeting the Pamai at Frenchmen's Creek (modern Arroyo Salado) in northern Coahuila on May 27, 1691 (Hatcher, 50). Espinosa met the tribe on the Medina in Bexar County on April 11 and 12, 1709 (Tous, 4, 5). Espinosa saw them again, this time with some Payaya, Cantona, and other Indians, on June 13, 1716, near the Brazos River in Burleson County (Tous, 17). Alarcón found them with other friendly tribes (Payaya and Xarame) at Mission de Valero when he returned to San Antonio from East Texas in January 1719 (Hoffmann, 86). *HOT*, 3:692; *HONAI*, 10:345, 349, 355.

84. *Pamoque* (PAMACA)

Lafora found some Pamaca at the San Antonio missions on August 24, 1767 (Kinnaird, 160). *HOT*, 3:692; *HONAI*, 10:356.

85. *Pampopa* (PAMPOA, PAMPOSA)

Espinosa found some Pampopa at a village near the Medina River in Bexar County on April 12, 1709 (Tous, 5), and saw them again on April 24 (13). Rivera listed them among the Indian nations living somewhere in the Province of Texas in 1727 (Porras, 125), and Barreiro listed them among the tribes living in the Province of Coahuila at the same time (Naylor and Polzer, 222).

Lafora reported that they lived in the Province of Coahuila in 1767 (Kinnaird, 155). Lafora also found some members of the tribe in the San Antonio missions in August 1767 (160), and Solís saw them at Mission San José de Aguayo on April 6, 1768 (Kress, 51). *HOT*, 3:692–693; *HONAI*, 10:349, 350, 356.

86. *Papanac* (PANAC, PAPANACA)

Massanet (with Terán) recorded meeting this tribe on the Frio River near Frio Town in northwestern Frio County on June 10, 1691 (Hatcher, 53). *HOT*, 3:695; *HONAI*, 10:345, 349, 355.

87. *Parchaque* (PARCHACA, PARCHIQUI)

Massanet met some Parchaca or Parchiqui at Juan's Creek (modern Salado Creek) in northern Coahuila on May 27, 1691 (Hatcher, 50), and again near the Frio River in Frio County on June 10 (53). *HOT*, 3:696.

88. *Parchina* (PACHINA)

Both Rivera (1727) and Lafora (1767) reported that members of this tribe were living somewhere in the Province of Texas (Porras, 125; Kinnaird, 185). Captain Orobio Basterra reported that the Pachina lived east of Trinity Bay (Béxar Translations, vol. 17, 70).

89. *Pastaloca* (PASTALAC, PAESTLALOCA)

Massanet met this tribe on June 5, 1691, at Comanche Creek in southwestern Zavala County (Hatcher, 52). *HOT*, 3:707; *HONAI*, 10:349, 355.

90. *Pastia* (PAXTI, PASUA, PAESTIA)

Espinosa met the captain of the Paxti nation with some Pampopa on the Medina near San Antonio on April 24, 1709 (Tous, 13). In 1767, Lafora reported that the Pasua were living in the Province of Texas (Kinnaird, 185). Solís found some tribal members at Mission San José de Aguayo on April 6, 1768 (Kress, 51). *HOT*, 3:708; *HONAI*, 10:349, 350, 356.

91. *Pataguo* (PATAVO, PATAGUA)

Massanet and Terán met the Patavo on June 10, 1691, near the Frio River crossing in northwestern Frio County (Hatcher, 53). Espinosa recorded finding Patagua in several separate encampments near the Leona River along the Zavala-Frio County line on May 7 and 8, 1716 (Tous, 7). *HOT*, 3:708–709; *HONAI*, 10:356.

92. *Patas de Perro*

On August 24, 1767, Lafora reported meeting this tribe with more than fifteen other Indian nations at one of the missions in San Antonio (Kinnaird, 160).

93. *Patchal* (PACHAL)

Massanet (with Terán) reported meeting this tribe on June 10, 1691, near the Frio River in northern Frio County (Hatcher, 53). See the entry "Pachal Indians" in *HOT*, 3:682.

94. *Patsau* (PATZAU)

Massanet (with Terán) met the Patsau on June 10, 1691, in Frio County (Hatcher, 53). See the entry "Patzau" in *HONAI*, 10:345, 349, 356.

95. *Pausane* (PAUJANE)

Lafora noted in 1767 that this tribe was living in the Province of Coahuila (Kinnaird, 155). *HOT*, 3:711.

96. *Payaguan* (PAYAVAN)

Massanet and Terán met the Payavan tribe at the crossing of the Frio River in north-central Frio County on June 10, 1691 (Hatcher, 53). In 1727, Rivera (Porras, 131) reported that the tribe lived in Coahuila; forty years later, Lafora again reported them living in Coahuila (Kinnaird, 154). *HOT*, 3:713; *HONAI*, 10:356.

97. *Payaya* (PEYAYE)

Terán met members of this tribe near San Antonio on June 13, 1691 (Hatcher, 14), and Massanet said that the captain of the tribe guided Terán's party to the large gathering of Jumano ("Chomanes") camped west of the present-day city of San Marcos (55). Salinas found them near San Antonio and also near the Medina River on July 1 and 2, 1693 (Foster and Jackson, 306–307).

Espinosa saw members of the tribe near San Antonio on April 11 and 12, 1709 (Tous 4, 5). In 1716, the padre met them with Ramón on May 28 in Williamson County and on June 13 at the Brazos crossing in Burleson County (Tous 13, 17). The Frenchman Derbanne saw the "Paillaille" on April 9 and 10, 1717, 3 leagues east of the Colorado River in Travis County (Bridges and De Ville, 248). Alarcón used a member of the tribe as a guide in September 1718 and saw several members in January 1719 near San Antonio (Hoffmann, 59, 87).

Rivera found them living with some Mesquite and Aguastaya near the San Antonio missions on August 16, 1727 (Porras, 111). Lafora reported that they were at one of the San Antonio missions on August 24, 1767 (Kinnaird, 160). *HOT*, 3:712; *HONAI*, 10:331, 349–350.

98. *Pelone*

Rivera reported that this tribe was living somewhere in Texas and in Nuevo León in 1727 (Porras 125, 132). Lafora also said they were in Texas and Nuevo León in 1767 (Kinnaird, 195). *HOT*, 3:718; *HONAI*, 10:352, 353, 368, 391.

99. *Piedras Blancas*

Salinas met some members of this tribe on May 9, 1693, near the Rio Grande crossing into Maverick County (Foster and Jackson, 283). *HOT*, 3:731; *HONAI*, 10:356.

100. *Piguique* (PIGUICANE)

Lafora reported that this tribe was living in the Province of Coahuila in 1767 (Kinnaird, 155). Solís met some Piguicane at Mission La Bahía del Espíritu Santo on March 9, 1768 (Kress, 46). *HOT*, 1:377; 3:733; *HONAI*, 10:356.

101. *Pita*

Rivera reported that this tribe resided in the Province of Coahuila in 1727 (Porras, 131), and Lafora noted the same in 1767 (Kinnaird, 155). *HOT*, 3:736; *HONAI*, 10:356.

102. *Pitahay* (PUTAAY, PITANAY)

Massanet and Terán met the Pitanay tribe on June 10, 1691, near the Frio River crossing in Frio County (Hatcher, 53). *HOT*, 3:736; *HONAI*, 10:349, 356.

103. *Pitalac* (PITALA, PETALAC)

Rivera reported that this tribe resided in the Province of Texas in 1727 (Porras, 125), and Lafora said the same in 1767 (Kinnaird, 185). *HOT*, 3:736; *HONAI*, 10:349, 356.

104. *Quem*

De León and Massanet met members of this nation near the Rio Grande crossing in Maverick County on April 1, 1689 (Bolton, *Spanish Exploration*, 355), and a member of the tribe helped guide their expedition party from the Rio Grande to Matagorda Bay that year and again in 1690 (373). Massanet reported seeing the Indians again on June 5, 1691, at Comanche Creek in Zavala County, and a member of the tribe again served as a guide (Hatcher, 52). *HOT*, 3:765–766; *HONAI*, 10:356, 349.

105. *Quichuixe*

On April 28, 1768, Solís met members of this tribe with the Tejas (Asinai), Bidai, Deadose, Tawakoni, and other Indians and reported that the tribe then lived between the Navasota and San Juan Creek in Houston County (Kress, 59). The name may be a variant of Quidehai or Kichai.

106. *Sacuache* (SAQUACHE)

Salinas met the Saquache on May 12, 1693, on Comanche Creek and saw them a few days later on the Leona River near the Zavala-Frio County line (Foster and Jackson, 285, 287) *HONAI*, 10:349, 356.

107. *Sadujane*

In 1727, Rivera reported that this tribe was living in Coahuila (Porras, 131); forty years later, Lafora made the same report (Kinnaird, 154, 155).

108. *Salinero* (SALINA)

In 1727 Rivera reported that the Salina were living somewhere in the Province of Texas (Porras, 125); in 1767, Lafora reported the same (Kinnaird, 185). In Rubí's *dictamen* (Article 14), he stated that the tribe resided in Coahuila and ranged north to the Rio Grande. *HOT*, 2:533; *HONAI*, 10:248, 389.

109. *Samampac*

On June 10, 1691, Massanet met members of this tribe near the Frio River in Frio County (Hatcher, 53). *HOT*, 3:833; *HONAI*, 10:349, 356.

110. *Sampanal* (SANPANAL)

Massanet and Terán met the Sanpanal on June 10, 1691, near the crossing of the Frio River in Frio County (Hatcher, 53). *HOT,* 3:833–834; *HONAI,* 10:349, 356.

111. *Sana* (SANAC, XANAC)

De León found the "Chana" with several other tribes (including Tohaha, Cantona, and Cava) on June 18, 1690, near the crossing of the Colorado at La Grange in Fayette County (Bolton, *Spanish Exploration,* 384). Salinas first met them on May 26, 1693, near the Fayette-Lavaca County line along the old Indian trade route to the Colorado crossing; he saw them again on June 25 near the same location (Foster and Jackson, 292, 304).

On April 14, 1709, Espinosa suggested that he had sent members of the tribe in advance of his party to locate the Tejas Indians whom the padre was to meet (Tous, 6). On September 30, 1718, the Xanac tribe asked Alarcón to establish a mission for them on the Guadalupe in Gonzales County (Hoffmann, 69). At that time, they were located a few miles east of the Colorado River in Colorado County, meeting with several other tribes including the Emet, Toho, and Mayeye.

On February 2, 1721, Peña reported that members of the tribe had given Aguayo information about a large Indian multitribal meeting with some French liaison officials on the Brazos (Santos, 25). A squad of the tribe dressed in Spanish clothing paid their respects to Aguayo on May 19, 1721, near the Blanco River in Hays County (37). *HOT,* 3:852.

112. *Saquita* (SAQUI, CACQUITE)

On June 25, 1693, Salinas found a large gathering of this nation along the old Indian trade route about 26 miles southwest of the Colorado River crossing near La Grange in Fayette County (Foster and Jackson, 304). A Spanish-speaking member of the group guided the governor along a new route farther west and southwest from Fayette County to the present-day San Antonio area and then southwest to the Frio crossing below the Hondo junction. Saquita may be a variant of Cacquite or Catqueza.

113. *Siguase* (SIGUANE, SIGUARE)

In 1727, Rivera listed the Siguase among the Indian nations that lived in the Province of Coahuila (Porras, 131). In 1767, Lafora also listed them as residents of Coahuila (Kinnaird, 155). See the entry "Siausi" in *HONAI,* 10:355.

114. *Sijame* (CHIJAME, SIXAME, XIXAME)

On April 13, 1709, Espinosa found members of this tribe near San Pedro Springs, Bexar County (Tous, 5). On June 13, 1716, Espinosa and Ramón met them with other tribes (Xarame, Mescal, and others) at the Brazos crossing near the Burleson-Brazos County line (Tous, 17). In 1727, Rivera reported that they were residing in the Province of Coahuila (Porras, 131). *HOT,* 3:880; *HONAI,* 10:346, 355.

115. *Silanguaya* (SILLANGUAYA, TILIJAYA)

In 1727, Rivera reported that this tribe was living in the Province of Coahuila (Porras, 131), and Lafora reported the same in 1767 (Kinnaird, 154). See the entry "Tilejayas" in *HONAI*, 10:356.

116. *Simaoma* (SIMAOMO, SIMOMO)

Salinas encountered this tribe on May 26, 1693, on the upper Lavaca River in Lavaca County; on June 24, he met them with some Asinai on Buckner's Creek near the Colorado crossing at La Grange in Fayette County (Foster and Jackson, 303). Espinosa met the Simomo on the Colorado River about 15 miles downstream from Austin in Travis County on April 19, 1709 (Tous, 8). See the entry "Siamomo" in *HONAI*, 10:357.

117. *Siupan*

On April 13, 1709, Espinosa met the Siupan near San Pedro Springs, Bexar County with Chalome and Sijame (Tous, 5). See the entry "Siupam Indians" in *HOT*, 3:888; *HONAI*, 10:356.

118. *Tacame* (TACOMO, TECAMO, TACONE)

Rivera listed this tribe among the several nations living near Espíritu Santo Presidio on the Guadalupe in 1727 (Naylor and Polzer, 159). Rubí found some Tecamo at one of the San Antonio missions on August 24, 1767. Lafora listed the Tacame as residents of the Province of Texas in 1767 (Kinnaird, 185). Solís found the tribe at Mission San José de Aguayo in 1768 (Kress, 51). *HOT*, 3:947; *HONAI*, 10:349, 356.

119. *Taguaya* (TAOVAYA)

On September 9, 1767, Rubí commented that during his stay at the "Mission de Nacodoches," the captain of the Taguaya, Eyasiguechi, came to visit him and renew his pledge of friendship, along with the pledge of their allies the Taguacana and the Yscani. At that time, Lafora listed the tribe, along with the Yscani, as living in a settlement to the north of the Province of Texas (Kinnaird, 185).

120. *Tamique*

Rubí found this tribe at the Espíritu Santo Mission on the San Antonio River in Goliad County on October 31, 1767, and Solís reported the same on March 6 of the following year (Kress, 46). *HOT*, 3:949; *HONAI*, 10:331.

121. *Tawakoni* (TAGUACANA, TAQUACANE)

Lafora (with Rubí) wrote that the Taguacana lived somewhere in the Province of Texas in 1767 (Kinnaird, 185). Rubí specifically mentioned the tribe in his diary as friends of the Taguaya in his entry on September 9, 1767. Solís met Taguacana with the Bidai, Deadose, and other tribes between the Navasota and the Trinity in Leon County on April 28, 1768 (Kress, 59). *HOT*, 2:709.

122. *Tejas*

See the entry "Hasinai" above.

123. *Tepacuache* (TEPAQUACHE)

Salinas found the Tepaquache on May 12, 1693, near the Nueces River crossing in Zavala County (Foster and Jackson, 285). *HOT*, 1:724; *HONAI*, 10:349, 356.

124. *Terocodame* (THEZOCODAME, THEROCODAME)

Rivera in 1727 (Porras, 131) and Lafora in 1767 (Kinnaird, 154) reported that the Terocodame lived in the Province of Coahuila. *HOT*, 3:963; *HONAI*, 10:331, 342, 344, 353, 355.

125. *Tilijae* (TILISAYA, TILIXAI)

In 1767, Lafora reported that the Tilixai were living in the Province of Coahuila (Kinnaird, 155). *HOT*, 3:1010; *HONAI*, 10:349, 356.

126. *Timamar* (TICMAMAR)

Espinosa met the Ticmamar with some Tejas (Asinai), Mesquite, and Ervipiame on June 10, 1716, about 18 miles east of the Brazos crossing in Burleson County (Tous, 16). In 1767, Lafora reported that the Timamar were living in the Province of Coahuila (Kinnaird, 155). *HONAI*, 10:355.

127. *Tlaxcalan* (TLASCALTECA, TLAXCALTECO)

Terán reported that he used the Tlascaltecan guide Pablo on his return march from East Texas to Matagorda Bay in February 1692 (Hatcher, 43). Rivera met the Tlaxcalteco near Parras in Nuevo León (Porras, 103) and near Monclova, Coahuila, in 1727 (107). He found them again on February 13, 1728, near Monterrey, Nuevo León (129).

According to his diary account, Rubí met them near Saltillo on June 6, 1767, and on December 5 of the same year near Boca de Leones. In 1767, Lafora (with Rubí) also reported that they were living in the Province of Coahuila (Kinnaird, 155). *HOT*, 3:1013.

128. *Toboso*

On May 11, 1693, Salinas was warned by Pacuache Indians near the Rio Grande crossing that the Toboso (with the Jumano) intended to attack the captain's convoy at the crossing of the Colorado (Foster and Jackson, 284–285). Salinas did not later definitely identify any members of the tribe; but ten days later, along the Indian trade route, he did capture some hostile Indians with the Jumano (290). Rivera listed them as residents of the Province of Coahuila in 1727 (Porras, 131), and Lafora reported the same in 1767 (Kinnaird, 154). Rubí met them on December 22, 1767, near Monterrey. HOT 3:1015; *HONAI*, 10:122, 329, 330, 333.

129. *Tohaha* (TOAA)

Massanet and De León found a village of Tohaha (with Toho) on April 16, 1689, on Big Brushy Creek in Lavaca County (Bolton, 359). In late April, De León recovered the two Frenchmen, Jacques Grollet and Jean L'Archevêque, at one of their villages along the old Indian route near the Colorado crossing at La Grange in Fayette Country (363). De León again met the tribe at the La Grange crossing of the Colorado on June 18, 1690 (Bolton, *Spanish Exploration*, 384). *HOT*, 3:1016.

130. *Toho* (TOO)

De León and Massanet found the Toho (with the Tohaha) on April 16, 1689, on Big Brushy Creek in Lavaca County (Bolton, *Spanish Exploration*, 359). De León found them near the crossing of the Colorado River near La Grange on June 18, 1690 (384). The same day, as the governor led a small party south from the Colorado crossing toward Matagorda Bay, he found a village of Toho ("Tho ó") on Sandy Creek, Colorado County (420n2). On De León's return trip from the Guadalupe to the Rio Grande on June 28, he passed a Toho encampment along the Indian trade route near the Atascosa River in Atascosa County (423n2). On May 26, 1693, Salinas noted that the Toho were on the upper Lavaca meeting with the Mescal and Simaoma (Foster and Jackson, 293). Alarcón met them with several other large tribes (Sana, Emet, and others) near Columbus in Colorado County on September 30, 1718 (Hoffmann, 69). *HOT*, 3:1016.

131. *Tonkawa* (TANCAHUE, TANCAQUA)

Lafora noted in 1767 that the Tancahue lived somewhere in the Province of Texas (Kinnaird, 185). On April 25, 1768, Solís reported seeing the Tancagueye at the Brazos crossing in Burleson County (Kress, 58). *HOT*, 1:788, 789; *HONAI*, 10:348, 362, 366.

132. *Tusonibi* (TOSONIBI)

There was only one recorded meeting with this tribe on an expedition. Espinosa met the Tusonibi or Tosonibi near the Colorado River about 15 miles southeast of Austin on Wilbarger Creek on April 19 and 20, 1709 (Tous, 8). See the entry "Tusolivi Indians" in *HOT*, 3:1032.

133. *Vanca*

Massanet and Terán met members of this tribe on June 10, 1691, at the Frio River crossing in Frio County (Hatcher, 53). *HOT*, 3:1057.

134. *Venado*

Lafora found some tribal members at one of the San Antonio missions in August 1767 (Kinnaird, 160). *HOT*, 3:1061; *HONAI*, 10:357.

135. *Xarame* (SARAME, JARAME)

On April 8, 1709, Espinosa met two members of this tribe on the Leona River in Frio County with a small number of Pacuasin Indians (Tous, 4). Espinosa met them again near the Brazos crossing in Burleson County with the Pamaya, Payaya, Sijame, and other tribes on June 13, 1716 (Tous, 17). In January 1719, Alarcón found them (again with the Pamaya and Payaya) at Mission San Antonio de Valero (Hoffmann, 86). In 1767, Lafora (with Rubí) reported that the Sarame were at one of the missions in San Antonio (Kinnaird, 160). *HOT*, 3:1134; *HONAI*, 10:346, 356.

136. *Xauna*

On April 6, 1768, Solís identified members of this tribe at Mission San José de Aguayo in San Antonio (Kress, 51). See the entry "Xanna Indians" in *HOT*, 3:1134.

137. *Xiabu* (IJIABA)

On March 29, 1689, De León met them with three other tribes on present-day Salada Creek (earlier called Juan the Frenchman Creek) in northern Coahuila about 15 miles south of the Francia crossing on the Rio Grange (West, 389).

138. *Yojuane* (YOJANE, YOJUAN, TOJUANE, JOJANE)

Espinosa met the Yojuane on Wilbarger Creek near the Bastrop-Travis County line on April 19 and 20, 1709 (Tous, 8). Rivera (1727) and Lafora (1767) included them in their lists of Indian nations living in the Province of Texas (Porras, 125; Kinnaird, 185). Solís met the Jojane with the Coco and Mayeye near the Brazos River crossing in Burleson County on April 25, 1768 (Kress, 58). *HOT*, 3:1138.

139. *Yorica*

On May 27, 1691, Massanet reported seeing this tribe on Juan's Creek in northern Coahuila about 15 miles south of the Rio Grande crossing (Hatcher, 50). Salinas met them on July 14, 1693, at a *paraje* called Pescado between the Rio Grande and the Sabinas River in northern Coahuila (Foster and Jackson, 311). *HOT*, 3:1138; *HONAI*, 10:349, 355.

140. *Yscani* (ISCANI)

Rubí refers to the friendly Yscani in his diary entry on September 9, 1767, as a tribe associated with the Taguaya and the Taquacana. In his *dictamen* (Article 16), he listed the tribe among the Norteños. The same year, Lafora reported that the tribe was living in the country north of the Province of Texas (Kinnaird, 185). *HOT*, 2:949.

NOTES

1. INTRODUCTION

1. For a summary of the limited 1675 Bosque-Larios reconnaissance that ventured up to 100 miles north of the lower Rio Grande and the 1683–1684 expedition led by Domínguez de Mendoza from El Paso to the Pecos River, see Donald E. Chipman, *Spanish Texas, 1519–1821*, 67–70. Fernando del Bosque's 1675 expedition diary was translated into English by Herbert E. Bolton in *Spanish Exploration in the Southwest, 1542–1706*, 283–309.

2. Carlos E. Castañeda outlined the events leading to Padre Salas's 1632 six-month visit with the Jumano in "Earliest Catholic Activities in Texas," *Preliminary Studies of the Texas Catholic Historical Society* 1, no. 8 (October 1931), 6–8. See Marion A. Habig, *Spanish Texas Pilgrimage: The Old Franciscan Missions and Other Settlements of Texas 1632–1821*, 148–152; and Oakah L. Jones, "Settlements and Settlers at La Junta de los Rios, 1759–1822," *Journal of Big Bend Studies* 3 (January 1991), 43–70.

3. Robert S. Weddle suggests that the misdirection reflected the prevailing ignorance of La Salle's time concerning the northern Gulf shore (*The French Thorn: Rival Explorers in the Spanish Sea, 1682–1762*, 15–25).

4. Although some site controversy continues, the weight of evidence suggests strongly that the French fort and community were located on Garcitas Creek, which currently forms part of the boundary between Victoria and Jackson counties. The present study supports this assessment.

5. Elizabeth A. H. John describes Retana's March 1689 meeting with Juan Sabeata and the Cibolo and Jumano Indians. She also notes that an earlier Spanish expedition led by Antonio de Espejo had found friendly Jumano Indians in the same region. In the summer of 1583, the Espejo expedition reported that several Jumano buffalo hunters served as guides to lead the expedition to the junction of the Rio Grande and the Conchos River in present-day Chihuahua, where the Jumano and the Toboso Indians then lived. See Elizabeth A. H. John, *Storms Brewed in Other Men's Worlds: The Confrontation of Indians, Spanish, and French in the Southwest, 1540–1795*, 30–33, 180–185.

6. De León's diary of the 1686 expedition is quoted in Chapa's *Historia*, which also includes a summary of De León's 1687 expedition. See Juan Bautista Chapa, *Historia del Nuevo Reino de León de 1650 a 1690*, ed. Israel Cavazos Garza, 123–135.

7. Ibid., 136–139.

8. The Spaniards, who had killed a number of Indians after capturing them and extracting information, took Géry prisoner and began to question him. Under this life-threatening pressure, during his interrogations in Monclova and later in Mexico City, the Frenchman gave conflicting answers, a not unusual occurrence in such circumstances. Before he was taken prisoner and later when he served as a guide, Géry was alert and impressive. He could speak the Coahuiltecan dialect with his Indian friends along the Rio Grande; three weeks and 300 miles later, he spoke in a second Indian language (Sanan) to some Toho and Emet Indian friends in DeWitt and Lavaca counties. The Frenchman was, perhaps first and foremost, a shrewd survivor. With his Indian wife and child, he had assimilated into the life of the natives—a development that some observers (such as Fray Massanet) apparently distrusted or found objectionable. Robert S. Weddle portrays Géry as "the demented Frenchman" in *Wilderness Manhunt: The Spanish Search for La Salle*, 132–148.

9. See David J. Weber, *Myth and History of the Hispanic Southwest*, 6, 19–32; and Donald E. Chipman, "In Search of Cabeza de Vaca's Route across Texas," *Southwestern Historical Quarterly* 91 (October 1987), 127–148.

10. The Texas Highway Department in 1991 presented a comprehensive study of Spanish expedition routes into Texas that includes the distances and directions recorded; unfortunately, the expedition route projections made by the state-financed study are not based on a careful chronological comparison of the different names used for the same river or stream by diarists during the expedition period. This failure has led to significant errors in route projections presented in the 1991 study. See A. Joachim McGraw, John W. Clark, Jr., and Elizabeth A. Robbins, eds., *A Texas Legacy: The Old San Antonio Road and the Caminos Reales, a Tricentennial History, 1691–1991*.

11. Buckley wrote that the early routes were "so varied and distinct" and names were "so profusely and promiscuously . . . scattered on the rivers" that a clear picture was difficult to find, and "it is hard to make any safe generalizations." She adds that "of all the diaries studied no two seem to follow exactly the same course" ("The Aguayo Expedition into Texas and Louisiana, 1719–1722," *Quarterly of the Texas State Historical Association* 15, no. 1 [July 1911], 33–34).

12. Castañeda's lack of confidence, or even interest, in De León's diary account of the direction taken is reflected in his rendition of De León's first expedition. From the Rio Grande crossing, Castañeda states that "if we take a compass and set the distance traveled until April 4, when they came to the Nueces, after going twenty-three leagues, we will find that the point of intersection is in the neighborhood of present Cotulla, which lies east-northeast from the starting point indicated. It was somewhere in the vicinity of this area that De León must have crossed the Nueces" (*Our Catholic Heritage in Texas, 1519–1936*, vol. 1, 333–335). Castañeda makes no reference to the directions given in the diary accounts for the three days' journey: north-northeast, not east-northeast.

13. Chipman, *Spanish Texas*, 82.

14. J. W. Williams, *Old Texas Trails*, ed. and comp. Kenneth F. Neighbors.

15. Map projections prepared by diary translators have been included in several translations, including those of Espinosa in 1709 and 1716, of Alarcón in 1718, and of Aguayo in 1721–1722. Carlos Castañeda also presented maps of the expedition routes along the lines of the march as he understood them. However, these maps do not include a daily route table giving camp locations to support the projections made.

16. The abridgment of Henri Joutel's journal prepared by Jean Michel (1713) and translated into English and edited by Isaac Joslin Cox and Henry Reed Stiles only occasionally gives the daily distance and direction traveled on La Salle's last journey. However, detailed daily route information is found for La Salle's last trip in Joutel's unabridged and untranslated journal (Pierre

Margry, ed., *Découvertes et établissements des Francais dans l'ouest et dans le sud de l'Amérique Septentrionale, 1674–1754,* vol. 3, 120–534), which I am preparing for publication.

17. William C. Foster and Jack Jackson, eds., and Ned Brierley, trans., "The 1693 Expedition of Gregorio de Salinas Varona to Sustain the Missionaries among the Tejas Indians," *Southwestern Historical Quarterly* 97 (October 1993), 264–311.

18. One of the clearest statements that time was a factor considered in computing the distance traveled was made by the experienced traveler Fray Espinosa. On April 23, 1709, after leaving San Antonio to return to the Rio Grande crossing, Espinosa noted that his party had traveled 16 leagues according to his time (*según el tiempo*). See Gabriel Tous, ed. and trans., "The Espinosa-Olivares-Aguirre Expedition of 1709," *Preliminary Studies of the Texas Catholic Historical Society* 1 (March 1930), 13.

19. Charles W. Polzer, Thomas C. Barnes, and Thomas H. Naylor, *The Documentary Relations of the Southwest: Project Manual,* 39–47. See also Thomas C. Barnes, Thomas H. Naylor, and Charles W. Polzer, *Northern New Spain—A Research Guide,* 68.

20. The topographical maps used for northern Mexico were Estados Unidos Mexicanos, Secretaría de Programación y Presupuesto, Carta Topográfica, 1:250,000 *Monclova,* G14-4, and *Piedras Negras,* H14-10; and Instituto Nacional de Estadística, Geografía e Informática, Carta Topográfica, 1:250,000, *Nueva Rosita,* G14-1. The topographical maps used for the Texas areas are United States Geological Survey maps, Western United States, 1:250,000 Series, *Eagle Pass,* NH14-10; *Crystal City,* NH14-11; *San Antonio,* NH14-8; *Seguin,* NH14-9; *Austin,* NH14-6; *Beaumont,* NH15-4; *Palestine,* NH15-1; *Tyler,* NI15-10; *Del Rio,* NH14-7; *Beeville,* NH14-12; *Bay City,* NH15-10; *Houston,* NH15-7; *Llano,* NH14-5; *Waco,* NH14-3; *Laredo,* NG14-2; *Shreveport, Louisiana,* NI15-11; and *El Dorado, Arkansas,* NI15-8.

21. Juan Agustín de Morfí, *History of Texas, 1673–1779,* ed. and trans. Carlos E. Castañeda, 77n84.

22. David J. Weber, *The Spanish Frontier in North America,* 10. See also Jean M. Grove, *The Little Ice Age*; LeRoy Johnson and Glenn T. Goode, "A New Try at Dating and Characterizing Holocene Climates, as Well as Archeological Periods, on the Eastern Edwards Plateau," *Bulletin of the Texas Archeological Society* 65 (1994), 1–51.

23. Susan L. Swain, "Mexico and the Little Ice Age," *Journal of Interdisciplinary History* 2 (Spring 1981), 633–648.

24. See Harlan Hague, "Guides for the Pathfinders: The Indian Contribution to Exploration of the American West," *Pacific Historian* 26 (Fall 1982), 54–63. The author's thesis is that "most explorers did not hesitate to credit Indians with valuable assistance, but historians have not been so obliging" (54).

25. Cynthia Irwin-Williams, "Post-Pleistocene Archeology, 7000–2000 b.c.," in *Handbook of North American Indians,* vol. 9, 31–42.

26. Alonso de León, Juan Bautista Chapa, and Fernando Sánchez de Zamora, *Historia de Nuevo León, con noticias sobre Coahuila, Tamaulipas, Texas y Nuevo Mexico.* For an English translation, see Carl L. Duaine, *Caverns of Oblivion.*

27. De León et al., *Historia,* 93. See also Morfí's account of the epidemic in the 1680s that struck Parras: Fray Agustín de Morfí, *Viaje de Indios y diario del Nuevo Mexico,* 217–218.

28. Juan Bautista Chapa, *Historia del Nuevo Reino León de 1650 a 1690,* 117–120.

29. Peter Gerhard, *The North Frontier of New Spain,* 24. See also David E. Stannard, "The Consequences of Contact: Toward an Interdisciplinary Theory of Native Responses to Biological and Cultural Invasion," in *Columbian Consequences,* ed. David Hurst Thomas, vol. 3, 519.

30. Gerhard, *The North Frontier of New Spain,* 23, 24, 169, 331, 339–340; Timothy K. Perttula, *"The Caddo Nation,"* 18–85.

31. Stannard, "The Consequences of Contact," 535. See also Alfred W. Crosby, "Summary on Population Size before and after Contact," in *Disease and Demography in the Americas,* ed. John W. Verano and Douglas H. Ubelaker, 277–278.

32. William B. Griffen, "Southern Periphery: East," in *Handbook of North American Indians,* vol. 10, ed. Alfonso Ortiz, 329–342. For a broader geographic treatment of agriculture as practiced by the native population in North America, including the introduction of plants such as corn and beans from Mexico to northern North America, see Charles B. Heiser, Jr., "Ethnobotany and Economic Botany," in *Flora of North America North of Mexico,* ed. Nancy R. Morin, vol. 1, 199–206.

33. Thomas N. Campbell, "Coahuiltecans and Their Neighbors," in *Handbook of North American Indians,* vol. 10, ed. Alfonso Ortiz, 343–358.

34. Ibid., 345.

35. Weber, *The Spanish Frontier,* 312. Del Weniger is the most prominent Texas historian to use narrative materials as a baseline for understanding the natural world at the time of early European and American contact in Texas. See Weniger, *The Explorers' Texas: The Lands and Waters.*

36. William W. Newcomb, Jr., "Historic Indians of Central Texas," *Bulletin of the Texas Archeological Society* 64 (1993), 24.

37. Michael Gannon, "The New Alliance of History and Archaeology in the Eastern Spanish Borderlands," *William and Mary Quarterly* 9 (April 1992), 321–334.

38. Contact between the Tejas and the Spaniards during the 1670s is summarized in Francis B. Steck, "Forerunners of Captain de León's Expedition to Texas, 1670–1675," *Preliminary Studies of the Texas Catholic Historical Society* 2, no. 3 (September 1932), 5–32.

2. IN SEARCH OF LA SALLE

1. The account of Governor De León's 1689 expedition is based primarily on a manuscript copy of his diary in the *Texas Documentary History,* vol. 1, *Mexico (Viceroyalty), [AGN] Provincias Internas,* in the Manuscript Division of the Library of Congress. A Spanish transcript of the diary is found in Lino Gómez Canedo, ed., *Primeras exploraciones y poblamiento de Texas (1686–1694),* 89–104. An annotated translation of this diary by Elizabeth Howard West was published in *Texas State Historical Association Quarterly* 8 (January 1905), 199–224. For this study, I made a comparison of the Library of Congress manuscript and the West translation. For the most part the West account was accurate; however, De León's diary entry for March 29 was omitted from West's published translation. The party on that date traveled 5 leagues to the northeast, one-quarter north. By mistake, West gives De León's March 30 entry for "Tuesday, the 29th" and omits any diary entry for March 30. West's translation of De León's 1689 diary with the editor's annotations is included in Herbert E. Bolton, ed., *Spanish Exploration in the Southwest, 1542–1706,* 388–404, but Bolton does not mention consulting the more complete manuscript copy held in the Library of Congress.

2. De León's 1688 diary is found in Walter J. O'Donnell, "La Salle's Occupation of Texas," *Preliminary Studies of the Catholic Historical Society* 3, no. 2 (1936), 12–13. Juan Bautista Chapa described the short expedition and capture of Géry in his *Historia del Nuevo Reino de León desde 1650 hasta 1690,* 136–137.

3. Chapa gave the names of the soldiers on the expedition (ibid., 142–143).

4. The 1690 letter from Fray Massanet to Don Carlos de Sigüenza has been translated by Lilia M. Casís, *Texas State Historical Association Quarterly* 2 (April 1899), 253–312. A typescript

copy of Fray Massanet's letter addressed to the viceroy dated September 1690 is in the Manuscript Division of the Library of Congress, under the title "Testimonio de autos an orden a las dilix [s] [y] resulta de ellas P [a] la entrada P [r] Tierra a los Paraxes de la Vahya del Spiritu s [to] S.[rio] D[n] P.[o] de la Cadena," 75–84, Sevilla, [AGI] México, 61-6-21.

5. Chapa, *Historia*, 142–157.

6. Ibid., 123–132.

7. Ibid., 58.

8. Spanish diarists continued to refer to Indian tribes as "nations" throughout the colonial period, and today the issue of sovereignty is critical to native populations in the United States and abroad. See Howard R. Berman, "Perspectives on American Indian Sovereignty and International Law, 1600 to 1776," in *Exiled in the Land of the Free: Democracy, Indian Nations, and the U.S. Constitution*, 125–188. The use of the term "groups" as a substitute for the term "tribes" or "nations" ignores the sovereignty question, as well may be the intent of those who use it. The term "groups" is avoided in the present study because it fails to convey this autonomy. It also fails to convey the close cultural bond that gave specific identity to the tribes.

9. Isaac Joslin Cox, ed., *The Journeys of René Robert Cavelier, Sieur de La Salle*, vol. 1, 285–296; vol. 2, 57–99.

10. An anonymous sketch map showing where Géry was captured, the route to La Salle's settlement, and a list of Indian tribes that lived north of the Rio Grande was published in Robert S. Weddle, *The French Thorn*, Fig. 5, 74–75. Weddle suggests that the map was based on Géry's report to Spanish officials and was prepared by either Captain Diego Ramón or De León himself (72). According to my understanding and reading of the manuscript, the Indian nations listed on the map include the Payaya, Moruame, Mesquite, Pampoa, Paestia, Yopane, Chane, Panaca, Aguafraya, Pumaya, Chupane, Yezipiamo, Patloa, Cantuna, Chulasame, Chijame, Paestlaloco, Timamar, Churame, Mescal, Paguache, Ocane, Tilisaya, Pajalaca, Vitlata, Palsua, Aguitaya, Hape, Yorica, Tilisaya, Churisame, Puapu, Paesa, and the Texas or Assinai. The friends of the Assinai who lived near the sea were the Vida, Yadosa, Uadesa, Cassi, Sunni, Cadiatridi, Saco, and Aulto.

11. In 1673 and again in 1675, over one hundred Spanish troops with several hundred Indians from near Monterrey marched north to attack Cacaxtle encampments along the Rio Grande and in the northern Webb-Duval County area (Chapa, *Historia*, 62–63, 68–69).

12. The first day the governor traveled 12 miles northeast to locate the campsite at the water pools in the bed of the creek, still called Cuervo Creek. With only a few exceptions, subsequent expeditions over the next forty years also moved north-northeast and visited Cuervo. The crossing of the Rio Grande and the *paraje* Cuervo, about 12 miles from the Rio Grande, can be inferred from the details of the area found on the Texas General Land Office map of Maverick County (March 1879), which confirms the location of Cuervo Creek, and from the location of both Cuervo Creek and Cueva Creek (both mentioned by Captain Ramón and Fray Espinosa on their 1716 expedition), as identified by name on USGS map *Eagle Pass*, NH14-10.

13. Carlos E. Castañeda placed De León's 1689 route crossing the Nueces about 50 miles farther southeast and downstream in La Salle County, following a course to the east-northeast, rather than northeast and north-northeast, as stated in De León's 1689 and 1690 diary accounts. This mistake is compounded by Castañeda's projection that De León crossed the Frio River below the Leona. Robert S. Weddle repeats the errors (*French Thorn*, 73).

14. Carlos E. Castañeda confused this river with the present Frio River (*Our Catholic Heritage in Texas*, vol. 1, 335 and map). The map projects De León traveling too far east and crossing the Frio below the junction of the Leona. The confusion may have originated with Fray Massanet, who referred to the same stream on May 7, 1691, as the Rio Frío. The Texas historian J. W.

Williams recognized that the Sarco named by De León is the present Leona River (*Old Texas Trails*, 113).

15. A 1991 study by the Texas State Department of Highways and Public Transportation (SDHPT) mistakenly identifies the April 6 camp location on the Río Hondo as being about 20 miles farther north on present Hondo Creek (A. Joachim McGraw, John W. Clark, Jr., and Elizabeth A. Robbins, eds., *A Texas Legacy: The Old San Antonio Road and the Caminos Reales, a Tricentennial History, 1691–1991*, 131). The mistake made in the SDHPT study is an example of the problems that occur when route projections are made on the assumption that the names of rivers and creeks used 300 years ago are the same as those used today. Finding the correct location warrants careful investigation to discover the carvings.

16. Richard I. Ford, "Inter-Indian Exchange in the Southwest," in *Handbook of North American Indians*, vol. 10, ed. Alfonso Ortiz, 717–722. The author adds, "Major trails connecting villages were well known and sometimes marked by shrines, petroglyphs, and debris (potsherds). Many trails originating in antiquity became the route followed by early explorers and settlers, and have become highways" (717).

17. The clear statement that the river flows east and southeast from the overnight camp where the crosses were found precludes any serious consideration that De León's party was on the present Hondo Creek (which runs north to south) on April 6 and 7 as projected in the SDHPT study (*A Texas Legacy*, 131).

18. Projections of De León's crossing of the San Antonio River many miles upstream near Floresville by J. W. Williams in *Old Texas Trails* and even farther upstream near the junction of the San Antonio River and the present Medina River in the SDHPT study (62) are based on erroneous estimates of where De León crossed the Nueces and Frio rivers. Moreover, these projections ignore the distances in leagues repeatedly given in diary entries between the San Antonio crossing, the Guadalupe crossing, and Matagorda Bay. The distance between the Guadalupe crossing and the French settlement near the bay was about 20 leagues or 52 miles (as given by De León on four occasions). If the Guadalupe crossing (reportedly 17 leagues east-northeast of the San Antonio River crossing) had been made near Seguin, as suggested by the projected San Antonio crossing in the SDHPT study, the distance between the Guadalupe crossing and the bay would have been about 120 miles rather than the 52 miles cited in the diaries.

19. Robert S. Weddle, *Wilderness Manhunt*, 145.

20. The ca. 1807 map by Manuel Agustín Mascaró was published in an article by Jack Jackson, "Father José María de Jesús Puelles and the Maps of Pichardo's Document 74," *Southwestern Historical Quarterly* 91, no. 3 (January 1988), Figs. 3 and 4.

21. Bolton suggests that the Guadalupe crossing by De León occurred below Victoria (*Spanish Exploration in the Southwest, 1542–1706*, 394n2); Castañeda, *Our Catholic Heritage in Texas*, vol. 1, 335, agrees with Bolton, stating that De León reached the Guadalupe River in the vicinity of Victoria. Weddle's *Wilderness Manhunt*, 183, is the most precise. Weddle, citing Massanet, describes the camp as being "5 miles" (rather than "5 leagues" as reported by Massanet) beyond the Guadalupe and relies on a broken astrolabe reading to place De León's base-camp "eight miles southeast of present-day Victoria." Weddle repeated his mistake in *French Thorn*, 73, as did Donald E. Chipman in *Spanish Texas, 1519–1821*, 82–83.

22. A recent study of the language of the Indian tribes that resided between the Guadalupe and the Colorado rivers concludes that a language called Sanan was spoken by several local tribes including the Emet, Cava, and Toho. Sanan is different from Coahuilteco (spoken by some tribes in northern Coahuila and South Texas), from Karankawan, and from Tonkawan (LeRoy Johnson and T. N. Campbell, "Sanan: Traces of a Previously Unknown Aboriginal Language in Colonial Coahuila and Texas," *Plains Anthropologist* 37 [August 1992], 185–212).

23. W. W. Newcomb, Jr., *The Indians of Texas from Prehistoric to Modern Times*, 136.

24. Ibid., 280; Weddle, *Wilderness Manhunt*, 181*n*16.

25. Chapa, *Historia*, 146.

26. Pat I. Nixon, "Liotot and Jalot: Two French Surgeons of Early Texas," *Southwestern Historical Quarterly* 43 (July 1939), 42–52.

27. See Weddle, *Wilderness Manhunt*, Map 8, following 136.

28. Bolton, *Spanish Exploration*, 410*n*4.

29. Chapa, *Historia*, 154.

30. O'Donnell, "La Salle's Occupation of Texas," 10.

31. Robert S. Weddle, ed., *La Salle, the Mississippi, and the Gulf*, 237.

32. Horses were reintroduced into North America by the Spaniards, who brought them north to the Rio Grande and New Mexico in the 1600s. The Apache and Jumano got horses through raids or trade from the Spaniards in West Texas, Chihuahua, and New Mexico. The Jumano, in turn, traded Spanish horses to their friends the Tejas in East Texas. La Salle then traded French items with the Tejas to secure mounts. See Henry Reed Stiles, *Joutel's Journal of La Salle's Last Voyage*, 123–127.

33. Weddle, *La Salle*, 238.

34. Peter Nabokov notes that similar distances were covered within a comparable time by Indian runners from tribes in New Mexico and New England in *Indian Running*, 11–36.

35. Cox, *Journeys of La Salle*, vol. 1, 220.

36. The depositions of the Frenchmen are found in O'Donnell, "La Salle's Occupation of Texas," 15–20.

37. Chapa, *Historia*, 155.

38. Later, Pierre Meunier testified that some inhabitants of the French colony had died of pestilence (Weddle, *Wilderness Manhunt*, 221*n*9). Despite the numerous reports of the smallpox epidemic at the bay, Weddle's assessment is that De León jumped to a conclusion in reporting the epidemic (195*n*13).

39. See Francis B. Steck, "Forerunners of Captain de León's Expedition to Texas, 1670–1675," *Preliminary Studies of the Texas Catholic Historical Society* 2, no. 3 (September 1932), 5–32.

40. Stiles, *Joutel's Journal of La Salle's Last Voyage*, 123–129.

3. A MISSION FOR THE TEJAS

1. The 1690 route of Governor De León is tracked from his expedition diary, a typescript copy of which is in *Texas Documentary History*, vol. 1, *Mexico (Viceroyalty), [AGN] Provincias Internas*, in the Manuscript Division of the Library of Congress. See also Herbert E. Bolton's annotated translation of a manuscript copy of De León's diary in AGN, Mexico, Provincias Internas, vol. 182, published in Bolton, *Spanish Exploration*, 405–423. I am preparing for publication an annotated translation of two manuscripts relating to the 1690 expedition which are held by the Beinecke Library, Yale University: Juan Bautista Chapa's *Historia* and De León's revised 1690 expedition diary.

2. See the entry "caramanchel," in *Diccionario de la lengua española*, 20th ed. (Madrid: Real Academia Española, 1984), vol. 1, 270.

3. Alonso de León to Viceroy, August 28, 1689, AGI, Mexico, 61-6-21, 75–77.

4. Bolton, *Spanish Exploration*, 408*n*1.

5. Ibid., 409*n*1. Bolton correctly states that the crossing was at the crossing location in 1689.

6. Captain Salinas and Captain Martínez were responsible for taking latitude readings on this

expedition, as Chapa had been on the trip in 1689 and on De León's 1686 expedition (Chapa, *Historia*, 165).

7. De León's personal praise of Géry to the viceroy contradicts the negative impression of Géry held by Padre Massanet and by several Texas historians (see Weddle, *Wilderness Manhunt*, 208; Chipman, *Spanish Texas, 1519–1821*, 80–82); letter from Alonso de León to His Excellency, Rio Grande, July 12, 1690, included in typescript of the "Testimony of the Activities and Their Results of the *Entrada* by Land to the *Parajes* to the Bay of Espíritu Santo, 1691," Secretary Pedro de la Cadena, Library of Congress, Manuscript Division.

8. Weddle, *Wilderness Manhunt*, 208.

9. Massanet described the route as passing through an area of thieves or "mariscar," a term that Lilia M. Casís incorrectly translated as "this sea region" (Massanet's letter to Don Carlos de Sigüenza, translated by Lilia M. Casís, published in *Texas Historical Association Quarterly* 2 [April 1899], 281–312). The correction is noted as a reminder that many of the documents concerning De León's expeditions including his diaries were translated and published eighty to ninety years ago with few route or other annotations and without the benefit of relevant materials found or developed in recent decades.

10. Bolton suggests that De León was traveling across the headwaters of the Lavaca and Navidad rivers close to Hallettville, several miles to the south of where the party was traveling, but he correctly places De León's crossing of the Colorado near La Grange (*Spanish Exploration*, 410n4; 411–412n2).

11. In the 1690s, the Tejas Indians had large horse herds in East Texas that had been developed from stock traded to them by the Jumano and other West Texas tribes that in turn had earlier secured the horses by trade or theft from the Spaniards in El Paso, Chihuahua, and New Mexico. Pierre Talon testified in 1698 that the Tejas used horses to transport cargo, particularly bison hides and meat taken many miles from their villages in East Texas (Weddle, *La Salle, the Mississippi, and the Gulf*, 230).

12. William E. Dunn, *Spanish and French Rivalry in the Gulf Region of the United States, 1678–1702*, 88.

13. Bolton also suggests that Pierre Talon was recovered a short distance north of Gonzales (*Spanish Exploration*, 412n3).

14. Weddle, *La Salle*, 235–236.

15. H. E. Bolton correctly states that the crossing occurred above the mouth of the Navasota River, which De León named the Arroyo San Juan (*Spanish Exploration*, 413–414n5).

16. Chapa, *Historia*, 173.

17. Bolton, *Spanish Exploration*, 420n3.

18. Weddle, *La Salle*, 241.

19. Bolton, *Spanish Exploration*, 384n3.

20. Weddle, *French Thorn*, 79.

21. Bolton, *Spanish Exploration*, 420.

22. Weddle, *La Salle*, 242.

23. Letter from Fray Massanet to Viceroy, September 1690, included in typescript of the "Testimony of the Activities and Their Results of the *Entrada* by Land to the *Parajes* to the Bay of Espíritu Santo, 1691," Secretary Pedro de la Cadena, 75–84, Manuscript Division, Library of Congress.

24. Jack Jackson and Winston De Ville, "Le Maire and the 'Mother Map' of Delisle," in Jackson, Weddle, and De Ville, *Mapping Texas and the Gulf Coast, 33*.

4. SAN ANTONIO DE PADUA

1. Eugenio del Hoyo, *Historia del Nuevo Reino de León (1577–1723)*, 469.

2. The manuscript copy of Governor Terán's 1691–1692 expedition diary is in *Texas Documentary History*, vol. 1, *Mexico (Viceroyalty)*, *[AGN] Provincias Internas*, in the Manuscript Division of the Library of Congress. An English translation of the diaries of Governor Terán and Fray Massanet by Mattie Austin Hatcher is found in "The Expedition of Don Domingo Terán de los Ríos into Texas," *Preliminary Studies of the Texas Catholic Historical Society* 2, no. 1 (January 1932), 10–67.

3. Herbert E. Bolton, *Spanish Exploration in the Southwest, 1542–1706*, 292–296.

4. Robert Weddle, *San Juan Bautista: Gateway to Spanish Texas*, 15. The map of Terán's route prepared by Carlos E. Castañeda which accompanies *Our Catholic Heritage in Texas*, vol. 1, misplaces the crossing of the Rio Grande used by Terán. The ford was the one used by De León in 1689 and 1690, allowing some deviation resulting from temporary changes in the local conditions. Partly as a result of this threshold error, Castañeda's projection of Terán's route of exploration between the Rio Grande and the Frio River is seriously defective.

5. Massanet reported that the following Indian nations were received at their camp on the Frio River on June 10: Sanpanal, Patchal, Papanaca, Parchiqui, Pacuachiam, Aguapalam, Samampac, Vanca, Payavan, Patavo, Pitanay, Apaysi, and Patsau.

6. See T. N. Campbell and T. J. Campbell, *Historical Indian Groups of the Choke Canyon Reservoir and Surrounding Area, Southern Texas*; and Donald E. Chipman, "In Search of Cabeza de Vaca's Route across Texas: An Historiographical Survey," *Southwestern Historical Quarterly* 91 (October 1987) 127–148.

7. Some Texas historians have made the mistake of locating Terán and Massanet's encounter with the large congregation of Indians near New Braunfels rather than San Marcos. See Robert S. Weddle, *The French Thorn*, 88; and Donald E. Chipman, *Spanish Texas*, 96.

8. Isaac Joslin Cox, ed., *The Journeys of René Robert Cavelier, Sieur de La Salle*, 222–240.

9. Elizabeth A. H. John, *Storms Brewed in Other Men's Worlds*, 182.

10. Cox, *Journeys of La Salle*, vol. 1, 223.

11. Castañeda, *Our Catholic Heritage in Texas*, vol. 1, 337.

12. The tribe's identification became significant two years later when Governor Salinas reported recruiting a guide a few miles west of the Colorado River from the Saquita Indians, which may be a variant of the name Catqueza.

13. Some confusion as to the camp location has occurred as a result of the diary translator, Mattie Austin Hatcher, rendering the Spanish word *monte* as a mountain rather than as a thick forest as Massanet intended ("The Expedition of Terán," 61).

14. Carlos E. Castañeda suggests that Terán's camp on the Colorado was 10 to 15 miles south of Austin, but states that the exact place where he struck the river cannot be definitely ascertained (*Our Catholic Heritage in Texas*, vol. 1, 365). Since Martínez stopped the first night at a well-known and frequently used location near La Grange (Jesús María y Joseph Buenavista) after traveling 10 leagues from the camp, Terán's campsite can be accurately sited, contrary to Castañeda's conclusion. The 1991 Texas Highway Department study repeats Castañeda's mistake and places Terán's crossing of the Colorado and camp near Austin rather than below Bastrop (McGraw et al., *A Texas Legacy*, Fig. 6, "Projected Route of Terán's and Mazanet's Expedition, 1691," 75). The map has Terán crossing the Brazos too far north, at the junction of the Little River. The route confusion was further aggravated by the Highway Department map projecting Terán's route to Los Adaes, a post that was not established until over twenty-five years after Terán's expedition.

15. The manuscript copy of the diary of Captain Martínez is in *Texas Documentary History*, vol. 1, *Mexico (Viceroyalty), [AGN] Provincias Internas*, in the Manuscript Division, Library of Congress.

16. Robert S. Weddle, ed., *La Salle, the Mississippi, and the Gulf*, 227–228 and *n*6.

17. Ibid., 252.

18. See Robert S. Weddle, *Wilderness Manhunt*; and Weddle, *La Salle*.

19. Weddle, *La Salle*, 238, 249.

20. Alonso de León, Juan Bautista Chapa, and Fernando Sánchez, *Historia de Nuevo León*, 22, 23.

21. Weddle, *French Thorn*, 90.

22. Hatcher's translation of Terán's diary omits July 23 and misnumbers July 24. According to the manuscript copy of the diary held in the Library of Congress, Terán traveled 3 leagues through heavy timber "north, a quarter northeast" on July 23.

23. Timothy K. Perttula, "*The Caddo Nation*," 84–89.

24. Peter Gerhard, *The North Frontier of New Spain*, 23–24.

25. Perttula, "*The Caddo Nation*," 19, 87. See USGS maps *Austin* (NH14-6) and *Beaumont* (NH15-4) and the Texas General Land Office map *Natural Heritage of Texas* (1986).

26. Eugenio del Hoyo described the smallpox epidemic near Monterrey, Nuevo León, in 1636 in his *Historia* (413); Alonso de León wrote of an epidemic near Cadereyta in 1646 in his *Historia* (148); Juan Bautista Chapa wrote of an unidentified epidemic depopulating Indian tribes in Coahuila in the 1650s in his *Historia* (117–120).

27. In 1693, Salinas confirmed that this was the crossing that Terán used in 1692. In his diary, Salinas comments that he had used the same crossing twice before (with Terán in 1691 and De León in 1690). It should be noted that the distance traveled by Terán's party on October 7 (4 leagues) is omitted in Hatcher's translation, but the manuscript copy of the diary held in the Library of Congress includes the distance notation.

28. The story of the misadventures and escape of Terán's young African-American bugler is related and well documented in Anibal Gonzalez, "Terán's Young Bugler," *Sayersville Historical Association Bulletin* 3 (Spring 1983), 1, 14.

29. See Carl L. Duaine, *With All Arms*, 210.

30. See comments on "Negros" or mulattoes in Nuevo León and Coahuila in the eighteenth century in Peter Gerhard, *The North Frontier of New Spain*, 332, 354.

31. See Thomas N. Campbell's entry on "Tlaxcalan Indians" in *Handbook of Texas*, vol. 3, 1013.

5. TO RESUPPLY THE MISSION

1. The route of Governor Salinas is based on a manuscript copy of his diary held in the Archivo General de Indias, Sevilla (AGI), Audiencia de Guadalajara (Guad.) 151 (old 67-4-11). The typescript of the manuscript is found in the Library of Congress, "Viaxe que hizo El Capitan de Caballos Corazas Don Gregorio de Salinas Varona, Gobernador de la Provincia de San Francisco de Coahuila, y Nueva Estremadura, a la Provincia de los Texas." The Spanish version was published in Lino Gómez Canedo, ed., *Primeras exploraciones y poblamiento de Texas (1686–1694)*, 277–307. For an English translation and annotation of the Salinas diary, see William C. Foster and Jack Jackson, eds., and Ned F. Brierley, trans., "The 1693 Expedition of Governor Salinas Varona to Sustain the Missionaries among the Tejas Indians," *Southwestern Historical Quarterly* 97 (October 1993), 264–311.

2. Robert S. Weddle has correctly observed that Salinas did not follow Terán's route and that "a succession of travelers beginning with Alonso de León" helped to define the Camino Real across Texas (*The French Thorn*, 97).

3. See William B. Griffen, "Southern Periphery: East," in *Handbook of North American Indians*, vol. 10, ed. Alfonso Ortiz, 329. Juan Bautista Chapa described these engagements in his *Historia*, 62, 63, 68.

4. Herbert E. Bolton, *Spanish Exploration in the Southwest*, 297, 308.

5. Salinas letter to viceroy, AGN, PI 182, 391–392.

6. Isaac Joslin Cox, ed., *The Journeys of René Robert Cavelier, Sieur de La Salle*, vol. 1, 223.

7. William R. Swagerty, "Indian Trade in the Trans-Mississippi West to 1890," in *Handbook of North American Indians*, vol. 4, 352, Fig. 1. See also William R. Swagerty, "Protohistoric Trade in Western North America: Archaeological and Ethnohistorical Considerations," in *Columbian Consequences*, ed. David Hurst Thomas, vol. 3, 471–499.

8. It is confusing that explorers used the same name for different rivers and different names for the same river. The confusion is evident in the treatment of the Salinas expedition in the 1991 publication by the Texas State Department of Highways and Public Transportation entitled *A Texas Legacy: The Old San Antonio Road and the Caminos Reales, a Tricentennial History, 1691–1991*. The study tracks the Salinas route across the Río Frío, Río Hondo, San Marcos, and Colorado along a projected line that assumes, incorrectly, that the names used for rivers several hundred years ago are applicable to the same rivers today (81–88, 245–265). To the contrary, not one of the names of the four rivers given by the early explorers and used by Governor Salinas can be properly applied to the Texas rivers that carry those names today. The governor was referring to the present Leona River when he cited the Río Frío; his reference to the Hondo meant the modern Frio; the San Marcos referred to the Colorado; and his Colorado was the Navasota.

9. Carlos E. Castañeda, *Our Catholic Heritage in Texas*, vol. 1, 373.

10. Letter dated August 19, 1693, AGI, Guad. 67-4-13.

11. Robert S. Weddle correctly identifies this location as Peach Creek, a tributary of the Guadalupe in Gonzales County (*The French Thorn*, 97). Fray Massanet reported that the Muruam tribe lived near the Guadalupe River at the time Governor Terán recovered five captive Muruam children from the Jumano in June 1691.

12. Since Salinas was unfamiliar with the new route he was taking to San Antonio and back to the Frio crossing, the recently acquired guide may have been responsible for correctly identifying the river. Salinas (with the guide's help) accurately thereafter identified the Cibolo and Salado creeks as tributaries of the San Antonio (Medina) River and correctly identified the upper stretch of Hondo Creek. Few Indians native to the immediate area between the Guadalupe and Colorado would have had an opportunity to learn Spanish (training usually found near existing Spanish missions). This suggests that the tribe may have lived elsewhere in New Spain south of the Rio Grande but was familiar with a route to San Antonio and south to the Frio crossing. The several lists of Indian tribes that lived in Coahuila and Vizcaya during the Spanish colonial period do not include a tribe called Saquita. However, both Rivera and Lafora listed the Cacquite among the tribes living in Coahuila. It is possible that Saquita is a variant for Cacquite.

13. See T. N. Campbell's extensive study of the Payaya Indians in *The Indians of Southern Texas and Northeastern Mexico: Selected Writings of Thomas Nolan Campbell*, 97–116.

14. William E. Dunn, *Spanish and French Rivalry in the Gulf Region of the United States*, 142–144.

15. Jack D. Eaton, "The Gateway Missions of the Lower Rio Grande," in *Columbian Consequences*, ed. David Hurst Thomas, vol. 1, 245–258.

16. Robert S. Weddle, who describes the exercise in graphic detail, notes, "The epidemic left

the mission of the Rio Grande depopulated to such an extent, says Father Espinosa, that [Espinosa] was obliged to go with a force of soldiers . . . to seek other rancherias of natives to replace those who had died in the mission" (*San Juan Bautista*, 73–86).

17. Isidro Félix de Espinosa, *Crónica de los colegios de propaganda fide de la Nueva España*, 775–778.

18. Diego Ramón, "Diario de la jornada que ha executado el Sargento mayor Diego Ramón," March 9–April 8, 1707, AGN, Provincias Internas, vol. 28, 53–71.

6. NEW ROAD TO THE COLORADO

1. See Jack D. Eaton's recent study of the missions in the area, "The Gateway Missions of the Lower Rio Grande," in *Columbian Consequences*, ed. David Hurst Thomas, vol. 1, 245–258. See also Marion A. Habig, *Spanish Texas Pilgrimage*, 248–250.

2. Robert S. Weddle gives an excellent account of events that occurred near San Juan Bautista leading up to the initiation of the expedition (*San Juan Bautista*, 92).

3. The diary of Espinosa was edited and translated into English by Gabriel Tous, "The Espinosa-Olivares-Aguirre Expedition of 1709," *Preliminary Studies of the Texas Catholic Historical Society* 1, no. 3 (March 1930), 3–14. A typescript copy of the manuscript of Espinosa's diary is held in the Manuscript Division of the Library of Congress, Sevilla, [AGI] México, 62-2-29.

4. Espinosa's exceptional ability as a chronicler is seen in his treatment of the early history of the missions, Indian customs, wildlife, and vegetation in Coahuila and Texas in *Crónica de los colegios de propaganda fide de la Nueva España*.

5. Robert S. Weddle, *The French Thorn*, 191.

6. Martin Salinas, *Indians of the Rio Grande Delta*, 116. Espinosa later said that the rats found by the Indians were the size of rabbits and were eaten as a meal (*Crónica*, 764).

7. The Texas State Department of Highways and Public Transportation's 1991 study of Spanish expedition routes incorrectly marks as inaccurate Espinosa's report that his party ascended the Arroyo Chapa (San Miguel Creek) on his movement northeast from the Frio crossing to the Medina (A. Joachim McGraw et al., *A Texas Legacy*, 355–357). Espinosa's reference to San Miguel Creek as Arroyo Chapa is accurate. De León named the creek on April 16, 1690, and Espinosa's route did follow the creek upstream toward the Medina.

8. Espinosa's reference to the stream as the León may have been made on the assumption that this was the first creek east of the Medina (San Antonio) River further south, called Arroyo del León.

9. William E. Doolittle excludes from agricultural areas all of Texas except East Texas and that area of the state along the Rio Grande from near the Mexican Conchos River to El Paso ("Agriculture in North America on the Eve of Contact: A Reassessment," in Karl W. Butzer, guest ed., *The Americas before and after 1492: Current Geographical Research, Annals of the Association of American Geographers* 82 [September 1992], 386–401).

10. United States Geological Survey, *Geological Survey Research 1980*, Professional Paper 1175, 222.

11. Alonso de León et al., *Historia de Nuevo León*, 47; Espinosa, *Crónica*, 761.

12. Espinosa, *Crónica*, 684.

13. T. N. Campbell, "Espinosa, Olivares, and the Colorado River Indians, 1709," *Sayersville Historical Association Bulletin* 3 (1983), 2.

14. The location for Espinosa's base-camp on the Colorado River on Map 10 is near the

location projected by Anibal Gonzalez, "The Overlooked Entrada," *Sayersville Historical Association Bulletin* 2 (1981), 4–7.

15. Tous's map incorrectly places San Juan Bautista several miles upstream on the Rio Grande. The ford of the Nueces is also placed too far upstream. Tous shows Espinosa crossing the Frio River near the ford used by Governor Terán, which is a serious error. As stated, and as reflected on Map 10, the padre crossed the Frio below its junction with the Hondo and then turned northeast. A similar misunderstanding by Tous is reflected in his projection of Espinosa's return route.

16. Espinosa, *Crónica*, 764.

17. Isaac Joslin Cox, ed., *The Journeys of La Salle*, vol. 1, 290.

18. Espinosa later wrote more about the birds and fish found in Coahuila and Texas at that time and noted that some *piltontes* (yellow catfish) in the Rio Grande grew to an enormous size. The padre reported, "The fish are called *piltontes*, which in Mexican language means boys [*muchachos*], because the fish is as big as a boy. Once one of these was brought to me and another priest by a soldier with Martín de Alarcón, and the fish was tied by the gills with a rope to the horn of a horse's saddle and its tail was dragging on the ground" (*Crónica*, 768).

7. IN QUEST OF COMMERCE

1. The comments on the route of the expedition are based primarily on Fray Espinosa's diary of the 1716 expedition, edited and translated by Gabriel Tous, "Ramón's Expedition: Espinosa's Diary of 1716," *Preliminary Studies of the Texas Catholic Historical Society* 1, no. 4 (April 1930), 4–24; and Captain Ramón's diary translated by Paul J. Foik, "Captain Don Domingo Ramón's Diary of His Expedition into Texas in 1716," *Preliminary Studies of the Texas Catholic Historical Society* 2, no. 5 (April 1933), 3–23. A typescript copy of the manuscript of both diaries is found in the Barker Texas History Center (AGN, Provincias Internas, vol. 181).

2. Tous's "Map of Espinosa-Ramón's Route in 1716" suffers from one of the same significant defects as the map he compiled of Espinosa's 1709 expedition: the crossing on the Rio Grande at San Juan Bautista is located more than 30 miles too far upstream. This initial mistake perhaps contributed to Tous's misplacing the crossing of the Nueces a few miles below the northern Zavala-Uvalde County line, rather than in southern Zavala County, and the crossing of the Frio River in Uvalde County rather than in Frio County, as seen in Map 11.

3. Jack Jackson, Robert S. Weddle, and Winston De Ville, *Mapping Texas and the Gulf Coast*, 12.

4. The history of the Tejas along the Rio Grande and in the missions of Coahuila is summarized by Francis B. Steck in "Forerunners of Captain de León's Expedition to Texas, 1670–1675," *Preliminary Studies of the Texas Catholic Historical Society* 2, no. 3 (September 1932), 5–32.

5. Robert S. Weddle, *San Juan Bautista*, 102.

6. Confirmation of Saint-Denis's use of this lower route south of the San Antonio area was given by Gregorio de Salinas Varona in his letter to the viceroy in January 1717. Salinas described the route taken by the Frenchmen in close detail and from reliable resources as moving southwest from the Brazos to the Colorado crossing (near present-day La Grange) and then due south for 20 leagues to the Guadalupe (near present-day Cuero) and west for 30 leagues, past the Leones River (Arroyo del León) to the San Antonio River, and continuing west for 30 leagues to the Frio crossing. These directions and distances are consistent with a journey from the Colorado along the lower route followed by De León and the Tejas in 1689 and 1690, but are inconsistent with a movement from the Colorado through San Antonio area to the Frio.

7. Robert S. Weddle incorrectly says that Saint-Denis visited San Pedro Springs at present-day San Antonio on his 1714 trip to the Rio Grande (*The French Thorn*, 318n19).

8. The romantic and intriguing story of the marriage of Saint-Denis and María Sánchez, niece of Captain Domingo Ramón, and its commercial and political significance is far beyond the boundaries of this study of early expedition trails. But it does help explain why a French commercial adventurer was hired to guide a Spanish expedition and was supplied with a caravan of mules and an armed escort back to San Juan Bautista the next year. See Charmion Clair Shelby, "St. Denis' Second Expedition to the Rio Grande, 1716–1719," *Southwestern Historical Quarterly* 27 (January 1924), 190–216.

9. The birds were identified as *gallos de la tierra*, a term that Espinosa equated with turkeys in 1709.

10. Patagúo Indians (or Patagua, as noted by Ramón) were recorded in the same general area in 1691 by Massanet on Terán's expedition. See Thomas N. Campbell's entry "Patagúo Indians" in *The Handbook of Texas*, vol. 3, 708.

11. The riverbank grape is the only vine identified by Robert A. Vines (*Trees, Shrubs, and Woody Vines of the Southwest*, 718–719) that attains the trunk size measured by Espinosa. Old trunks with a girth of 5 feet have been reported.

12. The route followed by Ramón and Espinosa to San Antonio is described by J. W. Williams (*Old Texas Trails*, 141–180). He traced the trek from the Francia crossing to the crossing of the Nueces near Crystal City, to Tortuga Creek, to the Leona River crossing near the boundary between Zavala and Frio counties, to the crossing of the Frio below the Hondo and north past the Pita campsite to the Medina. Williams claims that Ramón's expedition was the first to blaze this trail, which he calls "Ramón's Road." He apparently did not understand that Ramón's expedition with the help of Espinosa was faithfully following De León's route to the Frio crossing, Salinas's 1693 trip south, and Espinosa's 1709 trek north of the Frio past Pita to San Antonio.

13. According to the USGS map *San Antonio*, NH14-8, the reading is approximately 29°35', a variance of only 3 minutes or about 4 miles from Espinosa's reading.

14. Unfortunately, Espinosa discontinued reporting latitude readings at his campsites with the report from Brushy Creek.

15. Herbert E. Bolton, "The Founding of the Missions of the San Gabriel River, 1745–49," *Southwestern Historical Quarterly* 17 (April 1914), 328n8.

16. The 1991 Texas State Department of Highways and Public Transportation study mistakenly projects that Ramón and Espinosa crossed the Trinity River on June 15, 1716 (A. Joachim McGraw et al., *A Texas Legacy*, 89, 93, 101). On June 15, Ramón's party crossed the Brazos; the Trinity was not crossed until June 22 and 23.

17. See Williams, *Old Texas Trails*, 151, 166. Gabriel Tous includes a small map of Espinosa's route with his published translation of Espinosa's diary. Although Tous's route projection places Espinosa's crossing of the Nueces, Leona, and Frio 20 miles or more too far upstream (as does his map for Espinosa's 1709 trip), he correctly illustrates in his map that Espinosa moved southeast from the San Gabriel and crossed the Brazos well below the junction with the Little River.

18. See the USGS map *Austin*, NH14-6. Although J. W. Williams confuses the location of the crossing of the Brazos, placing it at the Little River junction, he correctly identifies present-day Cedar Creek, which crosses the Brazos-Robertson County line, as the Corpus Christi Creek named by Espinosa and Ramón in 1716 (*Old Texas Trails*, 152–153).

19. Stephen F. Austin's map was included in the portfolio of Robert S. Martin and James C. Martin, *Contours of Discovery*. Jean Louis Berlandier also mentioned stopping at the Corpus

Christi campsite a few leagues west of the Navasota River crossing on his return to San Antonio from the Trinity in 1828. The naturalist was following the road to the crossing of the Brazos near its junction with the Little Brazos (Brazo Chico), but from the Brazos to the Colorado there was no cleared road through the Monte Grande to the present Bastrop city area (*Journey to Mexico*, 332, 333–339).

20. A recent study of the western Caddoan tribes (which includes the Asinai or Tejas) describes their tribal range as extending west of the Trinity only for purposes of hunting. This assessment of the region occupied by the Tejas in the early eighteenth century (at least to the extent of having agricultural operations) seems to ignore the historic evidence found in the expedition diaries that Tejas farmers had fields between the Navasota and the Trinity (Timothy K. Perttula, *"The Caddo Nation,"* 251–252).

21. Isidro Félix de Espinosa, *Crónica*, 689. Some experts believe that the sunflower was domesticated in eastern North America before corn and beans arrived (by overland trade routes) from Mexico (see Charles B. Heiser, Jr., "Ethnobotany and Economic Botany," in *Flora in North America North of Mexico*, ed. Nancy R. Morin, 200).

22. Marion A. Habig, *Spanish Texas Pilgrimage*, 156–157. Peter P. Forrestal describes Margil's movement east to San Augustine and Robeline, Louisiana, in "The Venerable Padre Fray Antonio Margil de Jesús," *Preliminary Studies of the Texas Catholic Historical Society* 2, no. 2 (April 1932), 23, 24.

23. Katherine Bridges and Winston De Ville, eds. and trans., "Natchitoches and the Trail to the Rio Grande: Two Early Eighteenth-Century Accounts by the Sieur Derbanne," *Louisiana Historical Association* 8, no. 3 (Summer 1967), 239–259.

24. An annotation in the Bridges and De Ville translation of Derbanne's diary notes that the Indian attack occurred on the west side of the Brazos River, but this is an error. The distances from the attack to the San Marcos, the Guadalupe, and the San Antonio rivers indicate that the incident occurred west of the Colorado River.

25. Lester G. Bugbee, "The Real Saint-Denis," *Texas Historical Association Quarterly* 1 (April 1898), 275.

26. Shelby, "St. Denis' Second Expedition," 199–200.

8. A WAY STATION AT SAN ANTONIO

1. The *Diary of the Alarcón Expedition into Texas, 1718–1719* by Fray Francisco Céliz, translated by Fritz Leo Hoffmann, covers Alarcón's trip from the crossing of the Rio Grande on April 9, 1718, to February 10, 1719. The annotated translation by Hoffmann includes an extensive introduction.

2. The diary kept by Fray Pedro Pérez de Mezquía covers the expedition from February 16 to June 25, 1718. See Fritz Leo Hoffmann, "The Mezquía Diary of the Alarcón Expedition into Texas, 1718," *Southwestern Historical Quarterly* 41 (April 1938), 312–323. A typescript copy of the Mezquía diary is held in the Manuscript Division of the Library of Congress, in the papers of the Foreign Copying Program, Mexico, Box 4886: "Diario Derrotero q se formó con toda legalidad en la entrada q hizo en Gen. D. Martín de Alarcón a la Proa de los Texas" [the Mezquía Diary of the Alarcón Expedition in Texas, February 16–June 25, 1718], México, Colegio de la Santa Cruz de Querétaro, letter K, file 1, no. 13, 13.

3. The map is included in Herbert E. Bolton's *Texas in the Middle Eighteenth Century*. Bolton's map identifies a route that he calls the Camino Real, which commences at Monclova and runs to

San Juan Bautista. He mislocates San Juan Bautista, placing it about 30 miles too far upstream on the Rio Grande, as measured according to the longitude and latitude references given on his map. The Camino Real then runs from San Juan Bautista to Béxar (or San Antonio) along a route that crosses the Nueces a few miles above Comanche Creek, which is the route followed by every expedition from De León's in 1689 to Rivera's in 1727. Bolton's road crosses the Leona River and then the Frio below the Hondo. From there, it generally follows the San Miguel north-northeast to the Medina and San Antonio. The first expedition to cut farther east from the Nueces and cross along the route Bolton calls the Camino Real was Fray Espinosa's in 1709, although Governor Salinas earlier returned to the Rio Grande from the San Antonio area to the Nueces crossing along the same Camino Real in 1693.

4. The same stream was identified as the Caramanchel by Terán (June 5, 1691), Salinas (May 12, 1693), Espinosa (April 7, 1709), and Ramón (April 29, 1716). Robert S. Weddle agrees with Hoffmann and has also suggested that Caramanchel might be spelled Carabanchel to conform to the name of "a town in the Madrid province of Spain" (*Wilderness Manhunt*, 179).

5. Hoffmann is uncertain as to where Alarcón crossed the Leona River or the Frio, as indicated in his annotations to Fray Céliz's diary entitled "Notes to the Diary" (92nn23, 24, 25). On the map "Texas in 1718—Alarcón's Routes" included in the translation (110), Hoffmann draws Alarcón's route too far north, crossing the present-day Frio above the Hondo junction with the Frio and then crossing Hondo Creek before reaching the Medina and San Antonio. His annotations and the map reflect his confusion in the names used for the present-day Leona, Frio, and Hondo rivers.

6. Hoffmann's translation of Mezquía's diary drops the entry for April 24, which describes the crossing of the Medina.

7. The padres kept separate diaries of the short journey and both include unusually perceptive and colorful comments. Despite the existence of two diaries, however, the most prominent translator, Fritz Leo Hoffmann, incorrectly states that the party moved down the left bank of the Guadalupe from New Braunfels, returned along the right bank of the San Marcos River, and then followed "the road to the Tejas" back to San Antonio. The route in fact took the party first to the San Marcos River, downstream along the right bank to the junction of the San Marcos and Guadalupe rivers, upstream on the Guadalupe along the left bank to a camp near Seguin, away from the Guadalupe north to the San Marcos crossing near the present day city of San Marcos, and then back to San Antonio along "the road to the Tejas."

8. Carlos E. Castañeda, *Our Catholic Heritage in Texas*, vol. 2, 136.

9. Hoffmann places the camp on September 15 near the present town of Nursery, about 10 miles below the DeWitt-Victoria County line.

10. Castañeda mistakenly places the camp where Alarcón left his main body and supplies on the Guadalupe River rather than the Colorado River, which Alarcón called the San Marcos (*Our Catholic Heritage in Texas*, vol. 2, 100–102). He states that Alarcón struck the bay near Port O'Connor, in Calhoun County. On Castañeda's "Map of Texas 1683–1731," he shows Alarcón leaving San Antonio and descending the left bank of the San Antonio River to the Cibolo and then turning southeast to a campsite on the Guadalupe below present-day Victoria. This route map in vol. 2 reflects Castañeda's misunderstanding of Alarcón's route. As indicated in Table 7 and Map 13, Alarcón was on the opposite side of the bay.

11. Hoffmann's map and annotation suggest that Alarcón visited present Lavaca Bay about 10 miles farther west, but the distance traveled and description of the bay area do not support this conclusion.

12. The Sana, Emet, Toho, and Mayeye were noted as friendly Indians by De León, Terán, and

Salinas. T. N. Campbell considers the Huyugan to be a group from northern Coahuila who had immigrated to Texas to avoid the Apache threat or the Spanish influence (*The Handbook of Texas*, vol. 3, 426). The Curmicai are not otherwise noted on any expedition or at any mission.

13. Hoffmann admits that the Little River junction that he projected is northwest of Alarcón's camp, not north-northeast as recorded in the diary. He mistakenly attributes the inconsistency between the diary account and his projection of the crossing location to an error in the diary (*Diary of the Alarcón Expedition*, 103*n*157, 159, 160, 163, 165). The crossing at the junction of the Little Brazos (as shown on Map 14) is consistent with the directions given in Céliz's diary account. The 1991 state-supported study of expedition routes repeated the same mistake (A. Joachim McGraw et al., *A Texas Legacy*, 361).

14. On November 9, the governor named a river with many cypress trees the Río San Francisco de Sabinas. Typically, Céliz overstated the distances traveled each day, thus making stream identifications difficult. However, it appears that Alarcón was naming the present Sabine River.

15. Hoffmann, *Diary of the Alarcón Expedition*, 26–27.

9. BACK TO THE BAY

1. The Spanish retreat from East Texas in 1719 is described in an article by Eleanor C. Buckley, "The Aguayo Expedition into Texas and Louisiana, 1719–1722," *Quarterly of the Texas State Historical Association* 15, no. 1 (July 1911), 8–20.

2. The Mexican historian Vito Alessio Robles describes the land holdings of the marqués and provides a sketch map of the land area held by the Aguayo family (*Coahuila y Texas en la época colonial*, map following 292).

3. A manuscript copy of Fray Peña's diary is held in the Manuscript Division of the Library of Congress, *Texas Documentary History*, vol. 1, *Mexico (Viceroyalty), [AGN] Provincias Internas*. Peña's diary is translated with very modest annotations by Peter P. Forrestal: "Peña's Diary of the Aguayo Expedition," *Preliminary Studies of the Texas Catholic Historical Society* 2, no. 7 (January 1935), 3–68. See also the fully annotated translation of Peña's diary by Richard G. Santos, *Aguayo Expedition into Texas, 1721: An Annotated Translation of the Five Versions of the Diary Kept by Br. Juan Antonio de la Peña*. The manuscript copy held by the Library of Congress is a sixth version of the diary.

The translation by Santos includes a description of the route of the expedition. He correctly notes that Aguayo generally followed Espinosa's 1709 route from the Rio Grande to San Antonio, but he misstates where the route crossed the Nueces and the Frio. See "Route of the Aguayo Expedition" (106, 107). Santos's map of the route is not to scale and does not include longitude and latitude marks, making detailed route comparison impossible.

4. In the manuscript copy Peña refers to the "Nadadores" swimming with the barges (*balsas*) across the Rio Grande. Forrestal translates this as "swimmers"; Richard Santos translates it as "Nadador Indians," who lived along the Rio de los Nadadores (114*n*59). T. N. Campbell does not include the "Nadador" Indians in the extensive list of Coahuiltecan tribes noted in his article "Coahuiltecans and Their Neighbors," in *Handbook of North American Indians*, vol. 10, 343–358. The tribe was not included in the lists of Indians living in Coahuila by either Barreiro or Lafora. This study leaves the question of whether "Nadadores" was the name of an Indian tribe unresolved.

5. Alonso de León et al. *Historia de Nuevo León*, 79, 80.

6. The *paraje* Ojo de Agua was used by Espinosa and Captain Ramón in 1716; Caramanchel

(Comanche Creek) was named by De León in 1690 and was noted on all later expeditions. Santos incorrectly suggests that the Caramanchel was present-day Turkey Creek, east of Comanche Creek (*Aguayo Expedition*, 115n74).

7. La Tortuga campsite is on the headwaters of present Tortuga Creek in Zavala County. The camp was also used by Espinosa and Ramón in 1716 and on all expeditions between 1716 and 1727. Santos incorrectly states that the Nueces was crossed below Crystal City (*Aguayo Expedition*, 115n77).

8. Forrestal notes that the Frio canyon is particularly attractive, but mistakes Peña's Río Frío or present-day Leona for the present-day Frio River. Santos does not make the same mistake; he recognizes that the present-day Leona was called the Río Frío and that the present-day Frío was called the Hondo by Peña (*Aguayo Expedition*, 116nn80, 86).

9. Although Peña and other diarists frequently mentioned seeing deer and antelope north of the Rio Grande, they seldom recorded seeing the animals along the expedition routes below the Rio Grande. Espinosa clarified the matter in his description of wildlife in northeastern New Spain in the early 1700s, in which he reported that both deer and antelope ranged in northwestern Nuevo León and northeastern Coahuila (*Crónica*, 764).

10. The route followed by Aguayo from the Rio Grande to San Antonio is tracked on a map included in Buckley's article about the Aguayo expedition (following 32). However, this map is not drawn to scale. From the location of the river crossings, it appears that Aguayo's route from the Rio Grande to San Antonio, as drawn by Buckley, is very similar to that found with more detail in Map 15. The route crosses the Nueces a short distance above the mouth of Comanche Creek, crosses the Frio a short distance below Hondo Creek junction, and follows the San Miguel Creek to the Medina River.

11. Buckley, "The Aguayo Expedition," map following 32; Charles W. Hackett, "The Marquis of San Miguel de Aguayo and His Recovery of Texas from the French, 1719–1723," *Southwestern Historical Quarterly* 49 (October 1945), 204, 205. Hackett incorrectly assumed that the road to the Tejas ran east from San Marcos as drawn on Buckley's map and that Aguayo's route northeast from San Marcos toward the crossing of the Colorado below Austin was new.

12. The 1991 map "Texas Historic Routes of the Caminos Reales and the Old San Antonio Road" marks the "Camino de los Tejas (1691–1800)" as running from the San Antonio area through the Austin area and crossing the Brazos above its junction with the Little River. No Spanish expedition from New Spain between 1691 and 1768 followed the route marked on this map (A. Joachim McGraw et al., *A Texas Legacy*, Fig. 1 on 9). Aguayo crossed the Brazos River near Waco. All other expeditions crossed the Brazos near its junction with either the Little Brazos or the Navasota.

13. The Sana were a local tribe first seen on an expedition by De León.

14. Buckley's map correctly describes Aguayo's route between San Antonio and the Colorado River, but the comments in the article also compare Aguayo's route with the routes of earlier expeditions and with that of Rivera in 1727. After stating that the comparison "lays no claim to strict accuracy," Buckley suggests that no two expeditions followed the same course. This conclusion is disputed by Maps 3 to 17, which show that the expeditions that used the Francia crossing area, without exception, followed De León's route from the Rio Grande to the Nueces River crossing and that every expedition, with the sole exception of Terán, crossed the Frio River where De León first crossed, a few miles below Hondo Creek and west of present-day Pearsall. Maps 3, 4, and 8 show that the route from the Frio crossing east toward Matagorda Bay and East Texas crossed the San Antonio River near Falls City, the Guadalupe River near Cuero, and the Colorado River near La Grange. Map 8 shows Salinas returning in 1693 from San Antonio south-

southwest down the San Miguel Creek to De León's crossing location on the Frio and every expedition from Espinosa's brief trip in 1709 thereafter following the same route to the north-northeast upstream along the San Miguel, past Pita to the Medina. From San Antonio to the Colorado River, every expedition (again, except Terán's) followed the same route to present New Braunfels, to San Marcos, to Onion Creek, and to the Colorado River crossing a few miles above the creek. Buckley's inaccuracies extend to having Terán cross the Colorado near La Grange.

15. The reading was consistent with that given by Espinosa on May 25, 1716, near the same Colorado River crossing.

16. Santos mistakenly cites San Buenaventura Creek as a branch of Gibbons Creek, east of the Navasota River. The Navasota River was called San Buenaventura first by Espinosa on June 19, 1716; by Fray Céliz with Alarcón on October 7, 1718; and now by Peña. This mistake illustrates the need for a cross-document analysis in studying expedition routes.

17. It appears reasonably certain that the Tejas woman named Angelina was the same person who had served as an interpreter for Ramón and Espinosa on July 2, 1716, and who had been described as the sagacious Indian woman interpreter by Fray Céliz with Alarcón on October 19, 1718.

18. Buckley's map of Aguayo's route between San Antonio and the crossing of the Guadalupe River in DeWitt County is similar to Map 15 except that Buckley's map fails to show where Aguayo struck the river near Sandies Creek.

19. Buckley, "The Aguayo Expedition," 58–60, and associated map. The projection that Aguayo was on the Lavaca River, rather than on Garcitas Creek, when he directed the establishment of the presidio in 1721 has been repeated more recently by Santos (*Aguayo Expedition*, 131n365). Santos correctly places Aguayo's party on Garcitas Creek (called the San Joseph River by Peña) on March 23, 1722, but incorrectly has the party crossing Garcitas Creek the following day and moving east to the Lavaca River. Peña's entry for that day (March 24) does not note that the party crossed the San Joseph; the diary states only that the party moved east then southeast, crossing two creeks, to arrive at the presidio. As seen in Table 8 and Aguayo's route map, the directions and distances given are compatible with the location of the presidio on the lower Garcitas and incompatible with a site on the Lavaca.

20. Herbert E. Bolton, "The Location of La Salle's Colony on the Gulf of Mexico," *Southwestern Historical Quarterly* 27 (January 1924), 171; Robert S. Weddle, *The French Thorn*, 84. See the report on a study of the site prepared by Kathleen Gilmore, "La Salle's Fort St. Louis in Texas," *Bulletin of the Texas Archeological Society* 55 (1984), 61–72.

21. Kathryn S. O'Connor, *The Presidio La Bahía*, 12–13.

22. Charles W. Hackett, ed. and trans., *Pichardo's Treatise on the Limits of Louisiana and Texas*, vol. 2, 109–118.

10. THE PRESIDIOS REVIEWED

1. See the excellent recent study of Pedro de Rivera's inspection compiled and edited by Thomas H. Naylor and Charles W. Polzer, *Pedro de Rivera and the Military Regulations for Northern New Spain, 1724–1729*.

2. Rivera's route is tracked from an untranslated portion of his diary account published in 1945: *Diario y derrotero de lo caminado, visto y obcervado . . . D. Pedro de Rivera*, ed. Guillermo Porras Muñoz. The historian Jack Jackson kindly directed my attention to the diary. Jackson and I are currently preparing an annotated translation of the diary for publication.

3. A summary of the trip through Texas is found in Retta Murphy, "The Journey of Pedro de Rivera, 1724–1728," *Southwestern Historical Quarterly* 41 (October 1937), 125–141.

4. The brigadier listed the following nations residing at missions in Coahuila: Therocodame, Pacpul, Cacquite, Ocane, Payaquane, Cibolo, Cano, Catujane, Pachoche, Hape, Colorado, Obaya, Toboso, Sixame, Sillanquaya, Sadujane, Siguase (Siause-Bar), Pita, Pacuache, Pajalatame, and Carrizo. Barreiro named the same tribes in his description of the Province of Coahuila, except he omitted the Therocodame and added the Pampopa (Naylor and Polzer, *Pedro Rivera*, 209–224).

5. Isidro Félix de Espinosa, *Crónica,* 761–765, 769.

6. Robert S. Weddle, *San Juan Bautista,* 172.

7. Eleanor C. Buckley, "The Aguayo Expedition into Texas and Louisiana, 1719–1722," *Texas Historical Association Quarterly* 15, no. 1 (July 1911), 34, 35*n*1, contributed by Herbert E. Bolton; A. Joaquim McGraw et al., *A Texas Legacy,* 38, 187.

8. No comments were made in the diary account on the condition of these two posts, but the presidios were considered fully in Rivera's *proyecto* of 1728 and in the subsequent *reglamento* of 1729. The report (*proyecto*) of the inspector was organized in a logical sequential order, commencing with a description of the conditions of the post (*primer estado*), then the actions taken by the inspection at the presidio (*segundo estado*), and finally the recommendations for future action (*tercer estado*). The formal action later taken on his recommendations (which was usually in line with his suggestions) was expressed in the *Regulations of 1729.* See Naylor and Polzer, *Pedro de Rivera,* for details.

9. The confusion over the location of the presidio on the Guadalupe can be seen in Carlos E. Castañeda's map, found in *Our Catholic Heritage in Texas,* vol. 2, which mistakenly places the fort below the present city of Victoria. See also Charles W. Hackett, ed. and trans., *Pichardo's Treatise on the Limits of Louisiana and Texas,* vol. 2, 109–118. The location of the mission, which was also relocated from Garcitas Creek to the Guadalupe in 1726, has been marked by the State of Texas.

10. Jack Jackson, *Los Mesteños: Spanish Ranching in Texas, 1721–1821,* map on 324.

11. Governor de León named the present-day Atascosa River the Robalos in 1690.

12. Charles W. Ramsdell II, "Spanish Goliad," typescript in the Barker Texas History Center (2R, 157), Austin, Texas.

13. A report by Governor Winthuysen made four years before the reported celebration at the presidio on the Guadalupe states that the mission was located only 2 leagues from the presidio at that time (1744), but does not comment on whether the mission was across the river (Governor Tomás Felipe Wintuisen Report, August 19, 1744, Béxar Archives Translation [hereafter cited as BAT], vol. 15, 59–60, at BTHC). See also Russell M. Magnaghi, "Texas as Seen by Governor Winthuysen, 1741–1744," *Southwestern Historical Quarterly* 88, no. 2 (1984), 167–180.

14. Naylor and Polzer, *Pedro Rivera,* 159.

15. Adaes, Aes, Aynay, Nacodoche, Necha, Nozone, Nabidacho, Naconome, Yojuane, Aname, Ervipiame, Cusane, Malleye, Pampopa, Pastia, Coco, Coapite, Copane, Carancaquaze, Tacame, Araname, Atastagonie, Pelone, Salina, Parchina, Anna, Pacao, Pajalat, Pitalac, and "others not recalled."

16. Barreiro identified the following Indian tribes living in the Province of León: Bocarro, Xanambre, Gualaquise, Borrado, Pelone, Posuama, Zalaya, Malahueco, Pitisfiafuli, Guachichile, Tajaquiche, Alazapa, and Pajalto (Naylor and Polzer, *Pedro Rivera,* 222).

17. Ibid., 279–280.

18. Marqués de Rubí, *Dictamen* (April 10, 1768), Article 30.

19. Weddle, *San Juan Bautista*, 191–193; Castañeda, *Our Catholic Heritage*, vol. 2, 294.

20. Fray Juan Agustín de Morfí, *Viaje de Indios*, 331–353.

21. Herbert E. Bolton offered the following comments on the period: "For the period from 1727 to 1767 we have no diaries across Texas, but it is interesting to note that there is evidence that by the middle of the century the direct route from San Antonio to the Trinity was abandoned for the Bahía road, through fear of the Apache" (Buckley, "The Aguayo Expedition," 35*n*1, contributed by Bolton).

22. Governor Tomás Felipe Winthuysen Report, BAT, vol. 15, 59–60; also Buckley, "The Aguayo Expedition," 34, 35.

23. Carlos E. Castañeda, *Our Catholic Heritage in Texas*, vol. 3, 92–93.

24. See October 1745 to April 1746 letters between Joachín de Orobio Basterra and Governor Francisco García Larios, BAT, vol. 17, 1–80.

11. THE FRENCH THREAT FADES

1. Herbert E. Bolton, *Texas in the Middle Eighteenth Century*, 102–109; Lawrence Kinnaird, ed. and trans., *The Frontiers of New Spain: Nicolás de Lafora's Description, 1766–1768*, 31–33.

2. The Marqués de Rubí's route to East Texas and back to the Presidio La Bahía and San Juan Bautista is based in part on a newly acquired untranslated manuscript of his diary: "Itinerario del Mariscal de Campo Marqués de Rubí en la inspección de los presidios internos . . . en esta N. España desde 1766 a 1768," Thorn Family Spanish Colonial Documents Collection, Barker Texas History Center, University of Texas, Austin. Jack Jackson graciously directed me to the previously unknown document, recently acquired by the BTHC.

The account is also based on Lafora's diary account found in Vito Alessio Robles, ed., *Nicolás de Lafora, relación de viaje* (Mexico City, 1939); and the translation of Lafora's diary by Kinnaird, *The Frontiers of New Spain*.

3. Jack Jackson and I are preparing the recently acquired Rubí diary for publication.

4. Robert S. Weddle, *The San Sabá Mission: Spanish Pivot in Texas*, is an excellent history of the mission and the condition of the presidio at the time of Rubí's visit.

5. Marion A. Habig, *Spanish Texas Pilgrimage*, 176.

6. Ibid., 154–156.

7. See T. N. Campbell's entry "Coco Indians," in *The Handbook of Texas*, vol. 3, 181; and W. W. Newcomb, Jr.'s entry "Karankawa," in *Handbook of North American Indians*, vol. 10, 359–368.

8. Governor Tomás Felipe Winthuysen Report, August 19, 1744, Béxar Translations (hereafter cited as BAT), vol. 15, 59–60, at BTHC. See also Russell M. Magnaghi, "Texas as Seen by Governor Winthuysen, 1741–1744," *Southwestern Historical Quarterly* 88, no. 2 (1984), 167–180.

9. Later an officer and twenty men were stationed at the post, which guarded movements between San Antonio and La Bahía and the traffic to East Texas, as well as those who took the route from the Cibolo east to Vado de Adayseños on the Guadalupe, used by Fray Solís and his large military convoy the following year. See Kinnaird, *The Frontiers of New Spain*, 33. For an excellent history of the fort on the Cibolo, see Robert H. Thonhoff, *El Fuerte del Cíbolo*.

10. Paso del Gobernador on the Guadalupe above Victoria was later mentioned with reference to the location of Captain Ewen Cameron and his unit of rangers in 1842. See Joseph M. Nance, *Attack and Counterattack: The Texas-Mexican Frontier, 1842* (Austin: University of Texas Press, 1964), 286–287.

11. Mascaró's map is found in Jack Jackson, "Father José María de Jesús Puelles and the Maps of Pichardo's Document 74," *Southwestern Historical Quarterly* 91, no. 3 (January 1988), Fig. 3, 332. Manuel Agustín Mascaró, who prepared the detailed map in 1781, was a young officer in the Spanish Corps of Engineers stationed at the time in Arispe, the provincial capital of Sonora in northern New Spain. He was born in Barcelona, Spain, in 1747, and studied at the academy in Barcelona while in the Royal Guard. As an engineer, Mascaró was recognized for his architectural work, but he produced several geographical maps of significance. His 1781 map, which gives the names and locations of twenty-two crossings of the Guadalupe River, was based on reports and diaries available to him, since he had not visited Texas. See Janet R. Fireman, *The Spanish Royal Corps of Engineers in the Western Borderlands,* 150–165.

12. Carlos E. Castañeda incorrectly indicates that Rubí crossed near Hochheim. In a mistaken effort to relate the name of the ford to some governor who might have crossed the Guadalupe there, Castañeda suggests that "perhaps it was at this point where Alarcón came near drowning in 1728 [sic]" (*Our Catholic Heritage in Texas,* vol. 4, 228–229). As noted in Chapter 8, the governor had his narrow escape in the Guadalupe near New Braunfels rather than in DeWitt County.

13. Castañeda incorrectly concludes that Rubí crossed the Colorado at Columbus, Colorado County (ibid., 229).

14. *Our Catholic Heritage,* vol. 4, 229.

15. Corpus Christi Creek (named by Espinosa in 1716) is the largest stream that intercepts the open corridor that runs northeast from the junction of the Brazos and the Little Brazos to the Navasota. It was identified by the same name as late as 1828, when the scientist Jean Louis Berlandier traveled from the Trinity River crossing area in Leon County toward San Antonio. On June 1, 1828, moving west, he crossed the Navasota River and crossed Corpus Christi Creek about 3 leagues beyond. Several days later, still moving west, he reported crossing the Brazos near its junction with the Little Brazos and soon thereafter entering the dense Monte Grande. Berlandier found at that time there still was no identifiable path through the area called the Monte Grande (*Journey to Mexico,* 332–340).

16. Timothy K. Perttula reviews the early investigations of the Caddo Mound Builders in East Texas in *"The Caddo Nation,"* 46–47. See also the comments on the Caddoan Mounds State Historic Site along the Camino Real followed by Rubí in Parker Nunley, *A Field Guide to Archeological Sites of Texas,* 116–127.

17. Herbert E. Bolton refers to a letter written by Athanase de Mézières to Croix (March 18, 1778) in which he described his trip from Béjar to Nacogdoches along a route he called the Camino Real that ran southeast of Béjar to Fort Santa Cruz on Arroyo del Cíbolo and again "picked up the Camino Real" below the customary crossing of the Guadalupe (in DeWitt County). Mézières was following the route taken by Rubí (*Athanase de Mézières and the Louisiana-Texas Frontier 1768–1780,* 187).

Bolton notes that Vial only mentions two settlements he visited on his trip from Nacogdoches to San Antonio: Rancho del Retén and Rancho Chayopines, both along the lower route southeast of San Antonio. Bolton concludes that Vial followed the earlier route taken by Rubí and Solís (*Texas in the Middle Eighteenth Century,* 131–132).

18. See March and April 1746 letters to the governor from Orobio Basterra, BAT, vol. 17, 33–80. Basterra reported that east of the Orcoquiza villages near present Trinity Bay lived the Pachina and to the west were the Coco, Cujane, and Carancaguaze.

19. Ibid. In his instructions to the captain, Governor García Larios also referred to the route followed from the lower Guadalupe to Los Adaes as the Camino Real.

20. The DeWitt County map, compiled in 1860 by the Texas General Land Office, is published in Joe B. Frantz, *The Lure of the Land* (College Station: Texas A & M University Press, 1988), 34. See also the USGS map *Seguin*, NH14-9.

21. Fray Solís reported crossing the "creek of the Monaquía" a short distance before reaching the San Antonio River near La Bahía. "Monaquía," Solís explains, refers to the numerous "hermaphrodites" or homosexuals among the Karankawa.

22. Lafora listed the following Indian nations that lived in the Province of Texas and Coahuila (which at that time extended north to the Medina and San Antonio rivers).

In the Province of Coahuila: Terocodame, Pacpole, Cacquite, Ocane, Payaguane, Cibolo, Cano, Ostujane, Pachoche, Ape, Colorado, Obaya, Toboso, Xixame, Silangaya, Sadujane, Siguane, Pita, Pacuasin, Pajalatame, Carrizo, Conhumeno, Timamar, Pampopa, Tilixai, Mescal, Borrado, Pausane, Manos de Perro, Piquique, Julimeño, and Tlaxcalteca.

In the Province of Texas: Adaes, Ais, Ainai, Nacodoche, Necha, Nazone, Nabidoche, Naconome, Tojuane, Aname, Ervipiame, Cujane, Mayeye, Pampopa, Pasua, Coco, Coapite, Copane, Carancaguca, Tacame, Taraname, Astastagonia, Pelone, Salina, Parchina, Anna, Pacao, Pajaloc, Petalac, Orcoquiza, Vidai, Atacapa, Apiluca, Borrado, Tancahue, Taguacana, and Taguaya and Yscani (farther north).

23. Henry F. Dobyns, *Their Number Become Thinned*, 14.

12. REVIEW OF THE ZACATECAN MISSIONS IN TEXAS

1. The route of Fray Solís is traced from his diary of the expedition found in three manuscript copies. One copy that apparently has not been consulted in preparing any English translation is in the Manuscript Division of the Library of Congress, *Texas Documentary History*, vol. 1, *Mexico (Viceroyalty), [AGN] Provincias Internas*, #2176, 249–286. A second manuscript copy of Solís's diary is in the Barker Texas History Center, Documents, History, Texas Archives of Mexico, 248–298. This copy was translated by Margaret Kenney Kress, "Diary of a Visit of Inspection of the Texas Missions Made by Fray Gaspar José de Solís in the Year 1767–68," *Southwestern Historical Quarterly* 35, no. 1 (1931–1932), 28–76. A second translation has been prepared by Peter P. Forrestal, "The Solís Diary of 1767," *Preliminary Studies of the Texas Catholic Historical Society* 1, no. 6 (March 1931), 3–42. A third manuscript copy is in the Thorn Family Spanish Colonial Documents Collection, Barker Texas History Center, University of Texas, Austin.

2. Martín Salinas comments on the western Carrizo in *Indians of the Rio Grande Delta*, 92–93.

3. Herbert Bolton, "Tienda de Cuervo's Ynspección of Laredo, 1757," *Quarterly of the Texas State Historical Association* 6 (January 1903), 187–203.

4. Fray Espinosa's description of the winter weather conditions about 40 miles south and west of Laredo is graphic: "During the winter, the north wind blows almost continuously, freezing the water and bringing snow for days. Many domestic animals die as a result of the cold weather, and some young chickens have died while hiding under their mother. Even pumpkins, watermelons, and fruit are frozen" (*Crónica*, 761).

5. W. W. Newcomb, Jr., *The Indians of Texas*, 59–85. See also W. W. Newcomb, Jr., "Karankawa," in *Handbook of North American Indians*, vol. 10, ed. Alfonso Ortiz, 359–368. T. N. Campbell also identifies the Coco as Karankawa ("Coco Indians," in *Handbook of Texas*, vol. 3, 181).

6. Castañeda stoutly denies that force was used by the missions or the presidio troops to keep the Indians under mission control in "Pioneers in Sackcloth," *Preliminary Studies of the Catholic Historical Society* 3, no. 5 (October 1939), 20. He was wrong.

7. Alonso de León et al., *Historia de Nuevo León*, 41–43.

8. Jean Louis Berlandier, *Journey to Mexico,* vol. 2, 351.

9. Newcomb, *The Indians of Texas*, 74.

10. Carl L. Duaine, *Caverns of Oblivion*, 37.

11. David E. Greenberg, *The Construction of Homosexuality*, 40–56.

12. Father Anastase Douay, "Narrative of La Salle's Attempt to Ascend the Mississippi in 1687," in *The Journeys of La Salle*, ed. Isaac Joslin Cox, 222–240.

13. In 1766, Diego Ortiz Parrilla reported Manos de Perro near Corpus Christi Bay. See Salinas, *Indians of the Rio Grande Delta*, 72.

14. Roy Bedichek, *Karankaway Country*, 92–93. According to a current authoritative field guide to Texas trees, the huisache is still found in Wilson County and adjacent counties to the south and southeast, but after over 200 years has not spread northwest to adjacent Bexar County. See Benny J. Simpson, *A Field Guide to Texas Trees*, 40.

15. See Marion A. Habig, *Spanish Texas Pilgrimage*, 161.

16. The translation of Solís's diary by Margaret Kenney Kress requires correction at this point. There were 100 individuals going to Adaes, not 200, as stated by Kress.

17. The number of leagues Solís traveled each day is entered as an Arabic number at the close of each day's entry. The manuscript copy of Solís's diary translated by Kress did not include numbers indicating distance traveled on several days of the trip between San Antonio and the Colorado River, but the manuscript copy of Solís's diary held by the Library of Congress did provide this missing information.

18. Carlos E. Castañeda describes the severe ice and snow conditions encountered by Captain Orobio Basterra in *Our Catholic Heritage in Texas,* vol. 3, 143.

19. Some caution is required in attempting to follow the distances that Solís recorded in his diary. The padre, who was not an explorer or professional engineer, grossly overstated the distance traveled between identifiable camps or rivers. An example of such overstatement is the distance Solís recorded between the Colorado crossing and their camp on Bernabé Creek. Lafora and Rubí gave the distance as 12 leagues, but Solís recorded a total of 31 leagues. The measured straight-line distance is about 12 leagues. Rubí and Lafora were consistently closer to the mark not only in recording the distance traveled, but also in including the direction followed each day.

20. J. W. Williams, *Old Texas Trails,* 166–180. Williams takes the mistaken position that both Rubí and Solís crossed the Brazos at its junction with the Little River.

21. LeRoy Johnson and T. N. Campbell, "Sanan: Traces of a Previously Unknown Aboriginal Language in Colonial Coahuila and Texas," *Plains Anthropologist* 37 (August 1992), 185–212.

22. Berlandier, *Journey to Mexico*, 310, 311.

23. See W. P. Clark, *The Indian Sign Language;* and William Tomkins, *Indian Sign Language.* The following is a random list of words for which Indian signs and American Sign Language signs are the same or very similar: above, across, advance, afternoon, all, alone, among, another, arise, astride, baby, bad, below, big, bird, boat, bowl, brave, carry, chop, close, cold, come, cry, deer, depart, die, dismount, distant, done, eat, end, equal, exchange, fall, few, fish, flag, forest, future, give, go, grass, hand, high, increase, keep, large, least, little, man, meet, moon, night, pipe, quiet, rain, see, tent, tell, trade, tree, and walk.

24. Solís's diary entry for April 26 again illustrates his exaggeration of distance traveled: he reported moving 12 leagues between El Paes and Corpus Christi, while Rubí reported 8 leagues.

25. Although the diary account is very specific as to the burial of guns with the deceased Tejas, archaeological records from sites in Northeast Texas apparently fail to support the account. See Timothy K. Perttula, *"The Caddo Nation,"* 206.

26. No mention is made that Mission Orcoquisac was moved from the Trinity Bay area to East Texas in the history of the mission by Habig (*Spanish Texas Pilgrimage,* 174) or in *The Handbook of Texas,* vol. 2, 294. For a local treatment of the mission and post, see Darlene Houseman, "El Orcoquisac: Spain's Frontier on the Trinity," *Touchstone* (Texas State Historical Association) 13 (1994), 58–70.

27. Forrestal, "The Solís Diary of 1767," 36.

BIBLIOGRAPHY

ARCHIVAL SOURCES

Archivo General de Indias (AGI), Sevilla
Archivo General de la Nación (AGN), Mexico City
Bancroft Library (BL), University of California at Berkeley
Barker Texas History Center (BTHC), University of Texas at Austin
Béxar Archives (BA), University of Texas at Austin
Library of Congress, Manuscript Division (LCMD), Washington, D.C.
Beinecke Library, Yale University, New Haven

PUBLISHED SOURCES

Alessio Robles, Vito. *Coahuila y Texas en la época colonial.* Mexico City: Editorial Porrúa, 1978.
———, ed. *Nicolás de Lafora, relación de viaje.* Mexico City, 1939.
Barnes, Thomas C., Thomas H. Naylor, and Charles W. Polzer. *Northern New Spain—A Research Guide.* Tucson: University of Arizona Press, 1981.
Bedichek, Roy. *Karankaway Country.* Austin: University of Texas Press, 1974, 1983.
Berlandier, Jean Louis. *The Indians of Texas in 1830.* Ed. John C. Ewers. Washington, D.C.: Smithsonian Institution Press, 1969.
———. *Journey to Mexico during the Years 1826 to 1834.* Trans. Sheila M. Ohlendorf, Josette M. Bigelow, and Mary M. Slandifer. Austin: Texas State Historical Association and the Center for Studies in Texas History, University of Texas at Austin, 1980.
Berman, Howard R. "Perspectives on American Indian Sovereignty and International Law, 1600 to 1776." In *Exiled in the Land of the Free: Democracy, Indian Nations, and the U.S. Constitution,* 125–188. Santa Fe: Clear Light Publishers, 1992.
Bolton, Herbert E., ed. and trans. *Athanase de Mézières and the Louisiana-Texas Frontier, 1768–1780.* 2 vols. Cleveland: Arthur H. Clark, 1914.
———. *Coronado on the Turquoise Trail: Knight of Pueblos and Plains.* Albuquerque: University of New Mexico Press, 1949.
———. "The Founding of the Missions of the San Gabriel River, 1745–49." *Southwestern Historical Quarterly* 17 (April 1914), 323–378.

———. "The Location of La Salle's Colony on the Gulf of Mexico." *Southwestern Historical Quarterly* 27 (January 1924), 171–189.

———, ed. *Spanish Exploration in the Southwest, 1542–1706.* 1916; reprint, New York: Barnes and Noble, 1963.

———. *Texas in the Middle Eighteenth Century: Studies in Spanish Colonial History and Administration.* Austin: University of Texas Press, 1970.

———. "Tienda de Cuervo's Ynspección of Laredo, 1757." *Quarterly of the Texas State Historical Association* 6 (January 1903), 187–203.

Branda, Eldon Stephen, ed. *The Handbook of Texas: A Supplement.* Vol. 3. Austin: Texas State Historical Association, 1976.

Bridges, Katherine, and Winston De Ville, eds. and trans. "Natchitoches and the Trail to the Rio Grande: Two Early Eighteenth-Century Accounts by the Sieur Derbanne." *Louisiana Historical Association* 8, no. 3 (Summer 1967), 239–259.

Buckley, Eleanor C. "The Aguayo Expedition into Texas and Louisiana, 1719–1722." *Texas State Historical Association Quarterly* 15, no. 1 (July 1911), 8–35.

Bugbee, Lester G. "The Real Saint-Denis." *Texas Historical Association Quarterly* 1 (April 1898), 266–281.

Cabeza de Vaca, Alvar Nuñez. *Cabeza de Vaca's Adventures in the Unknown Interior of America.* Ed. and trans. Cyclone Covey. New York: Crowell-Collier, 1961.

Campbell, T. N. "Coahuiltecans and Their Neighbors." In *Handbook of North American Indians,* vol. 10, ed. Alfonso Ortiz, 343–358. Washington, D.C.: Smithsonian Institution Press, 1983.

———. "Espinosa, Olivares, and the Colorado River Indians, 1709." *Sayersville Historical Association Bulletin* 3 (1983), 2–16.

———. *The Indians of Southern Texas and Northeastern Mexico: Selected Writings of Thomas Nolan Campbell.* Austin: Texas Archeological Research Library, 1988.

———. "Name All the Indians of the Bastrop Area." *Sayersville Historical Association Bulletin* 7 (1988), 7–10, 16.

Campbell, T. N., and T. J. Campbell. *Historical Indian Groups of the Choke Canyon Reservoir and Surrounding Area, Southern Texas.* San Antonio: Center for Archeological Research, University of Texas, 1981.

Casís, Lilia M., trans. "The 1690 Letter from Fray Massanet to Don Carlos de Sigüenza." *Texas State Historical Association Quarterly* 2, no. 4 (April 1899), 253–312.

Castañeda, Carlos E. "Earliest Catholic Activities in Texas." *Preliminary Studies of the Texas Catholic Historical Society* 1, no. 8 (October 1931), 1–18.

———. *Our Catholic Heritage in Texas, 1519–1936.* 7 vols. Austin: Von Boechmann–Jones, 1936–1958.

———. "Pioneers in Sackcloth." *Preliminary Studies of the Texas Catholic Historical Society* 3, no. 5 (October 1939), 5–22.

Céliz, Francisco. *Diary of the Alarcón Expedition into Texas, 1718–1719.* Ed. and trans. Fritz Leo Hoffmann. Los Angeles: Quivira Society, 1935.

Chapa, Juan Bautista. *Historia del Nuevo Reino de León de 1650 a 1690.* Ed. Israel Cavazos Garza. Monterrey: Gobierno de Estado de Nuevo León, 1990.

Chipman, Donald E. "In Search of Cabeza de Vaca's Route across Texas: An Historiographical Survey." *Southwestern Historical Quarterly* 91 (October 1987), 127–148.

———. *Spanish Texas, 1519–1821.* Austin: University of Texas Press, 1992.

Clark, W. P. *The Indian Sign Language.* Lincoln and London: University of Nebraska Press, 1982.

Cox, Isaac Joslin, ed. *The Journeys of René Robert Cavelier, Sieur de La Salle*. 2 vols. 1922; reprint, Austin: Pemberton Press, 1968.

Crosby, Alfred W. "Summary on Population Size before and after Contact." In *Disease and Demography in the Americas*, ed. John W. Verano and Douglas H. Ubelaker, 277–278. Washington, D.C., and London: Smithsonian Institution Press, 1992.

Dobyns, Henry F. *Their Number Become Thinned*. Knoxville: University of Tennessee Press, 1983.

Doolittle, William E. "Agriculture in North America on the Eve of Contact: A Reassessment." In *The Americas before and after 1492: Current Geographical Research*, guest ed. Karl W. Butzer. *Annals of the Association of American Geographers* 82 (September 1992), 386–401.

Doughty, Robin W. *Wildlife and Man in Texas*. College Station: Texas A & M University Press, 1983.

Doughty, Robin W., and Barbara M. Parmenter. *Endangered Species*. Austin: Texas Monthly Press, 1989.

Duaine, Carl L. *Caverns of Oblivion*. Corpus Christi: Carl L. Duaine, 1971.

———. *With All Arms*. Edinburg: New Santander Press, 1987.

Dunn, William E. *Spanish and French Rivalry in the Gulf Region of the United States, 1678–1702*. Austin: University of Texas Press, 1917.

Eaton, Jack D. "The Gateway Missions of the Lower Rio Grande." In *Columbian Consequences*, ed. David Hurst Thomas, vol. 1, *Archaeological and Historical Perspectives on the Spanish Borderlands West*, 245–258. Washington and London: Smithsonian Institution Press, 1989.

Espinosa, Isidro Félix de. *Crónica de los colegios de propaganda fide de la Nueva España*, ed. Lino Gómez Canedo. Washington, D.C.: Academy of American Franciscan History, 1964.

Ewers, John C. "The Influence of Epidemics on the Indian Population and Cultures of Texas." *Plains Anthropologist* 18 (1973), 104–115.

Fireman, Janet R. *The Spanish Royal Corps of Engineers in the Western Borderlands: Instruments of Bourbon Reform, 1764–1815*. Glendale, Calif.: Arthur H. Clark, 1977.

Ford, Richard I. "Inter-Indian Exchange in the Southwest." In *Handbook of North American Indians*, vol. 10, ed. Alfonso Ortiz, 717–722. Washington, D.C.: Smithsonian Institution Press, 1983.

Forrestal, Peter P., trans. "Peña's Diary of the Aguayo Expedition." *Preliminary Studies of the Texas Catholic Historical Society* 2, no. 7 (January 1935), 3–68.

———. "The Solís Diary of 1767." *Preliminary Studies of the Texas Catholic Historical Society* 1, no. 6 (March 1931), 3–42.

———. "The Venerable Padre Fray Antonio Margil de Jesús." *Preliminary Studies of the Texas Catholic Historical Society* 2, no. 2 (April 1932), 5–33.

Foster, William C., and Jack Jackson, eds., and Ned F. Brierley, trans. "The 1693 Expedition of Governor Salinas Varona to Sustain the Missionaries among the Tejas Indians." *Southwestern Historical Quarterly* 97 (October 1993), 264–311.

Gannon, Michael. "The New Alliance of History and Archaeology in the Eastern Spanish Borderlands." *William and Mary Quarterly* 9 (April 1992), 321–334.

Gerhard, Peter. *The North Frontier of New Spain*. Rev. ed. Norman and London: University of Oklahoma Press, 1982, 1991.

Gilmore, Kathleen. "La Salle's Fort St. Louis in Texas." *Bulletin of the Texas Archeological Society* 55 (1984), 61–72.

Gómez Canedo, Lino, ed. *Primeras exploraciones y poblamiento de Texas (1686–1694)*. Monterrey: Instituto Tecnológico y de Estudios Superiores, 1968.

Gonzalez, Anibal. "El Monte Grande." *Sayersville Historical Association Bulletin* 4 (1983), 2–6, 14.

———. "The Overlooked Entrada." *Sayersville Historical Association Bulletin* 2 (1981), 4–7.

———. "Terán's Young Bugler." *Sayersville Historical Association Bulletin* 3 (Spring 1983), 1, 14.

Greenberg, David E. *The Construction of Homosexuality.* Chicago: University of Chicago Press, 1988.

Griffen, William B. "Southern Periphery: East." In *Handbook of North American Indians,* vol. 10, ed. Alfonso Ortiz, 329–342. Washington: Smithsonian Institution Press, 1983.

Grove, Jean M. *The Little Ice Age.* London and New York: Methuen, 1988.

Habig, Marion A. *Spanish Texas Pilgrimage: The Old Franciscan Missions and Other Settlements of Texas 1632–1821.* Chicago: Franciscan Herald Press, 1990.

Hackett, Charles W. "The Marquis of San Miguel de Aguayo and His Recovery of Texas from the French, 1719–1723." *Southwestern Historical Quarterly* 49 (October 1945), 193–214.

———, ed. and trans. *Pichardo's Treatise on the Limits of Louisiana and Texas.* 4 vols. Austin: University of Texas Press, 1931–1946.

Hague, Harlan. "Guides for the Pathfinders: The Indian Contribution to Exploration of the American West." *Pacific Historian* 26 (Fall 1982), 54–63.

Hatcher, Mattie Austin, trans. "The Expedition of Don Domingo Terán de los Ríos into Texas." *Preliminary Studies of the Texas Catholic Historical Society* 2, no. 1 (January 1932), 10–67.

Hatcher, Mattie Austin, ed., and Margaret Kenney Kress, trans. "Diary of a Visit of Inspection of the Texas Missions Made by Fray Gaspar José de Solís in the Year 1767–68." *Southwestern Historical Quarterly* 35, no. 1 (July 1931–1932), 28–76.

Heiser, Charles B., Jr. "Ethnobotany and Economic Botany." In *Flora in North America North of Mexico,* ed. Nancy R. Morin, vol. 1, 199–206. New York and Oxford: Oxford University Press, 1993.

Hoffmann, Fritz L. "The Mezquía Diary of the Alarcón Expedition into Texas, 1718." *Southwestern Historical Quarterly* 41 (April 1938), 312–323.

Houseman, Darlene. "El Orcoquizac: Spain's Frontier on the Trinity." *Touchstone* (Texas State Historical Association) 13 (1994), 58–70.

Hoyo, Eugenio del. *Historia del Nuevo Reino de León (1577–1723).* Monterrey: Publicaciones del Instituto Tecnológico y de Estudios Superiores de Monterrey, 1972.

Jackson, Jack. "Father José María de Jesús Puelles and the Maps of Pichardo's Document 74." *Southwestern Historical Quarterly* 91, no. 3 (January 1988), 317–347.

———. *Los Mesteños: Spanish Ranching in Texas, 1721–1821.* College Station: Texas A & M University Press, 1986.

Jackson, Jack, Robert S. Weddle, and Winston De Ville. *Mapping Texas and the Gulf Coast: The Contribution of Saint-Denis, Oliván, and Le Maire.* College Station: Texas A & M University Press, 1990.

John, Elizabeth A. H. *Storms Brewed in Other Men's Worlds: The Confrontation of Indians, Spanish, and French in the Southwest, 1540–1795.* College Station: Texas A & M University Press, 1975.

Johnson, LeRoy, and T. N. Campbell. "Sanan: Traces of a Previously Unknown Aboriginal Language in Colonial Coahuila and Texas." *Plains Anthropologist* 37 (August 1992), 185–212.

Johnson, LeRoy, and Glenn T. Goode. "A New Try at Dating and Characterizing Holocene Climates, as Well as Archeological Periods, on the Eastern Edwards Plateau." *Bulletin of the Texas Archeological Society* 65 (1994), 1–51.

Jones, Oakah L. "Settlements and Settlers at La Junta de los Rios, 1759–1822." *Journal of Big Bend Studies* 3 (January 1991), 43–70.

Joutel, Henri. *Joutel's Journal of La Salle's Last Voyage, 1684–87.* Ed. and introduction by Henry Reed Stiles. 1906; reprint, New York: Corinth, 1962.

Kinnaird, Lawrence, ed. and trans. *The Frontiers of New Spain: Nicolás de Lafora's Description, 1766–1768.* Berkeley: Quivira Society, 1958.

Kutac, Edward A., and S. Christopher Caran. *Birds and Other Wildlife of South Central Texas.* Austin: University of Texas Press, 1994.

León, Alonso de, Juan Bautista Chapa, and Fernando Sánchez de Zamora. *Historia de Nuevo León, con noticias sobre Coahuila, Tamaulipas, Texas y Nuevo Mexico,* ed. Genaro García. Mexico City: Bouret, 1909.

Magnaghi, Russell M. "Texas as Seen by Governor Winthuysen, 1741–1744." *Southwestern Historical Quarterly* 88, no. 2 (1984), 167–180.

Margry, Pierre, ed. *Découvertes et établissements des Français dans l'ouest et dans le sud de l'Amérique Septentrionale, 1614–1754.* Paris. Maisonneuve, 1876–1886.

Martin, Robert S., and James C. Martin, *Contours of Discovery.* Austin: Texas State Historical Association and the Center for Studies in Texas History, University of Texas at Austin, 1982.

McGraw, A. Joachim, John W. Clark, Jr., and Elizabeth A. Robbins, eds. *A Texas Legacy: The Old San Antonio Road and the Caminos Reales, a Tricentennial History, 1691–1991.* Austin: State Department of Highways and Public Transportation, 1991.

Morfí, Fray Juan Agustín de. *History of Texas, 1673–1779.* Ed. and trans. Carlos E. Castañeda. 2 vols. Albuquerque: Quivira Society, 1935.

————. *Viaje de Indios y diario del Nuevo Mexico,* ed. Vito Alessio Robles. Mexico City: Bibliófilos Mexicanos, 1935.

Murphy, Retta. "The Journey of Pedro de Rivera, 1724–1728." *Southwestern Historical Quarterly* 41 (October 1937), 125–141.

Nabokov, Peter. *Indian Running: Native American History and Tradition.* Santa Fe: Ancient City Press, 1987.

Naylor, Thomas H., and Charles W. Polzer, eds. *Pedro de Rivera and the Military Regulations for Northern New Spain 1724–1729.* Tucson: University of Arizona Press, 1988.

Newcomb, William W., Jr. "Historic Indians of Central Texas." *Bulletin of the Texas Archeological Society* 64 (1993), 1–63.

————. *The Indians of Texas from Prehistoric to Modern Times.* Austin: University of Texas Press, 1961.

————. "Karankawa." In *Handbook of North American Indians,* vol. 10, ed. Alfonso Ortiz, 359–368. Washington, D.C.: Smithsonian Institution Press, 1983.

Nixon, Pat I. "Liotot and Jalot: Two French Surgeons of Early Texas." *Southwestern Historical Quarterly* 43 (July 1939), 42–52.

————. *The Medical Story of Early Texas, 1528–1853.* Lancaster, Penn.: n.p., 1946.

O'Connor, Kathryn S. *The Presidio La Bahía del Espíritu Santo de Zúñiga, 1721–1846.* Austin: Von Boechmann–Jones, 1966.

O'Donnell, Walter, J. "La Salle's Occupation of Texas." *Preliminary Studies of the Catholic Historical Society* 3, no. 2 (April 1936), 5–33.

Perttula, Timothy K. *"The Caddo Nation": Archaeological and Ethnohistoric Perspectives.* Austin: University of Texas Press, 1992.

Polzer, Charles W., Thomas C. Barnes, and Thomas H. Naylor. *The Documentary Relations of the Southwest: Project Manual.* Tucson: University of Arizona Press, 1977.

Porras Muñoz, Guillermo, ed. *Diario y derrotero de lo caminado, visito y obcervado . . . D. Pedro de Rivera.* Mexico City: Porrúa, 1945.

Ramón, Domingo. "Captain Don Domingo Ramón's Diary of His Expedition into Texas in 1716." Trans. Paul J. Foik. *Preliminary Studies of the Texas Catholic Historical Society* 2, no. 5 (April 1933), 3–23.

Reindorp, Reginard C., trans. "The Founding of Missions at La Junta de los Ríos." *Supplementary Studies of the Texas Catholic Historical Society* 1, no. 1 (April 1938), 5–28.

Salinas, Martin. *Indians of the Rio Grande Delta.* Austin: University of Texas Press, 1990.

Santos, Richard G., ed. and trans. *Aguayo Expedition into Texas, 1721: An Annotated Translation of Five Versions of the Diary Kept by Br. Juan Antonio de la Peña.* Austin: Jenkins Publishing, 1981.

Shelby, Charmion Clair. "St. Denis' Second Expedition to the Rio Grande, 1716–1719." *Southwestern Historical Quarterly* 27 (January 1924), 190–216.

Sibley, Marilyn McAdams, ed. "Across Texas in 1767: The Travels of Captain Pagès." *Southwestern Historical Quarterly* 70 (April 1967), 593–622.

Simpson, Benny J. *A Field Guide to Texas Trees.* Austin: Texas Monthly Press, 1988.

Stannard, David E. "The Consequences of Contact: Toward an Interdisciplinary Theory of Native Responses to Biological and Cultural Invasion." In *Columbian Consequences,* ed. David Hurst Thomas, vol. 3, 519–539. Washington, D.C.: Smithsonian Institution Press, 1991.

Steck, Francis B. "Forerunners of Captain de León's Expedition to Texas, 1670–1675." *Preliminary Studies of the Texas Catholic Historical Society* 2, no. 3 (September 1932), 5–32.

Swain, Susan L. "Mexico and the Little Ice Age." *Journal of Interdisciplinary History* 2 (Spring 1981), 633–648.

Thonhoff, Robert. *El Fuerte del Cíbolo: Sentinel of the Béxar–La Bahía Ranches.* Austin: Eakin Press, 1992.

Tomkins, William. *Indian Sign Language.* New York: Dover Publications, 1969.

Tous, Gabriel, ed. and trans. "The Espinosa-Olivares-Aguirre Expedition of 1709." *Preliminary Studies of the Texas Catholic Historical Society* 1 (March 1930), 3–14.

———. "Ramón's Expedition: Espinosa's Diary of 1716." *Preliminary Studies of the Texas Catholic Historical Society* 1, no. 4 (April 1930), 4–24.

Tull, Delena, and George Oxford Miller. *A Field Guide to Wildflowers, Trees, and Shrubs of Texas.* Houston: Gulf Publishing Company, 1991.

Verano, John W., and Douglas H. Ubelaker, eds. *Disease and Demography in the Americas.* Washington, D.C., and London: Smithsonian Institution Press, 1992.

Vines, Robert A. *Trees, Shrubs, and Woody Vines of the Southwest.* Austin: University of Texas Press, 1960.

Wauer, Roland H. *A Naturalist's Mexico.* College Station: Texas A & M University Press, 1992.

Weber, David J. *Myth and History of the Hispanic Southwest.* Albuquerque: University of New Mexico Press, 1988.

———. *The Spanish Frontier in North America.* New Haven and London: Yale University Press, 1992.

Weddle, Robert S. *The French Thorn: Rival Explorers in the Spanish Sea, 1682–1762.* College Station: Texas A & M University Press, 1991.

———, ed. *La Salle, the Mississippi, and the Gulf: Three Primary Documents.* Ed. Mary Christine Markousky and Patricia Galloway. Trans. Ann Linda Bell and Robert S. Weddle. College Station: Texas A & M University Press, 1967.

————. *San Juan Bautista: Gateway to Spanish Texas.* Austin: University of Texas Press, 1968.

————. *The San Sabá Mission: Spanish Pivot in Texas.* Austin: University of Texas Press, 1964.

————. *Wilderness Manhunt: The Spanish Search for La Salle.* Austin: University of Texas Press, 1973.

Weniger, Del. *Cacti of Texas and Neighboring States.* Austin: University of Texas Press, 1988.

————. *The Explorers' Texas: The Lands and Waters.* Austin: Eakin Press, 1984.

West, Elizabeth H., trans. "Governor Alonso de León's 1689 Expedition Diary." *Texas State Historical Association Quarterly* 8 (January 1905), 199–224.

Williams, J. W. *Old Texas Trails.* Ed. and comp. Kenneth F. Neighbors. Austin: Eakin Press, 1979.

INDEX

Indian tribes with variant names are indexed under the name found in Appendix IV.

Rubí inspection tour, 187, 188, 194,
195; Solís inspection tour, 209, 211;
Terán expedition, 64, 65, 66, 69, 73, 74
Turkeys, 98, 100, 104, 108, 115, 118, 119,
131, 136, 148, 149, 151, 155, 172,
182, 184, 185, 204, 207, 209, 210,
227, 244–245, 304n.9
Tusonibi Indians, 102, 288
Typhoid fever, 24, 65, 211, 263, 264

Uadesa Indians, 295n.10
Urjataña, Captain, 210
Urrutia, Joseph de, 90, 177, 182

Vanca Indians, 2–3, 288, 299n.5
Venado Indians, 182, 183, 288
Venereal disease, 24, 211, 262, 264
Vial, Pedro (Pierre), 188, 223, 312n.17
Vigotes, Captain, 210
Vitlata Indians, 295n.10

Walnut trees, 86, 119, 120, 154, 169, 187,
188, 256
Water control, 99, 130, 132, 133, 135, 188
Weather. See Climate
Weber, David J., 6, 10, 12, 14, 228
Weddle, Robert S., 6, 22, 23, 39, 44, 63, 64,
156–157, 173, 296n.21, 301nn.1–2,
301–302n.16, 304n.7, 306n.4
Weniger, Del, 294n.35
Wichita Indians, 2–3
Wilbarger Creek, 103, 106, 159, 174
Wildcats, 167, 204, 245

Wildflowers, 130, 149, 205
Wildlife, list of, 233–246. See also specific
animals
Williams, J. W., 6, 7, 131, 296n.18,
304nn.12,18
Willow trees, 60, 89, 100, 116, 206, 207,
260
Winthuysen, Governor Tomás Felipe, 173,
183, 310n.13
Wolves, 24, 167, 200, 204, 210, 227, 246
Women: in Alarcón expedition, 130; as
Indian leaders, 120, 139, 153, 210,
214, 230, 309n.17; living with or
captured by Indians, 32, 44, 45, 61, 63,
193; in Ramón expedition, 109, 112,
115; sterility of, in Texas, 193. See also
names of specific women

Xanambre Indians, 310n.16
Xarame Indians, 2–3, 98, 118, 140, 182,
183, 288–289
Xauna Indians, 204, 289
Xavier Road, 118, 140, 151, 169, 186, 221–
224
Xiabu Indians, 2–3, 18, 36, 289

Yadosa Indians, 295n.10
Yojuane Indians, 102, 208, 289, 310n.15,
313n.22
Yopane Indians, 295n.10
Yorica Indians, 2–3, 54, 90, 289, 295n.10
Yscani Indians, 2–3, 289, 313n.22
Yucca plants, 116, 191, 200, 227, 258